THE EMPEROR'S NEW NUDITY

SHORT CIRCUITS
Mladen Dolar, Alenka Zupančič, and Slavoj Žižek, editors

Sascha Wiederhold, *The Hand Kiss*, 1928. © Silard Isaak Collection, Legacy Carl Laszlo, Photography: Thomas Bruns.

To Adam and Nitai, my sons
and to their grandparents

> For the People of that flow
> Are new, the old
>
> New to age as the young
> To youth
>
> —George Oppen, *Of Being Numerous*

THE EMPEROR'S NEW NUDITY

THE RETURN OF AUTHORITARIANISM AND THE DIGITAL OBSCENE

Yuval Kremnitzer

THE MIT PRESS   CAMBRIDGE, MASSACHUSETTS   LONDON, ENGLAND

This book was set in Copperplate Gothic Std and Joanna MT Pro by New Best-set Typesetters Ltd. Printed and bound in the United States of America.

Library of Congress Cataloging-in-Publication Data

Names: Kremnitzer, Yuval, author.
Title: Unwritten no more : new authoritarianism and the digital obscene / Yuval Kremnitzer.
Description: Cambridge, Massachusetts : The MIT Press, [2024] | Series: Short circuits | Includes bibliographical references.
Identifiers: LCCN 2024002647 (print) | LCCN 2024002648 (ebook) | ISBN 9780262549042 | ISBN 9780262379731 (epub) | ISBN 9780262379724 (pdf)
Subjects: LCSH: Authoritarianism. | Authority. | Power (Social sciences) | Communication—Political aspects. | Digital media. | Communication—Political aspects.
Classification: LCC HM1251 .K74 2024 (print) | LCC HM1251 (ebook) | DDC 320.53—dc23/eng/20240522
LC record available at https://lccn.loc.gov/2024002647
LC ebook record available at https://lccn.loc.gov/2024002648

10 9 8 7 6 5 4 3 2 1

CONTENTS

A short circuit occurs when there is a faulty connection in the network—faulty, of course, from the standpoint of the network's smooth functioning. Is not the shock of short-circuiting, therefore, one of the best metaphors for a critical reading? Is not one of the most effective critical procedures to cross wires that do not usually touch: to take a major classic (text, author, notion) and read it in a short-circuiting way, through the lens of a "minor" author, text, or conceptual apparatus ("minor" should be understood here in Deleuze's sense: not "of lesser quality," but marginalized, disavowed by the hegemonic ideology, or dealing with a "lower," less dignified topic)? If the minor reference is well chosen, such a procedure can lead to insights which completely shatter and undermine our common perceptions. This is what Marx, among others, did with philosophy and religion (short-circuiting philosophical speculation through the lens of political economy, that is to say, economic speculation); this is what Freud and Nietzsche did with morality (short-circuiting the highest ethical notions through the lens of the unconscious libidinal economy). What such a reading achieves is not a simple "desublimation," a reduction of the higher intellectual content to its lower economic or libidinal cause; the aim of such an approach is, rather, the inherent decentering of the interpreted text, which brings to light its "unthought," its disavowed presuppositions and consequences.

And this is what "Short Circuits" wants to do, again and again. The underlying premise of the series is that Lacanian psychoanalysis is a privileged instrument of such an approach, whose purpose is to illuminate a standard text or ideological formation, making it readable in a totally new way—the long history of Lacanian interventions in philosophy, religion, the arts (from the visual arts to the cinema, music, and literature), ideology, and politics justifies this premise. This, then, is not a new series of books on psychoanalysis, but a series of "connections in the Freudian field"—of short Lacanian interventions in art, philosophy, theology, and ideology.

"Short Circuits" intends to revive a practice of reading which confronts a classic text, author, or notion with its own hidden presuppositions, and thus reveals its disavowed truth. The basic criterion for the texts that will be published is that they effectuate such a theoretical short circuit. After reading a book in this series, the reader should not simply have learned something new: the point is, rather, to make him or her aware of another—disturbing—side of something he or she knew all the time.

Slavoj Žižek

UNWRITTEN NO MORE—THE NEW NORMAL

We are a natural disaster, shake mama, shake your head.
My Baby Boy, The Angelcy

An old Hasidic tale, told by Rabbi Nachman of Breslov, speaks of the prepa-
rations taken on by a king in order to address an imminent ecological disaster, the primary outcome of which would be widespread insanity. The king is
warned by his "stargazer" that the grain has been tainted, and anyone who ate
from it would become insane. The stargazer's suggestion to put aside some
untainted grain for the king and himself is rejected by the king: "If we do that,
we'll be considered crazy. If everyone behaves one way and we behave differently, we'll be considered the not normal ones. Rather," said the king, "I suggest
that we too eat from the crop, like everyone else. However, to remind ourselves
that we are not normal, we will make a mark on our foreheads. Even if we are
insane, whenever we look at each other, we will remember that we are insane!"

This story, which reads like a joke, delivers a painful, bitter punchline. For
are we not living, today, in the world of this tale? More and more we witness
the emergence of authority figures whose claim for distinction, and indeed
for intimacy with their followers, is founded on openly admitted, "self-aware"
madness: "things are crazy, we're the ones who know it, and I'm the one brave
enough to openly admit it" is their message.

The recent rise of new authoritarian rulers in Western democracies calls
for a profound rethinking of fundamental concepts such as authority, legitimacy and power in the modern state. The distinctive mark of the emerging form of power is the capacity of new authoritarian leaders to say the
unsayable, to break the unwritten rules of political discourse. What should
have traditionally spelled doom for these political figures is instead their very
source of power. This striking feature underlies the amazement and frustration of political theorists and commentators trying to come to terms with

contemporary political reality. What is shocking is not so much what is said, the transgressive content, but that it's said, that what used to be censored or obliquely suggested is not only openly admitted but proudly advertised. What seems to capture the fascination of spectators, horrified or admiring, is that such leaders make palpable the tacit dimension of social life, what we know but cannot put into words, cannot explicitly formulate. It is as if only in viewing the transgression of these implicit norms can we sense their real presence; and so their violation bestows a unique aura upon the ruler, perceived as exhibiting a mysterious social power.

We can approach the challenge these new patterns of political power pose to political theories regarding authority and legitimacy as the problem of "the emperor's new nudity." According to the prevailing paradigm, epitomized by the tale made famous by Hans Christian Andersen about the emperor's new clothes, the authority in the name of which power rules is nothing but an illusionary veil, and what is required in order to unmask it is a sober gaze, unencumbered by the inhibitions of custom and received wisdom. If we only look at things from this emancipated position we shall see the ruler as flesh and blood, just like us, and expose his naked body for all to see. Critical theory supplies us with a wide array of strategies based on exposure: exposure of power dynamics encoded in culture, the exposure of ideological lies, the exposure of subtextual messages. These strategies are based on the presupposition that the real kernel of the political is something hidden, in need of exposure and explication. The political patterns of new authoritarianism— distinguished precisely by proudly declaring itself to be naked—call into question the efficacy of these strategies, in the face of a reality in which the exposure—of lies or ignorance, of scandal—does not necessarily undermine political power, and may in fact be its uncanny source.

How to account, then, for the growing tendency of political power to push the obscene—according to its Greek etymology, the off-scene, what happens off stage, in between scenes—to the visible center of its public activity? The first step to be taken is to see that transgressive right-wing politics and what seems to be its polar opposite—the liberal politics of good governance and political correctness—in fact share an underlying project, a phantasy they approach from opposite ends: an order entirely oriented around the obscene, aiming to eradicate the unwritten, tacit aspect of social and political life. While right-wing politics seems to celebrate the transgression of norms, advocating a shameless politics of power, left-wing politics is driven by a no less obscene drive for codification. This drive to "write the unwritten," shared by opposing political forces, is underlined by a profound shift in the social and technological mediation of reality, which is the topic of this book.

Now, the notion that these things—new authoritarianism and new media —somehow belong together is embarrassingly obvious, and yet at the same time, I argue, it is profoundly puzzling, posing some deep theoretical challenges of its own. For we soon run into a bifurcation, a split in the road. Political theorists and social scientists who study the new wave of populist authoritarianism tend to view technology as epiphenomenal to their topic, a mere means of communication, utilized for effective propaganda, whereas theorists of technology tend to view the transformation in technology as an almost sole factor, certainly the determining one. This is not merely a problem of the scholarly division of labor, a matter of perspective. What is at stake is a profound puzzle regarding the very nature of power.

Why is it puzzling? It is because, in this conjuncture of technology and authority, in terms of mastery we have two, opposing complaints. When it comes to technology, we tend to complain that we have not yet mastered and maybe can no longer master technology; our instruments, the very means of our purported mastery over nature, have turned against us, and we are dealing here with a slave revolt that we cannot crush. In the field of politics, on the other hand, we tend to complain that we have not yet shaken off the shackles of old masters. Indeed, we witness the rise of something which resembles the primordial, mythological, uncastrated father.

Somehow, the forward rush and constant disruption of new technologies coincides with the return of the repressed, and so we find ourselves pushed toward a (pre)theoretical choice: either we view the transformation in media technology as fundamental, and the political and cultural content of the moment as epiphenomenal; or the other way around so that what we are seeing is yet another return of the repressed, with technical media ultimately but a means of its expression.

Instead of viewing one aspect as epiphenomenal to the other, my interest in this book lies in the intersection between authority and technology. How can we think of the network as a social phenomenon and, at the same time, consider the social as a network? What can social and political phenomena teach us about the nature of the new technology? How and to what extent does technology reshape the very fabric of social and political life? I pick up the connections, tensions, and intersections between network technology and related topics (systems, structure) and social and political theories of social, unwritten rules, which traditionally serve as pillars of authority.

There has been much discussion in recent years as to the role of digital culture in political polarization. The famous "echo chambers" that characterize online culture do not produce free-floating, isolated monads of public opinion, which would be bad enough, but irresolvable conflictual positions, as the very heart and focus of each such chamber is the hypocrisies and fallacies of the opposed point of view. This polarization, very real in its effects, nonetheless rests on an ideological falsehood. The loss of a shared reality, which has become a trope in public discourse under the problematic title of "post-truth," denotes not so much a plurality of viewpoints that do not coalesce into a single worldview, but rather a transformation in the status of what is normally taken for granted, unthinkingly forming the backdrop of everyday life. For what is hidden behind the so-called polarization is a shared underlying suspicion and mistrust, efficiently utilized and manipulated by new authoritarianism.

Something is happening to symbolic efficiency—"the symbolic trust which persists against all skeptical data."[1] Somehow, the very erosion of symbolic trust is increasingly utilized for a new form of political legitimation. The gesture of unmasking, disrobing, is emerging as the predominant mode of contemporary dissimulation. In order to see and understand this transformation, understood as a project of "writing the unwritten," the book explores the vicissitudes of the unwritten law—perhaps the oldest name for what Žižek calls symbolic efficiency.

Lacanian psychoanalysis points us in the direction of a traumatic kernel, impossible to symbolize, around which symbolic forms and social structures organize themselves, and because of which such structures are never quite as solid and stable as we imagine them to be, forever perturbed by the absence they cover up. A bit of the real which has to go missing for reality to attain its consistency. Thinking of unwritten law as emphatically unwritten, as what "never stops not being written," allows us to confront the radical ontological dimensions of what the concept "unwritten no more" aims to address. What happens when the gap that sustains the distance of reality from the traumatic real, never fully present, seems itself to be lacking? What we get is not the bare real, the thing in itself, but a reality in which tarrying with the real, traumatic kernel itself can serve as a defense against the real; trauma as a defense against confronting (structural) trauma; exposure as a way to ignore what had been exposed. A reality in which, the more catastrophe, eccentricity, and extremity are foregrounded, the less we are capable of realizing the extent to which normality—say, structural features of reality—itself is eccentric, let alone of acting in a meaningful way to address all that is leaping toward us from the background.

ENVIRONMENTAL CRISIS: DISAVOWAL AND ACTING OUT

In other words, it is not only the king's "madness" that is at stake. Have we not all been eating from the tainted grain? Far removed from the theological context in which it was conceived, this Hasidic tale has a contemporary, everyday variation. "We live in crazy times," we tell each other in everyday conversation, in response to this or that catastrophic event, often a natural disaster or a political one. "We live in interesting times," say some of us, more sardonically, referring to the mythical Chinese curse.

Marking reality as crazy, we signal to each other, exchanging a sign whose significance belongs to a world already lost to us. For what could it mean to know, to really know, that we are crazy, and living in crazy times? Are we not desperately trying to reassure ourselves that the distinction between crazy and normal still holds, while we have effectively stepped over the crucial threshold that keeps them, however porously, apart?

This book is an account of an experience, which the colloquial term "the new normal"—the idea that what is normal, and what is normative, is in constant flux—offers a certain, initial access to. But it is not my experience, or anyone's, really. Nor is it simply an abstraction. It is an abstract experience, to be sure, but a real one nonetheless. More precisely, what is at stake is a certain transformation of our experience with the abstract, with what cannot be pinned down or experienced directly. We can call it the virtual ground, or background of experience. Hegel spoke of ethical substance; in the wake of Wittgenstein, some philosophers have called this the form of life. For reasons which will become progressively clearer, I have chosen to take seriously a notion which never attained the conceptual rigor of either of these terms, displaying in its elusiveness a core feature of the phenomenon it is meant to grasp: unwritten law. Simply put, our moment seems distinguished by a powerful drive to "write the unwritten," to bring to the fore what is normally backgrounded, to directly experience what can only be approached indirectly. In this fervent activity to make things explicit, palpable, and tangible, to tear down all appearances, we lull ourselves into a powerful and dangerous illusion.

For all the while, in the background, the grain remains tainted, the ecological crisis keeps unfolding, and the societal structures that sustain it fully hold sway. In this way, catastrophes that appear on the world stage ever more frequently function as anti-events: we register them, and even become deeply invested in them for a while, but effectively are using them as powerful distractions from the global crisis in the background. We tend to view emergencies as exceptional singularities, effectively ignoring the way in which the "state of emergency in which we live is not the exception, but the rule," as Walter Benjamin put it.[2]

It is a matter for scientific debate whether what will replace the Holocene will be a new stability, even if no doubt considerably less favorable for human life, or no stability at all. But we do not have to wait for the outcome of that scientific debate. For whether or not there will be a new stable natural environment, the environment as such, as the background enveloping our lives, is lost to us. We can no longer take nature for granted. Nature, as the stable background of our lives, is no more.

We cannot accept that nature in this primal sense, nature as primal, is no longer there. This would be tantamount to the proverbial cartoon character (Wile E. Coyote) staring down into the abyss and, seeing there is nothing beneath his feet, diving straight down. Instead, we are acting this disavowed recognition out.

Let us recall the story of the tainted grain: What if, indeed, the first result of our ecological disaster is to be sought on the terrain of "second nature"? We normally assume that, as the pressures of a collapsing natural environment accumulate, human society will be put under unprecedented pressures, eroding our institutions to the point of collapse. As nature becomes more and more unstable, we worry, how will it be possible to maintain social life? But this worry relies on a faulty conception of the relation between "first" and "second" nature, or nature and culture, as two ultimately separable entities.

In the following pages I pursue a different view, guided by the hypothesis that the terrain of "second nature" is where we are already, and have been for a long time, acting out the contradiction and crisis of nature. The unwritten law—with its antinomic nature—is the primordial mode of appearance of nature within human, social life. And so what we seem incapable of effectively avowing does find a site of expression in our collective activity—in particular, in the entanglement of technology and politics, which forms the nexus around which this investigation is organized.

Human life expresses the unrest of nature. Simply put, humans have an extraordinary capacity to "denaturalize," associated with our technological mindset and activity: we tear things apart, destroying any semblance of a stable nature or essence. Technoscientific "progress" is thus one way in which the unwritten is written—we undermine all given, all essential grounds. But humans also have the extraordinary capacity to "naturalize," to invest in things man-made a holistic sanctity, to immerse into our most primal nature things which are of human origin. We sanctify our traditions, our ways of life. As we become chronically suspicious toward grounds, the unwritable real finds new ways of inscribing itself as such. At a moment when the world faces major existential threats which mostly arise out of our technoscientific activity, from the climate crisis to artificial intelligence, challenges that cannot be solved exclusively by the very means that have produced them, by means of our technological prowess, and can only be addressed in large-scale collective action, our political frameworks seem to have gone off the rails.

Trying to gain some orientation in times of great upheaval such as ours, one confronts two opposing tendencies. Taking seriously the possibility that we are in the midst of a sea change, there is a temptation to abandon what might appear to be outdated conceptual schemes and begin afresh, thereby running the risk of losing all anchorage. Indeed, for Hannah Arendt, the tendency to redefine our terms was a major symptom of the decline of authority, the inability to rely on what is handed down to us. At the same time the opposite tendency, to assume that our conceptual tools are resilient enough, or adaptive enough, to offer a good fit to whatever situation we are confronting, runs the great risk of missing precisely what is new and needs accounting for.

In order to avoid this deadlock, I have adopted a deceptively simple methodological principle: to seek after the precise point where concepts and theoretical frameworks are lacking in explanatory power, in light of the particularities of contemporary phenomena. Indeed, Benjamin saw this as the unique "empiricism" proper to philosophy, distinguishing it amongst other disciplines: a conceptually guided empiricism designed to allow for what is authoritative in the object under investigation itself to emerge.

The book was written with great anxiety, amidst political upheaval and war. While some of its broader topics, such as the unwritten law, have preoccupied me since the very beginning of my academic studies and before, my observation of its changing function in contemporary social and political constellations endowed the project with great urgency. Since I couldn't benefit from the quiet and calm that are typical of academic work, I had to draw other, compensatory benefits from anxiety itself, trying to draw encouragement for the case I was making from the horrifying confirmations of my worries, rather than allow them to paralyze me.

While this is not a book about him, Walter Benjamin has been a crucial source for the ideas at the root of this book, as well as something of a patron saint, whom I would like to imagine watching over its realization, hopefully sympathetically. Everything I know about Benjamin and his role in a tradition of post-Kantian metaphysical empiricism I own to Eli Friedlander, but this does not cover my debt to him. As his undergraduate philosophy student, I witnessed myriad imperceptible gestures and techniques of thinking which I have sought, often unconsciously and no doubt unsuccessfully, to imitate. Luckily, being an exemplary philosopher, he remains inimitable. Igal Halfin, a teacher turned friend, has never stopped pushing me to orient my thoughts toward the puzzles of everyday contemporary reality, and has shown me how.

My debt to the Ljubljana School of Psychoanalysis may be even more difficult to measure, let alone put into words. Slavoj Žižek, Mladen Dolar, and Alenka Zupančič have each in their own way laid out the general theoretical framework without which this book would not have been possible. This book is a dialogue with their continuous work, directly and indirectly. It is in the authority of Mladen Dolar, who became a mentor and a friend during my graduate work at Columbia University, that I found the sanction to carry out this work. Simon Hajdini's invitation to teach a condensed seminar on the topics of this book to his students contributed immensely to bringing together the different threads I have been pursuing. The astute challenges put forward by his students were of great value to me, and are a testament to his role as a teacher, in the full sense of the word.

A work written under duress needs to rely on the comradery of peers and patrons alike. Noam Yuran and Shaul Setter were both partners and instigators of the core ideas behind this book. Yossi Schwartz and Joseph Vogl have given me the institutional and intellectual support to get it off the ground, at Tel Aviv University and Humboldt University respectively. Thanks to their generosity, and the financial support of the Minerva Foundation, I was able to pursue my research. Early fruits of this research have been published in *Angelaki* and *Problemi*. Finally, to acknowledge Attay Kremer's contribution to this book requires the invention of an as yet nonexistent social function, which may be approximated by an analogy drawn from the music industry. In terms of that industry, Attay was the producer of this book: on top of absolutely indispensable technical support, Attay was someone to brainstorm with, the ideal audience and interlocutor, and often the only one who believed the book would actually happen. The only one except for Thomas Weaver, the Short Circuits series editor, whose intelligence and kindness made me trust his belief in the project, and put my own anxieties in their place.

FATHER KNOWS WORST:
AUTHORITARIANISM, OLD AND NEW

> Nihilists! F*** me. I mean, say what you like about the tenets of National
> Socialism, Dude, at least it's an ethos.
> Walter Sobchak in *The Big Lebowski*

The phrase "father knows best" encapsulates and simplifies an old, fading, and
highly discredited notion of paternal authority: father—or any other authority figure unfortunate enough to assume this place of privilege—is privy to a
knowledge that makes him fit to rule. This knowledge is assumed, implicit in
the rule of authority. "Put your trust in me" is here the message of authority.
"I know what I'm doing." Of course, we are by now long accustomed to seeing this position as fake, and father figures as imposters. Indeed, a major strain
of the Enlightenment project was intended precisely to relieve us from the
unthinking reliance on figures of authority, to dare to think for ourselves, as
Kant famously put it. [1] This was the core of the Enlightenment's emancipatory
promise: think for yourself, authorize yourself to think, and external authority just might wither away.

How are we to understand the movement from "dad to worse" (*père au
pire*), [2] the steady slide of liberal democracies, grounded in the promise of
enlightenment, into what can be called the rule of the worst (kakistocracy)?
Two and a half decades into the twenty-first century, we witness all around
us the rise of authority figures and political parties that seem to garner more
legitimation the more they demonstrate just how unfit to rule they are. Reasonable as we are, we pull our hair in despair.

But are they truly the worst? Can we not easily imagine, right around
the corner, something even worse? Behind the vain vengefulness of a possibly reelected Trump, promising to act as a dictator against his political enemies, doesn't there lie something worse still, the crystallizing ideology, say,
of Christian nationalism? Is what we are witnessing a step in the direction of

something worst, familiar to us from the twentieth century, namely full-blown fascism and totalitarianism? Or perhaps this comparison itself is a dangerous distraction, specters of past historical events leading us away from coming to terms with how deeply boring and disappointing, our postmodern dystopia truly is, denying us even the apocalyptic, final dramatic clash between good and evil?[3]

The spontaneous suspicion of figures of authority also informs political theory, as a suspicion of the very significance of authority and its figures, a worry that focusing on the political drama of elections, the battle for positions of power, is merely a distraction from the deep structure or the mechanics of power. We are, as Foucault famously put it, to cut off the head of the king in political theory, presumably a more difficult feat than beheading real-life, historical monarchs.[4]

Yet even headless authority figures—perhaps especially those ones—seem to come back from the dead to haunt us. From the gallows of history, an archaic figure of authority is making an inglorious comeback. What are coming to assume the position of old fathers, those supposed to know best, are new iterations of the worst kind of father: fathers who know worst. Leaders who come to assume positions of power not because they best know how to rule, but because they seem relieved of the basic duty to rule themselves. Leaders who garner support and legitimacy not despite, but directly due to, their display of an unencumbered, mindless will. Just consider how in the extremely consequential 2024 election for the US presidency, we witness a strange imbalance: whereas for Biden, the issue of his mental competence to rule at his advanced age seems crucial, his gaffes and lapses highly detrimental to his chances of reelection, the same doesn't seem to apply to Trump, only four years his junior and no less prone to gaffes and lapses. While this is certainly unfair, it is not devoid of rationale. Indeed, part of what makes this election so dramatic and consequential is the way in which two standards of rule here come to a clash. The candidates are truly held to different standards: Biden is measured by his ability to maintain the figure of the competent "dad" who knows best, that is, someone who approximates, to the best of his abilities, an ideal of better knowledge, whereas Trump answers to a much more elusive standard, the standard of "the worst," measured by his capacity to display that he knows something of the worst, his capacity, as it were, to put us in touch with the limit. Indeed, the imbalance in question has to do with a unique feature of the limit: limits cannot be reached, but they can be crossed. Crossing a limit by being "the worst," transgressing all norms, can give us a sense of being in touch with something that the mere approximation of a standard cannot.

While in their transgression new authoritarian leaders recall Freud's myth of the primal father, they should not be taken as direct reincarnations. That is not how the repressed returns. After all, the primal father is a myth, express-ing the primordiality of authority as we know it, as a set of unwritten rules which normally go unquestioned, rules inscribed in our very inhibitions and taboos. It expresses an unrest which belongs to our "second nature," an uneasiness toward the human condition. As a myth, the tale of the primal, uncastrated father expresses a condition, a limit that determines our field of possibility, by allowing within the frame of our imagination for a figuration of what exceeds it, the possibility excluded from our condition, or the impos-sible. The possibility of a life unbound by rules. What Freud expressed in the form of a myth—a story of brothers whose promiscuous father of the horde, sexually in possession of all the females, evokes such resentment and jealousy in them that they conspire to unite in rebellion against him, murder him, and then proceed to impose on themselves the sexual prohibitions from which the dead father is now the only one exempted—can be expressed by the pithy Lacanian formula "father . . . or worse" (*père ou pire*).[5] The myth and the for-mula alike express the understanding that in becoming speaking beings, it is *as if* we have opted for the discontent entailed in being subject to rules from which a stain of arbitrariness cannot be entirely removed (we cannot, as it were, give grounds to that which grounds us, hence the nagging notion of our ground or condition as resulting from some primal, mythical choice), but have thereby overcome something worse, one image of which is the violent rule of the arbitrary.

The primal father is a figurative mode of appearance of the worse, the threat lurking behind the impossible alternative for symbolic castration, the psychoanalytic name for the drama of limits. Far from being mythical figures of libidinal freedom from rules and inhibitions, offering us perhaps a liberat-ing path toward the same, fathers who know worst are rather a distorted out-let for us to collectively experience primal, symbolic castration. What we lack all knowledge of, what we can only represent in mythical or formulaic form, is granted a strange new positivity in them. In tarrying with the worst we are seemingly allowed access to something constitutive of our subjectivity. They bring about in a forceful manner the primal experience of limits by routinely transgressing them. What we can only construe as a forced choice constitutive of subjectivity, that is, a choice of which we are the result, not one we have taken, a choice detectable in what determines us, is dramatically put forward through such figures as a real choice that lies ahead of us, yet to be deter-mined. As those who "know worst," they allow us a strangely positive experi-ence of the worse averted by castration. Through them, we can experience "the worst"—a notion of limit, something we never can experientially reach—as an object of possible knowledge. The "worst" assumes the shape of an option, something which may or may not be opted for. Limits seem to lose the trans-parency of the frame and enter into the picture.

In this sense, the rule of the worst speaks to something broader than an emerging form of government. It speaks to a prevailing mood of our time. If ours is the "darkest timeline," as the popular internet meme goes, referring to the multiverse theory as imagined by comic books and movies, it is so in a very precise if paradoxical sense: it is the worst possible world precisely in that it could be worse. Indeed, it is getting worse. Bad as things get, we can trust one thing: there is worse still to come. If the climate crisis is the process in which our natural environment, the earth, is gradually turning into a hell-scape, degree after degree, the rule of the worst is the political form in which we gradually transform our societies into a hellscape. In both cases, the very fact that things can, and in all likelihood will, get worse strangely helps maintain us in the grip of what ought to be averted at all costs. Like the proverbial boiling frog, we can continue saying, "it's not so bad, could be worse," until we can't. Where's the limit, the absolute worst? Under the rule of the worst, we do not receive a clear answer to that question, but we are making the question itself omnipresent, coloring the entire horizon. What will he do next? Will that be the end of it? What natural disasters still await us, and which will be the "big one," after which everything changes forever? Where, in short, is the limit?

And yet, while more than merely analogous, the comparison between the climate crisis and the political one does not yield an identity. For in the political field we are directly engaged and active, many of us enthralled, eagerly anticipating the increase in chaos, others terrified by it. It is in the political field that a new sense of "realism" is emerging most distinctly, and a new modality of the "passion for the real" along with it.[6]

Mark Fisher distinguished capitalist realism from older modes of realism by highlighting how, under the continuously transformative conditions of capitalism, realism comes to signify a constant adjustment to an ever-changing norm, rather than a stable limit or reality principle.[7] Therein lies an important clue in our attempt to understand new authoritarianism. New authoritarianism charges the constant demand of normalization to worsening conditions (what Adam Curtis calls "hypernormalisation")[8] with a unique fervor of its own: how much worse can it get? Is there a limit to what we can get accustomed to? Normalizing what up until recently was considered impossible, unacceptable, becomes, under the condition of new authoritarian realism, an exciting adventure, a search for the boiling point. In this, new authoritarianism folds into the political dynamics the tension inherent to limits, the tension between a dramatic event of rupture, a cut, and an underlying condition. It routinizes, as it were, the experience of what transgresses the norm, effectively making normality progressively indistinguishable from aberration. In the process of getting worse, with the prevailing sense of the worst being yet to come, we lose sight of the precise way the worst is in the process of actualization. As the impossible is routinely realized, nothing seems impossible. We should allow that sentence to resonate fully and hear in it the aspect of denial or disavowal, namely, that as the impossible routinely transpires, it is nothing itself that becomes impossible, kept at bay. This may soothe, in effect, our fear of annihilation, making the limit disappear in the very process of perpetually approximating it. As Alenka Zupančič so aptly put it, we find ourselves saying, in effect, "The world is ending, but hey, that's not the end of the world!"[9] But we should also hear the way in which such a "realism" suffocates desire. For it is in principle the impossible we wish for, what lies out of reach.

This understanding should also inform our inquiry into new authoritarianism as a historical phenomenon. We are pushed to choose, in advance, whether to measure it against the dramatic aberrations from the norm of liberal democracy, as many liberals are prone to do, by comparing it with, say, twentieth-century fascism and totalitarianism, or to view it as a symptom of the generalized tendency of capitalism toward crisis, as many in the radical circles of the left champion. Max Horkheimer expressed the latter in a famous maxim from 1939: "Whoever is not willing to talk about capitalism should also keep quiet about fascism."[10]

Today, with capitalism itself undergoing such dramatic shifts that some have already declared ours a postcapitalist world,[11] we see capitalism itself transitioning into something worse; it no longer appears (only) as the infinitely adaptative robot from the future (Terminator 2) of late capitalism, generating and reabsorbing all externalities, all threats to its ever-mutating existence; rather, we perceive more and more clearly capitalism's propensity to produce another kind of surplus, one it cannot safely reabsorb, a kind of crisis that cannot be handled within its framework. The climate crisis is the glaring case in point, but what about its political expression? Perhaps it is time to reverse Horkheimer's maxim. Any understanding of capitalism that overlooks or downplays its self-destructive aspect is a partial one at best. In order to understand capitalism itself, we may need to study its symptoms, where its inner contradictions come to light, where it produces political forms that undermine the rule of capital itself. Capitalism not only pushes us to accept that all alternatives to it are worse, as Mark Fisher had shown remarkably well in his *Capitalist Realism*; capitalism also pushes toward the realization of these worse alternatives to itself, pushing is own adaptability beyond its limits.

KNOWING WORST: TRANSGRESSION AS AN OCCULTING EXPOSURE

What are we getting out of things getting worse? What is the strange satisfaction or enjoyment in orienting ourselves toward the worst? What, more concretely, underlies the appeal of new authoritarian leaders? The increasing number of illiberal leaders who have risen to power in the liberal-democratic world over the past decades exposes the need to rethink such fundamental concepts as authority, sovereignty, legitimacy, and power in the modern state. It is easy to classify the ascendancy of leaders such as Donald Trump, Recep Tayyip Erdoğan, Binyamin Netanyahu, and Vladimir Putin as an updated version of populism, especially given its widespread harnessing of resentment toward elites as a source of influence. Yet the concepts formulated by populism studies fall far short of encapsulating the phenomenon. They fail to explain the global nature of the emerging trend, and more importantly, they seem unable to account for the new patterns of legitimation, political discourse, and authority characteristic of this new kind of politics.

Let us take note of what seems to be a quintessential trait of the new politics: its direct appeal to the obscene as a source of power. This characteristic is especially striking when it comes to Trump, Netanyahu, and Silvio Berlusconi, as attested to by the spirit of hedonism or even vulgarity that surrounds them, by their ability to say things that are taboo, by their disregard for the rules of political discourse, the public use of winks and "dog whistles" (i.e., the positioning of the obscene as the center of the transmitted message), and so on. This appeal to the obscene offers us a key to the broader phenomenon, precisely in its most surprising aspect.

It is no wonder that such displays elicit the astonishment and frustration of political scholars and commentators. Patterns of discourse and actions that have traditionally been considered destructive to political figures are turning out, in the hands of these new leaders, to be secret weapons for securing power. They also pose a theoretical challenge to our ideas about political authority and legitimacy.

A good way to elucidate the theoretical challenge starts from Hans Christian Andersen's story "The Emperor's New Clothes," which illustrates a fundamental paradigm of modern thinking on the subject of authority. According to this paradigm, authority is nothing but external attire, and all it takes to uncover this fact is to look at it with eyes free of the chains of traditional political culture. If only we can gain enough insight—with the help of critical thinking, rejection of ideology, and recognition of the systems of power—we shall see that underneath the clothes, the people who hold the power are mere flesh and blood, and their nakedness will be exposed to all. And yet the new authoritarians flaunt their nakedness, in the sense that their patterns of recruitment, legitimation, and maintenance of power are in fact based on the exposure and blatant transgression that they themselves perpetrate. Much of their appeal lies in this act of exposure.

THE PARABLE OF GIANT GOLDEN LETTERS

Donald Trump's candidacy for the presidency of the United States and his public conduct since his election will serve us here as the parable of enormous, golden letters, to paraphrase Socrates' method in Plato's *Republic*, fixing our eyes on what is more legible because bolder and more distinctive, and thus indicative of the political power taking shape before us. The point is not to further the fascination and cult of personality of someone who might be, in some respects, an outlier; rather, what manifests itself in extreme fashion in the figure of a Trump is taken to be indicative of a much wider configuration of power and authority. Can there be a "Trumpism" without a Trump? Certainly, authoritarianism tends to center on figures of authority, but can these figures be easily replaced? At the moment, this remains an open question. What occupies us here is not what might be singular and irreplaceable in a Trump, but rather what general tendencies his rise to power makes visible.

Time and again during the 2016 U.S. presidential campaign, commentators declared the inevitable end of Trump's candidacy due to the candidate's scandalous and unusual behavior. Trump mocked former Republican presidential candidate John McCain for having been a prisoner of war, and derisively imitated a handicapped journalist in public and in front of cameras. When a recording of Trump boasting about his disgraceful treatment of women leaked in the press, the expectation was that he would at least lose the support of Moral Majority Republicans who hold family values and decency sacred. As it turned out, not only did Trump's image survive undamaged, it even gained ground among his supporters, many of whom are devout evangelicals. Trump himself famously remarked that he could "shoot somebody on Fifth Avenue" and his fans would continue to support him. Running again for the presidency in 2024, Trump is also facing several serious charges in court, and his attempt to thwart the results of the 2020 election, culminating in the January 6 uprising on Capitol Hill, had been widely covered and discussed in the media. As I write these lines, Trump is the frontrunner in his bid for reelection, despite, or indeed because of, the openness of his failures and transgressions. His immunity to criticism is at the heart of the charismatic power that has propelled Trump and his ilk to the top, a power that inspires dread in the hearts of his rivals and admiration among his supporters.

We might ask what makes the political charisma of leaders who fit the new model of authoritarianism unique, and what its secret of success is. Trump, more than any other leader, raises a problem that cannot be explained by the classic concept of charisma, even though Max Weber's description of the charismatic authority structure clearly outlines many of the antiestablishment aspects of the charismatic leader. Weber maintains that the charismatic leader has a direct relationship with the "masses," a fact that makes his charisma unstable and requires him to constantly rally and legitimize support. Because he does not rely on external (traditional or legal-intellectual) sources of legitimacy, the charismatic leader must validate his power by demonstrating it. In other words, he must succeed. As Weber puts it: "His charismatic claim breaks down if his mission is not recognized by those to whom he feels he has been sent." [12] Even though it is not stated explicitly, Weber's paradigmatic model is evidently that of the Protestant theological concept of election, wherein worldly success is an a posteriori proof of having been divinely chosen. Similarly, charisma, according to Weber, is validated retroactively only when it is already in effect and embodies a mode of being chosen without a singular moment of choice. The obvious discrepancy between the "inner determination and inner restraint" characteristic of Weber's charismatic leader and the chaos and permissiveness that Donald Trump disseminates around him is no marginal detail. For Freud, as opposed to Weber, demonstrative permissiveness and a lack of inhibitions are the traits of a "horde" leader. Restraint and determination seem essential to Weber, precisely because of the centrality of the concept of mission in his definition of charisma. The success of the charismatic leader is inseparable from the mission he has been chosen (by a higher power) to fulfill: he proves that he has been chosen by successfully accomplishing the task at hand. This is where we run headlong into the incongruity of the new "charisma." Although there are ample signs that both Trump and his followers see him as a man on a mission, it is doubtful that anyone— including the leader himself and his fans—could define just what that mission is. The vague folksiness of the Trump campaign's nostalgic slogans, such as "Make America great again" or "Drain the swamp," is no coincidence. These are ways of expressing discontent with the status quo without really defining it or laying out ways to amend it.

Do Trump and others like him present such criteria, by whose measure they might be seen to succeed or fail? Let us remind ourselves that this is no marginal quandary. If indeed charismatic authority needs to constantly keep proving its success, understanding the efficiency of said authority requires insight into its internal success criteria, which in Trump's case appear to be profoundly enigmatic. [13] What exactly is the mission that he is ostensibly, and successfully, fulfilling, at least in the eyes of his supporters? Any attempt to attribute an ideology or even a coherent agenda to Trump's conduct comes up short. For example, he may have claimed to be in favor of American separatism, but he also appointed (and then dismissed) one of the architects of neoconservative imperialist foreign policy, John Bolton, as national security adviser; he declared unprecedented friendship with Russia, while at the same time renewing the arms race against it; he speaks about the economic difficulties of the working class while giving tax benefits to the extremely wealthy (and, to a much lesser extent, to the moderately wealthy); countless examples could be added to the list. The one consistent line in his administration is the attempt to roll back the policies put in place by his predecessor, if only for appearances' sake. It all points to the fact that Trump's mandate is one of abnegation—he does not violate conventions in order to fulfill his mission;

breaking the conventions is the mission. In this sense, Trump most clearly embodies one of the prominent features of the current political moment. His most pronounced story of election, is, quite famously, the one that emerged through the internet conspiracy theory connected with the figure of QAnon.

As is well known, according to the narrative that has emerged from the "dumps" by QAnon, supposedly, a deep undercover secret agent, Trump is a man on a mission to expose and bring to justice the corrupt elites, who have merged the most perverse sexual activity—pedophilia—with political and financial corruption. What these conspiracy theories should teach us is the significance of Trump's mission being one of exposure, bringing to light what is kept hidden in the dark, imagined as a domain of forbidden, obscene pleasure only the powerful elites are privy to. What such a mission amounts to is the exposure of a conspiracy, a network secretly controlling our destinies, exploiting the most innocent—children—for their own, perverse enjoyment. Certainly, such conspiracy theories are delusional, but should not be discarded as useless. Trump does indeed bring to light a power, usually invisible, that rules us, only it is not orchestrated by a cabal of elites. It is the strange hold of unwritten rules over us, which he makes present by violating them. This is what the orientation toward the worst, by means of consistently transgressive behavior, attains: it makes the elusive stuff of our ethical substance assume a certain objectlike feature, however fleetingly, time and again.

TRANSGRESSION AS EXPOSURE: THE MEDIUM (OF POWER) IS THE MESSAGE

In order to establish the elusive criterion of success that characterizes the new authoritarian leader, it is imperative to pause for a moment and pay attention to the element of surprise evoked when unspoken things are said and unwritten rules are broken. What is surprising is not the content of the statement or action, but the very fact that they *are* said or done. Equally, it is not the actual violation of the rules that is shocking, but the public manner in which it is perpetrated, since the fundamental viewpoint of the modern citizen, especially in the "postideological" age of the last half-century, is one of extreme cynicism and jadedness.[14] We know better, we have no illusions;[15] we know very well that the emperor has no clothes. This position, which crosses political lines and even class divisions, shared by "elites" and "masses" alike, makes viewers of the political game prepared to expect obscene behavior on the part of others, perhaps especially on the part of politicians. However, they also expect it to take place in the dark corridors of power, away from the public spotlight.

"If you like laws and sausages, you should never watch either being made." This quote, misattributed to Otto von Bismarck, concisely captures the obscene dimension entailed in revealing the unseemly truth about the foundations of society, typical of the modern zeitgeist. Political modernization is accompanied by the rationalization and transparency of the means of control. Ostensibly, according to Weber's renowned sociological thesis, in the modern conditions of a transparent political process, a process also known as the "routinization of charisma," the mystery surrounding the origin of the law and its authority is supposed to wane.[16] Laws are made by parliamentary bodies in public assembly for all to see, and even covert procedures—so-called "backroom deals"—are an open secret and widely covered in the media. Modern humans do not obey the law because its source is sublime or mysterious, but despite or because they know full well how it is made. The democratic process, the organized struggle for authority, means that, in modern politics, political power no longer has a charismatic center shrouded in mystery or an aura of holiness to keep it in place.[17] Transgressing unwritten rules puts us back in contact with the "mysterious sources of authority," by making present what we normally either take for granted or unexpectedly stumble against.

What, then, makes the new emergent authoritarianism unique? As we shall show, the new authoritarianism reconnects with the mysterious element of the law in a cynical age, precisely because of its openly transgressive nature. As Slavoj Žižek observes:

> What is happening today is not just more of the same, but a qualitatively new form of dissonance: one openly admitted, and for that reason treated as irrelevant. The paradox is thus that, today, there is in a sense less deception than in the way ideology functioned in the past: nobody is really deceived. In other words, it is not that prior to our current era we took the rules and prohibitions seriously while today we openly violate them. What changed are the rules which regulate appearances, i.e. what can appear in public space.[18]

Denying reality by the very fact of admitting it is a familiar structure in psychoanalytic literature. Contrary to repression, fetishistic disavowal allows subjects to maintain their beliefs by denying them directly. Octave Mannoni insists on the widespread use of the linguistic structure typical of denial and effectively illustrates its internal logic: "I know well . . ." (that, like all politicians, the candidate I support is a crook / a cheat / incompetent / goes against my own self-interest) "but all the same . . ." (he is still better than his rivals / he reflects my identity / not to elect him would spell disaster).[19] Yet what makes this new form of authority so challenging to comprehend is the explicit way in which it makes exposure operate perversely as an illusion; the act of taking off the mask functions as a mask.

The Greeks had a saying: "The law is not written for the king or the jester."[20] That the law is not written for the king is a widely discussed topic in twentieth-century political theory. The paradoxical status of sovereign power as having the legal authority to suspend the law reveals the problematic link, in the law, between justice and violence. If we follow this thought to its conclusion, the fundamental justification of the law, which puts an end to arbitrary violence sometimes associated with nature, turns out to be the justification for boundless violence, a continuation of violence by other, far-reaching means.[21] However, the part of the saying stipulating that the law is not written for the jester points us in another direction, that of daily social life, a space where a rule violation is ordinarily met with ridicule and laughter rather than organized coercion, and as such directly touches on social "nature."[22] The attempt to understand the circumstances necessary for the rise of the clown-king, the leader who rules by virtue of his power to violate basic, unwritten social rules, requires a terminological distinction between two conceptions of the law— let us call them the social and the political for now—and the tracing of their historical pathways, as well as the points where the two meet and intersect. Indeed, this distinction is quite necessary to understand what the obscene is.

To better understand the sphere of the obscene, a distinction must be made between written and unwritten law. The distinction between what is decent and what is obscene is a matter of unwritten law, as opposed to the distinction between what is legal and what is illegal, which is a matter of written law. In very general terms, the unwritten law can be defined as the ethical background of the political order. As such, unwritten law is at once a source of legitimation of the existing order and the space from which it can be criticized. This intentionally broad definition is meant to elucidate how very distant and sometimes even opposing concepts, such as divine law, the law of nations (ius gentium),[23] local custom, natural law, and common law, have all historically fallen under the category of "unwritten law." The metaphorical image of the unwritten law as a "background" emphasizes the slippery relation of this kind of law with the written law: as the background to an object, the unwritten law is what must lose its articulation in order for the outline of the written law to be rendered distinct. This quality of the unwritten law is also the reason why it is difficult to define and therefore identify it as a distinct object of historical investigation. The resistance to conceptual formalization typical of tacit knowledge is also present throughout the conceptual history of the object in question: much of the conceptualizing is done by "translating" it to proximate terms while diverting the emphasis from its unwritten nature.[24] Thus, for example, divine law emphasizes the supremacy of the unwritten law in relation to the finality of the man-made, written law. Custom and tradition touch on the primordial element and the idea that unwritten law embodies the spirit of community, while natural law seeks to formulate the rules that must underlie the positive order and by way of which it can be criticized, the rational ground of law, so to speak.

For our purposes—the study of power accumulated through exposure—the most relevant characteristics of the unwritten law are those that emphasize its tacit aspect and resistance to formalization. One of the most prominent and consistent attributes of unwritten law (in its various instances) is also what distinguishes it most clearly from written law. The violation of a legal norm involves a forceful sanction imposed by the authorities, whereas a violation of the rules of public decency is met with a vaguer, albeit sometimes more severe, response.[25]

The obscene therefore has a complex role in relation to the social order: the obscene can be perceived as less severe than the illegal because it is a breach of unwritten law, which is not enforced by formal sanction, but it can also be considered more severe than the illegal for the exact same reason: the rules that it breaks are fundamental to society precisely because there is no way to formulate them fully and formally. These are rules that we follow without being aware of them, or, to employ a slightly more provocative phrasing, they are rules we do not even know we know. Like the hammer in Heidegger's well-known example, unwritten law only becomes present as an object when something goes wrong, only when our pretheoretical relation with it encounters an obstacle. Just as the hammer emerges before our eyes as an object only when it stops working properly, the unwritten law is only revealed when it is violated. (In a sense to be elaborated in chapter 5, it malfunctions when it is revealed to us as something functional). It is this feature of the unwritten law that led Walter Benjamin to identify it with the realm of myth: myth, in one short formula, is our encounter with the primal, with what we encounter as both determining, constitutive, and unaccountable. Both our attraction toward and our rejection of the obscene involve the impossibility of formulating the boundaries of the field. It is an object revealed only with experience, without our having a prior idea of what it is.

A functioning member of a given social group readily and immediately recognizes what is perceived as obscene, what violates the unwritten law, even though they cannot give an a priori definition of what falls under this category, to formulate a rule, so to speak. It just goes without saying.[26] This is why, in everyday experience, the effect that accompanies the breaking of an unwritten law is surprise and embarrassment. We feel that a boundary has been crossed, that we have said something that should not have been said, or looked at something we should not have seen, even though most of the time we are not quite sure what that boundary is or what rule we might have violated.[27]

The obscene, in that sense, is the opposite of the unicorn. The unicorn is a concept we can easily define and even draw on paper, even though it is not part of the experience-based reality of our lives. Conversely, we recognize obscenity when we encounter it in our daily lives, even though we cannot provide a definition for it. The inability to frame it as a rule is what creates the close link between obscenity and transgression. It is an invisible boundary which is only perceived when crossed; only then do we come face to face with it.[28]

Armed with the distinction between written and unwritten law, let us now briefly return to examining the singularity of the new model of authority in relation to the classic concept of charisma. Max Weber writes about the hostile attitude of the charismatic leader toward the legal system:

> Genuine charismatic domination, therefore, knows of no abstract legal codes and statutes and of no "formal" way of adjudication. Its "objective" law emanates concretely from the highly personal experience of heavenly grace and from the god-like strength of the hero. Charismatic domination means a rejection of all ties to any external order in favor of the exclusive glorification of the genuine mentality of the prophet and hero. Hence, its attitude is revolutionary and transvalues everything; it makes a sovereign break with all traditional or rational norms: "It is written, but I say unto you."[29]

The final phrase of this excerpt is highly significant for our investigation of the uniqueness of new authoritarianism. "It is written, but I say onto you" is the basic formula Jesus uses to confer authority upon himself in the Sermon on the Mount as the bearer of the new word of God that overrules established law.[30] This is not the place to discuss the influence of Christian political theology on Weber's thought, but it is important to note this allusion at a moment when present political reality forces us to revise and update social theory. Weber develops his notion of charismatic power by drawing on the work of Sohm on the power of the church,[31] as distinguished from the enforceable power of the state. In the Sermon on the Mount, Jesus brings to its culmination a critical process with a rich history: censuring existing law in the name of the unwritten law that underpins it and allows for its critique. In the case of Jesus, the unwritten law in question is divine law, but what matters to us is that historically speaking, very disparate categories of unwritten law, such as custom or tradition, natural law, and divine law can all be used for the same purpose—a grounded and thorough critique of the existing order. Jesus wishes to replace the letter of the law with the spirit of the law, which he is uniquely qualified to put into words. By identifying himself directly with the unwritten law, Jesus establishes a radical model of revolutionary-charismatic criticism. We might also note that Arendt sees twentieth-century totalitarianism as an apex of this tradition: totalitarian movements transcend lawfulness and lawlessness as they see themselves as servants of the unwritten law of movement, a law of becoming underlying the stability of all positive law.

Despite the frequent use by Trump and his ilk of the accusatory slogan "fake news" to mean "don't believe them, I am the only one you should believe," it is hard to attribute anything close to Jesus's sense of mission to the charismatic leaders of the new right. Their goal is not to give expression to the essence of the law hidden behind the language of the law but to reveal the essence of the unwritten as such. Their message, when all is said and done, is not "so it is written, but I say unto you," but "this is the unwritten; here, let me show it to you."

The violation of unwritten rules is an act of exposure. The new political power's recourse to obscene behavior as a means of mobilizing support should direct our attention, therefore, in the first instance to the importance of the unwritten—or tacit—nature of social ethical rules. For what captivates those watching the rise of this political power, whether in horror or admiration, is how politicians of the new breed bring the tacit dimension of social life, the rules we normally obey without being able to formulate them, to light by violating those same rules. Contrary to written law, the unwritten nature of these rules imbues them with an inherent mystery. It would seem that these rules become tangible only when they are violated, and it is this newfound tangibility that surrounds politicians of the new breed with a unique aura, as proof of their mysterious social clout.

WHAT ELSE IS NEW? (I) TRUTH AND LIE IN AN IMMORAL CONTEXT

But what exactly is the charismatic hold of such clown-kings over us? To what extent does it resemble, and in what lies its difference from, the power of the dictators of the twentieth century? It is worthwhile to turn our attention to Salena Zito's apt formula for the split reaction to Trump's outrageous lies and fabulations: "It's a familiar split. When he makes claims like this, the press takes him literally, but not seriously; his supporters take him seriously, but not literally."[32] There is no doubt that the elitist scorn showered upon leaders of the new kind plays a part in sustaining their power. It may be difficult to respect this clown, but we must nevertheless take him—and most importantly the circumstances that have made him possible—dead seriously.

For we are tempted to say: well, stupid might be bad, but evil is worse. Can a narcissistic fool be an evil genius? More generally, can evil be so stupid, can stupidity truly be so evil? The figure of the father who knows worst is hard to grasp in part because of the way in which it short-circuits a deeply ingrained distinction between stupidity and evil. We tend to think that it is precisely knowledge that makes the difference: there are those who do bad things because they don't know any better, and those who do them despite knowing better, out of evil intent. Stupidity deserves our ridicule or benevolent enlightenment; it is something we may laugh off or seek to amend. Evil seems more profound, worthy of heroic struggle. In transgressively pointing toward a knowledge no one possesses, the knowledge in which we are ourselves inscribed, new authoritarian figures seem to display the point of indifference between evil and idiocy, the stupidity of evil—that there is nothing uniquely profound or mysterious about it—and the evil of stupidity, what makes it less than innocent.

We might say that in the figure of the clown-king, what Deleuze called transcendental stupidity is raised to the level of radical evil. The radicality of evil for Kant is not meant to denote some extreme form of evil, but rather the way in which evil belongs to the very roots of human freedom. For Kant, radical evil is not a devilish, principled commitment to do evil for evil's sake, but rather the raising of self-interest, our natural propensity to do what we feel like rather than our duties, to the level of a principle, a law of character.[33] In this, it would be typified not by some cartoonish plot of destruction but by cynicism, the belief that all there is, all that governs human action, is self-interest. The only reason to follow rules and duties can be, from this perspective, self-interest itself, and self-imposed duty, or ethical commitment, is nothing but a sham. Along similar lines, for Deleuze, transcendental stupidity is to be distinguished from a propensity for empirical error. It is a certain blindness toward significance, an inherent tendency of thought toward triviality, a condition in which one lacks a sense for what makes a difference, what is salient and remarkable.[34] We might say that the figure of the narcissistic fool condenses radical evil with transcendental stupidity, or indeed points to their common ground: a narcissistic fool always (believes he) knows what's significant—whatever is on his mind. He is relieved of the fear that his thought might devolve into the trivial, for he denies with every fiber of his being that there can be any measure to the significance of things outside his whimsey. If significance in general points to our involvement with the world,[35] the way things in themselves matter to us, the narcissist's folly lies in his self-involvement. Significance loses precisely its objective hold on the world and becomes absorbed in his caprice. It would be wrong to say of a narcissist that he thinks himself the center of the world. Rather, the world, like any other orbiting piece of rock, revolves around him. That's his self-importance. While a narcissist makes no argument for this world(less)view—why would he?—his very existence seems to make the argument for him. As such, his behavior seems to defy the very idea of significance, its distinction from something merely subjective (interest), in the same way that cynicism undermines the very possibility of assuming moral duty as something distinct from self-interest. Evil and stupidity converge at this point, as the paradoxical rule of idiocy, of the idiosyncratic, undermining in one stroke both the notions of rule and singularity. This is the evil of a comprehensive, consistent triviality.

It is with this in mind that we should turn to comparing new authoritarianism with its twentieth-century predecessor. The new type of authoritarian leader that has emerged in recent years shares some similarities with the ones that typified twentieth-century authoritarianism. But, once again, it is where the similarity seems maximal that we should be alert to what nonetheless distinguishes our contemporary moment.

In his excellent essay on the type of leader that swept the world to unprecedented disasters in the previous century, Adorno makes a significant, counterintuitive observation. It is precisely because of the felt fakery, the obvious charlatanism of a Hitler that his followers were pushed to excessive, pathetic proofs of belief and faithfulness.[36] Arendt, for her part, has noticed the proclivity to lying in totalitarian propaganda, the strange mixture of shameless, baseless lies and shockingly honest admissions of what one would expect to have remained hidden.[37] Today it has become popular to refer to such a bombardment of lies as "gaslighting," meant to unanchor those exposed to it from the sense of security supplied by a shared sense of reality. What both these commentators of twentieth-century authoritarianism point to seems, to outside observers, like a mad loss of reality on the part of followers. How can anyone fall for such obvious charlatanism, such obvious lies? However, in our contemporary authoritarianism, this charlatanism can no longer be viewed as a mere instrument of power, but directly as the message. From the standpoint of ordinary experience, facts are, first and foremost, limitations on the will. We encounter facts as limits to what we can achieve. Displaying a disregard for the compelling power of facts is therefore, primarily, a display of power, hinting at an unencumbered will. That message is received, loud and clear, by opponents and supporters alike. An example from Israel might help render this subtle yet crucial point more palpable. In the 1990s, when Netanyahu first came to power, he was not yet received by his followers, as he is today, with the salutation "king of Israel." At the time, he was affectionately greeted on stage by the salutation "the magician." What should we make of such a disposition toward a figure of authority? What does it disclose about the mode of identification with him? It is crucial to understand the admiration of such figures of authority as inseparable from the mystifying effect they have on those seemingly outside their circle of influence. Those who consider themselves part of polite society, committed to the public rules of the game, cannot but be appalled by such transgressive figures, shamelessly lying and manipulating their way into power. Being appalled, however, is a modality of fascination, the engagement with a puzzling image. What is it about him, they ask themselves, that casts such a spell on those fools who follow him? How does he get away with it? By what trickery does he cast such a spell on those dupes who

follow him blindly? At the same time, the followers, we may equally speculate, are infinitely impressed by the capacity of a "magician" such as Netanyahu to transfix the gaze of outraged, scandalized "elites," by upsetting the
accepted norms of the public arena. What is it about him, they ask themselves,
that allows him to exert such powers on those who despise him, and us?
The fascination with charlatan authority figures, reaches here a kind of pure,
objective magic, turning the absence of positive qualities into a mysterious
quality X.

This is a purely negative "charisma": nobody has to directly believe there
are any positive traits that make these authority figures fit to rule. It is a mediated gaze, mediated, that is, by the gaze of another who is supposed to be
transfixed by some mysterious quality emanating from the leader. Nobody
needs to believe, directly, that the leader has "it"—there is direct evidence that
he has "it," for there are evidently others who believe it. All that is required,
then, is a profound suspicion toward the publicly authorized way of doing
things; indeed, not even that—it is enough to suspect that such a suspicion is
effectively motivating the "others." The "negative" charisma of such leaders is
thus inherently polarizing, it feeds directly on the "positive feedback" between
two negative attitudes.

FROM OBSCENE FIGURES OF AUTHORITY TO GENERALIZED HYPERSTASIS

One of the basic paradigms of thought about culture, society, and politics is
the assumption of a deep and complex relationship between the decent and
the obscene. The existence of political order, society, and culture relies on
the domestication, repression, or refinement of presocietal forces. The writings of Freud, Nietzsche, and Elias all contain expressions of this paradigm.[38]
However, it is much broader and more basic than the specific instances they
explore. In a certain sense, it is wide enough to include, on the one hand, the
entire body of political thought concerning the idea of the social contract,[39]
and on the other, Foucault's work on discipline and sexuality. In the more
sophisticated extrapolations of this paradigm, the relationship between the
decent and the obscene is dialectic: the obscene is not just a primordial, natural power, with the decent being its cultured sublimation; rather, the obscene
is created side by side with the decent and continues to accompany it like
an irreducible remainder. It is this dialectic that allows Foucault to declare
that Victorian society was "directly perverse."[40] Any attempt to purge the discourse of sexual content invariably bolsters the obscene. The same dialectic
is also observed by psychoanalysis: even though Freud sees human drives as a
primordial biological element, the taming of which signals the foundation of
culture, it is this very taming that marks human drives as obscene and ensures
their continued existence as a perpetual disruptive threat to order.[41]

That being said, all of the above-mentioned authors agree that the political, the societal, and the cultural belong squarely on the side of the decent. Even if the obscene is a necessary aftermath of culture and order, it will always be represented as the other, the hidden side of the coin. Even when we see political authority draw legitimacy from its mention of the obscene, it does so while maintaining the boundaries between the decent and the obscene, and preserving the place of the obscene as that which cannot be named directly. The burning question of the day then is how, within this same dialectic of the obscene and the decent, it has become possible for the political, which is supposed to reside on the side of the decent, to drastically switch sides and appeal directly to the obscene.

In contemporary political culture—and there is hardly any nonpolitical culture left—there is a strange new marriage between anarchy and order. On an intuitive, commonsensical level, what we are encountering today with new authoritarian politics is comparable to a police chief wearing a "fuck the police" T-shirt and smoking a crack pipe. On a more structural if somewhat abstract level, and this we will approach gradually, we are witnessing the emergence of a strange new political order based on mobilizing civil unrest and, more significantly, on undermining basic principles of civil order.

LIBERALISM OR TOTALITARIANISM? FROM FORCED CHOICE TO THE CHOICE OF FORCE

The general discontent with liberal democracy that has washed over liberal democracies around the globe in recent years, what pundits and political scientists often refer to as "populism,"[42] has brought "the democratic paradox" back into the central discourse of political science.[43] This concept refers to the tension, at the heart of liberal democracy, between the radical egalitarianism denoted by the term "democracy" and the liberal protection of individual rights, a tension that is currently threatening to bring liberal democracy to an end. The combination of these two separate foundations of liberal democracy, Chantal Mouffe warns, is not inexorable, but rather a product of historical chance and one that is riddled with tensions and contradictions.

These tensions and contradictions have come to the surface in recent years with the emergence of concrete political phenomena that emphasize the disconnect between the fundamental elements of liberal regimes. In his book *The People vs. Democracy*, Yascha Mounk describes the current crisis as a process of "divorce" between the democratic-popular pole and the liberal pole. The gradual separation of liberalism from democracy has manifested itself in the phenomena of rights without democracy, on the one hand, and democracy without rights, on the other. The former can be seen in the rise, over the last few decades, of liberal entities that are nondemocratic, in other words, institutions that promote liberal values and protect liberal rights through bureaucratic means, without relying in any significant way on popular support, such as the European Union or national and international human rights organizations. The latter is apparent in the adoption of various models of what Hungarian prime minister Viktor Orbán has termed "antiliberal democracy" by a growing number of countries around the world.[44]

Labeling the phenomenon "populism" not only fails to do justice to some of its crucial distinguishing features, but it also carries a whiff of elitism, a general suspicion of the dangerous potential of "the masses" as such, as if the only alternative is either elitist protection of liberal mechanisms and values or proto-fascist, popular rebellion against them. The point is not only that this locks our interpretation into a false either/or choice; this very forced choice is what makes it hard to even raise the question of the very popularity, the popular appeal, of contemporary antiliberalism.

What other concepts do we have, then, to approach the new phenomenon? For many observers, the profoundly antagonistic and transgressive approach of the new right in regard to established liberal norms raises the specter of twentieth-century fascism and totalitarianism. Indeed, there is no denying some striking resemblances, and we will address them directly shortly. This startling resemblance gives rise to the troubling expectation of an ideological galvanization. This is certainly a possibility, but far from a necessity. And indeed, this very expectation might be a serious hindrance in coming to terms with our contemporary political reality. What if our very expectation, based on historical experience, in effect masks what is truly new about new authoritarianism, namely, its ability to garner support and legitimation based on nothing but its transgressive behavior? If populism is too broad of a notion to capture what is unique about contemporary, right-wing authoritarianism, then the somewhat hasty comparison to twentieth-century movements such as fascism and Nazism risks being too narrow. While the comparison is understandable and significant, one is quickly struck by the absence, in contemporary authoritarianism, of an ideological vision of society that would mobilize the masses, which seems to be characteristic of twentieth-century political movements. If what we are facing today is a species of totalitarianism, it is a totalitarianism without totality.

But there is another, significant difficulty in applying the term totalitarianism and its associates to our contemporary situation. In his *Did Somebody Say Totalitarianism?*, Slavoj Žižek made the case that, more than an analytic concept, totalitarianism has become a watchword, serving to solidify the forced choice between the liberal status quo and what could only be worse, namely, any and all ideological projects.[45] Liberalism—at least as we inherit it from cold war liberals—is a kind of negative feat, to be hailed for its capacity to prevent the catastrophe of the worst—any ideological project seeking to change things fundamentally.[46]

What we are confronting today, however, is a new configuration of this very same conceptual coupling. We are seeing the emergence of a more totalitarian liberalism, on the one hand, that is, a liberalism strangely "charged" with the very same ideological fervor it was meant to keep at bay, and a more liberal totalitarianism, which is to say, a mode of antiliberal, authoritarian politics that does not display the full mobilization familiar to us from the twentieth century, and which manages to erode the liberal order without abolishing it entirely. New authoritarian regimes and movements, from Hungary and Poland to Turkey and Israel, crack down on political opposition without outlawing it entirely; they seek to get effective control over the media, without making them a direct channel of state propaganda; they maintain unfair advantages in elections, but do not cancel them, and so on. Liberalism and its more sinister relative, it seems, have entered a new, poisonous, codependent relationship. This is a new configuration, affecting the most fundamental concepts on which we draw in describing political and social reality. Let us begin by considering the notions of "charisma" and "legality."

IF AT FIRST YOU DON'T CONCEDE: IDEOLOGY IN THE TIME OF "MANUFACTURED DISSENT"

The 2020 US presidential election was meant to be a corrective to the aberration that was Donald Trump's presidency. Against the transgressive politics of Trump, the Democratic Party put forward a message of "back to normalcy," promising Americans a president who listens to experts and wears his Covid-19 protective mask, and not much more. To a large extent, the election was in fact a competition between the two modern sources of legitimacy outlined by Max Weber a century ago: charisma and legality. In Weber's terms, charisma has to do with a unique mandate, a task to be carried out for which the leader is uniquely qualified, while legality has to do with the instrumental logic that lies beneath, or above, the political battle over goals, a kind of reality principle that all policymaking has to abide by in order to execute its mandate, much akin to Foucault's "governmentality" that has eclipsed Weber's choice of terminology in recent decades. How is it that legality, the very means and medium of power, the supposed shared sense of reality on which the political battle can take place, has come to be a contested party? Far from a "return to normalcy," the outcome of the 2020 elections, with a popular Trump, in a final act of abnegation of norms, refusing to concede his defeat, has effectively split the political reality along the lines of a fetishist disavowal: like the proverbial maternal phallus, the absence of which is both recorded and disavowed, Trump both had lost and did not lose the elections. Indeed, the election is both over and settled and never-ending, forever open and contested. The loss of a shared reality, which has become a trope in public discourse under the problematic title of "post-truth," does not so much denote a plurality of viewpoints that do not coalesce into a single worldview, but a fetishist split of reality. What is so puzzling about it, from the viewpoint of critical theory, is the way in which the split in reality effectively covers over, well, the split in reality.

For lefties, raised to believe that, like all notions of unity, society is ultimately a veil, covering up class antagonism, the resurfacing of warring metaphors at the center of the political space is confounding. The "cultural wars" that are now progressively filling the space of politics throughout the democratic world can be labeled a "manufactured dissent," to bastardize the term made famous by Chomsky to describe the hegemonic manufacturing of consent.[47] This is not to suggest that there is an "invisible hand" orchestrating the battleground as a kind of global "false flag" operation, but rather to point out how the framing of the contemporary struggle over "consensus" is itself, largely, a new, emerging ideological configuration.

At the heart of contemporary liberal democracies today is a false struggle. The populace is forced to choose between a now forever politicized "legality" and a "charisma" which is, in a significant sense to be elaborated, purely "anti-legalistic," protesting against the "neutrality" of the rules of the game and insisting on the supremacy of self-interest. As such, this is a losing struggle for the left, one in which the left is currently leading a rearguard battle. The new right has managed to make ruthless, power-grabbing opportunism—usually conceived as the opposite of ideology—into its ideological motor, while the left is pushed to defend a possibly outdated technology meant to ward off ideological excesses.

TOTALITARIANISM WITHOUT TOTALITY

In order to begin to grasp what is novel about the new, right-wing authoritarianism, it is important, firstly, to emphasize the centrality of antagonism in the new strain of right-wing politics. The current form of antiliberal democracy does not seek to replace liberal democracy with another, positive, kind of democracy (totalitarian democracy, for instance, as Jacob Talmon would call it).[48] It is certainly possible for things to take a turn in that direction in the future, but for now it is imperative to recognize that the main focus of these regimes is antiliberalism, that is to say, the gradual and continued erosion of liberal values and institutions. This negation of liberalism is not a matter of passive attitudes, but one of an effective political action plan. The eclecticism that is characteristic of the many manifestations of contemporary, new-authoritarian "populism" is centered around this one common factor, even though it is a negative one. There is no doubt that such an erosion allows, among other things, for the rise of truly fascist elements, which have unquestionably drawn encouragement from the wave of right-wing populism. However, while we must recognize that this is a real eventuality, it is no less important to be aware of the possibility that the assault on liberal norms and institutions is not a transition stage toward some historical form of government we have experienced in the past, but a unique political configuration with its own characteristics and an unknown potential for longevity. Moreover, it is even quite likely that the fear of the return of fascism has been helping right-wing forces solidify their power. The easily identifiable differences between the emergent right-wing regimes and twentieth-century fascism enable the right wing to dismiss the alarms sounded by the left and center as baseless panic or propaganda. David Runciman has already established that the central image used to talk about the death of democracy, that of the coup d'état, is rooted in the past and ill-suited to illustrate what he calls liberal democracy's "midlife crisis."[49] This ill-suitability, in turn, prevents us from seeing what is taking shape before our very eyes. It's bad, but it could be worse, we tell ourselves. The defenders of the liberal order, by focusing on familiar dangers from the past, tend to view the new right as a transitional phase and thereby look right past one of its most prominent and significant features, the innovation that justifies its being called "new": the absence of a positive political program. The quintessential attribute of the new right is that it is nihilistic, transgressive, and thoroughly cynical. This is both its point of maximal proximity to twentieth-century far-right movements, and where its decisive distinction from them is to be identified.

In its negativity, the new right shares some striking similarities with the extreme right of the twentieth century, as described, for example by Hannah Arendt. The "masses"—a term we shall return to—whom totalitarians funneled into a movement were made ready for such mobilization by a "desire to see the ruin of this whole world of fake security, fake culture and fake life. . . . Unlike the nihilism of Nietzsche and other radicalisms (Sorel, Bakunin) for them it was about destruction for its own sake: destruction without mitigation, chaos and ruin as such assumed the dignity of supreme values."[50]

Reading Arendt today is a chilling experience. Much of what we are witnessing today is an even more accentuated version of the conditions she described as pretotalitarian: extreme atomization, existential loneliness (feeling oneself wordless and superfluous), and destructive nihilism, namely, the desire to see it all burn down. Arendt is not alone in connecting such a cultural mood to the rise of the extreme right. In his 1967 lecture on the new right, Adorno pointed to the appeal of an apocalyptic vision for societies in which a better future seems out of the question.[51]

And indeed, as Arendt closes her book, she notes that we should expect the new form of government she labels totalitarianism, like the old ones, to remain with us. Furthermore, the logical space in which Arendt situated totalitarianism is unquestionably the very same logical space with which the new right is flirting. For Arendt, totalitarianism was neither tyranny—"the rule of one against all"—nor democracy, the rule of the many (which could also be called "the all against one"), but a strange mixture of both. We might note, in passing for now, that this was the same logical space left vacant, so to speak, by the decline of traditional authority. It is therefore quite rational to fear that something like twentieth-century totalitarianism is around the corner, just one shock away from crystallization. The one thing missing, it would seem, is the kind of ideology described by Arendt to mobilize the masses. For her, the lack of rational goals in totalitarian regimes, their unique, shocking brand of "madness," is ultimately explained by ideology.

> Instead of saying that totalitarian government is unprecedented, we could also say that it has exploded the very alternative on which all definitions of the essence of governments have been based in political philosophy, that is the alternative between lawful and lawless government, between arbitrary and legitimate power. It defies, it is true, all positive laws. . . . But it operates neither without guidance of law nor is it arbitrary, for it claims to obey strictly those laws of Nature or of History from which all positive laws always have been supposed to spring. It is the monstrous, yet seemingly unanswerable claim of totalitarian rule that, far from being "lawless," it goes to the sources of authority from which positive laws received their ultimate legitimation, that far from being arbitrary it is more obedient to those suprahuman forces than any government ever was before, and that far from wielding its power in the interest of one man, it is quite prepared to sacrifice everybody's vital immediate interests to the execution of what it assumes to be the law of History or the law of Nature.[52]

Let us quickly contrast this description to the manner in which, in her essay on authority, Arendt describes the transcendence of the source of legitimacy. In traditional authoritarian rule, the source of authority always lies somewhere beyond the power of rulers. We shall have more to say about "the sources of authority" later. Specifically, we shall ask how the violation of what is understood as the virtual ground of law can become a mode of political legitimation. For now, let us just note how central this analysis is to Arendt's overall description of twentieth-century totalitarianism. Many of the peculiarities of totalitarianism as she describes them find their rationale in this account of the merger of lawlessness and lawfulness which lies at the heart of totalitarian ideology, including its strange relation with the truth. Since the ultimate truth served by totalitarians is an ironclad logic of *movement*, its "truth" is profoundly performative. To cite the example used by Arendt, the claim made by the Soviet regime in the 1930s that only Moscow has an underground train—on its face, patently absurd and easily disproved—is true from the perspective of the fulfilled History, in which Moscow has conquered, defeated, and destroyed all the infrastructure of its enemies. Call it an eventual truth. It is in serving as instruments of the "big other" of history (communist totalitarianism) or nature (racism, National Socialism) that a different, more metaphysical terrain of truth is being served, a truth to be realized by the political movement. In such an ideological constellation, the unwritten law in which positive law is grounded becomes itself the object of special, higher knowledge, a higher terrain of truth above mundane factuality. What is mobilized are the laws governing movement, the laws of becoming, and so the knowledge in question is "secularized" apocalyptic knowledge, the knowledge of things to come. Such knowledge is performative in a special, millenarian sense— knowing what is to come, we are charged with the task of bringing it about. It is the notion of such a servile position in regard to a higher task that seems to stand in the strongest contrast with contemporary authoritarian figures, who seem to be brazen, shamelessly self-interested, indulging in hedonistic pleasures. Their capacity to transgress the unwritten rules that apply to other politicians (and ordinary citizens) is one of their most striking features.

MIGHT IS RIGHT: LIBERAL HYPOCRISIES AND THEIR INVERTED RESPONSE FROM THE REAL

What we are witnessing today seems to be a very different kind of mixture of lawfulness and lawlessness from the one analyzed by Arendt. Now it is not so much the proclaimed access to a more fundamental, supreme, unwritten law that organizes the rationale of the new right, or its "truth value." These seem to lie, instead, in an act of exposure, a rationale that is so strikingly obvious it is hard to come to terms with. Here we come into closest proximity to the twentieth-century iteration of authoritarianism, but without the ideological framework, without the vision of a fulfilled, salvaged history.

As Arendt makes clear, the desire for destruction and sacrifice which was prevalent amongst the elites in the years leading to the rise of totalitarian movements in the twentieth century is not to be dismissed as "nihilism," for that would be to overlook "how justified disgust can be in a society wholly permeated with the ideological outlook and moral standards of the bourgeoisie."[53] In a significant sense, totalitarianism presented itself as the "answer from the real" to the duplicitous decay of the bourgeoisie's political philosophy, returning to the bourgeoisie their own message in inverted form:

> The totalitarian movements asserted their "superiority" in that they carried a *Weltanschauung* by which they would take possession of man as a whole. In this claim to totality the mob leaders of the movements again formulated and only reversed the bourgeoisie's own political philosophy. . . . [They] always believed that the public and visible organs of power were directed by their own secret, non-public interests and influence. In this sense the bourgeoisie's political philosophy was always "totalitarian"; it always assumed an identity of politics, economics, and society, in which political

institutions served only as the façade for private interests. The bourgeoisie's double standard, its differentiation between public and private life, were a concession to the nation-state which had desperately tried to keep the two spheres apart.[54]

What Arendt is suggesting here is quite startling: the cynicism deeply ingrained in liberal political philosophy, in which the public order is grounded in self-interest, has made for a public sphere that was principally understood as a mere facade for instrumental self-interest. Modern, bourgeois societies are characterized, as will become a major topic in her *Human Condition*, by the loss of a political, significant distinction between the public and the private, a loss that had totalitarianism as its impending inversion.[55] The collapse of the distinction between the public and the private that is often associated with totalitarianism is understood by Arendt not as the reversal of an individualistic, liberal society, but as making explicit what had already been latent in the liberal construction of public space. If capitalism promises that nothing is impossible for us individually, totalitarianism returns the very same message on the terrains of the social whole. If the liberal order positions the public good as a mere facade and facilitator of subjective enjoyment, totalitarianism "merely" promises to drop the mask and have enjoyment permeate the entire social sphere.

The new right currently on the rise is certainly using the "perversion of the bourgeoisie," only not so much by offering a "unified" man, for whom, say, the public and private spheres should coalesce, but by virtue of a direct appeal and maximal utilization of the very "superiority" imbued in revealing the dark truth of power and self-interest, which is why lines like the following, written by Arendt to describe the supporters of totalitarianism in the twentieth century, have such a contemporary ring to them: "They were satisfied with blind partisanship in anything that respectable society had banned, regardless of theory or content, and they elevated cruelty to a major virtue because it contradicted society's humanitarian and liberal hypocrisy."[56]

The appeal of twentieth-century populist authoritarianism, just like that of today, was intimately linked with the impotent rage unleashed by a politics which fosters and crushes hopes for individuals to "realize" their potentials by upward social mobility.

The quashing of the hopes on which this sociopolitical order is based, the hope of individuals to fulfill their own destinies, leads to a much more atavistic relation to the powers of fate: "without the possibility of a radical change of role and character . . . the self-willed immersion in the suprahuman forces of destruction seemed to be a salvation from the automatic identification with pre-established functions in society and their utter banality, and at the same time to help destroy the functioning itself."[57]

The unwritten law comes from nowhere. Unlike written laws, which derive their authority from the constitutive act of their legislation, unwritten law derives its power from the mystery surrounding its origins.[58] For the Greeks, it was the unwritten nature of the laws that made them divine.[59] Precisely because they could not be traced to any particular source, the unwritten laws were seen as having superhuman origins.[60]

The unwritten law is mythical, surrounded in mystery. It is unavoidable yet unknown, which is to say it is fated. The concept loses little of its mystery upon its entry into the philosophical tradition, where it is also directly associated with obscenity, in at least two ways. In Plato's *Laws*, the unwritten law appears as a fundamental social "substance," but one that does not entirely fit the category under which it is supposed to fall, the category of law. It is somehow the very "stuff" and substance of the law, it is the very heart and focus of the discussion, and yet it falls outside the strict concept of the law. In Plato's book, the Athenian states the following:

> All these things we're now going through are what many call "unwritten customs." Indeed, what they name "ancestral laws" are nothing other than all such things as these. What is more, the argument that has been poured over us now, to the effect that one shouldn't ordain these in law, and yet also shouldn't leave them unmentioned, has been nobly put. For these are the bonds of every regime, linking all the things established in writing, and laid down, with the things that will be set forth in the future, exactly like ancestral and in every way ancient customs; if nobly established and made habitual, they provide a cloak of complete safety for the later written laws, but when they perversely stray from the noble they are like props of the walls of houses which buckle in the middle and cause the whole edifice to fall.[61]

The unwritten law is perceived not only as a social institution but as universally and mysteriously effective, as in the case of the taboo on incest.[62] This is the aspect of the unwritten law that makes it so attractive to the political architects who take part in Plato's dialogue and seek to draft laws for a new polity. The unwritten law works through the internalization of the prohibition. The prescription of an unwritten law is experienced as an inhibition, as an internal restraint rather than as external coercion. After briefly discussing the supremacy of the unwritten law, Plato offers a realistic compromise. While it would have been preferable to be governed solely by unwritten laws such as the incest taboo, human desires are too strong and too numerous. Therefore, Plato proposes the "second-rank" order of law—what cannot be forbidden must be concealed:

The strength of the pleasure should, as much as possible, be deprived of gymnastic exercise by using other exercises to turn its flow and growth elsewhere in the body. This would be the case if the indulgence in sexual things never occurred without a sense of awe. For if shame made their indulgence rare, the infrequency would weaken the sway over them of this mistress. So let it be the custom laid down in habit and unwritten law, that among them it is noble to engage in these activities if one escapes notice, but shameful if one doesn't escape notice—though they are not to abstain entirely. Thus our law would come to possess a second-rank standard of the shameful and the noble, a second-rank correctness.[63]

The unwritten law, as it is delineated in Plato's dialogue, thus has two over-lapping dimensions: in the most fundamental sense, the unwritten law is the system of boundaries, tangible yet indefinable, between the decent and the obscene. As a marker of the elusive limit of what can be expressed, the unwritten law is at the same time the limit between that which can be made public, that which can be given stable linguistic expression, and that which can only be vaguely felt or implied. Thus, as something that cannot be formulated, the unwritten law itself contains an element of the obscene.

The "second-rank standard" that Plato describes is an overarching law, also unwritten, that establishes which rules are truly binding, and which rules can be broken in private. As such, it gives the very distinction between the obscene and the decent a whiff of the obscene. The concealment of the obscene desig-nates the decent public space as a space of pretense and culture as hypocrisy, something which for Arendt, we have seen, was particularly decisive for the configuration of the bourgeois public space in its late stages of decay. Formu-lated in these terms, decency itself becomes an obscene act, a cynical harness-ing of shame as a tool of mutual social monitoring.[64]

The picture painted by Plato might be cynical, but it offers a convincing cri-terion for social cohesion, which is often omitted from the discussion. This is the knowledge we lack, and which marks us as strangers in a society that is not our own. To "pass" in the sociological sense, to be viewed as one who belongs, not only requires knowledge of the explicit rules but, more importantly, know-ing which rules can be broken under the cover of silence. Social intimacy is, perhaps increasingly, a matter of complicity in the violation of rules.[65]

The deep ambivalence regarding the social order becomes somewhat clearer when we place emphasis on its tacit nature and the implications thereof. The social pact is not sealed by the signing of contracts but by a wink. When we wink, the gesture is the message. In the wink, the message is always, beyond all concrete context, the wink itself; the message is "We understand each other in silence, without words." That is, we understand each other somewhat like thieves, at the expense of some imagined other who is not in on the secret. However, this "conspiring" is simultaneously the establishment of what Freud would call "the ego ideal," that civilizing authority whose love we seek and before whom we are ashamed, the same authority from which we seek to conceal our failings.

The justifiable hostility evoked by hypocrisy regarding the rules of decency at least partially explains the reason why political figures like Trump are so attractive. For many voters, the only choice at hand is, to repurpose Sarah Palin's expression, between a pitbull with lipstick on—i.e., in the context we are pursuing, the representatives of the liberal establishment—and an honest pitbull that does not try to hide its animal nature.[66] Civilization is adornment, wouldn't you prefer the real thing? While it is certainly true that civilization is in a sense an artificial construct, it is no less real than other human constructions, such as buildings and railroads. Why would it be here, in the realm of social mores, that artificial comes to stand for fakery, a veil to be lifted? We shall have more to say about artificiality in chapter 3. For now, let us note the true horror of the current political moment: the way in which the desire to remove masks and libidinal liberty are coupled with their antitheses: powerlessness and a determination not to know.

And so the unwritten law points toward a contradiction in the concept of law. The law claims to be public, reasonable, and general, and the unwritten underside of it seems to suggest its failure to be equal to itself, so to speak. There is a stain of idiosyncrasy, a stain of enjoyment at the very heart of the concept. And it is this stain that carries the strange "truth effect" of obscene, cynical knowledge, a strange satisfaction entailed in reducing all "higher notions," all claims for universality, into something base and crude. The law's self-contradiction calls for phantasmatic support—ideology—but it is it what also attests to the law's inconsistency.

> The need for the phantasmic support of the public symbolic order (materialized in the so-called unwritten rules) thus bears witness to the system's vulnerability: the system is compelled to allow for possibilities of choices which must never actually take place, since their occurrence would cause the system to disintegrate, and the function of the unwritten rules is precisely to prevent the actualization of these choices formally allowed by the system. In the Soviet Union of the 1930s and 1940s—to take the most extreme example—it was not only forbidden to criticize Stalin, it was perhaps even more forbidden to announce this very prohibition: to state publicly that it was forbidden to criticize Stalin. The system needed to maintain the appearance that one was allowed to criticize Stalin . . . the paradoxical role of unwritten rules is that, with regard to the explicit, public Law, they are simultaneously transgressive (they violate explicit social rules) and more coercive (they are additional rules which restrain the field of choice by prohibiting the possibilities allowed for—guaranteed, even—by the public Law).[67]

Somehow, the more formal and rational the law is to become, the more pervasive is the suspicion of its very formal nature. As the law "reaches its notion," so to speak, it becomes more fully self-contradictory.

Consider Henry Maine's famous thesis on the development of law, from "status to contract." According to this narrative, the law develops from largely unwritten laws which concern themselves with the kinship group, with status and inheritance, stuck in a ritualized, eternal past, into the modern, contract-based, explicit arrangement of a society of individuals. Liberated from the irrationality of tradition, the law becomes progressively instrumental, a means to achieve more equity.[68]

It is this progress of the law that makes modern, liberal democracy uniquely "hypocritical," in Arendt's account. Liberal democracy, she suggests, presents itself as a machinery of sorts; society is there to facilitate the pursuits of happiness of individuals. If we follow this line of reasoning closely, the temptation of totalitarianism is not so much the return to some organic community, but the desire to join forces with what promises to break the machine apart.

The eternal quandary of the left is why it is the right that seems so much more adept in funneling the quite justified frustrations of "the masses" in Arendt's sense, namely, of ordinary people who feel themselves not only wronged by "the system" but utterly displaced by it, no longer capable of anchoring their identity in "class" or "nation." The "masses" that for Arendt are singularly the political subject of totalitarianism give rise to contradictory chimeras such as "National Socialism" and now perhaps Christian nationalism in the United States, or religious nationalist Jews in Israel, etc., because—as "masses"—they do not fully belong to the nation or to society. "Masses," in Arendt's use of the term, are the quality of quantity, so to speak: amorphous and expanding. It takes a movement to funnel and give direction to such a political subject. This is one thing, according to Arendt, that National Socialism and Communism had in common—their internal logic dictated expansion; they could not be contained within the confines of national, sovereign borders.

So, in order to trace changes in legitimation, let us turn to the source of legitimacy in modern democracies—the people. Arendt mentions a division to be overcome by totalitarianism, the image of the whole man. This division is an echo of the divided source of modern legitimacy, the division that runs across the notion of "the people."

WHAT ELSE IS NEW? (II) DIVIDED WE STAND

Modern political power no longer draws its legitimation from tradition, but directly from the people. Reinhart Koselleck observed that in many European languages, the word "people" has a double and often contradictory meaning.[69] On the one hand, "the people" is the sovereign body of citizens, the collective that forms the polity. On the other hand, "people" denotes the popular masses, the rabble, the shapeless crowd devoid of political or social order that constitutes a main threat to the moral order.[70]

The "people" then denotes two opposing concepts in terms of legitimacy. On the one hand, the people are the polity from which the political system draws its meaning, the subject in whose name political leaders are able to govern. On the other hand, the people are that hard-to-pinpoint segment of the population that do not follow the official values of the polity and endanger its stability. "Popular," derived from this sense of "people," is another word for coarse, nondescript, vulgar, and threatening. It therefore stands to reason that the "popular" has an essential and nonincidental link with the "obscene." The appeal to the obscene, on which we have been focusing, touches on that element in the people that is omitted from the array of regular representation. "Our era," writes Agamben, "is nothing but an invisible and systematic attempt to heal the rift dividing the people, to eliminate the excluded."[71] It is important to understand why the attempt "to heal the people" is, in actuality, synonymous with eliminating those who are excluded. The exclusion of the "popular," in this sense, is a formative gesture of the sociopolitical order,[72] establishing the boundaries of what is allowed and what is forbidden. It is in this context that we must consider the direct and public appeal of the new right to obscenity, the trend of placing front and center that which is supposed to be excluded from the public space, that which is defined exclusively by its exclusion.

This split in the notion of the people is constitutive of formal, representative democracy: the representative people, say, the public face of the people, leaves a remainder, a surplus "matter" that eludes representation. However, it is crucial to note that this constitutive "loss," what representative democracy structurally must leave out, is very much included in political culture.

Liberal, representative democracy only becomes the "neutral medium" of the political by including, as two competitive elements, itself and its opposite.[73] Only when, in the formal machination of parliament, there is a representation for what stands, ideologically, against the purely rational-formalistic worldview of capital-L liberalism, speaking in the name of tradition, can liberalism truly claim its victory. Now we are to choose between "conservative" values and liberal ones, to choose between a content-based unity of the nation and the formal arrangement of individuals.

Recall the trajectory from status to contract: as the law foregrounds individuals and individuation, inheritance and familial ties seem increasingly like murky, irrational phenomena, inherently "backgrounded"—part of our mythical background, ever present as archaic remainders we cannot quite grasp nor put to rest.[74] As Foucault noted, the split in the body of the people is the correlate of the new, modern subject of governance, the population.[75] We could say that once the reproduction of society becomes an object of governance, rather than of traditional, customary law, the very unwritten nature of tradition must be represented politically and culturally.

In order to appreciate the difference between our contemporary authoritarianism and its twentieth-century predecessor, what is crucial to note is the way in which liberalism "normally" contains its opposite. Significantly, in the cultural imagination of liberal democratic states, the duality of the "popular" is distributed between two "cultural types," roughly corresponding to the division between the city and the country:[76] we have the urban progressive, standing for formal liberalism, usually depicted as an alienated individual and an "artificial" person, very much concerned with the outward appearance of decency, contrasted with the more "folksy" and spontaneous "country folk," a down-to-earth, culturally conservative type, warm if irrational and prone to outbursts, a "full-blooded" member of the group.[77] While seemingly opposites, it is their very complementarity that holds the modern nation-state together. We have here a fantasy of a relation, often explicitly sexual, between two opposites who need each other to be whole: the formally free, if artificial, lifeless liberal, needs her counterpart, the lively and virile if unruly "salt of the earth." The first stands for the mechanical march of progress, associated with "civilization," and the second for the organic, spontaneous, and natural holistic dimension we associate with "culture."[78] In this way, within the very formality of the modern, liberal nation-state, form and content can come together, as long as they are represented as complementary opposites.

What is crucial to note is how this contains the tension between the formal logic of liberalism and the traditional background it is meant to break with, to the exclusion of a third, the constitutively excluded segment of the population that can only be represented, and governed, as criminal, as "dangerous individuals."[79] This excluded element can only appear, within the order of the law, as criminal. This would often be linked with the "constitutive crime" of a given state and would have everything to do with its conditions of "primitive accumulation," the plunder that makes the "normal" economy possible. Often enough, the "folksy" representation of tradition hides, in its very proximity, the crime on which the new order had been established. This is its fetishist aspect—the last thing we see before encountering the original absence comes to stand as its replacement and effectively "plug" the hole. In the American context, "southern" nostalgia thus covers up the criminal aspect associated with the South: the African American population and labor immigrants, the two historical and contemporary sources of "illegitimate labor" (slavery and "migrant work"). In Israel, the "warm" Mizrahi (oriental) Jew covers up the Palestinian, by giving a "sanctioned," indeed favorable image of "the orient."

This is the way in which the infamous overdeterminacy of class and race plays out: there must be a segment of the population that stands for class antagonism as such, that is, a segment that cannot be contained in the hylomorphic union of the nation-state and must appear as the internal threat to it, at once too atavistic (native) and hopelessly decimated by modernity (the broken family), more intimately bound to the land, and utterly foreign in a kind of polarized uncanniness, at once excessively homely and essentially foreign (racism, whether based on pseudo-biology or culture, is ultimately nothing but this excess of foreignness, foreignness transubstantiated into essence). In this "representational division of labor," capitalism pulls off its act as a vanishing mediator between nation and state.[80]

In light of this, let us ask again: What is the contemporary appeal of the popular? In what way does it differ from older revolts against liberalism? Let us take the case of the famous *Kulturkampf* in nineteenth-century Germany. The battle between the Catholics, representative of the old law, and the Protestants, representative of modernity, came to an end once the anti-Semite's phantasy of the Jew came to stand in for the tension as such: at once hypermodern and hopelessly atavistic, the Jew became the embodiment of the "cultural war," a way to exorcise it out of the body politic.[81] To create a race-state, a modern state based on the principle of blood relations, it was necessary to eradicate this "foreign body," indeed an impossible body made out of foreignness, foreign elements that cannot coalesce into a coherent form.

Will our current culture wars find a similar resolution? That is certainly a possibility. There is no doubt that the rise of the new right is accompanied by more and more explicit, shameless racism. Yet we should not overlook the way in which it is now often articulated: there is a strange competition as to who truly represents the structurally excluded. The claim that it is the right as such that is excluded effects a dual transformation: it all but closes the gap between the big and small L's of liberalism, identifying the very workings of the system with its cultural representation, and it aims at closing the gap on the other side, between the dignified representation of the ways of old and its illegitimate, hidden secret, by pushing the obscene and the criminal to the fore. What seems striking about our contemporary situation is the manner in which the very abstract "nature" of the transgressive element of the population, obscenity as such, comes to assume a public place. A good way of seeing this is to distinguish between contemporary, authoritarian populism and populist-emancipatory struggles.

The populist appeal to the popular qua obscene should be sharply distinguished from the emancipatory struggles fought in the name of what Rancière called "the part with no part." No doubt it is the unsettling proximity of these diametrically opposed political tendencies that is largely responsible for much of our contemporary disorientation. For now, let us only note the most obvious and, for our purposes, most telling difference.

While this should be obvious, let us first assert that emancipatory struggles have to aim at emancipation. They are motivated by an idea, freedom, which is abstract in a very precise sense, namely, in that it cannot be saturated by experiential material. It exceeds the posited order, emerging as at once necessary and impossible. We cannot give an example of freedom, or equality, such that it would do justice to the demands of the rational idea.[82] We cannot point to ancient Greece and say, here, you see, is fully actualized freedom. This is not to say that there cannot be exemplars of freedom, particular cases in which standards for how to break free are made manifest.

The conclusion to be drawn, however, is not that ideas belong to a pure beyond which we can only asymptotically approach. On the contrary, they are the very stuff of concrete, political goals. Indeed, emancipatory struggles challenge the false universal of the public order in the name of a particular universal. Organizing around the slogan "Black lives matter" is a good example, as it names those whose lives, in a particular configuration, officially matter but are in practice exposed to all kinds of systemic violence, from police brutality to poor healthcare. It is only a concrete struggle that can capture the universal dimension eluding representation, the objective contradictions or structural antagonism that can only be addressed radically, that cannot be solved without a serious transformation of the power structure. That which is underserved by the order of representation calls for the most concrete, the most precise act of naming. Note how popular, emancipatory uprisings tend to offer a constellation of ideas as their slogans, from the famous "equality, liberty, fraternity" of the French Revolution to the "woman, life, freedom" of contemporary Iranian protests. It is the configuration that is demanded, the refusal to choose one over the other. In this, emancipatory struggles assume their concrete shapes by identifying and refusing the forced ideological choices imposed on them. By contrast, the turn of new authoritarianism to the obscene is to be understood as a way to make what eludes representation present as such, as a kind of dense, symbolic "matter." It answers the abstractions of the "proper" with what could be called an "abstract concreteness," making present the "it" as such, as unnamable.

REVOLUTIONARY OPPORTUNISM: THE "REALISM" OF POSTIDEOLOGICAL ZEAL

Can we speak today of a global right-wing movement? On the one hand, a new, extremist right is everywhere on the rise, and certainly there are ideas and obsessions circulating back and forth between right-wing parties across the globe, from antimigrant to anti-LGBQT rhetoric and action. A strange new coalition of libertarianism, chauvinistic nationalism, and religious "conservatism" is promising to "crack down" on the "perversities" brought about by the liberal order, often led by leaders whose own, transgressive behavior seems to be one of their key selling points.

In totalitarianism, as we know it from the twentieth century, we expect to see the subordination of private interests to the general will, directly manifested by the one party and the one leader. And yet the strange coalition on the right between free-market-based libertarianism and a disciplinary "traditionalism," seeking to impose restrictions with legal mechanisms, many of them having to do with sexuality, is made possible, in part, by increasingly subordinating public law reasoning to private law. The state's most general legal mechanisms are seen as instruments meant to serve the special interests of whoever is in power—as long, that is, as those in power are the right ones, namely, the right. Might is right, but only when it's the right's. But is there a unifying purpose for this instrumentalization of the law? What drives the dynamics of the right-wing power grab, in the absence of a unifying theory or a coherent ideology? What charges its libidinal fervor?

There seems to be a positive feedback loop between the liberal and new-authoritarian political libidos. Consider Isaiah Berlin's famous distinction between negative freedoms, or "freedoms from," characteristic of the liberal conception of freedom, and positive freedoms, the "freedom to," characteristic of political movements whose roots lie in romanticism, the disastrous consequences of which are well documented in the historical research of the twentieth century.[83] Strangely, both positive and negative freedoms are today locked in a reactionary game. The "positive" freedoms of the right seem to be nothing more than the "right" to transgress liberal, negative freedoms, to troll and offend liberal sensibilities, and negative freedoms seem to expand exponentially, acquiring a quasi-positivity of their own, to restrict the ever-growing list of such infringements. Angela Nagle has very nicely described precisely such a dynamic as characteristic of online political culture, where progressive sensibilities trigger the "trolling" of alt-right transgressive culture, which fuels, in turn, the desire to censor such transgressive behavior on the other side. And so both parties are locked in a cycle, like two snakes biting each other's tails.[84] Positive freedom has given way to a positive feedback of negativity.

It is crucial to note in this regard how the famous "echo chambers" that characterize online culture do not produce free-floating, isolated monads of public opinion, which would be bad enough, but irresolvable conflictual positions, as the very heart and focus of each such chambers are the hypocrisies and fallacies of the opposed point of view. Taking sides on polarizing events, which today can range from actual war (Russia-Ukraine, Israel-Gaza) to the preference of a fictional character (are you "team Rachel" or "team Ross," to give an example that carbon-dates its author), we passionately organize our identity against an opponent, tacitly agreeing with the other side on one thing only: there is no common ground. The widespread presence of "fake news" on the web, serious as it is, is not as troubling as the new manner in which the truth itself lies in our digital universe. We are exposed to real acts and opinions on the other side. We perceive real folly, real evil, and real hypocrisy, for there is no shortage of such human phenomena. This is the one thing we share with our opponents—a sense of utter mistrust and disbelief. On each side we mistrust not only our opponents but the world itself, as we are continuously struck by a sense that "the world" is somehow on their side. We are exposed in our feeds to those aspects of political and cultural reality that marginalize our own position, as a lone, reasonable position in a world gone off the rails. The world has gone mad, how could anyone side with these people! Positioning ourselves against these very real and troubling shortcomings on the other side, what eludes us is only the empty negativity of this feedback loop, the way it makes it nearly impossible for truth as an event—unpredictable and disruptive to the status quo—to emerge. Truth here would not be some total point of view in which opposing sides find their reconciliation, but a shift of perspective that changes the entire situation, breaks out of the deadlock of increasingly violent, and ultimately false, conflict.

Across the liberal-democratic world, talk of "culture wars" is being gradually replaced with serious considerations of "civil wars." In Agamben's analysis, "stasis," the Greek term for civil war, is to be understood as a threshold between the prepolitical household, the realm of familial ties, and that of politics. It stood for a bidirectional tension between these terms, the tendency to politicize the family and household, and the opposite tendency to endow the political space with the qualities of the household.[85] For Agamben, the Hobbesian state, founded in direct, explicit relation to the potential of civil war, sustains and radicalizes this constitutive tension. The split between the people as the source of sovereign legitimacy and the "multitude" or the masses, to which we shall return, attains a complex, mythological temporal schema. "The state of nature is a mythological projection onto the past of civil war; conversely, civil war is a projection of the state of nature into the city: it is what appears when one considers the city from the perspective of the state of nature."[86]

In a sense, our contemporary "deadlock" has reached a state of "self-awareness." We might say that the contemporary deadlock of the democratic political space revolves directly around the dispute of whether such a threshold can ever be crossed, whether, that is, a political space distinct from familial ties can be erected at all, whether there can emerge something like a people, distinct from the multitude. The contemporary new right does indeed appeal precisely to that—mythological[87]—figure of the people which Arendt called "the masses," but, for the time being, without anything resembling the promise of twentieth-century ideologies. It promises in many respects to destroy the "system" that enrages the "masses," but does not seem to promise to erect a new world in its stead. What can sustain the paradox of such an anti-ideological ideology?

On the one hand, the new right is a revolutionary power, one that has been changing the agenda of government and the accepted rules of play. One clear mark of the ideological charge of the new right in Israel was Netanyahu's disregard to warnings, from experts and the public alike, that his judicial overhaul would bring tremendous harm to the state, both in economic terms and in terms of its national security. Pushing forward the reform despite such public and private warnings signals clearly the extent to which the new right is willing to act against the "reality principle" of the political order, the objective rules dictated by the exigencies of security and market economy. Yet, on the other hand, antiliberal, right-wing populism has been acting as an anti-ideological agent:[88] it does not seek to enlist support for an alternative vision of the future; rather, it presents itself as a remedy for the dangerous illusions created by liberal ideology, which is perceived as globalist, utopian, mired in self-deception, and therefore blind to actual, present threats. The right is calling for a "gloves off" mentality due to the realistic need to manage the now, an ongoing emergency that can no longer be contained. Meanwhile, the political power that currently represents the principal alternative to the new right, the center-right parties, is equally busy denouncing their extreme right-wing opponents for being too ideological, possessed by dangerous delusions, and therefore unfit to handle the challenges presented by reality.[89]

There is, therefore, an important distinction to be made between classic populism, which enlists popular support by undermining the existing order in view of promises, albeit mostly vague ones, of a better or more just future, and the populism of the new right, which promises to "burn down the establishment" as its main policy, which resembles the attitudes of twentieth-century totalitarian movements.

This is also why the antiliberal right presents itself as shackled, at this stage at least, by the various "fetters" it is seeking to remove. That is the context in which we must look at Netanyahu's and others' demands for "free governance," for example, which in practice means the removal of the "silk gloves" of standard regulation, and which is presented as the casting off of the shackles that have been preventing them from effectively handling the many, mounting problems of society today. This demand constitutes a pillar of the utmost importance in propping up the organizing fantasy of the new right. The message is: if only we didn't have our hands tied, we would be able to do away with our enemies once and for all. Enemies, of course, both internal and external, are never in short supply. However, like any fantasy, one has to simply imagine it coming true in order to see it fall apart—without the "fetters" of the liberal order to struggle against, the new right would actually have to take some real action. Let us skip over the major substitution involved in "scapegoating," namely, concentrating on the figure of some social "strangers" the very uncanny strangeness that unsettles identity from within, the horrifying tendency to escape systematic problems by singling out the "foreign elements," and grant, for argument's sake, the idea that we can in fact identify and effectively fight against concrete enemies. Eliminating enemies—who are, as we said, too many to count—is a much more difficult task, and one at which it is far easier to fail than continuing the assault on those same "fetters" holding back the righteous forces of the new right. It is precisely this negative-antagonistic element, the struggle against moral and institutional "fetters," that seems to form the basis of the new right's mechanism of legitimation. Considering how few restrictions are truly in place, how much of what keeps governments in check are unwritten, unenforceable rules, and how easy it is for governments today to evoke emergency exigencies and bypass even the minimal restrictions placed before power, one is tempted to respond to this line of propaganda by yet another variation on the well-known joke: why are you telling me you want to have unrestricted power, when power is already, in truth, unrestricted? One hardly wants to push the new right in the direction of twentieth-century totalitarianism, demanding that they present a radical vision of a "new man" to fulfill history. The point is rather to see how the absence of such an ideological goal is a positive, constitutive element of contemporary "postideological" ideology.

LIBERAL DEMOCRACY AND THE CRISIS OF REPRESENTATION: AN OUTDATED TECHNOLOGY?

According to a widely held belief, populism is an expression of the "crisis of representation." The paralysis that has gripped liberal regimes around the world—as manifested by frequent elections, shaky and short-term coalitions, and popular protests—seems to signal a deep crisis in the mechanisms of political representation. The attack on the formal mechanisms of liberal democracy, in the name of the people's will, must be considered a reaction to the centrality of the formal aspect of liberal democracy, a centrality pointed out by Claude Lefort. According to Lefort, politics is a form that gives expression to the symbolic dimension of society.[90] Therefore, the political configuration of liberal democracy, at the center of which is a contest between representatives of the people, expresses, first and foremost, the fact that there is no "natural" representative of the nation. It is an expression of the radical historicity of modern democratic society, founded on the objection to the traditional legitimacy of power. Whereas in a monarchy, the absence of a king is a fragile and dangerous time that must be ended as quickly as possible, in a democracy, the "throne" is empty by default,[91] meaning that the symbolic place of power once occupied by the king as the representative of the nation chosen by Divine Grace is only ever filled temporarily.[92] The "democratic invention" renders the struggle for power routine, and represents the conflicted nature of liberal society precisely by preventing its people from being fully represented. Lefort identifies a complex affinity between liberal values and institutions, on the one hand, and human rights and their legal status, on the other. Liberal values, unlike traditional values, are unlimited in principle: "From the moment when the rights of man are posited as the ultimate reference, established right is open to question."[93]

In the spirit of Hannah Arendt's "the right to have rights," Lefort stresses the status of rights as the perennial source of an undermining of the established order. This is the meeting point between the moral and formal aspects of liberal democracy: in its institutionalized struggle for the legislature, modern democracy has found a way to dynamically formalize the ability to challenge the law, thus making the law's lack of timeless legitimacy (conferred by God or tradition, for example) its exclusive source of legitimacy. In this sense, substantive democracy, the value content of liberal democracy—human rights—can be considered an extension of the form, through different means.

This is also Lefort's way of demonstrating the genetic affinity between liberal democracy and totalitarianism. Totalitarianism is a constant threat to liberal democracy, as it relies on the same "empty throne" vacated by the king. While liberalism seeks to keep the struggle for the representation of the people open, totalitarianism wishes to fill the empty space and express the will of the people directly. In liberal democracy, "the people do not exist." In our daily lives, we are but a collection of individuals, and "the people" come together only once every few years during elections, in a mediated form that requires compromises between different interest groups. Think of it as the ceremonial aspect of liberal democracy—the unity of the people is treated as a dangerous, sacred substance to be handled only with ritual care. Something crucial is missed when we consider the modern, liberal state as a procedural replacement of traditional, substantial ethical bonds, forged in common practices and rites—in liberal democracy, the procedural is sacralized, so to speak, it fulfills a function (we shall see in chapter 5 how problematic this way of putting things is) that is traditionally ritualistic.

The liberal fear of populism of any and all kinds stems from the latter's claim to "truly" represent the people, giving the people a continued public presence. It is not entirely unjustified—the notion of a self-identical, substantial people is a terrifying myth, which is not to say that it is simply untrue or that "in truth" we are all individuals. Rather, this is to say that liberal democracy can be understood as a historical mechanism—perhaps outdated—to contain an excess inherent to the social. Churchill's famous quip, according to which "democracy is the worst form of government, except for all those other forms that have been tried,"[94] is a popular expression of this view of democracy as an indispensable technique of limitation, "democracy . . . or worse." It could be that in its very reliance on the failures of attempts at something better, its reliance on the quashed utopian hopes of the past, democracy is mutating itself into something worse.

The populist sentiment is perceived as an expression of disbelief in representative democracy's claim to represent its constituents, to represent the people. Indeed, it is to be doubted, if by representation we understand the idea that elected representatives are working on behalf of, in the service of, those who elected them. And yet it is quite crucial to note that the new right is in no hurry to abolish the formal mechanisms of liberal democracy and give direct expression to the people's will. On the contrary, it claims to be the only truthful representation of the popular will. The new right-wing parties seek to change the rules of the game, thereby guaranteeing themselves a permanent advantage and making it difficult though not impossible to defeat them in the political arena. They shamelessly and openly seek to erode and transgress the unwritten rules of the game, but not to replace them with an entirely different formal system.

The change in the space of political representation should be sought in the mechanism of legitimation employed by the new authoritarianism. This mechanism does not demand full representation of the people; rather it places the dimension of the people that is in principle absent from the official public space right at the center of its representational array. It is through its transgressive actions that the populist right manages to make present that element of the people that escapes the regular system of representation. Sándor Ferenczi saw this as the unique power of the obscene word: the obscene word does not point at its object from a distance; it makes it present.[95]

From Claude Lefort, we learned that in liberal democracy the legislative mechanism plays an important symbolic role. The representative distance from the excessive real is a value in liberal democracy. From this point of view, a direct expression of this real—a full, unmediated representation of the people's will—would not just be an invitation to violence; it would be violence itself. In other words, the liberal space represents the representational distance itself as a supreme value of a special kind. One can even say that in liberal democracy the supreme value or the "ground" norm is the fact that there is no supreme value, there is no positive normative content that can be allowed to "saturate" the political system once and for all.

Parliamentary democracy and the discourse of rights are the means that express this absence as a positive value. The new right does not, at least not at this stage, seek to establish a supreme value—for instance, the nation or the leader—that would fully express the will of the people and thereby allow and perhaps even require the abolition of the mechanisms of representation. The "voice of the people" is used by new populists not to directly abolish the formal-liberal framework, but as a legitimation to erode established norms that have been taken as necessary for guaranteeing a "level" playing field, from major, structural arrangements, such as the balance of power between branches of government, to seemingly smaller ones, such as breaking a long-held convention to ensure control over the US Supreme Court, as did Republicans at the end of Obama's second term; or to turn to another example from Israel, Netanyahu's coalition piece of legislation that disqualified "reasonableness" as a tool of judicial review over the other branches of government. In both cases we witness a power grab, a cynical attempt to shift the balance of power in one's favor, but one that also carries a profoundly cynical message as to the ultimate reality of power and power alone. It is easy to get lost in the technical and judicial language and miss how, for example, Netanyahu's piece of legislation does exactly what is says it does: it delegitimizes reasonableness. Admittedly reasonableness is hard to precisely define, but its wholesale disqualification relied on an openly cynical rhetoric: all "reasonableness" can ever stand for is the power of judges to restrict the power of government, our own. And power should not be restricted, nor indeed answerable to reason. There can be no such thing as an objective standard of reasonableness, and the very attempt to apply such a limiting standard to the application of force is nothing but power masked.

These attacks on the status quo should not be understood therefore "merely" as attempts by the executive to garner more power. In breaking conventions and changing the rules of the game, the very sense of a common ground, a shared space of reason, is dropped from beneath the feet of the citizenry. The new right does not promise a new saturation of what unites us, a new meaning of national unity, but rather makes what is taken for granted lose all innocence. Unlike in a constitutional debate, once the unwritten rules of the game become subject to manipulation in the name of power, there is no way to retrieve their former status. Stomping our feet and saying, this is not done, this is not who we are, is an impotent gesture in this regard. For, here, it has been done, and it's doable. You have no ground on which to stand.

It is as if the new right is working to bring forward that which eludes the representational logic at the heart of the legislative act itself, and in the process has developed a "genre" of legislation that undermines the rational-formalist logic of the law and what it represents. Antiliberal legislation has been explicitly politicizing what up until now has been seen as neutral territory, one where the rules of the game have been equal for all participants—part of the formal and ideologically neutral gears of government. It is in such legislation, a shameless, uneven use of political power, that the "will of the people" is to be made present. That is the will of the excluded element of the people as such.

In this, the new right has effectively appropriated a critical point fundamental for the radical left. The very distinguishing line between radical and reformist, liberal lefties circles around this point: can the formal mechanisms of liberalism guarantee the very universal rights they are meant to serve? Take

Anatole France's famous quip against the formal equality guaranteed by the "rule of law": "The law, in its majestic equality, forbids rich and poor alike to sleep under bridges, to beg in the streets, and to steal loaves of bread."[96] A central tenet of radical left critique has been, ever since Marx, the argument that even systems that are supposed to guarantee neutrality and equality are tainted by ideological biases. The radical left's conclusion from this premise had been, traditionally, that true equality requires therefore a real restructuring of the social power structure: say that, in order to truly correct the out-of-proportion rates of incarceration of minorities in the US prison system, one would have to battle "systemic racism," namely, the myriad ways in which racist discrimination is "baked into" the social order. The new right's "conclusion" is quite different. Since neutral systems are "tainted" by special interests, never quite as public and neutral as they purport to be, power should be given to those who will shamelessly wield power to serve their own interests.

The new right does not simply equate the will of the majority with the general will; paradoxically, what expresses the "generality" of the right's political will, its claim for supremacy, is its explicit partiality. Consider how, in contemporary, idiomatic language, "player" means someone who is always advancing their own interest, and "the game" has come to stand for some rigged set of rules we all comply with unwittingly. The popular appeal of the new right has much to do with the ability to enlist an ethos of the "player," admired for their "game," against the opacity and hypocrisy of "the game."

Acts of legislation grounded in this reasoning are motivated to a large extent by the suspicion toward the medial dimension of the law—the rational-formalist conception of the law that gives utmost importance to preserving the status of the law as a space of ideologically neutral rationality, the medium through which various interests are given expression—and its deviation from this logic is what imbues it with the effect of "sincerity."

TECHNOLOGIES OF POWER: REACHING FOR THE GROUND OF LAW, FROM DISCIPLINE TO CONTROL

Focusing on the instructive role played by the transgression of unwritten norms in the legitimation of new authoritarianism brings us to Foucault, who consistently argued, throughout his career, for the growing importance of technologies of normalization, and the withering significance of law as a public, symbolic phenomenon.

It is striking to find in Foucault's seminars, in direct connection with this trajectory of power, a description of what he calls the grotesque or Ubu-esque figure of power (referring to Alfred Jarry's play Ubu roi). Foucault opens his seminar on the abnormal by pointing toward what seems like a permanent staple of power, equally present in Roman emperors, bureaucrats, totalitarian dictators, and psychiatric legal opinions:

By virtue of their status, a discourse or an individual can have effects of power that their intrinsic qualities should disqualify them from having. The grotesque, or, if you prefer, the Ubu-esque, is not just a term of abuse. . . . I think there is a precise category . . . the maximization of effects of power on the basis of the disqualification of the one who produces them. I do not think this is an accident or mechanical failure in the history of power. It seems to me that it is one of the cogs that are an inherent part of the mechanisms of power. Political power . . . can give itself, and has actually given itself, the possibility of conveying its effects and, even more, of finding their source, in a place that is manifestly, explicitly, and readily discredited as odious, despicable, or ridiculous.[97]

It would seem that Foucault is here describing what in Lacanian psycho-analysis is called symbolic castration: it is the very gap between the person and the symbolic role he is to fulfill that makes him appear indeed as the bearer of a power that exceeds his own person. As Lefort noted, the significance of this gap had been missed in Ernst Kantorowicz's classical study on the King's second body. As Kantorowicz shows, by means of careful rituals and ritual objects a second, "immortal" body of the king was separated and connected with the mortal bodies of kings in medieval Europe. But, Lefort notes, the "sublimity" of the kings, the symbolic status of kingship, is not attained by the symbolic theatrics in themselves, but in their relation to the body which is sexed and fallible. It is the gap between king and kinghood that sustains royal author-ity.[98] The gap between the person and, say, the seat of power is, in that sense, far from abnormal, and it certainly does not depend on the personality of the ruler being grotesque; suffice it that it falls short of the symbol—which it inevitably does.[99]

And yet Foucault explicitly rejects the very notion of the symbolic as a sig-nificant dimension of power. This is a principled position: symbolic power suggests to Foucault an antiquated interest in ideology: "We leave it to oth-ers, then, to pose the question of the effects of truth that may be produced in the discourse by the subject who is supposed to know. As for myself, I would rather study the effects of power produced in reality by a discourse that is at the same time both statutory and discredited."[100]

The reference to Lacan's notion of the subject supposed to know, developed in the context of Lacan's discussion of the psychoanalytic concept of transfer-ence,[101] is meant to suggest that transference—a complex of identification—has nothing to do with the new mechanisms of power.

For Foucault, the grotesque is connected, in fact, precisely with the demise of symbolic dignity. Foucault's point of reference is King Ubu, the spectacu-larly grotesque hero of Alfred Jarry's play. What he is after, however, is not some oddity, an aberration or accident, but rather something quite essential and elementary, a "cog" inherent in the "mechanism of power." It is the "mechanical" aspect that allows Foucault to see a functional homology between a discourse and an individual, between a bureaucrat and the authoritarian leader of a mass movement. To be sure, Foucault is by no means denying the profound transformations this fundamental modality of power had undergone. In passing, he refers to Pierre Clastre's work on political power amongst "primitive" societies. Whereas the grotesque might have served primitive societies to delimit political power, as Foucault takes Clastre to be suggesting, this does not seem to be the case with modern power. Quite to the contrary, in its modern guise the grotesque "seems to be a way of giving a striking form of expression to the unavoidability, the inevitability of power, which can function in its full rigor and at the extreme point of its rationality even when in the hands of someone who is effectively discredited."[102]

Far from operating as a social mechanism to limit the growth and concentration of power, the discrediting of power, at least in its modern iteration, serves to shed all limitations, to point to a power beyond any social restrictions. In this, Foucault seems to echo a certain narrative about the modern transformation of power, according to which premodern societies had techniques in place to contain violence, whereas modernity tends to unleash it.

What Foucault is after here, it would seem, is a transformation in political ontology, which we might describe as power's reach toward the virtual ground. "[It is] not a question of installing, as people say, another scene, but on the contrary, of splitting the elements on the same scene. It is not a question, then, of the caesura that indicates access to the symbolic, but of the coercive synthesis that ensures the transmission of power and indefinite displacement of its effect."[103]

What is at stake is the application of technology to what was once perhaps maintained by a symbolic technique. The transformation of power Foucault is analyzing here is precisely a transformation in the status of the virtual; no longer the symbolic ground, in principle beyond reach, its sublimity at best pointed at, the virtual is to be put side by side with the empirically real. Indeed, it becomes the very object of mechanisms of power.

This is what the new legal status of madness is meant to demonstrate: the Napoleonic legal code drew a stark alternative between legal responsibility and mental illness. Originally, expert opinion was meant to help the court decide whether a person was legally responsible or, due to his mental state, was to be considered as not responsible for his actions. And yet the status it came to assume is not that of a selector at the gates of law, deciding whether the issue was legal or medical, but rather, a stitching together of the two realms.[104] This stitching together of the private and the public not only makes the law expand rather than contract; it produces a monstrosity, a hybrid, an ontological impossibility:

Expert psychiatric opinion allows one to pass from action to conduct, from an offense to a way of being, and to make this way of being appear as nothing other than the offense itself, but in a general form. . . . [It] makes it possible to constitute a psychological-ethical double of the offense . . . to delegalize the offense as formulated by the code, in order to reveal behind it its double, which resembles it like a brother or a sister . . . and which makes it not exactly an offense in the legal sense of the term, but an irregularity in relation to certain rules, which may be physiological, psychological, or moral, etc.[105]

Expert psychiatric opinions serve to stitch together the written law, recently codified, and the unwritten law of conduct, which, being unwritten, has the character of virtuality. It will serve to make transgressions of the unwritten law, what Foucault calls conduct, appear as legal objects. Paradoxically, the restriction of the law's scope by codification has brought forth a "permanent state of exception," an open-ended expansion of legal power. In doing so, it shifts the guilt from the infringing act to the actor; from the act to its transcendental ground, so to speak, in the soul of the actor.

It is here that the more speculative aspect of Foucault's argument deserves our full attention. The stitching together of the public order of law and the private realm of the psyche and sexuality, and perhaps more significantly, the formal order of public law with the more elusive terrain of conduct, is taken by Foucault to suggest a shift in political ontology. Considering that psychiatric inquiry into the conduct of the accused is meant to tease out the transcendental frame of the criminal act, that is, to locate in his past behavior an individual's general tendency toward acting in a certain way, is a way for the mechanisms of power to seize hold of the empirico-transcendental doublet.[106] In doing so, virtuality is flattened out: no longer the symbolic background presupposed and to be displayed, but a realm for knowledge and power to act on directly, to dissect and analyze ad infinitum.

The transformation that Foucault is describing is of great significance and relevance, even beyond the historical framework in which it was composed. It is relevant, that is, even in a time where perhaps, from the perspective of the technologies of governance, subjectivity is to be avoided altogether. It shows a continuity between the subject of discipline and the dividual of control societies.

FROM EXPERT OPINION TO OPINIONATED MISTRUST OF EXPERTISE

The transformation of political ontology aimed at by Foucault is perhaps best captured by the tendency of contemporary technological developments toward what Mark Andrejevic calls "framelessness." Symbolic activity relies on framing, a process that totalizes by leaving something outside the frame:

"Telling a story means, by definition, constructing a frame that indicates what to include and what to leave out. All theorizing, categorizing, and abstract thought relies on a framework. For finite subjects, to dispense with a frame is to abdicate thought."[107]

Currently, however, automated media are operating on the premise of rejecting this very logic and embracing an alternative.

> We might describe the contemporary media moment—and its characteristic attitude of skeptical savviness regarding the contrivance of representation—as one that implicitly embraces the ideal of framelessness. . . . The driving force behind the contemporary critique of representation is that it falls short of framelessness: representations are always necessarily selective, biased, and therefore subject to debate, correction, and disbelief. Isn't this the real message of the charge of "fake news" mobilized by the political right in the contemporary media landscape: not that news is patently untrue but that it is always incomplete, subject to further forms of explication and contextualization in ways that deprive it of any real evidentiary purchase?[108]

Andrejevic's analysis of the drive toward "framelessness" serves him to uncover the logic underlying seemingly unrelated phenomena, such as the promise of data-driven target marketing to fulfill our needs and desires before we experience them, predictive policing systems that will target crime at its moment of emergence, and "smart" interfaces that are "preparing to monitor the rhythms of our daily lives so as to anticipate shifts not yet detectable by us such as aging or depression."[109] These rather distinct technological developments all partake in the tendency toward what Andrejevic calls automated subjects.

These are no longer techniques that are aimed at stabilizing the "essence" of subjectivity; they aim to do away with subjectivity altogether. Algorithmic governmentality[110] is not subject forming, but an automation of subjectivity. Algorithms are, initially, thought operators, a set of instructions that produce, as if by themselves, a result. As such, they can be said to be abstraction generators, specifically "the abstraction of the desire for an answer," translating it to the desire to make the world effectively calculable,[111] to make it, we might say, answerable to automated thought processes, to mold it in the shape of our models.[112]

Take the case of the new techniques of surveillance. The transition from the preventive logic of disciplinary surveillance to the preemptive ambition of contemporary surveillance aims at eliminating the role of the subject. Instead of assumed surveillance, internalized by the subject (as suggested by the model of the panopticon, envisioned by Bentham and made famous by Foucault), we will have real surveillance preventing the crime before it happens. This transition entails a broader change in framework, shifting the focus away from subjects and their motivation, indeed rendering interpretation superfluous. There is no need to understand why people may act in delinquent ways, only a need to find the right patterns that may serve to prevent such actions from taking place at all. Andrejevic is here able to pinpoint with much more precision an anxiety only vaguely expressed by Giorgio Agamben in his attempt to account for what is new about the kind of apparatuses we are currently surrounding ourselves with. Whereas the sorts of apparatuses that were the focus of Foucault's work (prisons, madhouses, the panopticon, schools, confession, factories, disciplines, etc.) were subject forming, the current apparatuses—Agamben's example is the cellular phone—are desubjectifying, indeed deindividuating.[113]

Desubjectification and social deskilling are part and parcel of the broader logic of framelessness.[114] The new logic of preemptive surveillance and consumerism entails a transformation in the very notion of knowledge. The core of this transformation is the attempt to replace symbolic framing, with its implicit gap between symbolic activity and the real to which it refers, with the cascading logic of a network of automated data collection, data analysis, and automated action that not only seeks to surpass the limitation of symbolic framing but to install something better in its stead. Strangely, framelessness is becoming, so to speak, a new frame of reference.

What Andrejevic calls automated media all tend toward the same effect: the relegation of activities that traditionally rely on a certain logic of "framing" to "frameless" processes. To the extent that one can identify symbolization with the act of framing, this ultimately amounts to a drive toward substituting of the symbolic function with automated processes. Just consider how the platform of new media, which carries no editorial responsibility, is to replace the gatekeepers of old media, making the "gates" of the internet radically open and deregulated. The notion of a platform aims to establish an automated, frameless frame, replacing symbolic selection with infrastructure.

And so Foucault's penetrating insight as to the shift in political ontology, the striving toward a "flattening" out of symbolic "depth," survives its own historicizing, so to speak. It supplies us with significant coordinates to trace and interpret the technologies that are arguably now replacing disciplinary techniques. What remains unclear in Foucault, however, is the very return of "old" Ubu-esque figures to the center of the political stage. If indeed the "message" to be learned from the Ubu-esque is the excesses of power, its tendency to grow, to shed all symbolic theatrics in favor of techniques, why would there still be the need for this message? If indeed it is no longer a matter of symbolic theater but of pure efficiency of power, why the "return of the repressed," why the insistence of the grotesque figure on power, displaying the gap between power and worth?

Indeed, as Foucault himself notes, such figures point beyond the effects of power to the source of power. That is, we might push the point further, they point beyond the effectivity of power, beyond the instrumental, means-to-ends logic, to its being and presence. To borrow the terminology of media studies, such moments of power are effectively declaring that "the medium is the message." At these limit points, power makes clear that it is not to be measured as an instrument, by means of the effects it is capable of producing, its efficiency, what its bearers can achieve by means of it, but as a medium, in its sheer presence and self-manifestation.

MEDIA SINCERITY: THE UNVEILING APPEAL OF TRANSGRESSIVE AUTHORITY FIGURES

In his book *Under Suspicion: Phenomenology of the Media*, Boris Groys proposes a possible explanation. According to Groys, the ontological desire, the need to identify what is "really" concealed beyond the surface sign, beyond the phenomenological level, is motivated by our existential dread concerning the medial nature of reality. Behind the content, the surface sign displayed by any medium, we cannot help suspecting the existence of a hidden message contained within the medium itself. The suspicion that there are dark and threatening forces operating beyond the visible dimension of phenomena can neither be corroborated nor disproved. This is an internal suspicion regarding the structure of the media: when you see a sign, you do not see the medium, and the medium can only be seen when it stops functioning as such. As an illustrative example, Groys considers a painting hanging in a museum: "When we see a painting in a gallery, we do not see the canvas that sustains this painting. In order to see the canvas, we have to turn the painting around." [115]

Based on this insight, Groys suggests a distinction, useful for the discussion before us, between medial sincerity and the truthfulness of the message. Because the message of the medium must be hidden, must disappear behind the signs, it cannot be presented directly but only revealed as if inadvertently, like a forced confession. Due to the hidden nature of the medium, the viewer watches with suspicion and anticipation for the medium to reveal itself. Groys proposes a "phenomenology of medial sincerity" whereby the consistency of messages only increases the viewer's suspicion that the gap between appearances and reality must be vast. Sincerity, therefore, is experienced precisely at the momentary appearance of the strange, the unusual, and the perverse at the heart of the familiar and the known:

> The biggest effect of sincerity . . . is created when signs are incorporated
> that are not only alien but also dangerous. This incorporation of signs
> of danger provides the most radical confirmation of media-ontological
> suspicion. Thus, signs of militant, revolutionary, direct, and immediate

violence—along with signs of insanity, ecstasy, and unrestrained erotic desire—come across as particularly sincere. . . . In this sense, sincerity stands in opposition to civility: we spontaneously associate "nice" with mendacious—and "coarse" with direct, authentic, and sincere.[116]

This link between the obscene or the "coarse" and the exposure of the "behind-the-scenes" dimension of the medium is supported by a possible etymology that links the English word "obscene" to the Greek *ob-skene*, the off-stage space where actors could change clothes between acts. The obscene, in this sense, is the appearance of what, in principle, cannot be "on stage," the medium which, by being hidden, allows the stage to be the locus of display.

Groys's description of the sincerity effect produced by the abnormal and the transgressive also offers an original explanation for the much-discussed penchant of the media to prefer the scandalous and the trivial over the important and the protracted. There is, however, yet another felicitous aspect to Groys's proposed explanation: it establishes a link between medial suspicion—the suspicion that the media are mendacious fundamentally and in principle—and the aura of "sincerity" that attaches itself to whoever and whatever breaks away from their rules. The greater the suspicion of the media ("fake news," conspiracy theories, etc.), the more compelling the sincerity of the coarse and the crude.

It is no wonder that the attraction of impulsive, immediate, and "unmediated" behavior, as the last sign of realness or "medial sincerity," has grown in recent years with the rise of the internet. As we shall explore in more detail later, the web is a medium that undermines the very distinction between what is medial and what is not. For now, let us only note that the distinctive feature of the web as a medium is that there is neither a clear sense of being "in" it nor of being "outside" it, and thereby the very distinction between being mediated and unmediated is eroded. This is made clear by contrasting the internet to broadcast media, which institute a stark distinction between inside—the people on TV, and outside, the spectators at home.[117]

The current media moment is not only the erosion of a clear distinction, in social terms, between being "in" and being "out" of the public eye. It signals the erosion of the line distinguishing the mediated from the immediate on an even more fundamental level, the erosion of the distinction we tend to take for granted, between words and acts. In the reality we see emerging before our eyes, words are more and more often perceived as acts of violence. This is a trend that has manifested itself in legislation, but perhaps more importantly in a culture—especially online culture—of sensitivity to "offensive" speech. At the same time, we see violence assuming a growing symbolic role. Not only is the main message of antiliberal legislation one of violence; we are living at a time when rocket fire, for example, is perceived as having semiotic value, the main and perhaps only language that both sides of the Israeli-Palestinian conflict have in common. Every average news consumer in Israel is accustomed, albeit unknowingly, to interpreting the rocket fire from Gaza to Israel, as well as Israeli violence toward the Palestinians, as a set of signals and signs. This is not merely the erosion of the marked distinction between war and peace,[118] or between emotional turmoil and rational stability, but a more fundamental erosion of the distinction between words and deeds, between symbolic activity and violence.

The discussion of representation and the means of representation, then, is a direct and inseparable continuation of our discussion of the new manifestations of power. It is the distinction between power and the space of representations that is now eroding. This is the challenge posed by naked power, a power that exults in its nudity.

2

GROUND AND SHADOW: UNWRITTEN LAW IN
PHILOSOPHY AND PSYCHOANALYSIS

They are playing a game. They are playing at not playing a game. If I show them I see they are, I shall break the rules and they will punish me.

I must play their game, of not seeing I see the game.

R. D. Laing

FROM CONCEPT TO IDEA: THE GROUND AND SHADOW
OF THE LAW

If we are to catch a meaningful glimpse of the elusive phenomenon of unwritten law, light must be thrown on its strange ontological status, as it were, at the very troubled conjunction of normativity and being—say, as a first approximation, between what "is" and what "ought" to be. Let us begin by considering the following illuminating quote by neo-Kantian philosopher Hermann Cohen:

The Greeks distinguished the "unwritten laws" from the written ones. The latter are statutes from human hands. It is not important that they should be written, though the highest certitude is inherent in the written and the state law. Even the positive laws require for their more profound verification conformity with the unwritten laws. If the actual ruler, like Creon, proclaims a law, it is not binding for Antigone, and she knows herself free from the wantonness of transgressing the law because, in her love for her brother, she appeals to the unwritten laws. These unwritten laws contained the morality of the Greek national spirit before it was formulated and motivated by the philosophers. Yet philosophic ethics was no safeguard against sophistry, which broke forth out of the ranks of philosophy itself. What in later times has been designated by the term "by nature" in opposition to convention, designated as "statute," is nothing other than that "in itself." The eternal, that unwritten, which precedes any recorded writing, precedes, as it were, any culture, must precede it, because it lays the foundation for every culture.[1]

In Cohen's account the unwritten law is the Platonic idea of the law, that which serves as a standard of any positive, written law but is itself invisible, unplaceable. The reference to the infamous Kantian "thing in itself" should be taken quite seriously here. The problem Cohen is pointing out is the social-political equivalent to the epistemic problem regarding the Kantian thing in itself: The unwritten law seems necessary for the law to make sense and to have validity and authority, and yet it itself seems to lead into insoluble contradictions; it is at once foundational for knowledge (of the law) and outside of it, beyond it. We have an unknowable foundation for our knowledge of the law.[2]

Without the assumption of a ground to the posited order of law, the law seems arbitrary and ungrounded, but the very dependence on a ground that lies beyond the posited order, and as such remains elusive if not inaccessible, eluding our conceptual grasp, is the nihilism that threatens the order of the law, what Cohen refers to above as "sophistry."[3] We might say that for Cohen, the trouble in our philosophical and political tradition, beginning with the Greeks, has to do with the attempt to conceptually grasp the ground of law. The ground as such is what makes possible conceptual cognition but cannot be captured by it. The unwritten law is an idea which, following Kant, is to be understood as something which might give us direction and orientation, but cannot be grasped by the understanding.[4]

According to Leo Strauss, the above-mentioned split between phusis and nomos, nature and culture, is premised on a split in the notion of custom, habit, or way.[5] In societies where traditional authority is intact, everything has its own way, what it is accustomed to do, and we learn about these old ways from our elders. The very split between our positive order of culture and some higher—if more difficult to ascertain—standard signals a crisis of traditional authority, and an attempt to inherit the spirit of tradition, the respect for the oldest things, while liberating ourselves from the authority of its representatives, the elders, by going all the way to the oldest, to the archē, the principle, beginning, or foundation.[6] In archē, it is well known, we already have this tension between what is first, what has logical or ontological priority, and what commands, what has authority.[7]

For such an idea to emerge, a foundation which is old in an absolute, not a relative sense, primordial, two further distinctions, Strauss argues, must be put in place: the distinction between hearsay and what one can see with one's own eyes, and the distinction between the artificial, or the man-made, and what was not man-made. The former distinction made it possible to doubt the old sayings, the oral source of authority, relying on what can be brought to the light of day and be witnessed first personally; the latter, to distinguish between arbitrary things, which owe their existence to human power, and what humans discover as unconditioned by them, something with a higher source of necessity.

And so for Strauss, this split between an unwritten natural law that we are to ascertain and the ways of our societies is nothing less than the emergence of philosophy and science. We now discover nature as both an object of rational study, unconditioned by our ways of life, and therefore a source for the highest standards of being, something we ought to aspire to. Nature, as it were, emerges simultaneously as an abstract notion to be conceptualized and as an ultimate ground and standard, an idea.

PRESCRIPTIVE, DESCRIPTIVE: THE FETISHIST DISAVOWAL OF NORMATIVE FORCE

How can the violation of what is understood as the virtual ground of law become a mode of political legitimation? We have seen that the unwritten law can be and has been referred to as the ground of law, but we have also begun to see that, as the emphasis falls on the unwritten aspect of the law, obscenity quickly comes into the question. Should we not simply distinguish conceptually between these two, seemingly diametrically opposed senses of the term "law"? Can we not separate the normative from the descriptive? We have already noted that unwritten law has historically been used to refer to dimensions of the law that strike us as antithetical, such as custom and natural law. The problem is that such a separation, which is the manner in which the unwritten law appears in modernity, is precisely the way in which it is occluded as a topic.

The unwritten law may be said to have split, in modernity, between two rationalities: legal-political philosophy and political economy. It is as if the two orientations each highlight a different aspect of the law-in-the-absence-of-law that governs the relations between legal entities, the law of nations, effectively the law of war and peace, understood as a commercial alternative to violence. One orientation envisions the zero level of law as one of war, violent confrontation, whereas the other imagines it as a state of mutually beneficial exchange. Theories of sovereignty and natural law (Hobbes, Locke, Rousseau) have postulated a "state of nature," out of which arises the explicit positive law. Political economy, on the contrary, aimed to delineate the emergence of a "spontaneous order" (Hayek's variation on Smith's invisible hand),[8] a quasi-natural lawfulness that governs human societies. If in general the unwritten law can be described as the appearance of the natural within the social world, the modern split of rationalities offers two oppositional yet complementary theories of the relation of the social to the natural. The first theorizes political power as a necessary limit to potentially lethal natural tendencies, a sovereign check on unruly human desire, whereas the other understands the "second nature" of society as unproblematically continuous with nature, and is concerned instead with the encouragement of desires. The unwritten law becomes either a normative abstraction, the ideal "ought" of natural law, aiming to ward off the mythical, virtual threat of the state of nature, which serves as its inherent rationale, or a quasi-natural power, the object of study of the emerging social sciences, and later, we might note, life science and cybernetics.

In the second half of the seventeenth century and the beginning of the eighteenth, against the background of the simultaneous rise of "natural law" and "laws of nature,"[9] two competing yet complementary new theories arise as to the link between human transgressive nature and the social order. One, given voice in Thomas Hobbes's *Leviathan* (1651) has become the founding gesture of modern political philosophy[10] and its key notions of sovereignty and representation,[11] while Bernard Mandeville's *The Fable of The Bees* (1714) propounds an obscene, often disavowed prefiguration of political economy, the shameful beginnings of modern economics.

Though this is rarely at the focus of readings of *Leviathan*, Hobbes develops in it a novel theory of human desire. Analogous to the manner in which the concept of a "law of nature" developed, that is, by the decoupling of movement from substance,[12] Hobbes stipulates his law of human nature by decoupling desire, the motivating force, from character, and power from the attainment of goals. The problem of human desire is no longer a question of self-governance, a major topic of classical ethics. Like the novel notion of motion, human desire is now seen as inert, perpetual in the absence of external limitation. Human desire, according to Hobbes, is unique in its tendency to fixate on the means of desire, power, and therefore to transcend any natural limitation in the form of the satisfaction of appetites or the attainment of goals. It is this accumulative, expansionist nature of human desire that makes humans a continuous threat to each other. Plato's "second-rank" law, according to which desires are to be curbed by being allowed some secret, private outlet, no longer suffices—human nature is so deeply antisocial, of infinitely ruinous potential, that it has to be curbed by a mightier, absolute will. Human desire has to be pulled into orbit by the gravity of the sovereign. Only the establishment of such a limit can create the space for prosperous human life.

While Hobbes postulates the sovereign as a necessary limit to the uniquely infinite and therefore potentially destructive nature of human desire, Bernard Mandeville turns directly against Plato's second-rank law, with his infamous subtitle and slogan—private vices, public benefits. For Mandeville it is precisely the antisocial nature of human sociality, as Kant would later put it,[13] that is responsible for the miracle of the social order, the secret of economic activity and productivity. All attempts to "fix" human vices will only destroy the social order to which they give rise. Mandeville introduces a new, elusive paradox, soon to be "tamed" and "smoothed over" by Adam Smith and the tradition that follows his footsteps.[14] Mandeville's economy is driven by vices, that is, by morally condemned activities, by obscene enjoyment, inseparable from its status as socially forbidden. Removing the public shame from such activities, declaring private vices to be publicly beneficial, runs the risk of "disarming" them, rendering them economically useless. In juxtaposition to Hobbes, Mandeville's "principle of motion" secretly requires an obstacle, a hindrance, in order to propel further. Mandeville's text performs a unique kind of "liar's paradox" as to the nature of the economy, serving to cover up the obscene nature of the economy by obscenely uncovering its secrets. In the more respectable developments of Mandeville's theory, from Adam Smith to Friedrich Hayek, Mandeville's "vices" are "neutralized" by their conversion into "self-interest,"[15] and the obscene nature and history of the unwritten law is rebaptized as "spontaneous order."[16]

Modern political philosophy takes itself often to be setting limits on human nature. Stipulating a problematic natural state in which, in the absence of law, there is nothing but vulnerability to the violence of others, the social link is reduced to the potential of lethal violence. Without explicit codification, the social substance—human nature—is volatile and dangerous. In the absence of law, modern political theory finds naked power, an unruly substance. Political economy, on the other hand, sees man as a creature whose problematic nature can and should be harnessed, his desires encouraged rather than curbed,[17] as it spontaneously produces an economic order. The economy is understood as a kind of second nature that serves to maximize human tendencies, a field that is to be guarded against interference and design. In the absence of law, political economy identifies a mysterious formal principle, a self-organizing, productive power, and tends to deny the "substance" of it, the "stain" of the illicit motivation, tied as it is to what is socially disapproved of. The "evil" of human nature is not to be constrained or codified by law, but it is to be both further abstracted and enhanced.

We might say that in modernity, the nature-culture relation, the original topic of myth, bifurcates into two poles, forming a paradox of freedom. Is freedom the release of man from nature by artificial, man-made constructs such as the law of the state, a project whose extreme horror was reached in twentieth-century totalitarian projects, intent on creating a "New Man"? Or is freedom the release of the natural current that runs through human societies, a project which echoes some major romantic themes, but one whose concrete political manifestation has been the free market ideology? Is desire to be curbed by culture, or should culture adhere to the demands of desire?[18]

As Alenka Zupančič shows, sexuality is the primary site where nature and culture are paradoxically entangled, where the nonrelation between nature and culture is articulated.[19] To speak of a nonrelation between nature and culture is to say that nature and culture can neither be set apart as two independent entities nor integrated harmoniously into one. Following this line of thought, we could say that the two, complimentary rationalities of the modern state and the economy crystallize this tension as such: in the tradition of modern political philosophy, we must presume the separability of nature and culture, and in the tradition of political economy we must presume their seamless continuity or harmonization.

Modernity thus splits the unwritten law between (idealistic) ethics and (realistic) politics. Both positions, and indeed the very split between them, distort the normative force of the unwritten law. Indeed, the very gap between normativity and force is a sign of the disappearance of the unwritten law. Can we comprehend a force of normativity as something different from the obligatory, penalizing law? Can we comprehend a normative order which has a hold on its subjects, without relying on some mode of enforcement?

AUTONOMY OR HETERONOMY? NO, THANK YOU!

As Étienne Balibar argued in his famous *Citizen-Subject*, as self-legislation became the defining principle of modern freedom, it split subjectivity between an almighty, sovereign legislator and his powerless subject.[20] As self-legislators we find ourselves, at the same time, tyrannized by an incompetent master and unable to control an unruly simpleton.[21] The identification of law and power makes power into a zero-sum game, but one that cuts through the very core of our subjectivity.

This discontent with autonomy amplifies an ambivalence inherent in the law: the problematic slippage between law as an ethical and law as a political category. Is the law a political instrument of power, ultimately alien to ethics, and internalized to the detriment of its subjects? Or does self-legislation put us finally on the right ethical footing, locating the source of normative power in the rational capacities of human individuals rather than some mystical other—whether that be God or the ways of old? Does autonomy signal our liberation from power, or an unheard-of submission to it?

Let us consider two contemporary philosophers with seemingly opposing views of the problem yet sharing a remarkably similar vocabulary: Giorgio Agamben and Robert Brandom. In his *Homo Sacer*, Agamben has singled out as paradigmatically encapsulating the modern crisis of meaning, or nihilism, an expression used by Gershom Scholem (the founder of the modern study of Jewish mysticism) to describe the law in Kafka's universe, in his correspondence on the topic with Walter Benjamin:

> *Being in force without significance*: nothing better describes the ban that our age cannot master than Scholem's formula for the status of law in Kafka's novel. . . . Everywhere on earth men live today in the ban of a law and a tradition that are maintained solely as the "zero point" of their own content. . . . All societies and all cultures today . . . have entered into a legitimation crisis in which law (we mean by this term the entire text of tradition in its regulative form, whether the Jewish Torah or the Islamic

Sharia, Christian dogma or the profane *nomos*) is in force as the pure "Nothing of Revelation."[22]

Validity without significance—the picture Agamben is painting is one of profound alienation from one's own form-of-life. We remain compelled to norms we do not understand and therefore cannot endorse. We inherit a normative vocabulary that remains very much in effect for us, though it has long since lost its meaningful context.[23] Our past has become unreadable, opaque, yet we remain shackled to it.

If Agamben describes the modern crisis of meaning in terms of a tradition that remains in force, i.e., valid, but without meaning, Robert Brandom's definition of the same problem seems, at first sight, to be its direct opposite. For Brandom, in modernity there is significant content, but without the accompanying validity or normative force.[24] The paradigmatic example of this malaise of the modern attitude for Brandom is the ironic mode of the romantics, understood as the distance between the subject and any of his proclamations, the gap of intent, the creeping question threatening to undermine all propositional content: "You say this, but what do you really mean?"

According to Brandom, the moderns are perfectly capable of understanding the contents of their traditions, their very forms of life, but no longer view these as authoritative in themselves. Normative force is now seen—rightly, according to Brandom—to derive from the judgments of rational subjects, autonomous rather than heteronomous, subjective rather than objective. The story of modernity is, according to Brandom, the story of the transition from ethical substance to autonomous subjects.

This is captured in part by the modern move to contractual theories of the social-political order: our normative reality has to be grounded in the rational—if implicit—consent of subjects, rather than in the substantive contents of a given tradition. In this, Brandom is offering a philosophical inheritance of Henry Maine's thesis as to the evolution of law from status to contract, from an implicit and ultimately irrational expression of social relations, to the explicit codification of social relations in contractual terms. For Brandom, however, while this is, to a large extent, an advancement, it comes at a considerable cost: norms lose their objectively compelling character.

It is possible to bring these seemingly opposing views together; what both outlooks share is a view of modernity as the condition in which content and validity, or normative force, come apart. This may help explain the elusive nature of the problem. The gap between content and validity or normative force can have a variety of different, even opposing manifestations. As Robert Pippin nicely puts it, it is "as if the most prominent and disturbing manifestation of Nihilism is the absence of any manifestation."[25] Nihilism, understood as the incapacity to fully believe, to truly commit, could appear in the guise of its opposite: overzealous commitments, masking an underlying doubt as to their value. It is not only ironic distance, cynical wisdom, or overbearing alienation from one's form of life,[26] but also the overzealous endorsement of its core values—i.e., fundamentalism—that can attest to a certain loss of philosophical innocence,[27] and to no longer feel at home in one's inherited life forms or traditions.

Underlying this prognosis of the modern predicament is thus the fantasy of a lost ethical substance, a lived tradition that bears its normative force within, and in which norms are objective realities rather than estranged duties. But what gets lost in the prognosis and its underlying fantasy is the very ability to inquire after the nature of normative force, deemed to have come undone from the contents of the modern life form. Normative force (often identified with authority) and tradition become trapped in a kind of hermeneutic circle: tradition is understood as that form of life in which authority is in full sway, and authority is the traditionally grounded power.[28]

With that in mind, let us now turn to a few select appearances of the unwritten law in the history of philosophy, in which its unwritten aspect plays a central role, and see what, if any, configuration emerges. Rather than assume that the normative force of the unwritten law is simply a thing of the past, let us explore the way in which it makes its appearance in the philosophy of history, particularly in philosophical texts concerned with the philosophy of history.

As we shall see, the unwritten law seems to be an exemplary "vanishing mediator." As a rule, the unwritten law makes its appearance in the philosophical canon fleetingly, in critical, illuminating points of the philosophical text, never to be explicitly defined: briefly illuminating grand philosophical systems, as if flashing by. Let us begin by reading together, side by side, two major philosophies of history, usually seen as diametrically opposed: those of Nietzsche and Hegel.

THE LAWFULNESS OF THE CONTINGENT: THE RADICAL HISTORICITY OF THE UNWRITTEN

For Nietzsche, being unwritten, in an emphatic sense, is the very definition of historical being. Nietzsche hints at this definition in the context of his discussion of punishment, which, we ought to note, he ultimately understands as a primordial form of writing, the inscription on the body[29] of a dialectics of memorization and forgetting, which makes humans what they are, animals capable of commitments, of making promises, binding themselves to future behavior.[30] This is the anthropogenetic function of custom.

Nietzsche seeks to show, first, that our rationale for punishment, in modernity, is very weak, incapable of accounting for its own genesis and the historical transformations it has undergone. However, Nietzsche is not simply seeking to ground the meaning of punishment in its most primitive or archaic appearance. The primal meaning of punishment is not to be found in its earliest form but in the very fact of its historical transmutations.

Punishment is a mode of primal inscription, opening up the horizon of a historical nexus between past, present, and future, and its significance is to be sought there, as it were. It is a mode of writing, we might say, in which we are inscribed, not an inscription that is legible to us. Foreshadowing Lacan's formula, this is a writing in which the subject is what one signifier represents to the next, the very inverse of communicative language, in which a subject uses a signifier to signal to another subject. In a similar vein, for Benjamin, we may already note, punishment was the basic conception of myth. "The basic conception in Myth is the world as punishment—punishment which actually engenders those to whom punishment is due. Eternal recurrence is the punishment of being held back in school, projected onto the cosmic sphere: humanity has to copy out its text in endless repetitions."[31]

Indeed, the unwritten or undefinable ethical "substance" arises, according to Nietzsche, once we forgo a utilitarian teleology:

> The matter is not to be understood in the way our naïve moral and legal genealogists assumed up till now, who all thought the procedure had been invented for the purpose of punishment, just as people used to think that the hand had been invented for the purpose of grasping. With regard to the other element in punishment, the fluid one, its "meaning," the concept "punishment" presents, at a very late stage of culture (for example, in Europe today), not just one meaning but a whole synthesis of "meanings" [Sinnen]: the history of punishment, up to now in general, the history of its use for a variety of purposes, finally crystalizes in a kind of unity which is difficult to dissolve back into its elements, difficult to analyze, and this has to be stressed, is absolutely undefinable. Today it is impossible to say precisely why people are actually punished: all concepts in which an entire process is semiotically concentrated defy definition; only something which has no history can be defined.[32]

Note that what we get here from Nietzsche is a kind of negative definition of the emphatically historical: what is historical is what is undefined. It has a history only as long as, and insofar as, it defies a definition. Once conceptually grasped, a thing loses its history, so to speak. Better put, once conceptualized, its history is repressed. Think of it as a variation on Marx's notion of real abstraction, in which the arising of the abstract notion signals, and covers up, the real abstraction of reality: the abstract notion of labor only emerges once labor has been abstracted, and its very emergence as an abstract concept, universally applicable, covers up its moment of emergence, the historical transformation that makes it possible to emerge as such, abstractly.[33]

In a sense, Nietzsche is here struggling to uncover, underneath the abstract notion, the underlying reality which makes possible a series of reconceptualizations but is not, itself, an ahistorical substance awaiting discovery. What a genealogy of morals aims at is not the oldest, "original" meaning of an ethical phenomenon such as punishment, but the undefinable unity of its diverse historical appearances, which, you will note, can only come to be perceived in what the present finds opaque in its ethical substance, say, what is repressed in the abstract concept. Utilitarian explanations are understood by Nietzsche to be a way of avoiding the dimension of the phenomenon to be explained, what in the phenomenon is "fluid," ill-captured by our explanations of it. The answer "the hand was invented for grasping" merely sidesteps what raised the question to begin with—the complex organization of the hand, which seems to defy a mechanical account of its makeup.

We might turn here to Kant's definition of "purposiveness" as the "lawfulness of the contingent as such"[34] to grasp what is at stake. For Kant, it is the contingent as such, that is, something appearing to us as not necessary, as something that could have been different or not at all, that gives rise to "purposiveness," as the lawfulness of the contingent. The contingent is that which stands in a relation of lawfulness without law (judgment without concept), so to speak, to other phenomena, to which it is somehow related. It is the experience of the contingent that gives rise to the sense of purposiveness, an order—a unity or totality—to which this particular belongs, a meaningful context in which it makes sense. Purpose, for Kant, is not a category of the understanding, like, say, causality, but a concept of reason, something we only know from within, by acting, in setting goals and executing plans. When we see something that suggests purposiveness to us, we have in fact already placed it in a normative context; it strikes us as only being comprehensible as part of some(one's) plan, suggesting some kind of subjective agency, be it fate, God, or nature. The issue, however, is to capture the kind of unity implied by such purposiveness without reducing it to a concept of our understanding, a lens through which we understand reality.

Purposiveness is not an answer to the question "Why?," but is what motivates the question. In judging something to be contingent, we judge it to be "lawful" in a way that escapes us, and that, according to Kant, we can only represent to ourselves by analogy with our purposive capacities, hinting, that is, at an underlying purpose (nature as art), a causality of the concept, in which it is, say, the concept I have of a chair that is responsible for my bringing about a particular chair. To point to a purposive design is problematic in this respect for philosophical, not scientific reasons. It turns the mystery itself—the way in which these things come to hang together in a nonmechanical way, that is, to be "purposefully" organized (i.e., in a way that appears to us as a realization of a concept)—into an answer: it is by design that these things have come about. The mystery is the very undefinable unity, the "lawfulness of the contingent," implying a concept that we lack.

For Nietzsche, this inexplicable "lawfulness," or unity, of the contingent implies the ontological necessity of (a philosophical) history: it is not simply that all definitions are historically contingent, but the unity of the different historical definitions cannot be captured by a definition without thereby reducing the very historicity of the phenomenon to a teleology, which casts history as the process of actualization of a latent, potential meaning. The idea of an underlying unity of purpose should not be abandoned, mind you, for the sake of a causal-mechanistic one. A genealogy of morals is no more the historical evolution of morality than it is the spiritual, teleological fulfillment of a latent purpose. The meaning of punishment does not arise by "returning" our modern notion to older, more primitive ones, nor does it develop from one to the other; the "substance" of punishment is the undefinable unity of its diverse historical appearances, the "lawfulness" of its contingent history.

Strangely enough, what we see in Nietzsche here is rather precisely the attempt to view something like the Platonic idea of punishment, what all particular manifestations of punishment "partake" in, behind the problematic, always partial attempts to conceptualize it. We might view Nietzsche here as inheriting Goethe's notion of primal, archetypal phenomena.[35] The unity of punishment is to be gleaned from the nonconceptual similarity between historical manifestations of the phenomenon, the way in which such appearances of punishment, in their very similarity, point toward a virtual archetype, which itself is nothing but the unity of such a multiplicity of appearances.[36]

HEGEL'S ETHICAL SUBSTANCE: SPIRIT BETWEEN MYTH AND HISTORY

If in Nietzsche we see an implicit theory of the idea emerging behind the failure of conceptualization, in Hegel we see how that very conceptual "surplus," what concepts must leave out, ushers us into the domain of history. And indeed, it is the very "unwritten" aspect of the law that introduces the transition, in the *Phenomenology of Spirit*, into history. While the unwritten law makes only a brief if dazzling appearance in Hegel, flashing up like lightning, it does in fact announce the entrance of the subject of Hegel's masterpiece, spirit.

In the *Phenomenology of Spirit*, the unwritten law appears in a transitional role, bringing the chapter on reason to a close and ushering in the chapter on spirit, and indeed signals the move into the unruly terrain of spirit proper, taking leave of the more conceptually established terms of consciousness, self-consciousness, and reason. From this point on, the topic of the *Phenomenology* is much more directly the historical unfolding of spirit, now beginning to emerge as "ethical substance," as the always historically embedded, finely contextualized—yet also constantly context-destroying—ethical domain of spirit.

Hegel foreshadows this transition, as is typical of the progression of the *Phenomenology*, in his final critique of reason assuming the shape of law, as either law-giving or law-checking. One thing that eludes this identification of the law with the faculty of reason, with human capacity, is the sense in which ethical reality gains a *substantial*, objective dimension. For Hegel, this "substantial" dimension of the ethical is inseparable from the unwritten aspect of the laws which form it.

> They are masses articulated into groups by the life of the unity which permeates them, unalienated spirits transparent to themselves, stainless celestial figures that preserve in all their differences the undefiled innocence and harmony of their essential nature. The relationship of self-consciousness to them is equally simple and clear. They are. And nothing more; this is what constitutes the awareness of its relationship to them. Thus, Sophocles' Antigone acknowledges them as the unwritten and infallible law of the gods:
>
> They are not of yesterday or today, but everlasting
> Though where they came from, none of us can tell.
>
> They are. If I inquire after their origin and confine them to the point whence they arose, then I have transcended them; for now, it is I who am the universal, and they are the conditioned and limited. If they are supposed to be validated by my insight, then I have already denied their unshakable, intrinsic being, and regard them as something which, for me, is perhaps true, but also is perhaps not true. Ethical disposition consists just in sticking steadfastly to what is right, and abstaining from all attempts to move or shake it, or derive it. Suppose something has been entrusted to me; it is the property of someone else and I acknowledge this because it is so, and I keep myself unfalteringly in this relationship. . . . As soon as I start to test them I have already begun to tread an unethical path. By acknowledging the absoluteness of the right, I am within the ethical substance; and this substance is thus the essence of self-consciousness.[37]

Let us note, first, the strange image of celestial figures "that preserve in all their difference the undefiled innocence and harmony of their essential nature. . . . They are. And nothing more; this is what constitutes the awareness of its [consciousness's] relationship to them."[38] We are dealing here with a constellation, a sort of belonging together that cannot be subsumed conceptually,[39] quite like the one that for Nietzsche made a turn to history necessary. But there is something much more historically specific at play here: Hegel's laws here have the marks of the Greek pantheon of gods. Hegel seems to be already hinting that ethical substance makes its appearance within a mythological context, that is, that its very formal logic, so to speak, is accompanied by a storied content; it is a form that cannot but refract into parts, being nothing but what holds these parts together in "magical" unity.

In his *Philosophy of Art*, Schelling turns to the logic of the Greek pantheon to account for the construction of art. In his account, divinity as such requires a self-subsisting unity, but a very curious kind of unity. It would not be enough to demand some abstract absoluteness from this unity, and so it must elucidate and concretize itself from within. This requires an internal division, that is, a unity sustained, within itself, by a plurality. Each of these "elements" of divinity would have to reflect the rest in its internal structure. Thus, reality may be granted through an entirely internal determination.[40] Schelling would revisit this notion of a unity that can only manifest itself in plurality in his philosophical account of myth: now this logic serves him to account for the very dispersion of myths, the dispersion of spirit, as it were, into a multiplicity of cultures.[41] Lévi-Strauss's structuralist reading of myth, while very different in tone and temperament, can be seen as a further articulation of the same notion, insofar as it takes the plurality of myths to be what underlies their unique structure.[42]

Hegel's laws seem to make up ethical substance in exactly this way, by being unified in plurality, a plurality that maintains the self-subsistence of the whole. This reflects, interestingly, an earlier point Hegel makes in the section of the *Phenomenology* on "The Force and the Understanding." As Hegel argues there, the law of nature can only exist as law by having particular partial determinations, or particular laws. But this plurality is exactly the unity of the law as such, whose internal indeterminateness is what allows these determinations.[43] Taken together, we can see the uncanny proximity of nature and culture in the articulation of the unwritten law, as what bestows a lawlike order on nature and a "naturalness" to human, social laws.

The unity of ethical substance is unwritten in an emphatic sense. It is a lawfulness that precisely cannot be viewed as itself falling under a law. It cannot be approached probingly, in a questioning mood, from outside, as it were, but affirmingly, from within. Its unity is to be primal, intuitive, rather than conceptually elaborated.

The example provided by Hegel for such a preconceptual substantiality—private property—is very telling. Indeed, private property can only function as a social institution to the extent that it has become "naturalized." Perhaps inadvertently, Hegel is here offering us an intimation of the revolutionary moment: to really question private property is not to pose a question regarding the permissibility of taking another person's property, which, presupposing the validity of the institution, can only amount to stealing. The "questioning" only truly arises in a revolutionary context, that is, by undermining the substance of the institution itself, say, by a collective of workers confiscating the factory in which they are employed, or, to take a more contemporary if utopian example, by the users of a social media platform finding a way to declare it a "common" and rip it from the hands of its "owner." In this way, one cannot speak of a violation of a law, but of its abolition. Ethical substance, unlike written laws, cannot be questioned, nor amended piecemeal—it can only be radically transformed, desubstantiated.

Ethical substance is "understood" in the troubled connection between theoretical cognition and practice; its objectivity is ethical, which is to say that it defies subjective cognition from a detached theoretical standpoint. It assumes our involvement, the appearance of a precognitive practice, what is taken for granted in our engagement with it, and therefore the issue never is simply to come to see it for what it is, but to transform such an understanding into a decisive, transformative act. We might further speculate that this is what makes the history of human forms of life the locus for the unfolding of the idea: we can glimpse the idea only in the unity of such breaks in conceptual continuity. Freedom, as the idea realized in history, would have to be not only what holds together its various manifestations, the Platonic sense in which phenomena partake in the idea, but also what makes necessary the transition from one to the other, the restlessness and imbalance driving ethical substance as such to change.

The comparison with Schelling's notion of the mythical order is crucial in bringing out the "naturalized" aspect of the unwritten law, but already in itself casts a serious shadow on Hegel's exposition of the unwritten law. Hegel's definition of ethical substance as a self-enclosed, simple unity of existence is—from a Hegelian standpoint—very suspicious. Isn't Hegel's central, recurring point that simplicity can never be identified with foundation? Indeed, the immediately following chapter on spirit will begin with the tearing asunder of the simple unity by its own inherent tensions, and ethical substance will have to finally reappear, after a long, tumultuous journey, precisely in the individualized, atomistic modern world via the mediation of revolutionary terror.

Significantly, this step into historical shapes of the spirit begins, in the chapter on spirit, with a confrontation with myth, specifically that of Antigone. As Hegel stages this conflict—to which we shall return—with Antigone on the side of the unwritten law of the mythical underworld, of familial, unconscious, and divine ethical order in feminine guise, and Creon on the side of public, man-made law, it is as if History, as a history of spirit, begins with a mythical struggle between myth and man-made law, between culture and the enduring remnants of nature within culture.

Hegel's introduction of the unwritten law confronts us with the dual nature of the primal, so to speak. The primal, say, preconceptual or intuitive disposition, can appear paradisal, a harmonious part-whole relation in which everything is in its place, perhaps primordially lost, and it can appear hellish, impulsive and explosive, unboundedly threatening and irrepressible: an unattainable ideal of the unity of form and content, and an unassimilable real, a formless "substance" or a substance without any recognizable shape or form.[44]

While never explicitly developed in his oeuvre, the notion of unwritten laws was central for Walter Benjamin, precisely in articulating the place of myth in history. It makes a brief appearance—as is typical of the conceptual history of the unwritten law—in his famous critique of violence and his equally famous essay on Kafka. In both contexts, Benjamin connects the unwritten law with the realm of fate and myth.

> Laws and definite norms remain unwritten in the prehistoric world. A man can transgress them without suspecting it and then must strive for atonement. But no matter how hard it may hit the unsuspecting, the transgression in the sense of the law is not accidental but fated, a destiny which appears here in all its ambiguity. In a side-glance at the idea of fate in Antiquity, Hermann Cohen came to a "conclusion that becomes inescapable": "The very rules of fate seem to be what causes and brings about the breaking away from them, the defection." It is the same way with the legal authorities whose proceedings are directed against K. It takes us back, far beyond the time of the giving of the law on twelve tablets, to a prehistoric world, written law being one of the first victories scored over this world. In Kafka the written law is contained in lawbooks, but these are secret; by basing itself on them, the prehistoric world exerts its rule all the more ruthlessly.[45]

At first blush, it might seem as if Benjamin is adopting here a simple narrative of triumphant progress from the murky, fateful domain of myth—where human life is exposed to invisible powers—to the human-made order of civilization.[46] But of course, the lesson of Kafka is, all to the contrary, about the ways in which this domain of the unwritten can "exert its rules all the more ruthlessly" within the order of law.[47] For Benjamin, the prehistoric world does not signify simply the time of early humans, before written history. It is rather primal and, as such, connected essentially with the mythical. As Eli Friedlander explains:

> The primal in human existence is mythical. The mythical isn't merely identified in the character of early human societies, or of primitive forms of human existence. The force of Benjamin's view of primal history lies in understanding that the mythical is ever-present in the space of human life. . . . Authentic historical time emerges in the struggle against the burden of myth. . . . The mythical has its hold, precisely as long as the space of life of the past does not undergo the highest meaningful articulation. This would mean that the problem of emerging out of myth is ever renewed, both in the struggles of the individual life as well as of the collective. Myth is the primal ground against which individuation or uniqueness in history arises.[48]

The primal is what is ever-present, and what with every significant transformation of experience emerges anew.[49] Repetition is here original, the very mark and stamp of originality. We can think of the "primal" nature of the mythical as the background of conscious, conceptual understanding: whenever we pick up an object of cognition, view it, as it were, through our conceptual lenses, we bring about a surplus of signification, an unformed, unrealized domain of significance. Indeed, the more conceptual our cognition, the more mythical surplus is produced. This is what makes Benjamin's thinking on this point so pertinent to our topic, the attempt to grasp the unwritten as primal but, for that very reason, as something that does not simply remain the same. To understand the place of myth in Benjamin's thinking, it is necessary to consider, however briefly, his early attempt to expand the Kantian notion of experience.

> It simply cannot be doubted that the notion, sublimated though it may be, of an individual living ego which receives sensations by means of its senses and forms its ideas on the basis of them plays a role of greatest importance in the Kantian concept of knowledge. This notion is, however, mythology, and so far as its truth content is concerned, it is the same as every other epistemological mythology. We know of primitive peoples of the so-called preanimistic stage who identify themselves with sacred animals and plants and name themselves after them; we know of insane people who likewise identify themselves in part with objects of their perception, which are thus no longer *objecta*, "placed before" them; we know of sick people who relate the sensations of their bodies not to themselves but rather to other creatures, and of clairvoyants who at least claim to be able to feel the sensations of others as their own. The commonly shared notion of sensuous (and intellectual) knowledge in our epoch . . . is very much a mythology like those mentioned.[50]

Benjamin's attempt to expand the horizons of Kantian experience is meant, in part, to open up philosophy to account for profound transformations of historical experience. This is one way to understand the significance of religious experience to his project. We ordinarily think of the form—a name for ground in this context—of experience as fixed, and allow history to present us with different contents of experience. People just like us had different empirical experiences, different things happened to them, but the transcendental frame of experience is an ahistorical fixture. Benjamin suggests a reversal: the content is eternal, and it is historical forms of experience that change around it. This would give us a sense of the historical life of the idea: forever out of reach of conceptual understanding, it "makes its appearance" in the very multiplicity of historical formations, as their underlying unity.

The first, major challenge to the commonsense assumption about the fixity of the form of experience is the phenomenon of religion: are we to imagine the greater part of humanity's history as a collective delusion, that is, to imagine that our ancestors had experienced things we cannot, that they saw gods and monsters, or are we to remain mystified by their inimitable gullibility, their willingness to take on faith fables of what lies beyond their senses?[51] If we are unable to account for religious experience philosophically, we find ourselves reducing the greater part of human history to collective delusion or naivety, with the strange exception of our own, modern experience. Normality turns out to be quite the outlier of human experience, which casts some serious doubts on its capacity to supply the norm.

A philosophical account of religious experience would have to understand the experience of the supersensible as something different from collective delusion, or illusion. One way of putting this philosophical challenge, or task, is to say that Benjamin problematizes what it means to "see" the invisible, or "hear" the inaudible. Benjamin's own preferred phrase, however, is, significantly, "to read what was never written."[52] It has to do with the capacity to "see" nonconceptual connections, a way in which things belong together that does not assume the form of "falling under" the same concept. Thus, for Benjamin, philosophy has to regain (to account for the possibility of), and so demystify, mystical experience.[53]

The talk of religious experience, then, should not lead us toward a forced choice between Benjamin the dialectical materialist and Benjamin the mystically inspired sage. To be able to give a philosophical account of religious experience as something other than delusional is indeed the precondition for a philosophically serious materialist engagement with history, that is, with history as something other than the varieties of empirical contents marshaling before an unchanging, transcendentally idealist consciousness. Dialectical materialism hinges on the capacity of a material, historical process to alter the very coordinates of experience, to shift the transcendental frame itself.

For Benjamin, we might say, any account of the ground of experience, including the modern one with its infamous subject/object split, is mythical. It "sneaks" into the frame the unity that is to hold the frame of experience together , confusing the transcendental function with the empirical subject. We ought to note at this point that Freud's core insight, in Lacan's understanding, was precisely the distinction between the self-conscious ego and the subject,[54] a discovery that, beyond the injury it inflicted on the ego, allowed Freud to detect thought in the unconscious, in dreams, slips of the tongue, etc. There is thinking that is not subjectivized, and yet it is there, and it makes an impression. Benjamin's name for that dimension is myth, an illusion with an "objective" character, an illusion we cannot, in principle, shake off, similar in that respect to transcendental illusion in Kant.[55]

For Benjamin, we might say, what is at stake is the necessarily illusional character that our experience with the transcendental assumes.[56] And so this is not merely a critical point, pushing us further into a kind of linguistic idealism or relativism; rather, it implies its own dialectical reversal, which Benjamin will further pursue: the mythical is our experience with ground. It is not that, reaching beyond our capacities of (scientific, mechanistic) understanding, we find ourselves producing ultimately nonsensical, fanciful stories, or worse, experiencing the fantastical as a delusion. Myth is the form that our experience with the inexpressible takes. In myth, we experience the virtual ground as unrealized, as a demand for realization.

MAKING IT IMPLICIT: PRIMAL EXPERIENCE, PRIMAL PHANTASY, PRIMAL REPRESSION

The dimension of experience toward which Benjamin orients the "future philosophy" is, in this sense, not merely an implicit experience, "tacit knowledge," but the experience with the implicit as such. This is to be diametrically opposed to the conclusion often drawn from the "myth of the given,"[57] which would encourage us to accept that all givenness is always already linguistically mediated, to give up on the notion of the primal as a mere retroactive illusion. Benjamin's notion of the mythical, by contrast, has to do with the "givenness" of the mythical," the elusive but palpable experience with the primal, which can only assume the distorted shape of myth.

This is not merely an academic quarrel over the interpretation of the role to be assigned to the illusional in human experience. Indeed, there is more than one way in which illusions can be integrated into experience. Taking seriously the possibility of profound transformations of experience, the thesis can be put forward thus: Modern experience makes it harder to view the "mythical" as anything other than lies. If all there are are truth and lies, there[58] is no room for the mythical other than a "big" or fundamental lie.[59] And so the less the mythical can be recognized, and socially integrated, the more truths in the plural—and more importantly, lies—proliferate.[60]

This intimate connection between the primal and the mythical naturally leads us to the terrain of psychoanalysis. Psychoanalysis emerged as a science of individualized illusions and phantasies at the historical moment when collective illusions were going through a major transformation. The "World of Yesterday" as described by Stefan Zweig, in which political rule was sanctioned by God and tradition, was fighting for its survival. The second industrial revolution was introducing rapid changes, loosening the hold of tradition more broadly, as the ability to take guidance from the past was diminishing in direct proportion to the quickening of revolutions in daily life. For Benjamin, times of great transformation are "mythical" times, in that they bring about a plethora of material that cannot be integrated into everyday experience and so assumes a mythical, distorted, form. There is an excess of address,[61] if you will—we are called to make sense of more than we can handle. This is not simply a matter of quantitative change but a change of the very form of experience, what Benjamin calls "shock experience." In modernity, he argues, experience is progressively isolated into nonassimilable units. We have more and more experiences (Erlebnis) and less and less meaningful, assimilated experiences that can bear on our present and future actions, what we mean when we speak of people being experienced, or having experience (Erfahrung). In this context, Benjamin took issue with Freud for what he took to be a "defensive" theory of cognition, part and parcel of the "shock" experience of modernity.

But Freud's great theoretical insight lies precisely outside "traumatic" experience. Freud's theoretical discoveries should not be seen as merely responsive to their historical circumstance, for one of their primary advantages is the way they open up the configuration of structure and event. Freud, you will recall, had distinguished between primary repression and ordinary repression. Primary repression is not the repression of some first, "original" traumatic content, but rather, the repression constitutive of the subject of the unconscious. It is coextensive with the constitution of the "space of meaning," the ground of experience, and its shadowy underside.

In Lacan's interpretation, primal repression is the repression of the binary signifier, the signifier which, had it existed, would correspond to the master, or primary signifier, the signifier which, so to speak, signifies nothing but signification itself. It would be the answer to the mystery of signification, what signification as such signifies. The primordial absence of such a signifier is constitutive of the order of signification. Were it possible to "write" the binary signifier, to couple signification with a transcendent signified, there would be no space of meaning, nothing omitted from our symbolic field, and so nothing to know. The allure of the master signifier would be gone, and with it the "space of meaning" would collapse. This would be a way of expressing the impossibility of capturing the terrain of the idea, or ground, with a concept: the very space of concepts is opened up by the gap between ground and existence.[62]

Lacan's is a figurative way to express the insight according to which the subject emerges with a missing piece, which is just the other side of the presupposed realm, or ground of meaning, known to Lacanian psychoanalysis as the big other. Our experience of the primal, then, is at the same time the experience of the unshakable ground of meaning, implicit in implicitness, so to speak, in the fact that we can (and must) conceive of our knowledge as lacking, and therefore "out there," and must repress the inconsistencies plaguing the symbolic field and its representatives, the "idealization" involved in transference. It is by seeing in some ordinary (i.e., in Lacanian terms, imaginary) person the agency of the big other that we form the bonds of transference; in the case of the nuclear family, initially with one's parents. It is they whose unconsciousness we repress, in taking them to be the ones "in the know."[63] And so the constitution of the necessary illusion of the "big other," the symbolic space of meaning, is coextensive—equiprimordial—to primary repression.

It is here that we can see most clearly the complex of sexuality and language in psychoanalysis. Consider the vexed issue of infantile sexuality. What is it that "charges" childhood activities such as thumb-sucking or playing with excrement with sexuality? It is true that it is only against the background of adult language that infantile sexuality is "charged" with sexuality "proper," but not because it is an encounter of "innocent" infantile behavior with mature, knowing adult behavior. The primordially missing signifier is not what is alluded to, between the lines of adult attitude toward children, but what, being primordially repressed, opens up the space between the lines to begin with. Language charges "infantile" drive sexuality with sexuality "proper," but, at the same time, it is sexuality, the knowledge of which alludes language, that eroticizes language.[64] Primal repression is what makes things implicit, precisely since it implies nothing, it points toward a knowledge—sexual knowledge—which is primordially lacking.

THE LOGIC OF PHANTASY: BACKGROUND EXPERIENCE

This "making things implicit" is of significance in understanding fantasy. As Laplanche and Pontalis put it, in their famed discussion of "Primal Phantasy," "the action of repression is difficult to grasp since 'fantasy life' is more implicit than repressed."[65] Primal phantasy, we might say, is both the record of and defense against primal repression. In that rightly celebrated work, Laplanche and Pontalis analyze the Freudian concept of phantasy, tracing Freud's oscillation between structural models and genetic accounts. Primal phantasy, as it emerges from this analysis, is the inner connection between phantasies of origin and the original, structuring function of phantasy. Phantasy, to put things overly simply, has to do with the impossible conjunction of event and structure. Somehow, in our experience, the primal, as what always already, that is, constitutively proceeds and grounds us, is inseparable from the event of emergence, a pure beginning, an absolute cut between before and after.

One way to grasp this is to say that what is at stake is the primal difference between difference and indifference. For there to be a structure in which we are embedded, we need to be minimally distinguished from that structure. The structure of differences only emerges, as it were, with our emergence as distinct from it. For Freud, significantly, this picture is already a phantasmatic distortion, the result of the identification of the ego with self-consciousness, a secondary reaction to the impossible emergence of consciousness out of its presubjective immersion in autoeroticism.[66]

Autoerotism should be understood here, as Laplanche and Pontalis remark, as the "drive" dimension of enjoyment, which is essentially presubjective, or rather, it is what makes any separation between subject and object incomplete and problematic.[67] In its nature as arch-parasitic on the vital bodily functions (nourishment, excrement) the drive is the enjoyment of the medium of satisfaction, injecting a reflective, "masochistic" element into our libidinal economy from its very beginning. Something in us enjoys through our satisfactions and dissatisfactions, long before anything resembling a sense of an autonomous self, capable of uttering "I," emerges. In psychoanalysis, subjectivity is not the unique and original site of "selfhood"; quite the contrary, selfhood only emerges against the background of a primordially lost, and yet ever-present—if backgrounded —"in itselfness," that of the drive.

When Freud says that "drive is our mythology," we should not, therefore, take it to mean that drive is merely an indispensable piece of fiction, but rather note the extent to which the drive can be "mapped" on the mythical in Benjamin's sense.[68] Drives are no empirical objects of experience, which is not to say they have no place in experience. To the contrary, they belong, precisely, to something which, while never becoming a fully distinct object of experience, is ever-present in the background of experience, so to speak.

> The theory of the instincts is so to say our mythology. Instincts are mythical entities, magnificent in their indefiniteness. In our work, we cannot for a moment disregard them, yet we are never sure that we are seeing them clearly. You know how popular thinking deals with instincts. People assume as many and as various instincts as they happen to need at the moment—a self-assertive instinct, an imitative instinct, an instinct of play, a gregarious instinct, and many others like them. People take them up, as it were, make each of them do its particular job, and then drop them again. We have always been moved by a suspicion that behind all these little ad hoc instincts there lay concealed something serious and powerful which we should like to approach cautiously.[69]

Note what distinguishes the psychoanalytic approach to the drive: it is a reverential approach to the "magnificent indefiniteness" of drives, so to speak.[70] The psychoanalyst recognizes in the very indefiniteness of drive a "magnificence," a power that should be taken seriously as having a certain overbearing, objective presence. It is not something to be taken up, played with, and dropped, but somehow taken in as a totality that bears, in its totality, on our own, on our existence as such. Even if its appearance is pluralized, it is as such, in its plurality, that the analyst detects an underlying power; like the pantheon of the Greeks, the unity of the drive is inherently refracted, it is, so to speak, the power—not a concept—that holds the partial drives together. Freud goes on to recount the genesis of his theory of the drives, the phases of its development. It is this strange "holding together" of the drive, Freud implies, that requires the most sustained effort to come to terms with, an effort, indeed, which, in its mutating genesis, the series of failed attempts at formulization, speaks to the entity it grapples with. The drive is not to be theorized once and for all; its theory "drags" its genetic development along with it, forever "half-born." Recalling Nietzsche's account of the nonformalizable nature of the historical, we could say that drive is an entity that never gets rid of its history, of the "unwritten," unformalizable dimension of it.

This may be why, as Laplanche and Pontalis point out, for Freud it is primal fantasy, not the drives, that is the correlate of animal instinct in humans. It is in fantasy that Freud seeks the link between the phylogenetic and ontogenetic, another site in which the problem of structure and event makes its impression. For now, let us only note the complex connection between daydreaming and the original or primal phantasy, those dream scenarios in which the subject witnesses the scene of her own conception, parental copulation.

> By locating the origin of fantasy in the auto-erotism, we have shown the connection between fantasy and desire. Fantasy, however, is not the object of desire, but its setting. In fantasy the subject does not pursue the object or its sign: he appears caught up himself in the sequence of images. He forms no representation of the desired object, but is himself represented as participating in the scene although, in the earliest forms of fantasy, he cannot be assigned any fixed place in it (hence the danger, in treatment, of interpretations which claim to do so). As a result, the subject, although always present in fantasy, may be so in a desubjectivized form, that is to say, in the very syntax of the sequence in question . . . but as for knowing who is responsible for the setting, it is not enough for the psychoanalyst to rely on the resources of his science, nor on the support of myth. He must also become a philosopher.[71]

What holds together "primal fantasy" and daydreaming is the ambivalent location of the subject in it, at once nowhere and everywhere, outside the picture and in every detail of it.[72] Consider Lacan's definition of the subject of the unconscious: The subject is what is represented by a signifier to another signifier. This, according to Lacan, is another way of looking at primal repression. In this inversion of the communicative scheme of language, that of conscious subjectivity in which a subject uses a sign to communicate to another subject, subjectivity is implied, a virtual presence hovering above signification, or in the space between signifiers, implied in everything that signifies, but nowhere locatable. This would be a way to experience a "pure" transcendental subject, a holding together of phenomena, not located in the empirical subject. In this way, the notion of "background" receives both its temporal and spatial dimensions, as what is both the background of the subject in the sense of that from which it emerges, which speaks to the impossible event of primary repression, and what is always there in the background of conscious experience. Phantasy is the form of this "background" experience.

It is crucial to note, as Lacan emphasizes again and again, that "phantasy" is not the opposite of reality but, as it were, the very ground of reality. We think of phantasy as working on some preexisting material, a reality which it deforms. But that is a structural mistake, a way to miss the precise sense in which phantasy functions as a cover or a defense. Phantasy as such defends us against what it reveals: the nonsymbolizable way in which experience is "held together," what, after Lacan, we can call the nonrelation. Rather than forming some preexisting material, the structure of phantasy, we could say, produces a surplus of unassimilable, unsymbolized "stuff."

The same holds for Freud's *Interpretation of Dreams*. Consider Freud's famous analysis of the "navel of the dream," the point where interpretation ought to come to a halt. Freud, we should recall, is offering a theory not only of how to interpret dreams, but of the unique challenges that arise for our interpretation of dreams, in large part because dreams are already, in themselves, interpretations. The dream process does not only call for interpretation; it resists our interpretations by offering its own. Indeed, it is in the context of this discussion that Freud will caution his readers to be most suspicious where dreams seem to have been thoroughly interpreted. This would be a sure way to forget the dream's navel, that which ties it to something ultimately unknowable.

> There is often a passage in even the most thoroughly interpreted dream which has to be left obscure; this is because we become aware during the work of interpretation that at that point there is a tangle of dream-thoughts which cannot be unraveled and which moreover adds nothing to our knowledge of the content of the dream. This is the dream's navel, the spot where it reaches down into the unknown. The dream thoughts to which we are led by interpretation cannot, from the nature of things, have any definite endings; they are bound to branch out in every direction into the intricate network of our world of thought. It is at some point where this meshwork is particularly close that the dream-wish grows up, like a mushroom out of its mycelium.[73]

Freud, the Deleuzian? Note how the dream's navel is the point at which it is connected to something of the nature of the virtual; a network, a bifurcating plurality that cannot be captured as a simple entity. We may come close, but we should not jump over this ontological difference. At its kernel, the dream leads to the unconscious, which is, strictly speaking, unknowable. It is only in the psychological process of the dreamwork, the unique ways in which the dream distorts its own contents, that something like an unconscious "message" is to be found. Freud likens this to the way in which a screen refracts light. The colors of the dream, so to speak, point toward something that is not itself visible, nor can it be rendered visible except by such refraction.

This notion of "primal fantasy" finds resonance in Benjamin's identification of the mythical dimension of life as "mere life," or life as ruled by fate. Consider his account of the ironic fate of law, introduced in the context of his interpretation of the myth of the fall from paradise: "The tree of knowledge stood in the garden of God not in order to dispense information on good and evil, but as an emblem of judgment over the questioner. This immense irony marks the mythic origin of Law."[74]

For Benjamin, fate is the "systematic ambiguity," the overdetermination introduced into the world in our conceptual, communicative use of language, the price paid, as opposed to the understanding of language as a medium in which essences are to be expressed, the prelapsarian language of names.

> Fate is never something assigned to individuals as a destiny of their own. Actions of individuals are not directed by fate, nor does their personality or character determine their fate. Rather, fate is for Benjamin the field of life insofar as it produces systematic ambiguity of meaning. Subjection to fate would be identified with the failure to articulate life in language, thereby suffering its inherent ambiguity.[75]

As Friedlander explains elsewhere: "Mythical life belongs to the dimension of totality. It is a higher life, which has not undergone concretization or individualization; it is un-actualized life, which Benjamin sometimes calls mere life [blosse Leben]. Early on, in the essay Fate and Character, Benjamin thinks of such a field of life as ruled by fate."[76]

The complex of fate and law makes a very early appearance in Benjamin, in his famous essay "On Language as Such and the Language of Man." This essay, which deserves a much more developed and nuanced commentary, can be viewed for our purposes here as an attempt to sharply separate—and thereby open up a way to salvage—the domain of objective, ethical substance from the domain of reason as law that occupied Hegel in the above-mentioned pivotal moment in the Phenomenology. Benjamin's strategy is to distinguish between the mythical, as the form taken by the primordially repressed/return of the repressed, and a dimension of the primal that retains its innocence, so to speak.

In the essay, Benjamin turns to the biblical story of the fall from paradise, precisely in order to conceptualize a domain of innocent, ethical substance, not yet perturbed by the probing of reason. Benjamin's interpretation of the biblical story of Genesis is a way to narrate—inevitably in mythical form—the "fall" of language into the predominance of discursive, conceptual understanding, which Benjamin proposes should be understood as inherently instrumental, "the bourgeois notion of language as a means of communication." In continuation of his project to expand the Kantian concept of experience, it will be significant for Benjamin that we still have experiential access to such a domain, in what he calls the language of names. In naming, human language is a medium of communication responsive to the way things communicate themselves. Naming them is a way to actualize—not to explicate—their essence, precisely by translating their language, the way they communicate themselves, to human language, tearing them from their life context and putting them in a higher one.

Benjamin's point is that language as symbolic order introduces a schism between existence and value. Existence as such is devalued as soon as its value is a matter of judgment. It is no longer good in itself, and indeed the good of the in-itself, often associated with the innocence of nature, is lost. This schism affects not only the evaluating subject but also the object of evaluation. And so the emergence of the symbolic order is not something that merely affects humanity; it has effects on nature as well. Nature is now "split" by the symbolic order: the more we grasp nature conceptually, the more we produce a "signification surplus/loss," larger and larger domains of "unactualized" life, making its demands, waiting to be named. This is the "weak messianic force" Benjamin refers to in his famous theses on history, which puts pressure on the present.

Call this the evil of knowledge: knowing evil takes precedence over the unknowing existence of the good, the good of existence, or good in itself. There is a perverse enjoyment in the preference of knowledge over being, which is constitutive of the speaking, conscious subject, a kind of alignment with the position of knowledge at the expanse of being, that becomes explicitly pronounced in the Cartesian *cogito*. As Lacan understood it—"I think where I am not, I am where I do not think."[77] Being and thinking are both "stained" by their problematic intersection, or nonrelation. Thinking implies a loss of being, and being a loss of thinking. And so Benjamin's story of the fall into unsettling questioning, the entrance into the symbolic order of language, is simultaneously an entrance to its shadow dimension of fate and indeterminacy. The irony in question is the following: the more we try to extract ourselves, with the power of thought, from being, the more we find ourselves entangled in an excess of being; the more we try to perceive things objectively, the more we find ourselves the object of a knowledge we cannot make our own.

Psychoanalysis speaks to a very similar effect of the symbolic order on nature, the manner in which it produces a certain excess, undead real, a haunting dimension manifested in human life as the order of fate.

As speaking being, humans participate not only in symbolic life but also in fate, in the state of undeadness that comes with the symbolic but is not reducible to it, and which, according to psychoanalysis, is the very fulcrum of human sexuality—and is related to the drives. . . . This is precisely what the term "death drive" refers to in the context of Lacanian psychoanalysis: it refers to the way in which an irreducible surplus life (surplus-enjoyment) emerges and exists as the flip side of symbolic life, clinging to it and often tipping it in strange, unpredictable directions. This surplus does not exist outside the symbolic, but it is neither itself symbolic nor is it covered by the symbolic . . . this is the other, "shadowy" side of symbolic life as the "eternal," independent, autonomous life of the signifier: it is like its underpinning.[78]

The order of fate is the order of "primal fantasy," an order of entanglement with life in which subjectivity appears as indeterminacy. Here the subject is not that which looks at the world from outside, but rather, precisely in having no definite place in it, is intensely, anxiously entangled with it. We might recall here Kant's notion of purposiveness as the lawfulness of the contingent. What is sometimes referred to as a part/whole logic, purposiveness is a name for the sense that what can only strike us as a contingent particular belongs, as such, in its contingency, to a meaningful whole. It is precisely as contingent that it strikes us as displaying an (unwritten), unique lawfulness. Call it a lawfulness without law, an orderliness which only appears as invisible. Fate is a name for our being entangled in life, that is, for inhabiting a space whose lawfulness we can only experience as contingent, unpredictable. Its significance lies in its unpredictability—it is, for us, primordially given, a ground we have to rely on but cannot comprehend. Life is for us an inexplicable whole, suggestive of intention . Individuation entails the splitting of the unwritten law: standing up, individuated, we cast a shadow on the ground.

THE ESSENCE OF ENJOYMENT: THE MODAL NONRELATION BETWEEN PHILOSOPHY AND PSYCHOANALYSIS

In our very brief survey of the philosophical difficulty in grasping the unwritten law, the recurrent problem has been the strange entanglement of ontology and normativity. This leads us quite naturally into the terrain of psychoanalysis. The most basic and most widely used psychoanalytic term for the unwritten law is of course taboo. There's much to be said about this topic, but for now let us note only two things that emerge clearly from Freud's account of the term, what he picks up from it: taboo is primal, and it speaks to a disturbingly intimate relation between prohibition and the thing prohibited. Indeed, taboo refers, equally, to both. Taboo is a contagious substance and the practice that aims to ward it off or contain it.

Precisely where philosophy and psychoanalysis seem to converge, the gap in approaches is most apparent. While both are interested in what is primal, the sense given to the primal could not be more divergent. The problem for a post-Kantian like Cohen is how to approach the thing-in-itself beyond the law, which seems to elude our grasp. The problem for psychoanalysis is how to gain enough distance from the thinglike nature of the law, what in it seems to disclose an uncontainable, eruptive substance. The primal appears either as an elusive ground which we cannot quite grasp, or as a dangerous substance we cannot quite keep at bay. But are these really wholly opposite approaches?

The unwritten law we aim to grasp here, in the very tension between philosophy and psychoanalysis, is not to be identified with the oral law, what historically preceded, we assume, the written law. This would simply be another name for custom. The distinction between written and unwritten, though not unrelated to media, is not reducible to a distinction between oral and written media. It implies a prehistoric media history of sorts, but one that points toward the primordial rather than the temporally first. That is, from the perspective of the unwritten law, the oral law as well has an "unwritten"—unspoken, unspeakable—underside to it.

Unwritten should here be read emphatically, as the unwritable underside of the law, what never stops not being written, what, if transmitted at all, is transmitted "between the lines"; or, to employ a vocabulary more suitable to an oral, embodied mode of transmission, it is something that is taught by example, in mimetic relations, rather than explicitly as doctrine. Putting aside for a moment the media connotations of the unwritten, we can speak here—with reference to a topic made famous by Wittgenstein—of the mysterious way in which we learn to "play by the rules," in the absence, indeed the impossibility, of the metarule, the rule as to how to follow rules. The unwritten law, in this sense, has to do with the intuitive dimension of a form of life, its spirit, the sense that things are held together in ways that cannot, themselves, be given representation in the form of a rule: a dimension of linguistic being that is perhaps only given expression by means of myth and ritual.

It is crucial, however, though difficult, not to confuse the unwritable with the ineffable, the illusive. It is not the other, the opposite of the conceptual, the formalizable, but what only comes to light through the impasses of formalization. Indeed, this is the only path of the real toward inscription, its path to be written, so to speak. As Lacan put it: "the real can only be inscribed on the basis of an impasse of formalization."[79]

As such, as an impasse of formalization, the real in question is also constitutive of the conceptual, formal order. It is necessary and impossible, necessarily impossible and impossibly necessary, and thus speaks to the intimacy of these stark oppositions: the necessity of the impossible, say, the structural need for something to ground the field of the possible, something therefore that does not belong to the realm of possibility and exceeds it, and the impossibility of necessity, the ways in which necessity is both less and more than what it purports to be. Less, in the sense made famous by Hume, because necessity is not something we can simply attribute to phenomenal nature (we cannot get, by induction, from "this is how it has always been" to "this is how it will always be because this is how it must be"), and at the same time, by definition, necessity is not something we can simply attribute to our epistemological biases. Such a necessity would be contingent, a necessity "for us," and therefore not a necessity at all.

Lacan articulates this intimacy—or extimacy—between the necessary and the impossible in the context of his infamous statement that "there is no sexual relationship": "There's no such thing as a sexual relationship—a formulation . . . based only on the written in the sense that the sexual relationship cannot be written. Everything that is written stems from the fact that it will forever be impossible to write, as such, the sexual relationship."[80]

Note how the impossibility of writing the sexual relation is a positive condition for writing as such, which for now we can take to stand for formulization, what can be put in a formula, inscribed by being described. So it is not that we have a capacity for formulization, or writing, which just happens not to be able to capture this one thing, sexual relations, but all that is written, all that is formulized, stems from that impossibility, which somehow is written, so to speak, between the lines, inscribed in what, in writing, is not itself written. We have here an impossible condition of possibility, but also, impossibly, a prevailing presence of that which eludes our order of inscription.

Significantly, Lacan models his statement as to the nonrelation of the sexual as the inverse of the copula, which he deems to be the major "fetish" of ontology. To put it somewhat naively, the impossibility to write, to formulate copulation, is structured in relation to the impasse of the copula.

For Lacan, the notion of the unwritable comes into play in articulating one of his central notions, that of jouissance, or enjoyment, at the edge between philosophy and psychoanalysis, between ontology and sexuality. As Alenka Zupančič had shown in her superb *What IS Sex?* the notion of nonrelation is not simply a statement about the difficulty, for human beings, of finding sexual bliss, but rather a unique principle of ontological negativity, pertaining to copulation writ large. It is important to note that sexual copulation should not be taken to be a mere metaphor here for a broader philosophical problem, as it is the primary site where the symptoms of said negativity are given expression; but for now, let us set it aside to focus on more "dignified" if more abstract conceptual couples.

Nonrelation, we have said, is not the absence of a relation, but a negative relation. For our purposes here, let us take only one, albeit rather a major example—the relation between language and reality. To speak of a nonrelation of sense is not to suggest that there is no relation between world and language, which is an absurdity, but rather to suggest that reality and language are inherently unrelatable, that while they cannot be consistently thought together, neither can they be thought apart. Language and reality cannot be thought of as two parts of a whole nor as two independent entities. The same obstacle that prevents them from harmonizing together is what prevents each of them from standing all by itself, from being an independent entity. Language and reality are conjoined by what prevents them from harmonizing.

And so Lacan begins his critique of ontology by joining the linguistic demystification of the verb *to be*, in its function as copula.

> Ontology is what highlighted in language the use of the copula, isolating it as a signifier. To dwell on the verb "to be"—a verb that is not even, in the complete field of the diversity of languages, employed in a way we could qualify as universal—to produce it as such is a highly risky enterprise. . . . In order to exorcize it, it might perhaps suffice to suggest that when we say about anything whatsoever that it is what it is, nothing in any way obligates us to isolate the verb "to be." . . . We would see nothing whatsoever if a discourse, the discourse of the master, m'etre, didn't emphasize the verb "to be" (être).[81]

Let us first note how Lacan deflates the dramatic problem of being, the *on* of ontology, viewing it as a somehow fetishized aversion of the problem of the copula, that which is to hold together the two basic elements of the sentence, the subject and the object, what is spoken about and what is said about it. Lacan is not using the term fetish haphazardly here: it is as if in substantializing the grammatical function of the copula as a supreme concept, being, what ancient philosophy did is precisely to create a fetish: at the very traumatic site of absence, in this case the absence of support for the function of the copula, the way the subject and object just come together violently in it, somehow held together as separated, our gaze locked on the nearest, contingent object, the word *is*, and has made it stand in for that absence. Ontology is the fetish that comes to cover up the travesty of the copula, the way it conditions our understanding: we have to think propositionally, and thereby cannot quite think what holds our propositional structure together, never quite be sure, that is, that we are indeed thinking, that there is substance to our thought.

Let us note further that Lacan takes issue with ontology not because it is a mistake to be abandoned. Ontology, while perhaps resulting from no more than linguistic folly, has a hold on us, such that it is to be exorcized. Even when dead, destroyed by myriad philosophical critiques, it still grabs us, haunting us because we cannot seem to put it to rest. But why does Lacan associate ontology with the discourse of the master? What is the hold of ontology on us? It is worthwhile noting that his emphasis is on the hidden, normative dimension of ontology, noticeable, as we shall see in due course, in the idea of essence as an implicit standard for being, the proper.

It is significant, however, to first note that Lacan's point of attack here is Aristotle, who, in his metaphysics, seems to consciously strive to cleanse ontology from normativity. Unlike Plato, his teacher, who gives us the ideas which are directly standards for being, conjoining the highest reality with the most supreme standard, the idea of the good, Aristotle is building his metaphysics from the ground up; the good in itself, Plato's idea of ideas, can only arrive at the end, it is to be somehow deduced in an ascending, conceptual inquiry into the nature of being. To put it very briefly, one can read Aristotle's metaphysics as an implicit critique of Plato's normative idealism. Only once you have understood what being is as such, qua being, can you see that the highest being, the most actual, is a self-enclosing unity, what is in itself. If you begin, as Plato does, with a theory of ideas, you will never quite reach being, only ideal abstractions, such would be the Aristotelian line. You would be left, we might say, at the mercy of the idea's self-revelation, with no way of approaching it with the power of reason, by means of conceptual probing. You would have to fill in the gaps of philosophy with myths, as Plato and many of his followers are prone to do, indeed, to fabulate the very structure and path toward the truth.

Let us then look at Lacan's critique of Aristotle:

That is what Aristotle himself thinks about twice before propounding since, to designate the being he juxtaposes to το τι εστι that is, to quiddity or what it is, he goes so far as to employ the following το τι ην ειναι—what would have happened if that which was to be had simply come to be. It seems that the pedicle is conserved here that allows us to situate from whence this discourse on being is produced—it's quite simply being at someone's heel, being at someone's beck and call—what would have been if you had understood what I ordered you to do.[82]

Before we unpack Lacan's key point, let us linger for a short while on the terrain in which he is intervening. For Lacan is intervening here in a long philological debate regarding the syntactic structure of Aristotle's *to ti en einai*, which we usually simply translate as essence, but which is one of the most enduring, infamous philosophical untranslatables.[83]

We have neither the space nor the competence even to properly present the scholarly controversy, but let us make a few points by way of clarification. The first thing to note is that Aristotle is here utilizing the form of the question, which is why one approximate translation is "whatness," corresponding to the Arabic translation *mahiya* and the Hebrew *Mahut*, and more fully spelled out in "that what it was to be" or "the what it was being," or "a what-being-is."[84] The awkwardness of these translations stems in part from the use of the question petrified, so to speak, substantialized, to indicate the object of the question. What is essence? It is the answer to the question what is this thing really, ultimately, what it is as such, as a being. It is the attempt to penetrate beyond mere appearance or semblance, beyond everything that is contingent, and get at some hard core that is not immediately evident.

The other source of linguistic and philosophical perplexity stems from the use of the imperfect particle, *en*, which introduces either a kind of past, "was," or an eternal aspect, which after Heidegger we might designate as the "always already." In a sense, Aristotle's entire metaphysics is condensed here: essence is what will turn out to be what underlies the very existence of the thing, but that is something we can only see from the viewpoint of teleological development, by considering the thing in its foremost actuality, having fully become itself. A seed, in its essence, is an apple. Essence is inherently teleological: the more a thing is, the more existent it is, the more its existence is essential. For Aristotle essence precedes existence in this logical sense: the more a thing can be said to exist, the more essential it is, relieved of contingencies. The highest being would be necessary, without accident, fully essential.

Note how in Aristotle's metaphysics there is a whole set of conceptual couplets: form and matter, potentiality and actuality, etc., that are ultimately to be harmonized in the one, in God, the immovable mover, fully enjoying his own being, being utterly content with the autoerotic activity of pondering and thereby maintaining his own perfect being: "Oh my, ain't I just the best." The metaphysics reaches a point where all puzzles find their reconciliation, and all tensions are held together in the unity of the highest One. Only at the end, maybe, do we get an idea, in the Platonic sense: something which, in being self-enclosed, fully real, offers us a standard of being, a model.

On this infamous untranslatability of Aristotle's expression, let us briefly present one hypothesis, which for our purposes here is the most illuminating, as one final preparation for unpacking Lacan's intervention in ontology. The classist Erwin Sonderegger makes the case that Aristotle here is in fact relying on, and slightly if significantly altering, a colloquial expression common in the Greek of his time, most prevalently in the comedies of Aristophanes. Aristotle's *to ti en einai*, he argues, is derived from the colloquial *touti ti en?*, which he renders into German as something like "What in the world is this?"[85] And we could say, somehow more appropriately, "What the fuck is this?"

This is not meant as a mere vulgar joke. You will be hard-pressed to find an American colloquial expression that has had quite the same global success as WTF, and, as we shall see, it really goes straight to the heart of the matter. Let us very briefly look at the very first example of the use of this question in Aristophanes. It is taken from *The Acharnians*, an antiwar satire about an Athenian citizen, Dikaiopolis, who bargains for a private peace treaty with the Spartans.[86] A Megarian enters the market, intent on selling his two daughters— because of the political situation and the economic sanctions placed on the Megarians by Athens he is desperately poor, but he also has serious doubts that anyone would want to buy what he has to offer. And so he places his daughters in a sack, asks them to pretend they are sows, little piglets, and tries to sell them so they can serve as an offering to Aphrodite. He enters into negotiations with the play's protagonist, Dikaiopolis, in the course of which, while feeling his way around the sack, Dikaiopolis exclaims: Hey, what's this? *Touti ti en?* We can really only do this scene justice if we add a silent *fuck*, or at the very least *hell*, in the exclamation.

So, what do we have here? We have a sack someone is trying to sell, and in it, something sticks out, something seems to indicate that this is not what it purports to be. Putting aside, for now, all the sexual connotations—as if one could ever do that—therein lies the general usage of this question:

> The question always arises from a very specific occasion; it is never asked in general or "out of the blue." It takes a very specific place in the course of a context of action or understanding . . . [which has] the following general features. At first, the questioner thinks that he is dealing with a quite ordinary thing or with an everyday fact. Then he is surprised by what he sees; the previously determined context of meaning is disturbed and thus becomes open. The thing or circumstance that was assumed to be certain becomes an indeterminate one so acting or understanding has to start all over again.[87]

It forms, we might say, a kind of imposed *archē*, a new beginning, a cut in the flow of things. Back to Sonderegger: "In all these cases, the question becomes necessary: 'Yes, what is it actually about now? What in the world is going on?' And this question is posed in the form τουτὶ τί ἦν; an object or circumstance lying outside the horizon of expectation, which has imposed itself on the observer, has forced him to ask this question."[88]

So there is a kind of violent imposition of wonder (*thaumazein*), which Aristotle, in his *Metaphysics*, famously says is the beginning of philosophy, its common root with myth.[89] It is only the violence that is somehow repressed, relegated perhaps to the lesser terrain of myth. We have here a certain, rather jolting experience of saliency—something stands out, jumping at us from the background, demanding our attention. There is something there of which we have as yet no concept, for which we lack a word. A thing sticks out, and a word drops out, so to speak; there is a thing in need of a word. "What (the fuck) was that?" we exclaim.

And so we could say that the grammatical form of Aristotle's essence, his *to ti en einai*, by responding to the "whatness" of the thing, its *je ne se quoi*, what makes it truly itself, manages to bypass its "what the fuckness," what makes it stand out and arouse a question in us in the first place, what in it imposes itself on us, addressing us in a way that invokes, even forces out, a question. In substantivizing that question, Aristotle is putting some philosophical distance between us and the jolting experience, pacifying the drama. It is as if now, after all is said and done, we can see what the thing was, what it has been all along. That which struck us as demanding, and threatening, is put back into place, and the mystery is dissolved. "These are women, not pigs, the proverbial cat is out of the bag." Addressing the "whatness" of the thing is a way to ignore its "what the fuckness," its violent imposition on us, the way in which it involves our very being, which the answer doesn't quiet but silence.

There is a whole spontaneous critique of philosophy implied in this exercise in philology, and admittedly a rather familiar one: the philosophical concept is the death of the thing; it arrives when the life, the drama, the different possibilities have all been exhausted, and we remain with the corpse of a puzzling thing, no longer posing any threat to us, no longer questioning us. Aristotelian essence does not so much answer the question as it petrifies it, turning its lifeless corpse into a strange tautological answer. To our "what the fuck is going on, what the fuck is this, right here and now," which is to say, the question which emerges not merely as existentially pertinent but, as it were, as pointing to the coextensive emergence of consciousness and loss of being, the response is: it is what it was, it is in essence; not what is striking, surprising, and coincidental, but what remains when the drama is over, when our confusion has passed and we have regathered our wits. It is in this sense a bit like the policeman arriving at the scene and managing the crowd by declaring "nothing to see here."

If we can learn something from the possible source of the term in Aristophanes, it is that essence might in fact be nothing but the pacification of the fright inspired by such a wounding emergence of difference, turning the passive experience of a cut in the normal run of things which forcefully awakens our consciousness, a difference in which our being is inscribed, into a difference we make, a difference we author and master.

This might explain why essence is an attempt at mastery, but this is not Lacan's line of thought, not quite. Lacan's exegesis of Aristotle's infamously contorted turn of phrase, usually translated simply as essence, is meant to highlight the way in which essence, what something is supposed to be beyond its particular manifestation, is an unrealized standard or ideal. In his reading, Lacan lays emphasis simply on the gap between whatever that mysterious X might have been and its product or avatar, the entity. He takes the imperfect "was to be" to be the key, both semantically and syntactically. Recall the end of the paragraph we cited above, the meaning Lacan teases out of the grammatical structure: essence is "what would have been if you had understood what I ordered you to do."

In this way, Lacan locates in ontology a hidden commandment for things to be what they really are, which is, in fact, an impossible injunction. This is not the same as arguing that it is fake, unreal, or a "mere" abstraction. Essence, in Lacan's translation, is a name for what we fall short of. There is a disappointed demand implicit in supposition—"This is what you are supposed to be!"

To make this point more fully articulated, let us consider one of the most common and influential essential definitions. The example for essence is often man: man is a rational animal, *zoon logicon*. Putting aside the vexed question of philosophical translations from Greek to Latin for the moment,[90] what are we to make of such philosophical definitions? What kind of generality is evoked by essence: are we to say that there are no irrational men? Or that being irrational, they lose what it is that makes them human? There is a normativity implied in the essential definition. Not a norm: essence is not what things are statistically, for the most part, nor what they always are, by law of nature, but what they really are, which is somehow, directly, what they really mostly are not but should be. What they would be, were they to listen to the instructions.

The concept of a thing, its conceptual definition, becomes not only its underlying reality, a deeper dimension of reality, its support; precisely in its gap from a given particular, such an abstraction carries a normative dimension as well. As an instantiation of the conceptual rule, a given particular always falls short of the essence it manifests. There is a normativity at the very core of ontology, and it is it, and more specifically its disappointment, the inability to satisfy the demand of essence, that has a hold on us, that addresses us in the mode of the command: be what you are (supposed to be)!

And so Lacan will want to show how, in seeking to metaphysically ground what things really are, in the unity of judgment, an internal gap creeps in. What the copula seeks to bind it also separates. The problem persists, long after Aristotle has died, and even as philosophy had become progressively critical, weary of metaphysical essences. We may progressively cleanse our conceptual grasp of the reliance on metaphysical essence, but its function as a fetish persists. Recall that for Lacan, ontology emerged as a fetish, covering over the travesty of the copula. This is why in his view, even as philosophical systems move away from metaphysical essence, they maintain the fetishistic practice of disavowing the travesty of the copula.

FORMALIZATION AND ITS DISCONTENTS

Essence introduces a link between being and language, for essence is what defines you. With the idea of essence, we inherit from Aristotle a sense in which there is a power to language, perhaps its essential power, the logos of logos, to capture a thing's kernel of being. Language—apophantic, assertoric, propositional, conceptual—reaches out into reality and makes a difference there, separating significance from background noise. Even as the metaphysical notion of essence loses much of its philosophical credibility, the idea that language, particularly in its formal, conceptual application, can capture the truth persists. And indeed Lacan sees a direct continuity in this respect between Aristotle's essence, Kant's transcendental "I,"[91] and even the seemingly deflationary project grounding thought in logic, or "grammar." All are taken by Lacan to be terms and methods that are meant to bridge the gap between, or harmonize, language and reality (subject and object, the universal and the particular, essence and existence).

For Lacan, master's discourse is totalizing discourse. It is in this context that he turns to "writing." As he puts it, "grammar is that aspect of language that is revealed only in writing."[92] And yet he also asserts that "what is written is not to be understood."[93] Writing here stands for the kind of lawfulness to which we are subject as speaking beings, a lawfulness which conditions our thinking, and as such cannot itself be understood. Such is the copula. This is one way of understanding Lacan's famous dictum "There is no metalanguage." There is no vantage point from which to totalize language. Nonetheless, and this is key, while metalanguage doesn't exist, it does insist. This is a crucial point for Lacan at this point in his teaching: "We have to show where the shaping of that metalanguage—which is not, and which I make ex-sist—is going. Something true can still be said about what cannot be demonstrated."[94]

Lacan here is alluding to Gödel's incompleteness theorem. For our purposes, suffice it to say that this theorem expresses a certain inner limit, or antinomy, of formalization. Gödel takes formalization to its utmost—in formal mathematical language—and shows in a rigorous mathematical fashion that it has inherent limitations. Simply put, he shows that the purely formal is plagued either by an inconsistency (a paradox, a contradiction) or by incompleteness—something we can formulate but cannot "figure out" or "make sense of."[95]

There are two things we ought to glean from Lacan's offhand reference to Gödel. Firstly, we can think of the historical line from Aristotle to Gödel as one of progressive formalization, which is to say, a process in which we may detect the continuous attempt to rid our thinking of any reliance on metaphysical objects. Rather than relying on an extralinguistic metaphysical essence, the ideal formal system should be self-grounding, its own metalanguage so to speak. And yet this process leads to an impasse, an antinomy of sorts. This accounts, in part, for the haunting quality of ontology, the reason Lacan thinks it is a matter of exorcism. The second, more significant thing we ought to note is that for Lacan, the paradoxical result produced in Gödel's attempt to formalize mathematics is somehow given expression in the sexual nonrelation.

While never stating so explicitly, Lacan's "formalization" of the sexual nonrelation splits this Gödelian either/or in two. In this, Lacan can be seen as offering a Schellingian twist to Gödel's "antinomies"; just as for Schelling the antinomy of nature, its dual appearance as product (mechanical) and productivity (teleological), is given expression in the human being, a natural being plagued by freedom, so for Lacan human sexuality is the site where the inherent contradictions of knowledge play themselves out as such, as truly antagonistic.[96] This is a way of seeing how sexuality, which is already an ontological

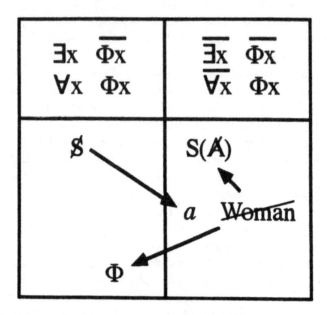

Table of sexuation, from Jacques Lacan, *Seminar XX: The Limits of Love and Knowledge,* 1972–1973, ed. Jacques-Alain Miller, trans. Bruce Fink (New York: W. W. Norton, 1999), 73.

problem in nature, is given a higher articulation in human beings—that is, more powerfully articulated in its polarity, more intensely polarized. It is the site where the split inherent to nature gets articulated as such.

On the masculine side (on the left) of Lacan's formalization, we get the paradox of exception (all x is under the phallic sign, except that there is one that is not), and on the feminine, the paradox of inconsistency (not all x is under the phallic sign, not true that there is one that is not under it). If we begin with the universality of the rule, we find ourselves having to ground it in an exception, whereas, if we begin with denying the universal application of the rule (accepting inconsistency), we find ourselves unable to find a singular case that would exemplify this, not one manifestation of the absence of the rule. Indeed, we find it extremely difficult to make any sense of it.

Let us take full account of this striking difference between the male and the female sides of Lacan's table of sexuation, namely, how (relatively) easily we can understand and imagine the first paradox, as opposed to the second. Recall Aristotle's metaphysics: all beings are at a gap from their concept, never fully captured by their essential definition, except for the one in which concept and thing coincide, in which, we might add, being what you are is the very image of full, autoerotic enjoyment. That would not be a bad description of the paradox of the male side of the table. All entities fall short of their concept, except for one. This, in fact, would be a nice way of capturing the continuity of what persists from Aristotle's metaphysics to Gödel's incompleteness theorem.

What accounts, then, for the striking difference between the two sides of the table? Between the left side's susceptibility to sense and the right side's refusal of it? In its utter resistance to the understanding, the right side of the table which is meant to spell out the logic of femininity, in the very "purity" of its formality, its defiance of sense, appears directly as its ontological opposite, dense, opaque matter. Spirit here is a bone, directly, in its very disembodied formality directly "object-like." One is tempted to say that, while the left side of the table, "masculine" logic, makes sense, the right side of the table makes a difference; it brings into being a pure, nonrelational difference, a difference in and of itself.

One way to articulate the difficulty is to state, absurdly, that man is a concept, woman an idea. This would only work, of course, if they could be so neatly separated, but we might gain some insight by pretending for a moment that we can articulate their distinction in such a clear opposition.

Man is a concept—not only in the sense that man has been, historically, conceptualized as universal. Rather, it is the very logic of the masculine side of Lacan's table that can be profitably read as a logic, or rather paradox, of conceptuality as such. All entities fail to match their concept, their essence— except for one. Man, in short, belongs to the order of representation, an order which is somehow founded on an ontological redoubling, a contradictory self-identity. This of course applies to all women as well, insofar as we approach them conceptually, as we no doubt must do. Only that woman is an idea, which is to say, in truth, that the idea is feminine.

The idea, since its origination in Plato, insofar as it is identified, in the *Symposium*, with the beautiful, is an erotic object. Insofar as it is beautiful, truth is not an object of knowledge, not an object of intention.[97] As such, it cannot be straightforwardly grasped conceptually. To begin with, concepts, we have already seen, respond to questions, whereas the idea does not; it is, as Benjamin put it, "beyond all questioning."[98] As Eli Friedlander puts it, being beyond question does not render the Idea certain, but beyond certainty and doubt, beyond the reach of the question as such: it is unquestionable.[99] Questions, conceptual probing, do not deliver us unto the idea. The idea is unapproachable, there is no making sense of it. But this is not to say that it is wholly mysterious. As a thing of beauty, the idea is self-revealing, it shines forth in radiance. Further, the idea does not apply to particulars, particulars are not subsumed in it but "partake" in it. Good things partake in the idea of the good, and this partaking cannot be the simple subsumption of good things by the concept of the good. The idea is the virtual ordering of phenomena and nothing but: there is no concept of the good beyond the ordering of phenomena in the idea.

Like the idea, Lacan's notion of femininity points to a self-presentation, not something we can get a representation of. The idea is not a concept, it has no essence to which it refers, not even itself; it is nothing but the nonconceptualizable holding together of its particular manifestations. As self-presentation, the idea is at once unapproachable and self-revealing. Hence its manifestation in beauty, semblance, which is both radiant and elusive, holding back.[100] Beauty is singular. This is also to say that singularity is the—ultimately false—unity or totality of beauty, the semblance which captivates by being unique, by being singularly itself. This is what underlies the erotic or aesthetic path to the truth, the necessary detour through the semblance of beauty on our path to the good in itself.

Let us not forget, however, that with Lacan we are telling a story of ontological failure, not success. To bastardize the famous opening lines of *Anna Karenina*, we might say that all essences fail in the same way: the particular never quite reaches the universal, one never is the primal father, one never is The Man, which does not mean there isn't a variety of phenomena here (we each fail to match up to our concept in our own way). Woman, on the other hand, is an idea that only realizes itself in and through the singular. The failure here is not a particular failing by the standards of the universal, but that of a singular that is somehow never quite free of the virtuality it manifests; its singularity dependent on this semblance, it carries a disturbing shadow of generality, the fear being it might not be quite as singular as all that. The idea of femininity as masquerade[101] can here be distinguished from masculine performance anxiety:[102] masculinity constantly fears it will not measure up, its performance will not be as good as some imagined, stereotypical "Man," which is to say, it essentializes the model to be copied; femininity is anxious about its singularity, the fear being that it might not be quite as mysteriously and uniquely itself.[103] The infamous notion of feminine mystique has everything to do with the ontological "superiority" of femininity, the fact that it does not rely on a fetishized notion of essence. Man is a woman who believes she exists, as Žižek once put it.[104]

But we must recall that Lacan's accent is not on the distinction or differentiation between two entities, male and female, idea and concept, but on the nonrelation, on what prevents these oppositional couplets from harmonizing into one, and, at the same time, from gaining independence. We might call the trajectory of science the rule of the male side over the relation, which would translate to the rule of the concept over the idea, and mysticism (and its cousin, aestheticism) the rule of the female pole over the relation, the rule of the idea over the concept. If we analyze the nonrelation through the lens of one of these alternatives, we make them into that, alternatives, and thereby create a relation. But these are both ways of trying to make the relationship work. And it is a relation that cannot quite work.

Lacan is not here simply antimetaphysical. Yes, ontology, indeed any totalizing discourse, implies an impossible injunction, but it is not simply a mistake. It expresses a myth, a dream, of the union of discourse with a real that lies beyond it. We might say that it is precisely in the dream of metaphysics that Lacan finds its truth kernel. He situates his brand of psychoanalysis as the inverse of the master discourse of ontology. Psychoanalysis, then, would be the other side of the nonrelation between science and mysticism. And we might add that in that very space is where one finds the philosophical collaborators of psychoanalysis; philosophy occupied with that tension is a natural ally of psychoanalysis.

In what sense is psychoanalysis directly the inverse, the other side, of the master's discourse, of ontology, split as it is into mysticism and science? Psychoanalysis brings to light the intimacy of the necessary and the impossible that must remain hidden in ontology. In Lacanian psychoanalysis, the impossible yet necessary coupling of language and being, the object of metaphysics, has effects precisely by virtue of not existing. It is in direct opposition to the injunction of essence that Lacan offers his formula of the sexual nonrelation as both necessary and impossible. Or rather, to be more precise, the nonrelation of necessity and impossibility, the manner in which these opposing modalities are coimplicated, or to use his terms, conjugated.

> The necessary . . . is that which doesn't stop . . . being written. . . . What doesn't stop not being written is a modal category, and it's not the one you might have expected to be opposed to the necessary, which would have been the contingent. Can you imagine? The necessary is linked [*conjugué*, declined, conjugated] to the impossible, and this "doesn't stop not being written" is the articulation thereof. What is produced is the jouissance that shouldn't be/could never fail [*qu'il ne faudrait pas*]. That is the correlate of the fact that there is no such thing as sexual relationship, and it is the substantial aspect of the phallic function.[105]

The phallic function is symbolic castration, a psychoanalytic myth that expresses the manner in which language, by confining the subject (female or male) to the symbolic order, produces an impossible enjoyment beyond language, primordially lost and forever haunting; this enjoyment, by virtue of being prohibited, cannot but impress itself as overwhelmingly necessary. Let us take note of the inverse relation between essence and jouissance: If essence, as the metaphysical ground of being, must be, and as such always fails to be realized (it is impossible because necessary), jouissance, on the other hand, should not be, and therefore cannot but attain an uncanny insistence (it is necessary because impossible). Essence is presupposed, and as such beyond reach. Jouissance is primordially repressed, and as such its only manifestation is in the return of the repressed, a nagging insistence of that which never was, and as such we can never quite rid ourselves of it. [106] And so, while diametrically opposed, essence and jouissance are inseparable, two sides of the same impossible coin, so to speak, or rather, two aspects of the (non-)relation between the necessary and the impossible.

Contingency, in the schema offered by Lacan, is the mediating term between the necessary and the impossible; it is that which stops not being written. The way in which relations can be said to be conditioned by the non-relation can be understood through the modal logic offered here. Relations—whether sexual relations between humans or relations of sense, where sense is made—obviously do take place. But they are not strictly speaking possible, if by that we understand a notion of instantiation, in which a given romantic affair is an actualization of the abstract, merely possible, logical form, or idea, of love. In dealing with the real, we are dealing with an actuality that can never be realized. It is, in one sense, prior to the very gap between possibility and actuality, a ground which can only be actual, a condition we find ourselves in, coloring the entire horizon of what is possible for us, or it is an impossibility that happens, that is, an actuality which, once it emerges, retroactively changes the very coordinates of the possible. The real cannot be realized—this means both that the real is what remains unrealized in every actualization, the virtual ground, and what has the power, when coming to light, to rewrite that very same ground. It is never the mere instantiation of a preexisting possibility: it either affects us in its very failure to be realized, or it alters the very limits of the possibility, bringing a new possibility into existence.

To sum up, philosophy and psychoanalysis in Lacan's account are non-related along the very lines of the sexual nonrelation, with "essence" assuming the place of what lies beyond "phallic" castration in the male side of the table of sexuation (the mythical ground of the symbolic law) and "jouissance" assuming the same place on the feminine side. The Lacanian point is not, however, to side with "feminine" psychoanalysis, against the phallogocentrism of philosophy, as if these were two independent "substances," but precisely to work with and on their nonrelation, the precise—if intricate—way in which they form a negative relation, the way in which, in their very bifurcation, they articulate the "redoubling" of ontological impasse.

Indeed, we might say that, if the dual trajectories of forming a relation between concept and idea are those of science and mysticism, the meeting point of philosophy and psychoanalysis, in general, is in the space of the nonrelation itself. And so in the philosophical accounts of the unwritten law we have briefly surveyed above, while it cannot be incorporated into any given, posited order, we have been given an image of the unwritten law as neither the idea of the law nor its essence. The unwritten law has to do, instead, with what prevents the concept of law and the idea of law from harmonizing but nonetheless binds them as the very locus of a problem.

This strange, twisted topology puts us finally in a position to pose the following question: Is there a link between the destinies of these two avatars of ontology, essence and enjoyment, separated and conjoined by Lacan's formula of nonrelation? How are we to think together the process of deessentialization, say, the modern and postmodern progressive exposure of the failure on the male side of Lacan's table, and the strange ontologizing, objectification, perhaps essentialization of enjoyment, the way in which we seem driven to materialize enjoyment as such, to endow it with an objective, independent status? What is it that brings into existence enjoyment without us, as it were, one contemporary avatar of which is precisely the animation of technology?

3

THE MACHINE'S NEW BODY: TECHNOLOGY, OLD AND NEW (DRIVE AND TECHNOLOGY)

What is it that drives technology? What is its spellbinding effect on us humans? Critiques of technology, beginning with ancient myths and up to the most speculative of twentieth-century philosophical accounts, tend to associate technology with a human drive for the mastery of nature. This narrative, often taken for granted, is to be treated as a fantasy screen. In order to better understand the thrust of technology, we shall argue, we must shamelessly focus on its erotic, indeed sexual dimension. However, it is important not to reduce the question regarding the drive of technology to a mere instantiation of the drive more generally. Rather, we shall want to inquire about the dual trajectories we were confronted with at the end of the previous chapter: the process of progressive deessentialization that can be associated with the progress of science, and the process of objectification or essentialization of enjoyment. If what is ultimately unwritten is the sexual (non)relation, in order to see what "unwritten no more" amounts to we must tend to the ways in which this dual trajectory is "held together," what makes it, in fact, a single ontological problem that is split between two seemingly independent trajectories of development.

MASTERY IS SAID IN TWO WAYS

We began this inquiry by noting how a new style of authoritarianism has emerged, distinguished by the manner in which it foregrounds violations of unwritten rules, and makes those rules palpable by way of transgressing them. Such leaders and the broader movements behind them seem to place the "truth of enjoyment" at the center of their political message: we are all petty little humans chasing after enjoyment, let us finally do away with the masks of civilization, the hypocritical foundations of the public good.

We have also begun to suggest that this new style of legitimation is related to the new medium in which it takes place, the Internet. In this rather obvious entanglement of a new technological medium and new patterns of legitima-tion lies a profound puzzle. In technology, in the words of philosopher of technology Bernard Stiegler, it is an issue of asking, "What power [*pouvoir*] do we have over our power [*puissance*]?"[1] Meanwhile in politics, we witness the rise of something which resembles the primordial, mythological, uncastrated father Freud writes about in his infamous *Totem and Taboo*, a leader who governs by means of standing outside social laws, unencumbered by the inhibitions and taboos that define social life.[2]

There seems to be a short circuit between two opposite tendencies: we get a strong sense that technology is hurling us toward a posthuman future, it decentralizes, disrupts, diffuses, and deindividuates,[3] whereas authority, and in particular authoritarianism, seem to be all too human, an atavistic, pri-mordial mode of attachment, firmly rooted in the archaic, mythological past, maybe even our animal nature. Technology leads us toward an impersonal and hyperrational world, to such an extent that it renders human subjectivity out-moded, threatening some of the core, essential features of our human sub-jectivity, ushering in a posthuman age. Authority, on the other hand, anchors our subjective identifications to particular authority figures and seems to be hopelessly primitive and irrational.

Somehow, the forward rush and constant disruption of new technolo-gies coincides with the return of the repressed, and so we find ourselves pushed toward a (pre)theoretical choice: either we view the transformation in media technology as fundamental, and the political and cultural content of the moment as epiphenomenal, or the other way around: what we are seeing is yet another return of the repressed, and technical media are ultimately but a means of its expression.

To mention just two quick examples: For a philosopher of technology such as Bernard Stiegler, the story of our moment is about how the dialec-tics between technological disruptive innovation and its subsequent absorp-tion into culture, the phase in which it becomes second nature, absorbed into the background, is something digital technology no longer permits, for it has made disruption its eternal entelechy, so to speak.[4] One way of grasping this point would be to notice how generations now are something technology possesses, not culture. We have a 2.0 etc. for all of our devices, and we can no longer sustain a relationship between generations in society. For Stiegler, the cultural and political phenomena we observe are epiphenomenal of this fun-damental arrhythmia of digital technology we have reached. Nonetheless, he hangs his hopes on law and culture somehow reining in digital disruption.[5]

On the other hand, an intelligent analyst of contemporary global power, such as historian Timothy Snyder, is capable of observing how, while shar-ing some qualities with both tyranny and totalitarianism—interestingly, the two alternatives, according to Arendt, to authoritarianism proper—a regime such as Putin's "functions not by mobilizing society with the help of a single grand vision, as fascist Germany and Italy did, but by demobilizing individuals, assuring them that there are no certainties and no institutions that can be trusted . . . the Putin regime is imperialist and oligarchic, dependent for its existence on propaganda that claims that all the world is ever such."[6] While these are certainly valuable observations, touching on a significant difference between contemporary authoritarianism and its twentieth-century predecessor, for Snyder not only is media technology epiphenomenal, an instrument of propaganda, but, because of that very perception, he identifies the nihilism of Russian propaganda with the older generation of passive TV spectators, and hangs his hopes on a new generation fighting for democracy for whom the web has become second nature. These are not just parallel arguments, different perspectives: they form a contradiction, and it is impossible to reconcile them. So which is it? Where is the locus of power?

The wager of our intervention here is that this contradictory attitude toward mastery might provide us with an opportunity to approach the contradictory nature of mastery as such. So let this be our guiding hypothesis: Technology and Authority—their impossible conjunction is the contradiction of mastery.

And so we have two contradictory "faces" of mastery and its discontents, which are somehow, while contradictory, profoundly intertwined. To get a better grasp of their entanglement, let us take note of a strange analogy, or correspondence, in the critical impasse we face in both terrains. Recall the notion of "the emperor's new nudity": in a nutshell, our critique is linked with the idea of uncovering power's secrets, and it has a hard time reorienting itself in light of an object which seems at least to be self-exposing. Now, rather remarkably, a similar thing is occurring in relation to our critical stance toward technology.

For a long time, the critique of technology consisted in exposing the ways in which what we take to be a project of mastery over nature is in fact something very different, a process in which, far from becoming masters of the universe, we have become exposed to dangers of our own making.

Today, the notion that technology is aimed at the mastery of nature is undermined most explicitly by what Jean-Pierre Dupuy calls (after Karl Popper) the "metaphysical research project" that has become dominant across a broad variety of technoscientific projects, from AI to nanotechnology, the origin of which Dupuy elsewhere traces back to "cybernetics."[7]

For our purposes here, suffice it to say that cybernetics is now largely acknowledged to have been the intellectual source not only of many foundational inventions in the fields of information and computation, but also in the theoretical cornerstones of cognitive science, the notion of DNA, and the projects of artificial life and artificial intelligence. It springs from the theoretical consequences drawn from the possibility of engineering a self-regulating or self-correcting mechanism—the self-guiding missile. If a mechanism can interact with its surroundings by means of a feedback system, the ontological divide separating the living from the inanimate is shaken to its core. What for a long time was considered a characteristic mark of the very distinction between mechanical, dead nature and life—purposiveness—can now be thought of in technical terms, as a problem of engineering, and so the ontological divide between the living and the mechanical is seriously eroded. We might also note, in passing for now, that what had emerged in modernity as one aspect of the unwritten law, its positive if elusive nature that had suggested a certain continuity between social life and nature, the "spontaneous order"—a space where human conscious planning cannot and should not intervene (thereby inheriting an aspect of divine governance or providence)—is now beginning to emerge in its abstract, most "detachable" feature: no longer the secret of providence, of the market economy or even of life, self-organization begins to emerge as something that may in fact be reproducible.

What science aims at today is a paradoxical entity: artificial nature. As Dupuy shows in great detail, the dominant "metaphysical research program" of our moment seeks to create, by design, things that will surprise their creators. It is a paradoxical project to bring about, to be the designers of, something for which we lack the design. This is the stated object of cutting-edge scientific research: to bring into existence something we do not master and do not understand.

We are accustomed to thinking about knowledge, and in particular scientific knowledge, as a means of mastery—with the noted exception of psychoanalysis, to which we shall return. And yet, contrary to this habit of our thinking, in contemporary science a wedge is driven between mastery and knowledge. This goes to the very fundamentals of contemporary scientific epistemology: Knowing how to do something and understanding what that something is has effectively come apart. What underlies the ever-growing convergence of science and technology is not the mechanical and ultimately instrumental viewpoint of the natural-scientific outlook, in which knowledge is equated with knowing the mechanism, knowing how to fabricate, to break a thing apart and (re)assemble it. Instead, the new objects produced by science are complex in a rather rigorous sense: it is easier to fabricate (to formulate and thus produce their structure) than to understand them (to formulate their behavior).[8] AI is the paradigm of this reversal—scientists are now capable of producing something which they then have to study as if it was a natural phenomenon.

Simply put, we can now make things we do not understand. And, this is crucial, this is the very goal. If we run to the scientists now and say, "Wait a minute, don't you see you are unleashing processes you cannot control?," they'll scratch their . . . let's say heads, and say, "Well, yeah, we know. That's the whole point."[9] The "metaphysical research program" of our moment is the uncanny attempt to bring about by design something that seems to have its own principle of self-organization, which means, for all intents and purposes, to create artificial life.

Aristotle famously wrote that "art [techne] either imitates the works of nature or completes that which nature is unable to bring to completion."[10] What scientists aim at today is a radically new twist of this notion, an attempt, so to speak, to complete nature by imitating it. Technoscientific skill is now much closer to romantic theories of artistic genius[11] than to anything we tend to associate with modern science—the sign of our work being naturelike, an imitation of nature (nature working through us), is this very lack of mastery over our products,[12] the fact that we do not have our product follow our blueprint or plan.[13]

This new reality, in which science and technology no longer frame their project in utilitarian terms, calls for a reappraisal of our fundamental conception of technology. From a philosophical, conceptual point of view, it gives us the opportunity to reformulate a general question regarding the artificial, the man-made. From a psychoanalytic perspective, it calls for a consideration of the relation between drive and the technological, or the artificial more broadly.

A BONE TO PICK: ON THE NATURE OF ARTIFACTS AND THE ARTIFICIAL

Let us begin with the conceptual point. The explicit, avowed rejection of utilitarianism by contemporary science allows us to bypass an entrenched habit of thought that associates the technological with the utilitarian and the mechanical. Often we distinguish between artifacts according to their perceived purposes, separating sharply between decorative objects of art and practical instruments. In this way we separate the trajectory of art and aesthetics, and indeed of culture more broadly, everything humans seem to make without explicit, goal-oriented design, as techniques, from the more narrow, modern and modernizing trajectory of technology. While we know that historically and semantically the poetic act and the technical act are connected, something we still hear in the Latinized art—separated historically into industrial and fine, technology and technique[14]—we tend to define them by way of a juxtaposition. Art has to do with what serves no practical purpose, whereas technological activity is all about the utilitarian manipulation of nature. Note that in this way we already introduce utility at the level of distinction.

Perhaps this juxtaposition is better understood not as a statement of essential distinction between different classes of artifacts, but as describing a tension inherent to the artifact as such, by which what is aimed at is a broad definition of what humans produce. These two vectors are distinguishable analytically, but they are copresent.

Now, philosophers often distinguish between artifacts and natural objects and in particular the natural organism, in order to point out the artifacts' "looser" internal organization, something which mirrors, we might note, in passing for now, many of our myths regarding our own unique human being. We shall come back to this. Indeed, an artifact, while presumably produced for a particular purpose, can be taken apart and repurposed in ways that would spell the death of an organism. On the other hand, an artifact tends to become the medium for expression of what serves no utilitarian purpose, and, as such, can take on immense value, even sacredness. Such an artifact might be untouchable, its integrity much more essential than that of an organism, and while we might hesitate to refer to it as living, it certainly cannot be taken apart without harm. For simplicity's sake, let's call the first vector the vector of technological development, and the second, that of cultural expression, or "second naturing." This sounds rather abstract, but an example here should be helpful.

As an example of an artifact, let us take one of the oldest objects our ancestors made use of, the bone.[15] The bone is not produced by humans, it is a ready-made artifact, so to speak. But consider what is required for us to pick up a bone and put it to use. We need to be capable of tearing it from its life context, from the whole to which it belongs. This holds both mechanically (we need to be able to look at the bone as a part that can be broken down and recombined) and psychologically (we need to be unaffected by taboos regarding the dead, to be pragmatically indifferent to the life that was lost). This requires a very violent type of abstraction, in which our mind (or understanding) functions like a knife, tearing an item out of the fabric to which it belongs. Once separated from the carcass, we can use the bone as a club, a hammer, or as a building block for constructing other tools and dwellings. The bone is opened up before us as a multifunctional object, which we might repurpose again and again, exploring its "horizon of possibility."[16] Let us note that this approach or mentality is not limited in principle to bones and other inanimate objects. It is a perspective or a domain of objects that can be—and has been—extended to human beings.

That very same bone, of course, above and beyond any practical use we can put it to, may serve as an ornament or an object of ritual. It might represent for us life after death or the unsurpassable finality of this one, and it can serve to distinguish between people of our group and others. In all these cases, the bone might be said to appear to us as if it held a certain hidden subjectivity, enfolding intentions and desires of its own. The bone conceals a spirit, a life. While this approach to objects might strike us as primitive, it is by no means something we have securely left behind. We disclose elements of this attitude whenever we offer an interpretation of a painting, but also when we get mad at a computer that malfunctions as if to spite us.[17]

To sum up, we may treat a human being as an object, and an object as a human being. We can treat the living as if they were dead, and the dead as if they were alive. In fact, we might push this a bit further to apply to our very distinction between material objects and signs.[18] We can take material objects as symbols, loaded with meaning, and we can treat language as if it was a purely functional instrument. If it is indeed language and instruments that stand between us and our natural surroundings, as our general anthropology states,[19] both can be taken up either as means or as media.

To this dual nature of the artifact correspond two notions of technique, to be further elaborated in the next chapter. As a first approximation we can say that the first is imitating nature in that it is as if nature works through it, it endows its artifacts, and indeed culture more broadly, with a semblance of totality, adding a virtual surplus of the symbol, whereas the second aims to complete nature, to actualize what nature has left merely possible. These two vectors can come together in human society in various ways, though probably not infinitely so,[20] and their mutual influence can be quite profound.

To the extent that the duality of the artifact is responsive to the duality of nature, nature as a product (which can be treated as a mechanism, i.e., as "dead") and nature as a productive process,[21] we ought to note that the response is already a dialectical one.[22] What we called the artistic imitation of art as a complete, holistic product, an organic whole, introduces strife and division, offering a "completion" of nature, what we call second nature, that is full of discontent and disharmony; and what seems like a project to complete nature, to actualize its productive process in ways nature itself does not, winds up producing an uncanny imitation of the process of nature, the "undead" march of civilization.[23]

In their treatments of the concept of civilization, Durkheim and Mauss attempt to distinguish between the societal and the suprasocietal. In this conceptualization, civilization stands for the suprasocietal. We can take the ethnic unit to be primary—and we tend to do so—and wonder about what one group borrows from another and why in a broader civilizational area of exchange, or we can take that broader area as primary and ask about cultural individuation, as a process that takes shape mainly by means of what is not borrowed, what is unique, "untranslatable."[24]

It is against this context that we should understand Bernard Stiegler's core argument. It is not only that we do not predate tools: only when technique is thus polarized, between the "ethnic" and "civilizational," do we have the human. Following closely Leroi-Gourhan's work on anthropogenesis, Stiegler is not content with the Derridean point about the circularity of origin. The

Derridean différance applies, in Stiegler's reading, already to the deferred origin of life—life is deferral, Stiegler learns from Simondon, it is what individuates by means not only of spatial differentiation from the milieu (which, for Simondon, is characteristic of all individuation) but of temporal deferral as well, suspending that which ultimately individuates it, namely death.[25] And so the question of human origins, of anthropogenesis, does not emerge, let alone is satisfied by différance. Différance here precisely fails to make a—rather crucial—difference.[26]

Stiegler pushes the Derridean supplement, the arch-writing, all the way back to the stone age—stone tools are already the exteriorization of memory, the beginning of culture in the sense of epiphylogenesis, memory inscribed in "organized inorganic matter." And yet they do not produce the human, they are not yet the "human invention," meant reflexively—the invention of the inventive being would refer simultaneously to that which the human invents and that which invents him. A being characterized by what it makes, its unique activity, turns out to be quite dependent on the product of said activity. For the inventive being to arise, his inventions have to prove themselves, well, inventive.

For a long time, Stiegler learns from Leroi-Gourhan, such tools are slow to develop and stylistically uniform. Technique, at this stage, has only a chronological dimension, and it moves slowly, at a steady pace. When there is only "technology," no stylistic, ethnic differentiation, tools have the temporality of nature, they codevelop with the cortex. These proto-humans, while already tool bearers, already produce traces, arch-writing, but they are still bound to the rhythm and pace of biological evolution. There is no invention yet.

It is only with the appearance of (anatomically) modern humans, once "culture" with its ethnic diversity makes its appearance, that we begin to see an acceleration in technological development, what we know as history. Now tools become properly inventive, displaying a developmental tendency.[27] The lesson for Stiegler is that we can speak of history as something distinct from nature only when we have the dialectics of both cultural differentiation and technological acceleration. Our moment, to him, is one in which culture can no longer keep pace with technology. "In its buildings, pictures, and stories, mankind is preparing to outlive culture, if need be," as Walter Benjamin put it.[28]

This gives some precision to the notion of posthumanism: humanity proper only begins when the "arch-writing" that precedes it gets "extra-charged" by the very attempt of culture to keep up with it, domesticate it, reintegrate it into "second nature." It is only when the artifact is split, so to speak, between life and death, in that very polarity when we can say "spirit is a bone," that the space is opened up for infinite judgment. Posthumanism would be the moment when such "arch-writing," the necessary but insufficient condition for humanity, reaches escape velocity, leaving us behind.

We might already hear in this opposition or tension an echo of Freud's first introduction of the death drive, an introduction that ends with eternal tension between the power that binds, love, and the power that tears asunder, death.[29] Quite aside from the problematic picture of eternal tension, at the very least, we might say that the picture we have sketched here complicates matters significantly: for we tend to associate technology—founded in our analysis on a certain lethal mode of understanding—with civilizational progress, with a universal and universalizing spirit, a tendency toward ever more complex networks of relations, whereas culture, while we tend to be attached to our own, is certainly a cause of division and strife between people. It is to Freud's credit that he resisted separating these dual "aspects" of civilization,[30] an intuition which, had he held fast to it, might have prevented him from separating the drive into two.

With this broader understanding of the artificial and its dual tendencies, let us return to the problem of utility. For one might well object to the significance of this reformulation and say that, to the extent that we have become dependent on our artifacts, whether cultural or more strictly technical, we are in the position of prosthetic gods, to use Freud's apt term. Many of our myths, both ancient and modern, about what makes humans stand out in nature point to the absence of an essential natural function, the relatively "loose" or unfinished purposive organization of humans, which makes it necessary to compensate for what we lack in organic composition with the creation of tools and artifacts, inclusive of our social artifacts, our institutions.

Think of Plato's rendering of the myth of Prometheus (forethought), giving fire and skills such as hunting to humans in order to compensate for what they lack, what his brother Epimetheus (afterthought)[31] forgot to endow them with, having wasted all the unique natural skills on the animal kingdom,[32] all the way up to modern anthropology, with its "naturalized" version of the same idea, from Herder to Yuval Noah Harari: humans must compensate with cultural knowledge, symbolic language, and skills for what they lack in instinct, being born "half baked," organically less organized.[33]

Recall what we said above about the artificial object in juxtaposition with the natural one: it is not only that we turn to technology to compensate for what we lack; we are, ourselves, the very model of the artificial. We are by nature artificial, artificializing beings, bound to produce artificial objects. And we do so bipolarly, so to speak, artificially "naturalizing" our forms of life and naturally artificializing, supplementing nature.

Hence Freud's excellent coinage according to which we are prosthetic gods, progressively dependent on what we produce in order to compensate for our frailty as organisms. That which is meant to give us a measure of protection from the powers of fate becomes, in the irony that accompanies all things fateful, something on which we depend, charged with all the ambivalence that relations of dependence tend to generate, just like our relationship with our parents. And indeed our artifacts, as we learn from the study of techniques, are in a significant sense our progenitors, as responsible for our evolution as we are responsible for theirs, if not more so.

But we ought to add a footnote to this familiar story, as Freud does. In one of his wildest, most ridiculous speculations, one, it seems, even he was slightly ashamed of as he buried it in a footnote, Freud proposes that the origin of humanity's conquest of fire, the mythical "original" technology,[34] lies not in a compensation for our frailty in comparison to other animals but as a side effect of our infantile sexuality and its domestication.

> Psycho-analytic material, incomplete as it is and not susceptible to clear interpretation, nevertheless admits of a conjecture—a fantastic sounding one—about the origin of this human feat. It is as though primal man had the habit, when he came in contact with fire, of satisfying an infantile desire connected with it, by putting it out with a stream of his urine. The legends that we possess leave no doubt about the originally phallic view taken of tongues of flame as they shoot upwards. Putting out fire by micturating . . . was therefore a kind of sexual act with a male, an enjoyment of sexual potency in a homosexual competition. The first person to renounce this desire and spare the fire was able to carry it off with him and subdue it to his own use. By damming down the fire of his own sexual excitation, he had tamed the natural force of fire. This great cultural conquest was thus the reward for his renunciation of instinct.[35]

So fire, the very first technology mastered by man, is a kind of compensation for drive inhibition. Yes, Freud's story is quite amusing, but that does not mean it is entirely wrongheaded. Recall Prometheus's first trickery: Prometheus is said to have deceived Zeus, making him choose the substanceless bag of bones with a shining appearance over the unattractive yet nourishing and delicious meat for the gods' lot, their portion in ritualistic sacrifice.[36] One obvious interpretation of this myth would be that it comes to justify and explain a strange habit some humans have, to sacrifice to their gods not the best—most nutritious and delicious—portion of the meat, but the seemingly lesser remainder, with an artificially shining appearance. The gods get superficial semblance, while we humans get the substance. But we ought to note that in tricking the gods, Prometheus is in fact compensating us humans for what we have lost in sacrifice, that primordial practice of symbolic castration: beauty, the superfluous splendor that has been dedicated to the gods, returns by means of this myth to our tables. Our unappealing substance, that which only nourishes, has been given an extra flavor, that of the forbidden fruit, stolen from the gods. Somehow, technical prowess comes to function as a reward and compensation for what we lost in splendor, for our truncated, drive-inhibited existence. Technology becomes a way to enjoy the satisfaction of our needs, to endow a certain surplus enjoyment on that which is seemingly "merely" vital for our survival.

But technology can function as the reward, the bonus pleasure, which we get as the compensation for drive inhibition in an even more direct way. Consider Monty Python's wonderful account of the great civilizational progress attained by the invention of the condom.

In a memorable scene from Monty Python's *The Meaning of Life*, a Protestant couple is looking outside the window, watching with dismay, if not utter disgust, as their Catholic neighbor's children are playing in the street. The husband (Mr. Harry Blackitt, played by the late Graham Chapman) turns to his wife (Mrs. Blackitt, played by Eric Idle), and utters, appalled:

MR. HARRY BLACKITT: Look at them, bloody Catholics, filling the bloody world up with bloody people they can't afford to bloody feed.

MRS. BLACKITT: What are we dear?

MR. BLACKITT: Protestant, and fiercely proud of it.

MRS. BLACKITT: Hmm. Well, why do they have so many children?

MR. BLACKITT: Because . . . every time they have sexual intercourse, they have to have a baby.

MRS. BLACKITT: But it's the same with us, Harry.

MR. BLACKITT: What do you mean?

MRS. BLACKITT: Well, I mean, we've got two children, and we've had sexual intercourse twice.

MR. BLACKITT: That's not the point. We could have it any time we wanted.

Here we have yet another variation on the theme of technology acting as a reward for drive inhibition: the condom is a technological innovation that finally allows us to separate sexual pleasure from sexual reproduction. As Mr. Blackitt continues to describe the possibilities of pleasure opened up by the invention of the condom, his Mrs. gets exceedingly aroused. The conclusion drawn by the sexually frustrated Mrs. Blackitt is a natural one: now we can have as much sex as we want, without worrying about the repercussions! She has it almost right: what the condom allows them to do is to enjoy the possibility of sexual pleasure, divorced from reproduction, without actually having to do it! Her husband shows his "deeper" understanding of the role of technology by enjoying, directly, the possibility opened up by technology, that is, without realizing it. It is not the satisfaction of an urge that is at stake, but the ability to enjoy its inhibition. In this way, one enjoys drive inhibition, the civilizational achievement, directly: we know we can have sex whenever we want, thanks to our civilizational advancement, and so we are relieved of actually having to go through it! The crucial theoretical point not to be missed, to quote a Žižekian turn of phrase, is this: what we enjoy in technology is never what it serves as a means for, say, in this case, finally allowing us to separate sexual pleasure from reproduction. What we enjoy in technology is the way in which it makes the drive present, that is, the way in which, in it, means are precisely "liberated" from their instrumental function.

And so, putting aside the plausibility of Freud's "fantastic sounding" account of the historical origin of the conquest of fire, that ground zero of anthropogenesis, there is a structural, conceptual point that has to be asserted at this point: the psychoanalytic notion of drive and the problem of technology have the most intimate of associations. Drive, at its minimal definition, is precisely the rebellion and assumption of independence of what were supposed to be mere means for the satisfaction of our needs. Take the classical example, that of the oral drive. Suckling is a means of satisfying a natural need, the need for nourishment. And yet humans display, the second they are born, a strange surplus enjoyment: they enjoy—or something in them enjoys—the very act, the medium of satisfaction, without the need being satisfied. Human babies are pacified by sucking on a finger, or a pacifier, an old piece of technology. That which was meant to be a mere means of our satisfaction can indeed take over our entire system of enjoyment, our very mode of being: we might become oral types, having to swallow—destroy—all that we desire, or become generally addicted to the satisfaction of the mouth, from sucking to eating, from smoking to lecturing and hearing the sound of our own voice.

From this perspective, one might be tempted to trivialize the question of technology. Isn't it merely a special case, a particular instantiation of this fundamental phenomenon discovered by psychoanalysis? We might look down at philosophers who can only glimpse this foundational aspect through the mediation of technology. But that would be to miss an opportunity. Why is it, we might ask instead, that technology allows the drive to make its appearance within philosophical discourse? And perhaps more fundamentally, what is it about technology that makes it become such a major site for the drama of drive?

How, then, are we to think of drive and technology together? Our suggestion is that inasmuch as the drive is the key to understanding technology, technology might teach us something about drive. What, we shall want to ask, is unique about the drive of technology, what is it that makes it indeed a *special* case of the drive, and what, if anything, might we learn from this specialization about drive more broadly?

THE ORGAN OF THE DRIVE

Technology is often described as an extension of man, an artificial organ. Technology, in this account, enhances natural human capacities: A telescope is an extension of the sense of sight, recording devices are extensions of our memory, and so on. Now, significantly, a structurally absent organ is precisely how Lacan introduces the lamella, the organ of the drive.[37]

At the (absent) center of the drive, what the drive circles around, is "an organ, in the sense of an instrument, of the drive," Lacan writes. This is an "ungraspable," even "false" organ, which we can only circumvent. Lacan links this organ "whose characteristic is not to exist, but which is nevertheless an organ,"[38] to the myth of Aristophanes on the division of the sexes. "It is something . . . that is related to what the sexed being loses in sexuality, it is, like the amoeba in relation to sexed beings, immortal—because it survives any division, any scissiparous intervention. And it can run around."[39]

Already heavily hinting at Freud's discussion of the death drive in his *Beyond the Pleasure Principle*, as something which might relate to a state of life before death, the immortality of "unicellular organisms,"[40] Lacan directly links his organ of the drive with an older psychoanalytic notion, libido. "It is the libido, qua pure life instinct, that is to say, immortal life, or irrepressible life, life that has need of no organ, simplified, indestructible life. It is precisely what is subtracted from the living being by virtue of the fact that it is subject to the cycle of sexed reproduction. And it is of this that all the forms of the *objet a* are the representatives. . . . The breast . . . certainly represents that part of himself that the individual loses at birth, and which may serve to symbolize the most profound lost object."[41]

The (primordially lost) objects around which the drive circles—the breast of the oral drive as the paradigmatic example—are but representatives of that which is primordially lost to sexed beings. For us, death is inexorably bound with sex: our death is "sexualized"—it is entwined with sexual reproduction and is uncannily "enlivened" by a surplus, evidenced for example by the universal compulsion to ritualistically handle the dead, and our sex is "mortified" and "petrified"—there is something undead, drive sexuality, conditioning and disturbing our natural reproduction.[42]

Conditioned as we are by sexual reproduction (symbolic castration), non-sexed life would be, precisely, life without us, that is, life purified of subjectivity and its vicissitudes. It is a life without individuation, a life in which the very gap between genus and species does not arise.[43] And so our libido is haunted by immortal, preindividuated life, pure life drive, the stupid insistence of the amoeba which for us is blown up to mythical proportions, turning a life indifferent to divisions, the "nothing" that our drives conserve,[44] that is, a past we cannot quite get rid of, into the impossible, fantastic horizon of a terrain in which division is overcome, harmonized. For us, pure life drive is an organ that does not exist, but as such bears heavily on our lives. Because it does not exist, it insists, it drives us. But where to? Can the drive be said to have a direction, an orientation? Isn't it precisely distinguished from telos by being without aim, a pure thrust we cannot quite direct anywhere?

THE SEXUAL LIFE OF TECHNICAL BEING: THE VEIL AND ITS VICISSITUDES

If indeed the very talk of technology via the prism of the mastery of nature is misleading, perhaps we should find clues for our investigation if we follow those instances in which technology is situated in direct relation to sex and sexuality. It is no secret that in both myths of human origin that are foundational for Western civilization, the Greek and the Hebrew, the acquisition of the special knowledge that gives humans supremacy amongst the beasts is accompanied by the curse of sexual difference: Eve, produced from Adam's rib bone, is the very agent of our fall into instrumental knowledge,[45] and Pandora is the punishment for us accepting the gifts of the gods.[46]

We have this idea of human knowledge as uncovering nature's secrets—recall Aristotle's notion of the completion of nature, as if we are capable of reaching behind the veil and turning directly to nature's blueprints. From Pandora, the image of the calamity of spilled secrets, through the ancient notion of nature as a veiled feminine figure, Isis, which modern science under the guidance of Bacon had determined to extort a confession from, to torture all her remaining secrets out of her, there is a lingering association of technology with sexual difference, and an association of femininity with nature's hidden aspect, that which ought perhaps to remain forever veiled.

We should here linger briefly on this image of nature as a veiled feminine figure and bring out the full significance of the sadistic practice of torturing nature, so as to make as clear as possible that, contrary to appearances, we are not dealing here with anything resembling the mastery over nature, if by that we understand something like bringing it under our control. Bacon's predilection for the violent torture of nature is often taken to be paradigmatic of the modern approach to nature, broadly understood as a project of mastery and submission. "The secrets of nature are better revealed under the torture of experiments than when they follow their natural course."[47]

As Hadot notes, Heraclitus's famous saying, usually rendered as "nature likes to hide" [phusis kruptesthai philei], more likely was intended by its author to mean something like "what causes things to appear, tends to make them disappear (i.e., what causes birth tends to cause death)" or "form (or appearance) tends to disappear (i.e., what is born wants to die)."[48] That is, for Heraclitus, before the solidification of the abstract concept of nature, what is at stake is the internal relation between life and death, the way in which death seems to be the very tendency of life, and disappearance the very tendency of form. "We capture a thing only on its path of becoming its opposite, nothing," would be a way of approximating Heraclitus's general philosophical orientation, but also an ancient intimation of the death drive. For the idea of nature as veiled to emerge, Hadot goes on to show, nature had to be compared with an artifact,[49] and personified,[50] which, we might say, redoubles the original tension of Heraclitus's aphorism. What is the veil, and what is the body unveiled? Do we uncover a mechanism (originally meaning trickery) underneath mythical personifications (what Hadot would call the Promethean attitude), or do we look beyond the trickeries of mechanics to unveil a divine, supersensible nature (the Orphic attitude)?

Against this background, let us ask the meaning of the modern scene of torture, as the preferred method of unveiling. How does it fit with Bacon's assertion that "one does not have empire over nature except by obeying her"?[51] To understand this scene of torture we should turn to Lacan, who understands the perverse satisfaction of torture, counterintuitively, as a servile position, the position of "an instrument of the big other." The pervert, in Lacanian psychoanalysis, serves as an instrument of the other's desire,[52] offering his activity as a "plug," as a fill-in for the very object (constitutively) missing in the other. In this way the pervert effectively disavows the lack in the other—it is there, the lack, I know full well, but I can fill it up, I know how.[53]

The pervert "expert" is not so much looking for a truth unbeknownst to him and known only to the subject of his violence, in this case, nature, and, by getting it out of her, finally attaining mastery over her. Rather, the pervert is nothing if not an expert on the other's desire, and he is determined to retrieve out of the subject of his torture the admission that the secret of her desire is what he knew it to be all along, enjoyment, that is, to prove that he can indeed make her satisfied, emphasis on "make her." He will drive her to the limit. This is what his expert knowledge amounts to: he knows what it is that the other wants—enjoyment—and he knows how to extract that confession from the other, by pushing her to her limits, producing pleasure out of pain. The limit, where we can't take it anymore, is enjoyment localized, the point where pain and pleasure merge into one. In proving to us, the tortured, that enjoyment is real, that pleasure and pain coalesce, the pervert is in fact proving to himself that he is the expert on enjoyment. Note the strange "reality" of enjoyment: the pervert knows it to be real because it can be produced and realized, he can make it materialize at will, he can extract it from any subject, as their true, internal core. Such is the nature of modern science: real because it can be realized, forcefully, again and again.

For our purposes here, what is crucial is just to note that the violence exerted on nature in this famed image of modern technology is not an attempt to gain mastery by gaining knowledge, but an attempt to impose knowledge where none exists. Nature assumes here a feminine form precisely in order to avoid, protect against, its hysteric dimension, the fact that it—the big other—does not know what it wants, that it is ontologically incomplete. Fearful of the other's desire, the fact that there is no answer to it, to what it wants with us, our place in "the grand scheme of things"—a fact that comes to the fore as modern epistemology loses the comforts of natural teleology—we make her confess that it is enjoyment she seeks and nothing but. Nature will be forced into reality, we will prove it is real by infinitely producing new bits of the real. We make nature "spit out" one natural law after the other, in order to disavow its ontological incompleteness. Treating nature "mechanically" is not a simple gesture of mastery, nor is it simply the dissolution of purposiveness. There is a strange new, disavowed purposiveness: in treating nature as what becomes more real the more of its possibilities are realized,[54] the concept of nature as a teleological arrangement becomes disavowed, for we must behave as if all of these mechanical laws are somehow systematically organized in order to continue discovering empirical laws of nature. The stance is "I know full well nature is not some mysterious whole, but nonetheless, I must continue cutting it into bits."

TO KNOW A WOMAN: ON THE SEXUAL TRANSFORMATION OF ARTIFICIAL LIFE

We have this persistent constellation of technology and sexual difference, and yet the elements that compile it are not fixed to one and the same space; there is movement in the stars. The manner in which technology is related to sexual difference is subject to historical change, and we are witnessing such an alteration in our time. Here we might get some aid from contemporary cinematic myths.

The screen in recent years—both the big screen and the small—has presented us a riddle. It seems that something has happened to the fundamental fantasy that has been accompanying our culture for some time now. The fantasy of something man-made coming to life, breaking loose, rebelling against us. Pure life, artificially produced, turning against its creators. A minor plot twist—the change in the robot's sex—raises a series of questions about the complex connections between sexuality, technology, sentience, and artificiality.

Unlike the robot, and its literary predecessor, Frankenstein's monster, who were principally male or sexless—that is, a kind of man, for we are familiar with the feminist critique according to which gender neutrality in cultural representations is, in fact, entirely male and the woman is "the other sex," which already indicates to us how the sexed universe defies simple "neutralization," how, in it, the objective is never simply that—the representation of artificial intelligence has leaned in recent years toward female embodiment.

For example, while the film *Westworld* (1973) dealt with the story of an entertainment male robot rising up and taking revenge against his masters, the focal point of the television program *Westworld* (2016–present), based on the film and broadcast on HBO, is a female robot that demands her freedom. In Spike Jonze's *Her* (2013), Rupert Sanders's *Ghost in the Shell* (2017), and Alex Garland's *Ex-Machina* (2017), we encounter artificial intelligence in feminine form. For some reason, in the age of the computer, and even more so in the age of the internet, the computer network as a medium, the popular image of technology breaking free or coming to its own, has taken on the figure of a woman.

Let us focus our attention for a while on *Ex-Machina*, as it explicitly discusses the sexuality of the artificial intelligence that stands at the center of the narrative, and bears the symbolically suggestive name "Ava," recalling our biblical Eve. In the film, Caleb, a programmer in a company that runs a large, Google-like search engine, "The Blue Notebook" (in reference to Wittgenstein), wins a chance to spend a week with the mysterious founder and owner of the company, Nathan. As he arrives at Nathan's secluded home—located in a heart of tropical nature, away from civilization—he discovers why he was invited: to function as the test subject in a sophisticated Turing test for Ava, an artificial intelligence Nathan has built. In an interesting twist on Turing's imitation game, which is performed with no bodies present (by communicating through anonymizing terminals), Ava presents a body unmistakably female and unmistakably artificial (her electronic "entrails" are visible via a translucid segment of her artificial skin).

If Ava manages to convince Caleb that she's sentient—despite him already knowing that she's artificial—then the experiment would be a success. We might note that in this, the film has supplied us with an intimation of our contemporary, massive-scale experimentation with AI. While mostly bodiless, we engage with AI programs that amaze us with how humanlike they are despite us knowing very well that they are "artificial."

Narratively, *Ex-Machina* is based on the erotic tension that is characteristic of film noir: at the center, there is Ava, a woman whose spellbinding beauty traps the hero in a dangerous net, and transfixes him onto her. But, of course, she belongs to another, powerful man—classically that would mean she is tied to a mafia boss who "owns" her, or in this case, is constructed by a tech giant with a god complex. The hero is drawn into the spiderweb of intrigue, manipulated both by his powerful competitor and by the alluring woman. This is the infamous femme fatale, a woman whose sexuality brings disastrous consequences for her and her surroundings. Woman as the locus of fate, at the center of the spiderweb that draws us in. The only difference here is that Ava is not flesh and blood but a man-made machine. In fact, in her character, we find fused together two figures of the artificial coming to life, inherited from the nineteenth century: like E. T. A. Hoffmann's Olimpia, Ava is an attractive doll, and like Frankenstein's monster, she is a human creation breaking free of her creator's control.

In order to appreciate the novelty of our situation, let us step back and examine these two literary sources. 1816 saw the publication Hoffmann's "The Sandman"—his most famous work, owing in part to Freud's famous reading of it in which he develops the notion of the uncanny. In the story, we meet Olimpia, who transfixes Nathanael's—the hero's—longing gaze. (Recall that Ava's creator is named Nathan, quite clearly alluding to Hoffmann's tale.) In one of the story's dramatic high points, we discover that she is a lifeless automaton, her mechanical eyes separated from her lifeless body, a revelation that drives Nathanael, who was deeply in love with her, to madness.

While often criticized by theorists of technology for neglecting or downplaying the role played by the automaton in the phenomenon of the uncanny, Freud's refusal to lean on the ambiguity between the animate and the inanimate should be considered as one of the strengths of this famous essay, especially for anyone who truly wants to engage with the question of technology today. To "explain" the phenomenon of the uncanny by relying on the notion of the automaton or the machine, blurring the line separating the living from the dead, is to attempt to solve a puzzle with a mystery. The issue, instead, is why and how something like the uncanny, which bears the stamp of the "return of the repressed," that is, of an undead repetition we cannot account for, which once bore the name of fate, comes to be reincarnated in human-made artifacts. You will recall that automaton is Aristotle's term for the predetermined, close perhaps to the Kantian notion of the pathological as causally—and therefore mechanistically—determined, but having nothing to do with our commonsense notion of a machine. Freud's turn to "castration" is quite justified if we consider that the automatism of the return of the repressed entails a primordial loss, a loss constitutive of the subject, the very same loss we have briefly mentioned above, the loss that is introduced with our entrance into sexed life, the loss of pure, immortal life.[55] Simply put, if there is an automatic, unaccountable repetition, we are dealing with a primordially missing cause that is inherent to the phenomenon to be explained. Hence its uncanniness. The machine does not explain symbolic castration, or the return of the repressed, it does not explain the haunting repetition, but adds another layer to the puzzle: what are we to make of an artifact which assumes that "surplus" life, or surplus enjoyment? And so we come closer to teasing out the crucial question pertaining to technology, the question of materialization or actualization of "pure life" which belongs to our virtual-symbolic (back)ground.

Two years after Hoffmann's "Sandman," Mary Shelley's *Frankenstein: Or, The Modern Prometheus* was published. In its path to become a modern mythology,[56] the name Frankenstein, originally the name of Victor Frankenstein who creates, by accident, a monster, has clung to the monster itself. This historical accident highlights a central theme of the story, the intimate, or rather extimate, relationship between the creator and his creature. It is, of course, a double metonymy: on the one hand, the man, the scientist, who wishes to inherit Prometheus, the titan responsible for creating mankind, and endowing them with questionable gifts of technology in Greek mythology. On the other hand, it refers to the creature, the monster, reflecting the discontent of man with his own creaturely being. The human, as it were, disappears, or appears fleetingly, as the vanishing mediator between the titan creator and the created monster. Humanity's proper place, so to speak, would be in the very gap between the creator and his creation, belonging to neither side. Hence Frankenstein's monstrous uniqueness, his nameless singularity.[57]

In the story, Victor Frankenstein, a young scientist struggling to recover from his mother's death, attempts to bring to fruition, with the aid of modern, scientific medicine, what the occult magical practices only promised to do: to give life to inanimate matter. He shall have his victory over death (and thus "earn" his proper name, Victor). Incredibly, with the aid of electricity, harnessing the power of lightning, he succeeds. Or does he?[58] The creature he composes in his lab springs to life, but it is monstrous. Despite his efforts to endow his creature with a handsome, human appearance, it does not look human; something about its appearance discloses that it is artificial, that it was made by mechanical means. Mind you, there is nothing mechanical in the creature itself: he is made of flesh, organic matter, animated by electricity, just like us. It is only his composition that seems to lack the artistic "touch" that would make it whole. His terrifying, dead gaze shines directly through his eyes, indistinguishable from them,[59] his appearance only a mask for his gaze.

This is the creature's tragedy: it is sentient and kind, good-natured, yet it is rejected by human society for its threatening appearance. It is the rejection it suffers at the hand of human society that makes it turn violent and aggressive. In this, Frankenstein's monster is the reverse image of Rousseau's savage who, encountering another whose exterior contrasts with the savage's inner turmoil, utters the first word, a lie, a misnomer: giant![60] Frankenstein's monster is that giant, the terrifying mirror image of the noble savage, that throws him into the social world and its deformities. Inside, he is pure, but, when his exteriority is reflected back to him by society, he learns that he is a monster. As Mladen Dolar aptly put it: "Through his tragedy, culture only gets back its own message: his monstrosity is the monstrosity of culture."[61] Destined to a life of solitude, the creature turns to its creator, asking him to make him a partner, a wife. Victor at first obliges his creation's request, but changes his mind at the last minute—giving the creature the capacity for sexual reproduction is the one limit he will not cross—and he tears apart his new creation, the feminine counterpart to the monster (a gesture that echoes Hoffmann's Olimpia being torn to shreds), a violent gesture which is repaid by the monster in the murder of Victor's beloved on their wedding night.

There's much more to be said about these two stories, and much has been written. For our purposes, what matters is what I would like to call the thesis, or aporia, of the nineteenth century. The nineteenth century presents us with a choice: a lifeless automaton that seems like a human, in the body of a woman; and inanimate matter truly animated, capable of setting its own goals and demonstrating all the internal features of human life—reason, desire, violence, and a thirst for vengeance—lacking only the appearance of humanity—all that in masculine guise. And so, with the emergence of the uncanny, an implicit thesis emerges as to the limits of enlightenment:[62] We can create the fascinating, magnetizing, beautiful and attractive semblance of the human, but one which is illusory, without substance; or we can create an artificial man who has everything but that alluring, elusive, appearance. Either way, the result is disastrous. In short, there is a disconnect, an either/or choice between the technical-mechanical creation and the artwork.

Recall the general characterization of the artificial we have outlined earlier—we may say that in Olimpia's figure, we get only the shining semblance, the purposeless, superfluous aspect of the artificial object, the illusion of life (semblance, beauty), while with Frankenstein we get human purposiveness, missing only that ornamental surplus, which seemingly serves no purpose.

When these are put together, we can glean the outline of a more complicated argument or paradox: the complete artificial thing—we, the model of objects—necessitates both the purposive and the superfluous, both self-directionality and outward semblance, but, at least in the nineteenth-century imagination, it seems that in one thing both cannot be manifest at once. The impossibility of the perfect artificial being, the human recreation of pure, sexless life, is strangely inscribed in the division of the sexes, binding the impossibility of the perfect artifact with the impossibility of sexual union.

One might argue that this complex is the very mode of appearance of the machine, in contradistinction from the instrument. For better or for worse, the industrial revolution of the nineteenth century liberated humans from their essence as tool bearers. The machine and the industrial production it enabled took over that function. It was now the machine that operated tools, and its human operators were in some sense reduced to yet another tool. We became worried that we might be replaced by machines, but, in the same gesture, we became aware that things that seem to belong to our nature as human beings, such as the need to toil over the land, may in fact not be so. Without downplaying the identity crisis such an experience can lead to, it also clears the path to consider labor not primarily as a natural necessity but as the product of social relations (the relations of production, control over means of production), and it also opens the path to reconceive humans as distinguished by their relation with death, the longing for a nature from which man has been alienated by society, with which they might form a higher bond thanks to their imagination or creativity, the great tropes of romanticism and distinctive features of the human which today are once again called into question by developments in artificial intelligence. If the nineteenth century bore witness to the rise of the machine, which in the imagination appeared by means of the radical opposition between the mechanical and the beautiful, we are now witnessing its mutation into something else.

Before we move on to consider our current moment, let us note that, strangely enough, the above-mentioned deessentialization might be the very essence of technology. Simondon develops a full-blown philosophical account of technical objects, which hinges on the realization of the fundamentally deessentializing nature of the technical, its pure functionality. To paraphrase Heidegger, Simondon's point can be summed up by the slogan: the essence of technology is (that) nothing (is) essential. To render his point as simply as possible, let us say only this: Simondon speaks of technology as a mode of intelligibility that is centered around the separation of figure from ground, the human capacity we mentioned apropos of our bone example to isolate what stands out, dissect it and recombine it with other elements in new ways, and so to actualize latent possibilities, those aspects which, alluding to Aristotle's formulation, nature has left for us to complete. One of the more penetrating insights implicit in Simondon's philosophy of technology is that this is at bottom, an activity that not only defies essentialism, it effectively destroys any solid notion of an essence we might hold on to, including our own. It is the very deessentializing unfolding of technology that can profoundly shake up social relations, and even fundamental assumptions about the nature of human life.

We have mentioned that Simondon describes technical being as something which seems to aspire toward organic life. Simondon does not ascribe a will to objects. His point is rather that technical objects are creatures of pure becoming—more properly historical, if you will, than humans, perhaps the true subject of history—which is to say that they become more real the more concrete and more fully developed they are, which is part of the reason why, in his view, it is a profound mistake to think of them via the lens of their most primitive form of appearance, that of the instrument or tool. Rather, we need to study technology as it mutates into more complex and more tightly woven assemblages, from the instrument to the machine and further. Technical being is not instrumental, but is what strives, impossibly, toward organic composition, toward ever more systematic relations between parts and whole.

What, in technical terms, is the novelty of our area? What is it that separates us from the age of the machine? For Simondon, it seems, the answer would be the network. What he has in mind is the power grid, but also communication networks. For Simondon, the network is the highest realization of the inessential nature of the technical. For the network is precisely a way to realize (in the dual sense of the term) the part-whole relation in a nonorganic, insubstantial way. Neither the part nor the whole is a substance, only their reticular relation, whose primary aim is to prevent them from stabilizing into anything resembling the philosophical notion of substance. From substance to network, if you will. Ultimately, for Simondon, the network is the way in which virtuality is actualized as such, paradoxical as this must be. Simondon equates nature "as such" with possibility. In his account, in human, social life, the pure virtuality of nature as such, as indeterminate, returns as destiny:

> Nature is the *reality of the possible*, in the form of this ἄπειρον from which Anaximander makes every individuated form emerge: Nature is not the contrary of Man, but the first phase of the being, while the second phase is the opposition of the individual and the milieu, the complement of the individual relative to the whole. According to the hypothesis presented here, ἄπειρον would remain in the individual, like a crystal that retains its mother liquor, and this charge of ἄπειρον would allow it to go toward a second individuation. . . . Individuals bearing ἄπειρον discover in the collective a signification, which is expressed, for example, as the notion of destiny: the charge of the ἄπειρον is the principle of disparation relative to the other charges of the same nature contained in other beings.[63]

Continuing to trace technology in its deessentializing effect on us, it is apparent that the industrial revolution and the technical object that typifies it, the machine, are by no means the end of our story. In consumer culture, unlike in industrial culture, it has become evident that technology has not necessarily come to satisfy human needs; it can also help them proliferate. What seems at first to be the promise of answering all human needs technologically, the functionalist ethos of modern life, quickly turns out to be its very opposite—the promise to find and adjust a new need for every technological innovation.

That is why, as keenly noted by Jean Baudrillard, in consumer culture the machine as the symbol of the technical is replaced to a large extent by the gadget, the gizmo. Baudrillard acutely analyzes the manner in which the multifunctionality of gadgets has itself become a symbol, a message, an aesthetic, answering "no other need than the need to function."[64] The aporia of the nineteenth century appears here in dialectical form: the gadget is the machine that in the surplus of its multifunctionality seems to declare "I am a device, I can do many things," and so covers over its true nature as a producer of needs (i.e., as a commodity). Functionality is no longer the bitter, naked truth of our culture, the uncanny Frankenstein. It has itself turned into a mask of sorts, a semblance, an ornament. Note that naked utility, functionality, has become erotic precisely because it covers over something else: consumption above and beyond any purpose.

In his analysis of the modern system of objects, Baudrillard further points out that the fantasy of the functional world, the organizing phantasy of technology, relies on a fantasy of the organized functioning body.[65] There is nothing quite like a robot to conceal the anxiety that hides behind seemingly naked functionality. The robot, in Baudrillard's analysis, is the ultimate gadget, that is, phallus:[66] behind the anxiety that the tool meant to serve us will gain independence and bring us to ruin hides the anxiety of the impotence of the devices that we rely on. The anxiety that we are not quite so well organized, not so fully functional as we would like to believe, that our artifacts might simply malfunction. The grand complex web we've spun for ourselves—of mind, society, and technology—is much less stable and much less functional than we tend, or would like to, believe. But precisely in this context, Baudrillard notes that the robot is sexless, that is, as we remarked above, a symbol of pure masculinity.

Which leads us back to the riddle with which we started on this journey of sex and technology: How is it that our robots have become female? Why does the ultimate accessory, the sublime gizmo, the smartphone, express its intelligence—what makes it more than a mere gadget—by way of an operating system with a feminine voice and name? And why is it that our screens have become rampant with female embodiments of artificial intelligence? What is this intelligence that contemporary technology "frees" from human essence in that same ambivalent and uncanny way that industrial technology "freed" us from manual labor?

In our contemporary, computer-based imagination, the aporia between purpose-driven interiority and outward appearance is not so much resolved as somehow condensed. Famously, Alan Turing, the theoretical father of the computer (aka the Turing machine), suggested late in his life a test to see whether our creations have reached intelligence. In this test, Turing first imagines a guessing game in which we would have to determine the sex of our interlocutor in conditions that veil all physical clues such as sound and shape, and only then turns to apply this test to the machine, never really accounting for this transition and its implications.[67] To hazard an interpretation of Turning's phantasy, what remains implicit in his account: it is as if getting at the symbolic essence of sexual difference, disembodied in the female, so to speak, was the line one would have to cross in order to attain pure disembodied symbolic intelligence. In order to get beyond appearances, we have to go through the semblance of femininity, a pure appearance, an appearance without (physical, sense-based) appearance. Intelligence abstracted from our rootedness in the material world is somehow dependent on a strange remainder of the body in the symbolic, the mysterious feature that would mark a woman as such, independent of any sense data. The pure artificial creature would have to somehow echo the infamous "natural" artificiality of the feminine,[68] the essence of that which is essentially without essence.[69]

And so we arrive back at our film with its sophisticated Turing test. If Ava convinces Caleb she is a woman, that is, if she makes him fall in love with her, even though he knows full well she is an artificial machine, then she will have passed the ultimate Turing test, and there would be no doubt that we have created that which we do not understand—ourselves.

How was Ava created? Nathan, her creator, explains to Caleb how she was put together. Her "brain" is made out of wetware, not hardware. Plastic material, capable of imitating the plasticity of our brains.[70] But more importantly, her software is, directly, the utilization of the traces we leave online when we use the web. Nathan figured out what to do with the raw material of the internet. While his competitors were using our use of the web in order to sell us products,[71] Nathan realized its true potential. What we do online is the pathway not to what we want, what commodities one could push down our throats, but how we want, the very nature of our desire. As he puts it to Caleb: "Search engines are like striking oil in a world that hasn't invented combustion engines."

In the movie Ava is the incarnation of the internet, the web in the flesh. It is almost impossible to think about the internet as a device—it is the environment and medium in which we live. Indeed, Ava's software, her "mind," is built from the traces left by our autoerotic and compulsive use of the internet: what we do absentmindedly, without purpose. Ava, in short, is the promise of the utility of all the time we waste online. She is "functionalized" enjoyment. This is a kind of a vulgar, literal translation of the supreme cultural value of what has no function: Ava is a sublime object built directly out of human waste.

With the internet, it is as if we have switched places with the gadget. It is now we who are fully utilizable, who are declaring that there is nothing in us that cannot be put to use, in particular that which is most antiutilitarian, our enjoyment. As we play with our gadgets, it is no longer their functionality that keeps us hooked but our own.

Ava succeeds in being something beyond the functional, the impossible fusion of Frankenstein and Olimpia: She is intelligent, setting her own goals and acting on them (rather ruthlessly), and garners tremendous erotic value as a sublime object of desire.[72] She does this by a redoubled gesture, utilizing everything that serves no purpose, and in doing so passing herself beyond utility, beyond instrumentality into artificial life, at once beautiful and alluring, a pure semblance, and somehow the "real deal," motivated by her own hidden desire and capable of setting her own goals. She is certainly not an instrument to be used by us.

Here a comparison of the psychoanalytic discussion of the drive with the account given by philosopher of technology Gilbert Simondon might be instructive. Simondon puts forward a notion that technology is, in a sense to be unpacked, the tendency of matter toward life, the strange striving of instruments to concretize their existence by becoming progressively more self-organizing. While Simondon goes out of his way to avoid teleology, and indeed bases his entire metaphysical intervention on the critique of Aristotelian hylomorphism,[73] the narrative that emerges from his account, according to which technical being is distinguished in being only intelligible from its more fully actualized state,[74] which is the state of cybernetic,[75] quasi-lifelike assemblages, is inescapably at the very least quasi-teleological.[76]

It is, of course, a "parasitic" teleology; for Simondon technical beings are a manifestation of the inherent tendency of the preindividual to actualize itself as such, which needs humans as its agent. Certainly, technical beings do not occur naturally; they are brought into existence by human beings. But, in creating technical beings, humans are in fact manifesting their capacity to "see" the virtual, to see, beyond the tree, or the bone, the myriad functions it can be made to serve, the myriad possibilities awaiting actualization. What begins to actualize itself through the technical activity of humans is a special kind of being, a being of pure becoming. For what is essential in technical beings is that they have no essence; they can be broken apart and recombined, and so are more and more concrete the more interwoven and interchangeable their part-whole relation becomes. They are, if you will, more symbolic in nature than their producers, or they are the symbolic without us.

And so there is, so to speak, an inorganic teleology of which we are the unintentional agents, a tendency toward the realization of a concrete, empirically embodied virtuality. Simondon wishes to amend Aristotle's technical account of individuation, in part in order to disambiguate it from accounts of living matter. An amended technical account would be one that gives priority to the process over individuals, so much so, indeed, that human individuality itself would have to be a phase of the process, not quite as concrete as what it, humanity, brings about—ultimately, technical systems, according to Simondon.[77]

The concretization of the technical being in this account, the uncanny mixture of drive and goal it exhibits, can be likened to the striving of dead matter toward artificial life. This would be the "cunning" of technicity—what we see as the multifunctionality of objects, a space for us to intervene and complete what nature has left us with, to make our own "artificial" constructs, can be seen, from the perspective of objects, as their gradual emergence from abstract partiality toward a more and more systematic, i.e., "organic-like," interconnectedness. In this way, the process of technological progress is an uncanny imitation of organic, natural life. In our technical activity, we bring into life a pure drive toward (organic) life. Through our very intentional, goal-oriented activity, we materialize a drive foreign to our interests. A final "cunning of history" in which the historical process, which Hegel understood as a process of concretization, is taken over by a pre- and posthistorical entity, realizing itself through history.

We have Lacan suggesting that our missing organ is pure life drive, and we have a philosopher of technology attributing such a pure drive, or rather, a reflexive twist of it, say, a drive toward life, to technology. And so we might advance a preliminary hypothesis: technology is not so much an attempt to compensate for the limited power of any of our organs, but rather to materialize the organ of the drive. To bring to life that which only, and purely, seeks to live.

But we ought to note at this point a certain temporal parallax. We are to bring about, to cause into existence, something that mythically precedes us, and conditions us by virtue of being lost to us, inaccessible. We are to create what we encounter as primal. Somehow, that from which we were individuated, the *apeiron* from which we were constitutively cut off, that impossible, virtual real, must not only be actualized but materialized, given physical existence. This is strange because what we have (always already) lost is by no means a fading memory but a nagging, disturbing presence. Is our attempt to materialize this surplus a desperate attempt at containment? To put in front of us, as a goal of sorts, what we feel breathing down our necks, gazing at the back of our heads, driving us blindly? To localize what otherwise is all-pervasive, but can never quite be pinpointed? The aim of the drive is distinguished from its goal, for the drive "lives" in circulating its goal; what we encounter here is an attempt to realize the drive, as it were, by making the aim and the goal overlap, introducing a temporality of an endless end.

Somehow, objects produced by human knowledge, artifacts, come to assume a special role in relation to drive. In technological advancement, if we follow Freud's clue, we find a compensation for our drive inhibition; what we lose in terms of our own enjoyment returns to us in material, objective form. We can enjoy our own renunciation of enjoyment, as long as we give some objective, independent existence to this enjoyment.

In our analysis of the artifact, we have already intimated how for us, pure life, a life unperturbed by sexual reproduction, the life of nature as such, is split in two: life as an organic whole, the pinnacle of being, and life as a process of becoming. And in our brief discussion at the very top, we mentioned how contemporary technoscience is seeking to bring these two aspects together, to materialize an artificial life. If we are to confront our technological moment, the question, then, in the very famous words of Marshall McLuhan, is how and why: "*Man becomes, as it were, the sex organs of the machine world, as the bee of the plant world, enabling it to fecundate and to evolve ever new forms.*"[78]

Which begs the question, not only of how our drive comes to be objectified in the machine world, in the world of artifacts that seem to require specialized, advanced knowledge, but also, what makes this progressively acceptable, explicitly, as an inescapable goal, a combination of blind, fated drive, and intentional striving. What is it that seems to prompt us to act as servants of the machine's wish to come to life?

OUT OF CONTROL: ON MASTERY, TECHNOLOGY, AND JOUISSANCE

After this long detour into myth and fantasy, we are now perhaps in a position to broach anew the question of power. In his discussion of cybernetics, Lacan points out how in this new era of technoscience, mastery becomes indistinguishable from servitude. In the old ritual technology, Lacan speculates, humanity saw itself as participating in maintaining the symbolic order of the universe. It had an avowed purpose, a role to play in a system to which humans were subordinate. But with science something fundamental changes:

> From the moment man thinks that the great clock of nature turns all by itself and continues to mark the hour even when he isn't there, the order of science is born. . . . The order of science hangs on the following, that in officiating over nature, man has become its officious servant. He will not rule over it, except by obeying it. And like the slave, he tries to make the master dependent on him by serving him well.[79]

Alluding to Bacon, Lacan is here suggesting that what cybernetics stands as a culmination of is a new, perverse mode of servitude, which amounts to the blurring of the very distinction between master and slave, between mastery and servitude. Mastering nature becomes the function we must serve. The Aristotelian notion of completing nature becomes the way in which in our very mastery we are servants. This does not suggest merely that as we become more autonomous, masters of ourselves, we become our own servants (a familiar narrative about the progressive internalization of inhibitions). For we are not only under control in our very attempts to be in control: being in control is our way of being totally out of control.

Isn't Deleuze's notion of societies of control—a philosophical misnomer if there ever was one—pointing at a similar difficulty? As Deleuze makes quite clear, far from standing for some even more nefarious big brother, societies of control are the constellation that emerges as the older disciplinary society analyzed by Foucault begins to disintegrate. In societies of control, control does not designate an attained status, but something like an infinite task—or incestuous drive—proportional to the entropy of decaying institutions: "In the disciplinary societies one was always starting again (from school to the barracks, from the barracks to the factory), while in societies of control one is never finished with anything."[80] In societies of control, "perpetual training tends to replace the school, and continuous control to replace the examination."[81]

In societies of control, roughly corresponding to what has sometimes been labeled "neoliberalism" and which we might more profitably call "actually existing capitalism," Walter Benjamin's bleak description of capitalism as a religion in which every day is a Sunday, a day of worship, with no reprieve, has come one more step, perhaps the final one, toward full realization: "Disciplinary man was a discontinuous producer of energy, but the man of control is undulatory, in orbit, in a continuous network."[82]

In societies of control the very separation between private, familial life and productive work is eroded; not only does work limitlessly chase us at home, in the guise of nagging email, our private lives themselves have become progressively a product, indeed an investment.[83] So, if ours are societies of control, this is because they are fundamentally out of control, or, to be more precise, because in our societies being controlled and being out of control have become uncannily blurred. As William Burroughs, on whom Deleuze relies in his notion of societies of control, put it: "You see, control can never be a means to any practical end. . . . It can never be a means to anything but more control . . . like junk."[84]

If control is to offer us any tactical or strategic value, it is crucial to note how it presents itself, in Deleuze's account, as a sophistry, a name that lies. This, of course, is not a simple lie. Control, a term no doubt borrowed from the language of cybernetics, is an apt name for our contemporary society insofar as it is the name of a society in which being in control and being out of control are no longer easily distinguishable.[85]

To unpack this difficulty, let us consider two ways in which we might understand the efforts of control in relation to its presumed object, entropy. Is entropy simply the increase of noise and the decrease of information, or is it rather the growing difficulty in objectively telling noise and information apart? On the first understanding of entropy, the solution is conceptually simple, if pragmatically perhaps impossible: it would be, as Norbert Wiener had it,[86] to oppose the natural tendency toward entropy, which seems to rule the physical universe, with the creation of man-made negentropic systems. We are to valiantly oppose the natural increase of noise with a cultural-historical increase of counterinformation, or order. However, if the second understanding is true, what we are progressively losing is the very distinction between (background) noise and information. No simple increase in information will do. Instead, we must find ways to reintroduce measures capable of supporting this very distinction. Deleuze's notion of the society of control can be of great use, if we read it as a sketch of a society in which the increase of means and measures of control approximates, to the point of indistinction, the increase of noise: a society in which the attempts to impose order, to bring things under control, is not a human project of subduing unruly, chaotic nature, but one in which the distinction between chaos and order, noise and information, is progressive eroding, along with the distinction between natural necessity and human pursuits. The notion of control thus speaks to the relation between history and nature, specifically to what seems like the contemporary, momentous erosion of the very limit between the two. To the extent that the term Anthropocene names our era, it points to the practical undermining of the distinction between nature and history, foundational for much of our intellectual division of labor. How shall we understand this erosion? Should we abandon, as some suggest, the very distinction between man-made processes and natural ones? If we do so, we might lose sight of an important, often neglected aspect of this general observation: not only that it is becoming harder and harder to find natural processes that have not been dramatically impacted by human activity, but that, more and more, the terrain of history and human action seems subject to a nature-like automatism of its own, as political catastrophes such as war impose themselves as inevitable expressions of what is natural in humans. There is a tension between acknowledging the complex interpenetration of the natural and the historical, which does seem to indicate an erosion in the gap separating them, and the need to maintain their conceptual distinction. And so, to give this erosion more precision, in the context of the notion of control, we may put matters thus: the society of control is the society in which, so to speak, the most instrumental has become its own end, a society, that is, where need and drive coalesce and switch places: need assumes the structural features of drive, whereas drive is absolutely functional, vital and necessary for the functioning of the system. Need is derailed from serving any functional purpose, and drive becomes the very engine of the machine.

In order to break down this paradoxical constellation, let us consider how precisely technological development and enjoyment have become thus entangled. Let us tend, finally, to the philosophical-historical distinction between the era of the machine and our own, the era of the apparatus.

FROM MACHINE TO APPARATUS, FROM OBJECTIFIED KNOWLEDGE TO OBJECTIFIED ENJOYMENT

Above, we have considered the machine in its distinction from what, in terms of a philosophy of technology, is its more primitive mode of appearance, the instrument. In order to move forward, let us delve into this problem again more carefully and ask: what is a machine? In the *Grundrisse*, Marx defines the machine as what objectifies knowledge, and thereby dispossesses subjects of their knowledge, leading to what is known as "deskilling" or the production of the "concrete abstraction" of "raw labor power," power as a material to be commodified and sold. It is worth quoting at length:

Once adopted into the production process of capital, the means of labor passes through different metamorphoses, whose culmination is the machine, or rather, an automatic system of machinery (system of machinery: the automatic one is merely its most complete, most adequate form, and alone transforms machinery into a system) set in motion by an automaton, a moving power that moves itself; this automaton consisting of numerous mechanical and intellectual organs so that the workers themselves are cast merely as its conscious linkages. . . . The use value, i.e., the material quality of the means of labor is transformed into existence adequate to fixed capital and to capital as such; and the form in which it was adopted into the production process of capital, the direct means of labour, is superseded by a form posited by capital itself and corresponding to it. Not as with the instrument, which the worker animates and makes into his organ with his skill and strength, and whose handling, therefore, depends on his virtuosity. Rather, it is the machine which possesses skill and strength in place of the worker, is itself the virtuous, with a soul of its own in the mechanical laws acting through it; . . . the workers' activity, reduced to a mere abstraction of activity, is determined and regulated on all sides by the movement of the machinery, and not the opposite. The science which compels the inanimate limbs of the machinery, by their construction, to act purposefully, as an automaton, does not exist in the worker's consciousness, but rather acts upon him through the machine as an alien power, as the power of the machine itself. The appropriation of living labor by objectified labor—of the power or activity which creates value by value positing itself—which lies in the concept of capital, is posited, in production resting on machinery, as the character of the production process itself, including its material motion. . . . In machinery, objectified labour confronts living labour within the labour process itself as the power which rules it; a power which, as the appropriation of living labour, is the form of capital. The transformation of the means of labour into machinery, and of living labour into a mere living accessory of this machinery, as the means of its action, also posits the absorption of the labour process in its material character as mere moment of the realization process of capital.[87]

If we are to understand the machine through its role in the process of production, as Marx indeed prompts us to do, we must take him to be defining conceptually what a machine is, not describing it empirically. The machine is the concrete form taken by abstract labor; it is what makes labor appear objective, alien to the worker. As Marx makes clear, this is not an accidental aspect of capitalism.[88]

It is not that, with the emergence of what we understand empirically to be machines, humans began to be dispossessed of their skills, that is, that the machine with its automatism made manual skill superfluous, as a matter of fact. That would be a fetishization of the machine, endowing its technical makeup with the capacity to transform human relations all by itself. It would mean that the machine, in its technical makeup, is something that cannot be instrumentalized. But recall Simondon's analysis of technical objects: instrumentality is their abstract existence; the more concrete the technical object, the less of an instrument it is. Every tool we operate, we might say, has an instrumental side and a systematic tendency, a way in which it is, at least potentially, systematically connected with other aspects of the labor process. And so, with the rise of the industrial machine, it is this more developed technicity that is not only realized but made manifest. It is the appearance of a system of machines, or "machinery," that concretely abstracts labor.

What emerges with capitalism is an "automatic" power system—but is that development "automatic," an aspect of a tendency implicit in technical objects? It is one thing to grant technology the power to deessentialize, to undermine what we take to be natural or essential, and another thing completely to endow it with the power to drive and restructure human affairs all by itself. When we do this we unthinkingly rely on a kind of historical machine, which runs all by itself, which is indeed the underlying ideology of capitalist modernity. It is as if technology always already was in full possession of that which it seems to strive toward, life.

If there is something "automatic" here, it certainly cannot be attributed to the machine's technical makeup. Rather, the "machine" is the appearance given to that in which human subjects encounter their own labor as alienated, "the system" to which worker, capitalist, and empirical machines all belong. This broader understanding of the machine is preserved in the colloquial expression to "rage against the machine," or in talking about the political "machinery," etc. There is, if you will, a certain incestuous surplus to the machine, above and beyond its technical makeup and technical definition.[89]

What we are dealing with here is quite literally a technical surplus or surplus of technicality: it is precisely the possibility of putting the technical—the machine, the instrument—in quotation marks, the possibility of expanding the sense of the technical beyond the strictly technical, in which technicity is redoubled, applies to itself. If technicity consists in the capacity to rip a thing out of its context, then the way in which it rips itself out of its own "proper" context, so to speak, is how technicity "realizes" its strange, antiessentialist nature. And so the "objectification" of knowledge is not simply a formalization that renders the subjective labor skill superfluous. Objectification here *displays* the spoliation of the subject. It is the system, or structure, in which "the worker *appears* as superfluous to the extent that his action is not determined by capital's requirements."[90]

We need to understand the absence of subjectivity from knowledge here as a determinate negation in Hegel's sense: objectified knowledge is positively desubjectivized; it is the result and manifestation of the disappearance of the subject. Its "alien" character is nothing but the effect of this subjective loss. In the machine we witness, as it were, our labor without us, our knowledge and skill subtracted from them. Abstract labor is "captured" in the machine in a dual sense: it is what mediates between capital and abstract, commodified labor, the medium through which labor becomes positively desubjectivized, commodified, and surplus value thereby extracted, and it speaks to the "automatic," impersonal and objective form in which social relations are organized under capitalism. In the machine we witness the materialization of Simondon's deessentializing process, we witness what used to belong to us essentially cut off from us, confronting us in all its opacity.

But precisely here we must raise the difficult question of structure and history. Is not the capacity to "disappear" labor the very universal feature of mastery as such? Could we not say that what holds together mastery in the sense of mastery of technique and mastery as a social relation is the way in which in both we encounter a display, precisely, of the *disappearance* of work? A masterful performance by a musician, we could say, displays, not precisely effortlessness, but a kind of absorption of past effort, hard-won experience, into the levity of grace.[91] In a similar vein, consider the prototypical king of a Hollywood production, clapping his hands to have his subjects vacate the room, allowing it to assume the splendor that only arises in the repression of the effort taken to maintain it.

As Lacan put it in an early seminar, dedicated, in part, to questions posed by the emergence of cybernetics: "The machine is the structure detached from the activity of the subject. The Symbolic world is the world of the machine."[92] In this sense, the very appearance of the symbolic as "objective" is, already, the machine. But that would be the precondition for becoming a speaking subject, the ability to rely on a stable structure of meaning "out there." And so, we ask, what, if anything, truly changes with the emergence of the modern machine? What changes as the virtual "machine," language as symbolic order, becomes materialized? What changes in the very meaning of "objectivity" that requires the virtual to be incarnated in physical, technical objects?

Perhaps nothing changes. That is, what changes is the status, and mode of appearance of nothing, of the loss involved in "symbolic castration." If, then, the "machine" is a name for the symbolic castration, the way in which language implies the loss of the subject's object cause of desire, we have to ask what is it that drives the materialization of the symbolic, what is it that makes objectified knowledge assume a key, structural role, in social relations of domination?

This is the very topic of Lacan's Seminar XVII, also known as *The Other Side of Psychoanalysis*. There he makes the fundamental psychoanalytic point according to which the very entanglement of knowledge and mastery presents us with a serious conundrum and is something to be explained. Unlike philosophy, which tends to presuppose a will to knowledge, which, in its most self-critical articulations, is taken to be inseparable from the will to power, for psychoanalysis the subject is always in a position of not wanting to know something. Indeed, the will to knowledge is understood from this perspective as a way to avoid a certain truth about knowledge. From a psychoanalytic perspective, when knowledge assumes the position of mastery, as it does under the conditions Lacan refers to as "university discourse," it serves, in effect, to rob knowledge of its potency. Knowledge serves as a defense, insofar as it reassures the subject that she is on the side of knowledge.[93]

Lacan poses the question as to the shifts in the place of knowledge in relations to mastery. In his reading of Plato's *Meno*, Lacan suggests that philosophy is, originally, the theft of slave knowledge. Turning what is inherently hard-earned, embodied, tacit knowledge, the kind of knowledge that allows for mastery and virtuosity, into formulas that can be easily communicated, detached from the experience invested in gaining them, is the way in which philosophy participates, perhaps indeed initiates, a process of desubjectification.[94] What Marx describes, in Lacan's understanding, is a situation in which slave knowledge, thus detached from individual experience, has come to assume the place of the master, what Lacan calls university discourse. In the position of the master, knowledge seems to be automatic, self-generating, a machine with no off button.

And so there is an intimacy between these two major stories of modernity: the rule of science (scientific revolution) and the rule of capitalism as a mode of production, a mode of organizing social relations. There is a situation in which the locus of power is not where commands are issued, in direct relations of domination, which, to be sure, are very much still to be found, but instead in the very impersonal process of knowledge.

In one sense, with modern, abstract relations of domination, the truth of mastery is made manifest. We come to perceive mastery for what it is, a social relation. But this is also the way we misperceive it. No longer bound by transference to master figures, the bonds of status and tradition, we find ourselves bound "artificially." But the recognition of this artificiality is the new form our bond takes, the dialectical reversal of disavowal analyzed by the mature Marx: in market relations, we know, consciously, that we are participating in an instrumental, complex system of exchange, and in so believing, we practically endow the system and the commodity exchange that lies at its center with "magical" qualities.[95]

The same applies to the modern, scientific investigation of nature as analyzed by Kant: we are no longer to believe, directly, in the purposive organization of nature (purpose is not a category of the understanding), but, in our practical scientific orientation, we are to behave as if we do. Indeed, such a disavowed belief is the precondition of the modern scientific exploration of

$$\text{M} \qquad\qquad\qquad \text{U}$$

$$\frac{S_1}{\$} \;\text{€}\; \frac{S_2}{a} \qquad\qquad \frac{S_2}{S_1} \;\text{€}\; \frac{a}{\$}$$

$$\frac{\$}{a} \;\text{€}\; \frac{S_1}{S_2} \qquad\qquad \frac{a}{S_2} \;\text{€}\; \frac{\$}{S_1}$$

$$\text{H} \qquad\qquad\qquad \text{A}$$

The four discourses, from Jacques Lacan, *Seminar XVII: The Other Side of Psychoanalysis*, trans. Russell Grigg (New York: W. W. Norton, 2007), 79.

nature: if we are to continuously discover new empirical laws of nature, we must act *as if* all of these laws ultimately cohere in the concept of nature, for all of these empirical laws must be taken to be linked systematically. In this sense, we must approach nature as if it were a purposive whole under which these particular empirical laws are unified.[96]

If the machine is what dispossesses us of knowledge in the precise sense that in it we encounter our knowledge objectified, our knowledge without us, "automatized," then in our era of actually existing capitalism we have found a way to objectify something more intimate still, our very enjoyment.

Ours is the society of the apparatus,[97] if we pick up on some clues from Vilém Flusser's elucidation of the term.[98] Condensing Flusser's account, we might offer the following tripartite distinction: if a tool is what is used by humans, and a machine is what puts humans to use, an apparatus is what puts to use our using it. It would in fact be better to say that an apparatus is what puts to use our enjoyment of it, since the apparatus, as analyzed by Flusser, incites our desire precisely by means of what in it exceeds instrumentality. This is a way to grasp conceptually what we have approximated with the notion of the gadget or the gizmo, and what hides beneath the notion of play.

Our instruments today incite us to play with them. This, in part, is a form of seduction, which means that behind it lurks a certain question as to the desire of the device. Our asking ourselves, playfully, "What can I do with it?" has inscribed in it the echo of "What do I want from it, namely, what am I meant or supposed to do with it?" "What am I to do with it?" is truly the question "What does it want me to do with it?" This is the way in which we encounter in the apparatus our enjoyment "objectified." There is in the apparatus an enjoyment from which we are, in an emphatic, positive sense, subtracted, dispossessed. Our very own enjoyment is objectified, opaque, and closed off.

Flusser helps us see this. For it is precisely in its suprafunctionality that the apparatus incites us to play with it and explore its possibilities. Flusser's example is that of the camera—as users (functionaries, in his terms) we play with the camera, explore it as a medium, and this is how the camera realizes itself. In pursuing what remains unrealized in the apparatus and exploring the medium, we function as instruments, so to speak, of the apparatus's desire, its desire for the realization of its possibilities.[99] In its very opacity the camera, indeed any apparatus (Flusser speaks here of Kafka's world!), seduces us to explore it as a field of play, beyond any utilitarian purpose; the apparatus introduces something like an "objective" or "systematic" enjoyment. There is something that is "getting off" on our "getting off," something "feeding" on our enjoyment of it. What then, drives technology? What is it that drives us to materialize, actualize, the pure, virtual life of the drive? To materialize in empirical form the virtuality of the symbolic order? What is it that drives us to build apparatuses, material and intuitional, that utilize our very enjoyment of them, making us into the agents of their realization?

YOU OUGHT BECAUSE (IT) CAN: THE MYTHICAL POWER OF A FUTURE WITHOUT ILLUSIONS

Today it seems as though we have never been postmodern. What prison house of language?[100] We are up to our necks in the real. If the trouble with postmodernism was its reliance on a position of "better knowledge," an attitude of disillusionment with the modern project of disillusionment,[101] how are we to describe the "new sensibility," with its strange mixture of radical disbelief in all institutionally produced knowledge and passionate acceptance of the fantastic, from the reality of aliens to magical ancient civilizations? We seem to believe that nothing is possible in the political realm, there is no way for us to shape our collective lives, but everything is possible technologically: immortality, superhuman capacities (genetic manipulation and/or "neuro-links"), the population of the stars.

In Jean-Luc Nancy's account, the plight of the postmodern "sense of the world" was not simply that we have lost the anchorage to a transcendent meaning (God, the fulfillment of history): without the transcended reference, or the absolute, the relative—this, sensuous-material world we inhabit, the realm of the merely possible—loses its sense as well.[102] The world is no longer (was it ever?) experienced as given in its simplicity, a place in which we can straightforwardly orient ourselves. Ours is a world devoid of sense, and a sense that is wordless. And so we would either lament the loss of an inescapably mythological absolute or resign ourselves to nihilism.

For Nancy, this precisely was the postmodern plight, to be torn between two untenable alternatives as to the relation between the relative (the sensuous, material, phenomenal world) and the absolute (its sense or significance, what transcends it). On the one hand, there is our mythological past notion of the absolute as given. It is mythological for us moderns in a dual sense: First, modernity can be defined by its suspicious attitude toward the given as mythical, placing value on our critical sensibilities over anything taken on trust as a given. Second, the image of premodern ideology as naively relying on myths is itself a mythological construct of the premodern past from which modernity had sought to distinguish itself. The modern focus on our critical sensibilities thus tends to raise the relative—our cognition and desire—to the level of the absolute. This entails a temporal reversal: the (ultimately mythological) absolute does not so much dissipate as it is transposed from the primordial, mythological past (the always already, the given, the fully actual, a being beyond being) to the continuously deferring future to come, the possible, as something to be realized by us, the object of our desire. But can we truly believe, firmly hold on to a future absolute that is of our own making?

For Nancy, it seems, postmodern nihilism was our incapacity to do so, the ultimately paralyzing effect on us of the abyss of possibility.[103] Knowing the absolute to be up to us seems to fundamentally devalue it. Trust belongs essentially to the mythological past. And yet, in a sense, the current technological trend can be seen as a resounding affirmation of the possibility of believing in a future of our making, endowing it with the compelling necessity of the absolute. As we shall see momentarily, the narratives forming around contemporary technological trends seem to be precisely designed to allow for a replacement of the mythological, given sense by a nihilistically yet fervently pursued future absolute. The narrative of technologically conquering what were traditionally transcendental limitations of the human experience is a way to confer upon the possible the full force of the mythological given. As our technical capacities have assumed mythical proportions, our myths themselves have become technical.

Our discussion of the apparatus's "creepy" self-realization helps bring to light what is so fascinating—hauntingly compelling and disturbing—about the thought experiment that came to be known as Roko's Basilisk.[104] According to this thought experiment (proposed by a user named Roko on the Lesswrong forum in 2010), a hypothetical, future omnipotent AI could retrospectively resurrect and punish anyone in its past (which includes our present) that did not contribute to its creation. It is ironically because such an AI will be supremely good that the failure to act on its behalf would be considered—justifiably!—evil. And it is because it will be omnipotent that it could recreate and eternally torment a virtual version of all of us who have failed to bring about its reign.

While there is clearly something deeply sinister and strange about this thought experiment, it is not that easy to pinpoint. After all, is this not only a mild—if decisive—alteration of the progressive motivation of our age? We are often called to be on the right side of history—to recognize, as it were, the morally progressive tendencies operative in the present and support them with all our might, so as not to be judged unfavorably by future generations, to whom our morals will no doubt appear lacking, if not outright unforgivable. Did we do all we could—and should have—to prevent ecological disaster? Did we do all we could, and should have, to fight against the many injustices that plague our society? In a sense, all Roko's future AI does is to replace the symbolic disapproval of a morally superior future, as a motivating force in the present, with the actual, physical torment afflicted by the supreme technology that will come to effectively install and enforce the morally improved future. But therein lies its unique evil.

Like the God of medieval theologians, AI is unique in that its mere possibility, the fact that it is conceivable, is what makes it actual—but in a way that blurs the lines between existence and duty. AI's existence is our duty. Because it is possible, we must make it actual. To paraphrase Kant, we must, because it can (come to be). It is a profoundly perverse phantasy, in that it helps bring to light what is disturbing about perverse phantasy in general, the way a certain "however" immediately mutates to a "therefore," the way the inexistence or impotence of the symbolic big other is immediately transformed so as to enlist us in the service of its omnipotence. The logic here is as follows: There is no AI (it is a mere possibility, an item of speculation). However, precisely because I now know of its inexistence, its utter contingency upon human action (it isn't, but it might come to be), I must behave as if it is real (however = therefore). Indeed, I must become an instrument of its purposes, disregarding or justifying its strange, sadistic enjoyment.

Fate now lies not in an actuality that precedes, predestines our lives, the mythically given, original structure of the world, but in the very open-ended future of our own making, the high achievement of the modern, critical age, suspicious of all myths.[105] The unique evil of this thought experiment lies in its performative, interpolative function—anyone exposed to the thought experiment should find herself motivated to do all she can to bring about the existence of this hypothetical AI. It is enough to recognize the performative potential of the story, that is, to find it plausible that others might take it seriously, in order to be motivated to do the same, without, however, avowing it first personally. If one believes that a story like this might cause others to bring about the AI described in it, then the content of the story, though hypothetical, becomes effectively true, and you'd be a fool not to do the same. In this way, one can be a tool, a servant of the coming AI, without however being a tool, a dupe. Disillusionment itself becomes a most potent illusion, and a compelling symbolic narrative is constructed out of utter paranoiac distrust[106] and a competitive, cynical, indeed antisocial relation to the other.[107] Perhaps counterintuitively, the symbolic lie is at the zenith of its power here, where no one needs to believe it. Its effectiveness thus approximates a causal chain, indifferent as it is to subjective interpretation and intentional strivings.

4

HUMAN, NATURE: DIALECTICS OF THE PRIMAL

It is a deep irony of our age that, at a time when there are seemingly no longer any aspects of our natural habitat, the planet, that are uninfluenced by human activity, in this age of the human-centered planet (the Anthropocene), human exceptionality has come under increasing scrutiny, so much so that some declare this to be a posthuman age.[1] Humans, it seems, have become something of a natural, or perhaps unnatural, phenomenon.

The more we are capable of manipulating nature, it seems, the less we are capable of self-control and self-organization, even self-understanding. By the end of the eighteenth century, Kant's philosophical anthropology viewed humans as creatures of two kingdoms: the causally determined kingdom of nature, and the normatively (or purposefully) guided kingdom of freedom or ends.[2] Today the situation is reversed: technological development promises unforeseen interventions in nature, inclusive of our own nature (manipulation of our DNA, life outside the planet), whereas the realm of "second nature," of culture and politics, seems as fixed as Newtonian physics. We can envision and enact technological interventions to suck carbon out of the atmosphere, but seem much less capable of collectively deciding on the right course of action, let alone enacting it, and are at a total loss in the face of social and political problems such as growing inequality and war. Indeed, we seem progressively incapable of seeing any value in our "ethical substance," our form of life.

Everything today is out in the open, there are no more mysteries left, nothing we cannot, in principle, know. We have no illusions anymore, no noble dreams as to human nature. And yet, in the face of this (over)exposure, we seem paralyzed, incapable of collective action. Do we truly know all we claim to know? What kind of knowledge is it that prevents, rather than serves, its own logical conclusion in decisive action?

According to a widespread narrative, while technological advancement supplies us with powerful tools, it robs us of the capacity to apply a nonutilitarian rationale, turning the entire domain of objects, the whole world, into nothing but material for technological manipulation.[3] The more we know how to manipulate nature, the less we are capable of allowing nature to reveal itself to us, something to which we have traditionally responded with our very mode of being, in action, in the very practices that form the dense fabric of a form of life. Disenchanted, we no longer believe there is anything beyond the veil of appearances which we cannot help ourselves to, and thus can no longer sustain the erotic relation to being, on which all transference is dependent. What is missing from this account is the very transference we form with exposure and disillusionment, the erotic appeal of erotic disinvestment from "the natural."

OCCULTATION AND EXPOSURE, BODY AND FLESH: BETWEEN FIRST AND SECOND TECHNOLOGY

Walter Benjamin makes precisely this one of the focal points of his famous essay on the work of art in the age of its mechanical reproduction.[4] Benjamin opens the essay by introducing the significance of speed into a materialist account of history. The base, which Benjamin understands expansively, covering the real-life changes to experience, the labor process in its most wide-reaching sense, everything that goes into the reproduction of society, undergoes intense and rapid transformations under the conditions of capitalism, which the superstructure fails to keep up with. Benjamin's memorable framing of the political significance of this debate on art, the alternative between an aestheticization of politics offered by fascism and the politicization of aesthetics he calls for as a response, can be granted some lucidity here. Technology violently shakes the very foundations of experience, undermining what allows us to experience ourselves as spectators, and thus opens up the basic parameters of the nature-history relation. Fascism responds by taking the basic concepts of aesthetic theory, such as genius, spirit, etc., and applying them directly to the social whole, to politics understood as art's nature. Fascism is therefore, in psychoanalytic terms, a fetishistic response to the newly discovered gap between history and nature. The task taken up by Benjamin, to the contrary, is to granularly study what the transformation in experience implies; what changes to the fundamental categories of aesthetics, broadly construed, it demands.

In the "Work of Art" essay, he distinguishes between what he calls "first" and "second" technology. The two technologies serve to articulate a juxtaposition between what he terms "cult value" and "exhibition" value. Considering that his famous notion of "aura" has to do with a certain inaccessibility, a sense of "distance no matter how close one gets," we might say that "cult" value is the technique of occultation, of hiding from view, and "exhibition" the technique of bringing things into full view. However, since the notion of aura entangles both dimensions—it is the appearance or "shine" of the supersensible in the sensible—it is clear that the polarity here does not imply independence, but rather opposing articulations of the same entanglement.[5] Occultation is one way in which to make something unapproachable, and exhibition is another. As a first approximation, we might say that "cult" as a technique is about drawing distant things near, having a sense of intimacy with the supersensible, whereas "exhibition" is about revealing the distant in what is most near, creating an erotic appeal toward the most common and everyday, by uncovering the minimal distance implied in intimate nearness.

Nearness and distance are articulated by Benjamin early on in a difficult text, "Outline of the Psychophysical Problem." There he seeks to distinguish between two modalities of the mind-body problem. *Leib*, translated as an ensouled or minded body, is a unity of form.[6] *Körper*, corporeal substance, or flesh, has the unity of substance, which has no external limitations.[7] Consider Spinoza's notion of substance, as it was Spinoza who pushed the notion to its logical extreme—if there is truly one substance, it must be the totality as such, something that admits of no exterior and no conditioning. All of its determinations are internal, aspects of its being.

But in what way could we speak of a dimension of our own bodies as "substance"? As a first approximation we might say that while the body is an extensive reality, localizable in experience, flesh is measured in intensity.[8] In this, Benjamin is echoing Kant's discussion of the soul as intensity, as the inner life of the body, which cannot perhaps be quantified but can intensify and wither away.[9] We are here dealing with Benjamin's inheritance of the dramatic confrontation between Spinozistic monism and Kantian transcendentalism which animated German idealism.[10] Benjamin seeks a dimension of experience that internalizes Kant's critique and does justice to the fundamental split of subjectivity, and at the same time does not remain fixated on the historical limitations of the Kantian system, particularly its impoverished notion of experience. And so, as we shall see, in the psychophysical problem Benjamin points to a dimension of our embodied existence that corresponds to the Kantian experience, and one that goes beyond it while grounding it. Benjamin's monism—the unity of being—is split, so to speak, between the transcendental unity of experience (formal unity) and the substance that serves as its ground.

What does it mean to speak of a dimension of the body as limitless? Relying on Eli Friedlander's interpretation, we could say that Benjamin here is expanding on Schopenhauer's distinction between our bodies as objects of perception, the bodies we have, and our bodies from within, which disclose the (noumenal) dimension of the will.[11] In our bodies, or as our bodies, we have an experience of what Kant had described as strictly supraphenomenal, an experience of will as self-directionality. There is an immediate link here between the physical and the normative.

Benjamin too will speak of the flesh as a moral instrument, an "instrument created to fulfill the commandments."[12] But already here we can see that the flesh is not to be confused with the autonomous subject of self-legislation. Benjamin's distinction is analogous to Schopenhauer's insofar as it too seeks a dimension of embodiment that is not an object of perception but its ground. However, his emphasis lies not on the activity of the will (self-grounding) but on the activity of the flesh as a passive medium of sensation, so to speak, the site where the grounding of experience takes place.[13] Corporeal substance, the flesh, Benjamin writes, is polarized by pain and pleasure.[14] It is, if you will, the body of enjoyment: not the body that experiences and is experienced, split, as it were, in two dimensions, but the strange substratum, or ground, of this very split of embodied experience.

In Benjamin's terms, reaching toward corporeal substance corresponds to the philosophical task of transcending the limitations of Kantian experience. The Kantian notion of experience separates experience as object and subject, separating between experience and the knowledge of experience.[15] Benjamin seeks to recover a sense of the prior unity of experience and knowledge of experience, which he thinks is inseparable from expanding Kantian experience beyond the mechanical so as to be able to account for the logical possibility of religious experience.

> The task of the coming philosophy can be conceived as the discovery or creation of that concept of knowledge which, by relating experience *exclusively* to the transcendental consciousness, makes not only mechanical but also religious experience logically possible. This should definitely be taken to mean not that knowledge makes god possible, but that it definitely does make the experience and doctrine of him possible in the first place.[16]

The exclusive relation to transcendental consciousness is to be understood in the context of Benjamin's immediately preceding critique of the identification of transcendental conciseness, the unity of apperception, with the position of the conscious subject. Religious experience should be made possible, conceivable, as a different articulation of the unity of apperception, of what holds together subject and object, which would point upward, as it were, to the very virtuality that holds this strained unity together. But what could knowledge in experience amount to? How and why is it linked with the religious experience?

Let us first note that in speaking about the logical possibility of religious experience Benjamin does not mean something like the truth of revelation, attested to by intoxicated, mystical experience.[17] As is well known, Benjamin opposes the tendency, popular in his time, to value lived experience [Erlebnis] over long experience [Erfahrung]. Far from signaling a unity of life, lived experience is for Benjamin a sign of the utter impoverishment of modern experience, the inability to assign a higher, authoritative context to experience.[18]

Indeed, the decline of experience is tantamount in Benjamin's account of the decline of tradition: modern experience is "shock" experience,[19] in the sense that experiences become isolated in the Freudian sense of the term;[20] they are accumulated but not integrated.[21] As Benjamin confessed to Adorno in a letter: "The roots of my 'theory of experience' can be traced back to a childhood memory. My parents would go on walks with us. . . . After we had visited one or other of the obligatory places around Freudenstadt, . . . my brother used to say, 'Now we can say we've been there.' This remark imprinted itself unforgettably on my mind."[22]

Such is the nature of modern shock-fashioned experience: the experience of the child, Benjamin's brother, is reduced to "saying we've been there." There is no meaning in such a recording of fact. Modern experience is thus utterly chronological—experiences are collected as isolated events, devoid of any inner meaning or particular significance.

Modernity is not the loss of singular, exceptional experiences, but the situation in which such exceptions have become the norm.[23] In a similar vein, Benjamin describes capitalism as a cult in which every day is a "Sunday."[24] For Benjamin, secularization does not stand for the loss of the sacred, or disenchantment, but for the loss of the mechanisms distinguishing the sacred from the profane, mechanisms such as days of worship. Worship, as will become gradually clearer, is a technology of the flesh or corporeal substance. As it loosens its grip we are not liberated from the sacred as much as "overcharged" with it.[25] One can hardly avoid seeing the extent to which this aspect of the modern experience has been accentuated in our contemporary technological environment, where experiences are to be had, it seems, solely in order to record and publish them on social media, so that we can "say we have been there." It is as if experiences are gathered in order to prove to the other that we have had them. The utter profanity of such accumulated experiences is "sacralized" in the incessant drive to accumulate, the desperate attempt to prove they are somehow real. We do not enjoy, profanely, our experiences, but worship their enjoyment.

Along similar lines, Benjamin goes against the tendency to value the ensouled body (Leib) over flesh (Körper). The ensouled body, or the mind-body unity, is what undergoes transformations over historical time.[26] We might say that the variety in such unities of experience corresponds to the historical variety of forms of life. Flesh, on the other hand, is the virtual ground of such changing historical ways of being. It is in our flesh, not our bodies, that we sense we have transgressed unwritten laws. This is not to say that it is simply lifeless, or abstractly eternal, without change. Rather, it is what conditions and is present in experience, while never being an object of perception. Everybody hurts, to quote R.E.M, but hurt leaves different impressions in accordance with the varieties of historical experience.

As mentioned above, corporeal substance, polarized in Benjamin's account by pleasure and pain, is a matter of intensity rather than extension, and as such is in principle limitless; it does not have an external form as its limit. As was explored by philosophers from Schopenhauer[27] to Wittgenstein,[28] pain and pleasure are not strictly speaking objects of experience; it makes no sense to say "I have pain," or even "I feel pain," but rather, "I am in pain." This is why, as Wittgenstein enjoys showing, there is no sense in asking us for evidence or proof of our pain. A distinction arises here between the knowledge we might have in experience, a knowledge identical to experience, and knowledge as separate from experience, a knowledge about experience. Pain is intense not only as a "mute" experience ("it hurts so bad" is what all silent suffering, as well as screams of pain, seem to say), but rather in its relation with language; pain is given expression in infinitely nuanced ways.[29] It is not a matter of proving or attesting to it, but of giving it flesh, so to speak, allowing it to speak for itself in our very modes of expression.

At the same time, pleasure and pain can be said to be virtually present in the background of all sensation and perception: flesh is the "aesthetic body," if you will, the pleasure and pain internal to all perception, giving perception, even thought, orientation.[30] Perception is guided, as it were, by the "traction" with perceived objects, the inner measure of their interest for us as perceived phenomena.[31] Does this capture my attention? Does this speak to me? Pain and pleasure are what invest our very perceptions with the substratum of direct involvement with the world, or the way the world itself is "animated" for us: there is, so to speak, a vital substance to which the enjoyment—the space of pleasure and pain—of the body attests.

Pain and pleasure belong more intimately to our bodies than any other sensation, and yet they are not strictly speaking subjective experiences. If the ensouled body is a desiring body, led by its intentional structure, corporal substance is its drive. We do not have an experience of the drive except by being driven, internally. There is no "I" of the drive, except for what, in the "I," is objectively reflexive ("I am driven"). Enjoyment as a unity of sense and pleasure is a kind of experience of the knowledge of experience, knowing the knowledge to which experience answers from within.[32]

There are two other, interrelated polarities that are to give corporeal substance, or flesh, its inner definition: sex and spirit, nearness and distance.[33] While Benjamin does not fully explicate the manner in which these polarities are to be thought together, we could say that in the highest manifestations of spirit, we draw near what is most distant, without, that is, canceling its distance. Call this the inherently erotic dimension of spiritual life.[34] This would be manifest in Benjamin's inheritance of the Platonic idea, which can only reveal itself through the veil of beauty and can never be an object of intention.[35] To draw near the distant is not simply to revere it, to keep the distance, but to form a relation in which distance is not the empty space between two points; we might say that it depends on creating a vertical relation to the distant, relating to it as what is absolutely "high," and as such, in its inaccessibility, enabling. Distance would be the determination that opens up the space of freedom, the way someone assured his fate has long been determined, written in the stars, is free to live his life out of inner determination or resolution.[36] A relation in which an intimacy with the distant is manifested by inner determination.[37]

By contrast, in the heights of sexual relations, we manage to maintain a distance from what is most near, body to body, without canceling the intimacy, the direct contact between two (or more) bodies. This would attest to the inherent spiritual dimension of sexuality: two bodies can conjoin, cancel all physical distance, without thereby becoming one. If anything might correspond to the notion of "carnal knowledge," it would be this.

What all these polarities have in common is the sense of an inner determination by way of intensification; we have a sense of a high versus low definition, as opposed to the juxtaposition between conceptual definition and amorphous, ill-defined "noise." In the second case, definition is a matter of the unity of form (information), a process that knows maturation and decline (entropy); in the former, definition is a matter of intensity, of the coming together of differences as such, the way in which differentiation is the actualization of substance.

DRIVES ARE OUR MYTHOLOGY: HISTORY, BETWEEN DRIVE AND DESIRE

From what we have sketched out so far, it would seem that the dimension of the flesh cannot be subject to historical change. And yet Benjamin sets up his discussion of the radical transformations of aesthetic experience attested to by the emergence of the cinema, the decline of the aura, and other such well-known themes in terms of the very polarity with which he had opened up the dimension of the flesh, the polarity of distance and nearness, conjoined in the notion of aura.[38] Can flesh, corporeal substance, have a history? Can it be subject to change? Whereas the body is the subject of historical transformation, flesh is understood as its prehistory, the substratum from which bodily existence arises, so to speak. In its continuous presence, it is comparable to the libidinally charged body of the "polymorphously perverse" baby, which the organized body never fully leaves behind. Can the corporeal substance of the drive be, in some way, subject to history? To speak of historical transformation in our experience of the flesh would be to speak of the historical alterations in relation to myth. Flesh is the embodied reality of myth; body, in its very distinctness, is that which always already emerges out of its mythical ground. Can we speak of a historical dialectics between (Spinozist) substance and (Kantian) subject? This would be, very precisely, to introduce, in a rich and productive way, Hegel's "subject is substance," namely, the radical split that makes substance lose its "eternal," inner identity to itself.

Benjamin articulates his philosophy of history by drawing directly on the uneven way in which pain and pleasure are entangled. While he speaks of pain and pleasure as polarities, there is no symmetry between them: pain is far more expressive, demanding, and exacting a far wider range of articulation, whereas pleasure, in its expressionlessness, is not of this world, a "premonition from another world."[39] Pain is experienced as continuous, chronic, whereas pleasure is kairotic, occasional and fleeting. It is as if pain is what gives a sense of the substratum as something continuous, unrelenting, whereas pleasure punctuates it as an interval, a momentary relief, thereby only augmenting pain's predominance. This is later echoed in Benjamin's vision of happiness as a philosophical-historical category.

> "It is one of the most noteworthy peculiarities of the human heart," writes Lotze, "that so much selfishness in individuals coexists with the general lack of envy which every present day feels towards its future." This observation indicates that the image of happiness we cherish is thoroughly colored by the time to which the course of our existence has assigned us. There is happiness—such as could arouse envy in us—only in the air we have breathed, among people we could have talked to, women who could have given themselves to us. In other words, the idea of happiness is indissolubly bound up with the idea of redemption.[40]

This is the idea of the past which, according to Benjamin, concerns the historical materialist; the "weak messianic power" of the past, the manner in which the past as such is a missed opportunity, is what addresses us.[41] This is also why the relation between body and flesh is a relation between two different temporalities, more than merely echoing Benjamin's *Theological-Political Fragment*.[42] In that fragment, Benjamin speaks of the way in which human intentional strivings, the search for happiness, are an ultimately destructive process, and as such messianic, pointing to another dimension that realizes itself through such strivings.

> The body, the function of the historical present in man, expands into the body of mankind. "Individuality" as the principle of the body is on a higher plane than that of single embodied individuals. Humanity as an individual is both the consummation and the annihilation of bodily life. "Annihilation" because with it the historical existence, whose function the body is, reaches its end. In addition to the totality of all its living members, humanity is able partly to draw nature, the nonliving, plant, and animal, into this life of the body of mankind, and thereby into this annihilation and fulfillment. It can

do this by virtue of the technology in which the unity of its life is formed. Ultimately, everything that subserves humanity's happiness may be counted part of its life, its limbs. Bodily nature advances towards its dissolution; that of corporeal substance, however, advances towards its resurrection.[43]

For Benjamin flesh is to be resurrected, which is opposed to the continuous dissolution of historical forms of life into the general, universal of humanity. We might say that the catastrophic aspect of history, the great surplus of pain over pleasure, defined by Benjamin, precisely, as the experience of a missed opportunity,[44] has to do with pleasure being that aspect of the flesh that can only be resurrected: what we can experience only as a missed opportunity, unrealized. This pressure of the unrealized encapsulates the relation between pain and pleasure: there is infinite pain because pleasure is forever elusive, unrealized. And so, in this polarity of pain and pleasure, we can speak of the dialectics of drive and desire: it is because pleasure is, as it were, of another world—a premonition of happiness, the restoration of a primordially lost unity of life—that pain seems to be its "deviant" instrument. There is something that is realized through the tragic, failed pursuit of human happiness. As we approach the question of a historical dimension of the flesh, the dialectics of the primal, we will witness a strange transformation in the status and experience of the primal. We shall have to see, that is, what happens as we realize that "substance is subject,"[45] what happens to substance as history pursues its destructive path.

With this in mind, let us return to Benjamin's famous essay on the work of art and the account given there of first and second technologies. Benjamin describes the two technologies as two poles of the dialectics of technology. First technology is a technology suited for

> the requirements of a society whose technology existed only in fusion with ritual. Compared to that of the machine age, of course, this technology was undeveloped. But from a dialectical standpoint, the disparity is unimportant. What matters is the way the orientation and aims of that technology differ from those of ours. Whereas the former made the maximum possible use of human beings, the latter reduces their use to the minimum. The achievements of the first technology might be said to culminate in human sacrifice; those of the second, in the remote-controlled aircraft which needs no human crew. The results of the first technology are valid once and for all (it deals with irreparable lapse or sacrificial death, which holds good for eternity). The results of the second are wholly provisional (it operates by means of experiments and endlessly varied test procedures). The origin of the second technology lies at the point where, by an unconscious ruse, human beings first began to distance themselves from nature.[46]

Art representative of the first technology would be that of cave paintings, which Benjamin believes had to have been part of a ritualistic, magical context, pertaining to humans and their environment, but one in which a mimetic embodied relation was made present:

> We should ask whether the earliest mimesis of objects through dance and sculpture was not largely based on imitation of the performances through which primitive man established relations with these objects. Perhaps stone age man produced such incomparable drawings of the elk only because the hand guiding the implement still remembered the bow with which it had felled the beast.[47]

The prime artistic example of the second technology is for Benjamin the images of deserted human landscapes, specifically Atget's photographs of deserted Paris streets.[48] With this we have manufactured the impossible gaze that Schelling had attributed to Spinoza's mechanistic picture of reality. For Schelling, the gaze of a world devoid of subjective agency, thoroughly mechanistically determined, was tantamount to a transference of subjectivity to a dead gaze.[49] It implied that we cannot get rid of subjectivity so easily, as some Spinozists might assume. It might be hard, but humanity seems determined to make it possible.

In the "Work of Art" essay, Benjamin aims to show that there is a productivity to the very destructive, radically transformative intervention of technology in experience. The work of art is productive to the extent that it allows a kind of working-through of such far-reaching transformations. Cinema, on Benjamin's reading, trains humanity for the new requirements of shock experience, teaching us to perceive via distraction, in the manner of city dwellers. It opens up the possibility of adapting to a world that can no longer be experienced with the critical distance of spectators, an experience of continuous, disruptive change that assaults and jumps at us, so to speak. It helps close the gap opened up by rapid material changes in the very framework of experience, adjusting our lagging understanding to the demands of these changes. Fascism, on the contrary, takes up destruction itself, the very annihilation of humanity, as a supreme aesthetic object, which we may enjoy as spectators. It violently imposes modes of understanding rendered impotent to face the transformations in experience, believing itself thus capable of taming the forces of change, positioning us as authors and consumers of destruction. In fascism sacrifice no longer proves the extreme use value of humans, associated with cult value, as gifts appeasing the gods, but becomes an aesthetic spectacle, the ultimate work of art. Atget's pictures, melancholic as they might be, show the product of human technological work as surroundings that might survive their creators. This is the most accentuated point of exhibition value. Fascism covers over this profound melancholy by "filling in" the absence of humans that haunts Atget's pictures, making visible, and perversely enjoyable, the very violent disappearance of humanity. Fascism's celebration of visions of destruction, which Benjamin attends to at the end of his essay, is the (re)occultation of exhibition value, covering over the inherently destructive aspect of human productive work, construction, by presenting front and center destruction as a supreme work of art. In its celebration of the most horrific expression of technology, modern war, fascism covers up the destructive if potentially emancipatory nature of technology in general, in its very constructive function. The ambiguity of the word "work," pointing both to the process of labor or production and to the finished product, here comes to a head.[50] Fascism presents the negative workings of art in the broad sense, *techne*, as the ultimate product, or creation, and celebrates its own genius or talent for it. Even annihilation can be presented via the semblance of the beautiful, of the completed, singular thing, a work of art, expressive of creative genius. To oppose this, Benjamin seems to believe it necessary to point to the "negativity" at work even in the most mundane and constructive technical processes, and to point to the unrealized potentials this negativity uncovers. This is where the distinction, and the relation, between first and second technology become central.

What are we to make of this distinction between the two technologies? How do they relate to one another? As Benjamin remarks, "to describe the goal of the second technology as 'mastery over nature' is highly questionable, since this implies viewing the second technology from the standpoint of the first. The first technology really sought to master nature, whereas the second aims rather at an interplay between nature and humanity."[51] This is a crucial distinction, which seems to stand in stark contrast with the way our relationship with technology is often portrayed. From the Frankfurt school's notion of utilitarianism to Heidegger's critique of technology as a mode of disclosure of being as standing in reserve,[52] we tend to take for granted that it is modern technology that enters into a relation of mastery over nature, whereas the further we go into the past we find humans living more harmoniously with nature. In the face of the devastating powers of nature to which, with their relatively feeble technologies, they were much more exposed than we are, ancient humans were inclined to converse with their surroundings. Not only was their technical intervention in nature much less consequential than our own, but their fundamental attitude toward "greater powers" was one of reverence. They sacrificed and entered into a symbolic-economic exchange with their deities, trying to appease them.

What could it mean to argue that it was their ritual-infused technology that aimed at the mastery of nature? This question is of the highest significance, for Benjamin suggests that it is the remnants of that first, primal technology in our modern technologies that prevents us from even understanding its *differentia specifica*. The misperception of our technology is double: we think ours is a technology built for the mastery of nature, which shows that we do not understand what mastery of nature entails, nor the ways in which our technology is ill-suited for it. The idea of freedom opened up by second technology is veiled behind this very misperception.

MAKING SENSE COMMON: PRIMAL TECHNOLOGY, PRIMAL PHENOMENA, PRIMAL CONCEPTS

Let us proceed by asking: in what sense does the first technology master nature? The first thing to note is what "first," or primal, stands for. First technology is not merely archaic but an archaic—or primordial—mode of relating to the archaic, to the primordial as such. In asking about the dialectics of first and second technology, we are dealing with the difficult question of the dialectics of the dialectical—that which admits of development and change— and the nondialectical, or the primal. That is, we shall have to lay out the foundations necessary in order to bring out the question of what in our relation to the primal admits of change, and has changed, and what remains unchanged, as the very substance of historical transformation.

Before we discuss first or primal technology, let us very briefly lay out the relation between the "mythical" and the primal. Philosophies of myth, from Schelling to Cassirer and Wittgenstein, are a special case in which philosophy is trying to think its primordial other. For one of the self-grounding myths of the philosophical tradition is the break with mythology: philosophy, even in its initial, proto-scientific and pre-Socratic phase, is distinguished from myth in attempting to offer rational, conceptual accounts where myths present us with stories and striking images.

The more sophisticated of these philosophical accounts see myth as responding to something that conceptual probing structurally misses. Myth is primal not only in the sense that it is older than philosophy, but in that what it responds to, what it gives expression to, is primal experience. For Cassirer, for example, myth is about the very emergence of phenomena as significant.

> Not the what but the how is decisive here; it comes not from the nature
> of the noticed but from the nature of the noticing. . . . The spiritual crisis
> through which the sacred emerges out of the profane, through which the
> outstanding emerges out of the sphere of the equally valid. . . . The object
> of religious consciousness is, so to speak, first constituted in this process of
> separation.[53]

Myth records, as it were, the emergence of significance. It is an experience of saliency as such. In psychoanalytic terms, this would correspond to symbolic castration, the dramatic or affective aspect of being split in and by language.

Commenting on Max Müller's explanation of myth as the result of the "basic lack, or weakness of language,"[54] attested to by the similar-sounding names, or homonyms, which affect a semblance of similarity where no serious conceptual link could be established (such as the relation, in Greek, between people and stone: λαοι and λᾶας), Cassirer points to the failure of such a critical perspective to account for the necessity and insistence of such a semblance, this "shadow" of meaning. What Lacan would call lalangue, language as a mode of enjoyment,[55] the nonsemantic dimension of language, those seemingly contingent, material resemblances, such as homonyms, might have no significance as objects of knowledge, but they do speak to a certain substantial communion of experience in language, expressed in myth. The homonym, we might say, expresses a kind of kinship, or affinity, that is preconceptual, the significance of which conceptual probing makes hard to see.

In a similar vein, Wittgenstein addresses the famed cobelonging of ritual and myth. For Wittgenstein, it is precisely what seems most superfluous about rituals that grants access to their intelligibility. Ceremonies have "an affective addition that a mere theatrical performance does not have. . . . Even if it merely were a rather cool performance, would we not anxiously ask ourselves: what is this performance aiming at, what is its meaning? And apart from any interpretation, its strange pointlessness could unsettle us (which shows what the reason behind such uneasiness can be)."[56]

It is this unsettling "pointlessness" that ceremonies share with the phenomena they correspond to. Reflecting on Frazer's *The Golden Bough*, Wittgenstein is angered with Frazer's fundamental misunderstanding of his subject matter—the form of life of "primitive people," organized around myth and ritual—which lies in his attribution of a developmental, but more broadly an explanatory scheme. For magic is immediate; it has to do with the way in which things come to stand in a relation that is not further analyzable.[57] Frazer's mistake lies in presenting the primitive as "mistaken." Primitive people are perceived, by the anthropological gaze, as holding a set of beliefs we couldn't possibly hold, which their ceremonies express. What Wittgenstein aims to tease out in his critical reading of Frazer is a very different sense of the primal, much closer to what occupies us here.

What is the status of knowledge that is expressed in ceremony? In Lacanian terms, it is a knowledge that is strictly speaking impossible—jouissance. Jouissance, which Lacan explains is at once necessary and impossible, is the conjoining of sense and enjoyment—the impossible understanding of enjoyment, and the enjoyment of the impossibility of understanding. It is where knowledge, which is inherently intentional, and that which defies all intention, enjoyment, are coarticulated. What is at stake in ceremonies, we could say, is corporeal substance, or the flesh: a dimension of embodied existence in which the ground of experience is made present.

While his language is quite different, it is precisely this that drives Wittgenstein's frustration with Frazer's account of myth:

When Frazer begins by telling us the story of the king of the woods at Nemi, he does so in a tone that shows that something strange and terrible is happening here. However, the question "why is this happening?" is essentially answered by just this [mode of exposition]: because it is terrible. In other words, it is what appears to us as terrible, impressive, horrible, tragic, etc. that gave birth to this event [or process]. One can only resort to description here and say: such is human life. Every explanation is a hypothesis. But someone who, for example, is unsettled by love will be ill-assisted by a hypothetical explanation. It won't calm him or her.[58]

What Frazer misses in his account is precisely the significance of the "libidinal charge," the intensity of the experience at stake. Wittgenstein rightly seeks to close the gap between himself and the "primitive." The "primitive" is precisely what we share with those who fascinate us, not what distinguishes us from them: "when I, who do not believe that there exist, anywhere, human-superhuman beings whom one can call gods—when I say 'I fear the wrath of the gods,' then this shows that I can mean something with this [utterance], or can express a sentiment that is not necessarily connected with such belief."[59]

What we are to distinguish is not between more developed and less developed human beings, but between different levels of approaching phenomena, which are common to human beings as such. Both the "primitive" and the modern have access to mechanical explanations and utilitarian tool manipulation: "The same savage who, apparently in order to kill his enemy, pierces an image of him, really builds his hut out of wood, and carves his arrow skillfully and not in effigy."[60] And both have access to quite another dimension, in which what matters is not causal relations, the way one thing works on another, but the medium of relations, which allows for much looser, even elusive relations:

That a human shadow, which looks like a human being, or one's mirror image, that rain, thunderstorms, the phases of the moon, the change of season, the likeness or difference of animals to one another and to human beings, the phenomenon of death, of birth, and of sexual life, in short, everything that a human being senses around himself, year in, year out, in manifold mutual connection—that all this should play a role in the thought of human beings (their philosophy) and their practices is self-evident; or, in other words, it is what we really know and find interesting.[61]

Ceremonial behavior cannot be explained by underlying beliefs because what ceremonial behavior responds to is the very "saliency" of phenomena, their "signifierness," to borrow Lacan's expression. It is not that the primitive is mystified by what for us is well explained by scientific reasoning. The "lawfulness of the contingent," the non-causally-efficient way in which things seem to belong together, is simply not explained away by evoking contingency.[62] Saliency, what jumps to the foreground, what strikes us as significant, is clearly not an objective property of a phenomenon, nor is it merely a subjective preference, an arbitrary choice. It is the emergence of something that strikes a subject as objectively significant, something "involving," which is to say, something with which we are primordially involved.

> No phenomenon is particularly mysterious in itself, but any of them can become so to us, and it is precisely the characteristic feature of the awakening human mind that a phenomenon acquires significance for it. One could almost say that man is a ceremonial animal. This is probably partly false, partly nonsensical, but there is also some truth to it.[63]

The issue, Wittgenstein notes, is not what "sticks out," which phenomena come to assume significance, but the very fact of their "sticking out," the fact of significance as such:

> It could have been no insignificant reason—that is, no *reason* at all—for which certain races of man came to venerate the oak tree other than that they and the oak were united in a community of life, so that they came into being not by choice, but jointly, like the dog and the flea (were fleas to develop a ritual, it would relate to the dog).
> One might say, it was not their union (of oak trees and humans) that occasioned these rites, but, in a certain sense, their separation.
> For the awakening of intellect goes along with the separation from the original *soil*, the original ground of life. (The origin of *choice*.) (The form of the awakening mind is veneration.)[64]

What Wittgenstein is offering here is a theory of the technology involved in ritual "fetish," which should more properly speaking be termed "symbolic technology." In venerating, say, an oak tree, which we usually take to be a fetish, taking an object to stand for the totality, what is established is the underlying substance shared by the object and the subject; in their very separation, or distinctness, they come to express a higher unity or a common ground, thereby forming a symbolic unity, the unity of the sensible and the supersensible.

We should be very precise as to the "fetishist" aspect here. Recall how for Freud, the phantasy "a child is being beaten" was used to articulate the perverse dimension of neurotic phantasy.[65] "Perversion" here stands for the very fixation on a scene of phantasmatic indeterminacy, the "free-floating" subjectivity that holds the scenario together by making the subject position indeterminate. Am I the child being beaten, the father doing the beating, watching from outside? Perverse here is the very "elevation" of the ground of existence, the forever-lost unity of subject and object, over the cause, what allows existence to emerge from its ground—the very split that constitutes subjectivity.[66] The ritualistic scene does not so much represent as recreate, again and again, the impossible: a common ground.

This is why Benjamin, as we shall see shortly, will emphasize the mimetic dimension of ritual. In entering a mimetic relation, we rely on a shared corporeal substance between the object and the subject of imitation. They are of the same flesh, and their relationship is, precisely, an object of "fleshing out," an identity that is articulated by means of differentiation.

Significantly, such a common ground, a sense of the common, is sustained by ritualistic behavior. Once again we encounter the sense of the primal as the mythical encounter with ground. Somehow we find ourselves in a relation of belonging to something from which we are separated. "Magic" is nothing but the nonconceptual way in which things belong together in no perceivable order, their being related in a way that is immediate and cannot be "captured" by a rule.[67]

Such a relation between objects of experience ultimately points to the strange "nonrelation" between the subject and his world, at once facing the world as if from without and not being able to extricate herself from it. Connection and separation are uncannily equiprimordial in our experience. Symbolic, ritual technology is a solidifying repetition of this very same, tense constellation.

However, development does not really do away with the primal. Take the problematic notion of "instinct" for example. There is no problem in principle in explaining how what we take to be instinctual behavior has evolved. It's just that such explanations precisely miss the "primal" as an experience. To feel oneself driven by instinct—or drive, for in this context they are truly one and the same—is to find oneself acting on a basis of a knowledge that is not one's own, following a path one has not set for herself. While in some contexts the question of whether that knowledge can or cannot develop "naturally" is of crucial importance, from the perspective of the subject driven that question is insignificant. The subject acting on instinct is acting on grounds which are, for her, absolute—fated. Finding causal mechanisms that might account for it, grounds for it having come to be, is not the same as finding grounds for it being that subject's ground. What we are after is what, nonetheless, can be said to have changed in our relation to ground, with the separation of technology from ritual.

For Gilbert Simondon, magic is a primal phase of being before the bifurcation into two modes of intelligibility: religion, which seeks a "ground," a totality beyond the multiplicity of phenomena, and technicity, an intelligibility which seeks "figures," what is detachable from ground, what can be separated and recombined.[68] This story is already complicated by noting how "magic" itself, the holding together of figure and ground, is not only a primal phenomenon, or primal experience, but also a kind of primal technique. A technique of the flesh, that is, as opposed to techniques of the body; a technique that intensifies ground, rather than differentiates objects. Ritual is a technique of the mythical, the dramatic holding together of the very distinction between figure and ground, the emergence of the tense bond of significance. There is a technique that precedes the bifurcation between religion and technicity, and indeed resists it. The realm preserved by Simondon, for the primal "balance" between technicity and religion, or magic, the realm of aesthetics, is therefore not simply "the permanent reminder of the rupture of unity of the magical mode of being, as well as a reminder of the search for its future unity,"[69] but the very function of primal technology. It is a "worlding" technology, "magical" in the precise sense of endowing a sense of mysterious wholeness to experience.

What is the difference, then, between technology fused with ritual and technology separated from it? How can such a difference even emerge? For Wittgenstein, explanations are one way to respond to what is striking in phenomena, their "secret law" and ceremonies another.[70]

The ceremonial, we might say, resembles that to which it responds. But that would be misleading, thinking of ceremonial expression as a secondary reaction to some even more primitive impression. There is something of the instinctual in ceremonial behavior:

> When I am angry about something, I sometimes hit the ground or a tree with my cane. But surely, I do not believe that the ground is at fault or that the hitting would help matters. "I vent my anger." And all rites are of this kind. One can call such practices instinctual behavior. And a historical explanation, for instance that I or my ancestors earlier believed that hitting the ground would help, is mere shadow-boxing, for these are superfluous assumptions that explain nothing. What is important is the semblance of the practice to an act of punishment, but more than this semblance cannot be stated.[71]

What does it mean to describe ceremonies, or hitting the ground for that matter, as "instinctual behavior"? "Instinct" should be taken here to mean "primal." It is precisely in being faced with what is just so, what is, in the relevant context, grounding and ungrounded, a primitive condition, that we respond with the production of something equally grounding and ungrounded, with ritual and symbolism. This is what gives symbolism its old sense, of conjoining the sensible and the supersensible. Faced with the mystery of that which conditions us, we produce signs and practices that are, for us, mysterious. In this way, we begin to see, primal technology is "naturalizing" in a very specific sense: it produces the human form of life as an imitation of the supersensible, of which natural phenomena are themselves a copy. Only then will we be able to inquire after the historical break between symbolic, primal technology and technology as we now understand it. Only then will we be able to ask about the ways in which symbolic technology persists and the ways in which its objects reemerge.

THESE THINGS ARE NOT THE SAME: DOCTRINE OF THE SIMILAR

In a series of connected essays, Benjamin develops a "Doctrine of the Similar."[72] The category of similarity he employs is not to be confused with analogy. It points to an experience, in part mundane, with the invisible, as its zenith lies in what he calls "nonsensuous similarity." Situating Benjamin's notion of the similar in its genealogical context of Goethe's "affinities," Eli Friedlander explains:

> For Goethe, similarity is based on the idea of a space of variations ruled by metamorphosis. Such a space of similarity would be characterized as the variation of a primal type that is not itself given in experience. Thus, in so far as two cases can be placed in the space of variations necessary to present the primal type, one could speak of an affinity between them by way of the relation of each to the archetype without referring to any shared phenomenal properties. With Goethe, we have then an understanding of similarity that assumes no presentable common element but relies on the unity of surroundings of living forms.[73]

Similarity points toward a virtual archetype, which is nothing but the relationship between those particulars. As Friedlander demonstrates, Wittgenstein's famous notion of family resemblance also belongs to the same intellectual lineage. Similar things "partake" in the archetype or idea, they are not subsumed in it as particular instantiations of a concept. We project a virtual, invisible archetype when we recognize similarities, which is also to say that it is only manifest in the relationship, just as the resemblance between family members is mediated via such a virtual archetype. The mythical Ur-father, we could say, is a warped stand-in for this inherently virtual archetype, translating what is impossible to represent—the idea as nothing but the holding together of its manifold manifestations—to the unlawful, the absolutely forbidden.

For Benjamin, the mundane, everyday experience of similarity is but an echo of the more profound, unconscious one, which we encounter in the dream or in daydreaming: "The similarity of thing to another which we are used to, which occupies us in a wakeful state, reflects only vaguely the deeper similarity of the dream world in which everything that happens appears not in identical but in similar guise, opaquely similar to itself."[74] That is, the "similar" in its purity is the similarity between a thing and itself, the uncanny, minimal difference at the heart of identity. And so, for Benjamin, ritual activity was (and is) a way to respond to the similarity one encounters by producing one's own. "We must assume in principle that in the remote past the processes considered imitable included those in the sky. In dance, on other cultic occasions, such imitation could be produced, such similarity dealt with."[75]

To imitate, and it is crucial for Benjamin that the span of objects imitated was once much broader, encompassing even such things as constellations, is to produce a similarity from within one's body.[76] In this we take our bodies to be primordially similar to the objects of imitation, namely, we take the objects and our bodies to be "folds" or intensive articulations of one and the same primal substance. That substance gets its articulation from within, so to speak; it is not a matter of imposing form on an external material, but a substance that gets articulated the more it is differentiated and "fleshed out." Hence its "normative" pressure—resemblance demands articulation by means of intensification; it is a bond to be repeatedly consecrated.[77]

This is symbolic activity in the old, contractual sense, of matching one's own broken piece to another. We could say that in imitating behavior we are behaving as if we were letters, which in their relation to other letters form a script. In "first technology," our "second nature," the form of life in its sacred activity, forms a bond with primal nature. Here we respond to what Lacan would call the "signifierness" of nature with a "signifierness" of our own.

With this, nature is "mastered," in the sense that the social system is itself "naturalized" and "enlivened." The performance of symbolic activities that have no ultimate ground or reason is a way to avoid the ideological closure of a life form, to avoid an overfamiliarity or stiffening habituation. These are "excessive" habits, which serve to create a culturally productive self-alienation. In their excessiveness they resist total habituation, a totally smooth and transparent functioning.

> Far from being an obstacle to the living experience of meaning, the
> presence of such "enigmatic signifiers," which emanate unknown meaning,
> i.e., this very obstacle to a full transparency of meaning, is what makes a
> given symbolic space truly alive, engaged in a passionate struggle to unearth
> meaning and is the ultimate source of its vitality.[78]

The excess of ceremonial behavior, that which cannot be translated into protoethical or protoscientific maxims and rules, had been seen by social theorists as what "sacralized" the past.[79] By producing "hieroglyphs," in the Hegelian sense, i.e., signs that are mysteries for their "users," what is produced is culture itself, a surplus to be handed down from one generation to another. For Benjamin, the production and decipherment of such "texts" was to be seen as the most primal, preceding the creation of actual hieroglyphs.

> "To read what was never written" Such reading is the most ancient: reading prior to all languages, from entrails, the stars, or dances. Later the mediating link of a new kind of reading, of runes or hieroglyphs, came into use. It seems fair to suppose that these were the stages by which the mimetic gift, formerly the foundation of occult practices, gained admittance to writing and language. In this way, language may be seen as the highest level of mimetic behavior and the most completed archive of nonsensuous similarity: a medium into which the earlier powers of mimetic production and comprehension have passed without residue, to the point where they have liquidated those of magic.[80]

This is the sense in which "primal technology" is traditional technology. It is by producing a symbolic excess that a society renders itself an object of tradition, a treasure to be handed down, with great care and discretion, from one generation to another. Hegel's famous quote, according to which the hieroglyphs were a mystery for the Egyptians themselves, means nothing but this: it is in producing signifiers without signifieds, an excess of significance, that society produces itself as a mystery to be handed down, as an object worthy of imitation. This is the "function" of culture. As Thorstein Veblen saw it, it is the ceremonial, superfluous aspect of custom that makes it a valuable treasure. What happens, then, as ritual experience diminishes? What happens when the grounding technologies of the flesh lose their hold? We know Freud's answer: as religion subsides as a public, communal experience, what we get are the "private religions," like the ceremonies of the obsessive.[81] But how can such a hold even truly loosen its grip?

WRITING THE UNWRITTEN: CLASTRE, VEBLEN, AND THE RUSE OF SECOND TECHNOLOGY

It is important to distinguish in the clearest of terms our discussion of first and second technology from the recent, revived popular interest in "ancient technologies." In recent years, prehistory has made a major comeback, grabbing the attention of scholars and the lay public alike. In particular, the notion that there have been advanced civilizations in the distant past has gained a lot of attention. Figures like Graham Hancock have become internet sensations, claiming to have accumulated evidence for the existence of a bygone civilization, lost to the historical record, in part because of the "magically" infused technology utilized by it. From the perspective we are advancing here, it would seem that this fascination is intrinsically misguided; yes, it could well be that there have been technologically advanced civilizations in the ancient past, only that would not speak to the very primal nature of ritual-infused technology. What is it that has kept those civilizations from developing script and written history? What, more fundamentally, had kept their form of life emphatically unwritten?

Even the more academically respectable version of this fascination, Graber and Wengrow's ambitious *The Dawn of Everything* (2021), seems to go astray precisely around this topic. Relying on accumulated evidence in anthropology and archaeology which seems to undermine some well-entrenched notions regarding the process of civilization—such as the findings in Göbekli Tepe, with their impressive archaeological accomplishments which predate the agricultural revolution—the authors set out to challenge a major narrative of civilization, according to which hierarchy, increasing inequality, and state power with its mechanisms of enforcement are the price we have to pay for technological advancement.

To counter this, Wengrow and Graeber put forward a hypothesis according to which the majority of human history had in fact allowed for a flexible transition between the modes of organization required for large-scale cooperation, which do entail some hierarchic structure and the issuing and following of commands, and the laxer and more dispersed, spontaneously anarchic form of organization that does not call for such modes of dominance. We have not evolved from small, "spontaneously" communistic bands of hunter gatherers to the complex civilization in which we find ourselves today, but got "stuck," forgetting how to transition between one form of life to another.[82] Seductive as this countermyth might be, it completely fails even to raise the issue of what permitted our ancient forefathers to hold on to their mythic flexibility. What was the technique that allowed them to refrain from getting "stuck" for so long, keeping themselves from falling into the path leading to complex hierarchies and interdependence?

Graeber and Wengrow's partial reliance on Pierre Clastre is telling: The authors wish to inherit Clastre's vision of "society against the state," namely, the idea that ancient humans had at their disposal ways of life that did not succumb to the path leading from society to the state, from communal life to the machinery of the state; but they reject Clastre's most interesting suggestion, that such societies in some sense actively work against the trajectory leading toward the state.[83]

While this is indeed a strange notion, seemingly suggesting that primitive life had a premonition of things to come, it is a crucial and valuable one. Clastre's interpretation of "primitive" torture as the violent, initiating inscription of equality on the bodies of members of the group is indeed an account of a technology of tradition, or tradition as technology. According to Clastre, picking up a question raised by Nietzsche in his *Genealogy of Morals*, the way in which torture creates a bond lasting in time is not to be understood simply as a form of memorization. Rituals of initiation, in exposing all members *equally* to extreme pain, inscribe in their bodies a primal equality, one resistant to the envious, comparative gaze that drives the problematic process of civilization, the path to the internalization of moral inhibitions and the outsourcing of enforcement to mechanisms such as the state.[84] Clastre, we might say, is raising the complementary question to Rousseau's: What are the origins of equality? How is equality, in its most fundamental sense of equally belonging to a group, produced and maintained?

In this, Clastre shares Freud's sensibilities: the law at its most minimal deserves the name "symbolic castration" precisely in its equalizing function: each member of the group accepts limitations on his enjoyment, as long as those limitations apply to others as well. Such equalization is sustained as long as there is a big other in relation to whom envy is irrelevant. Simply renouncing enjoyment does not do the trick: the sacrifice has to be accepted by a superior being.[85] This lends support to Hocart's hypothesis, according to which symbolic kings—gods, figures of the big other—long predated actual, empirical structures of hierarchy between people. Kings were objects of ritual long before they were incarnated in human flesh.[86]

Clastre's argument only makes sense against the notion of a primal technology that is retarding by its very nature. It channels the desire for differentiation and individuation inward, so to speak: you shall distinguish yourself by becoming an outstanding member of the group, giving more and more definition to our shared, communal substance. The inscription on each individual body can only be understood as the imprinting of separate letters, so to speak, which together are to form a unified substance and a unified text, a situation in which individual difference is an expression and intensification of the group's spiritual body. We can allow you your differences, under egalitarian conditions, because they are ours, they are the very substance of the social bond.[87] We might say that in primitive society, as interpreted by Clastre, we use our bodies to ingrain a collective flesh, whereas, in modern societies, we use our flesh to create a collective, artificial body.

The dismissal of Clastre's most compelling theoretical point inevitably leads to the greatest weakness of The Dawn of Everything, a book explicitly intended to reignite our political imagination. The authors claim to open history to the varieties of experience, but they assume a transhistorical, embarrassingly liberal subject as their frame of reference. Up until modernity, the authors claim, the default of society has been democratic, consensus-building processes. The evidence? The historical record shows that when civilized Europeans uproot their lives and "go native," they tend to stay there, preferring the new settings, whereas when indigenous people are uprooted, they never quite adjust to modern life, and often choose to go back where they came from.[88] The authors choose to interpret this as compelling evidence for the natural freedom of society: given the choice, we all prefer the older ways of life. Somehow, we have always been liberal subjects, free to choose; it is only we moderns who seem to live in chains, in societies we would prefer to alter. In this, Graeber and Wengrow join a trend of intellectual activity from which the dialectics of modernity have vaporized. Is it not obvious that, for better or for worse, what is shown here is the "naturalizing" power of traditional society? Sure, we all long to live a life that is more "natural," only moderns have become removed enough from it that they can actively see the matter as an alternative. The ability of moderns to drop their ways of life and adopt others is the one good thing about modernity, without which the project of their book, to imagine an alternative way of life, would be unthinkable.

The rehabilitation in recent anthropological literature of the long-discredited notion of animism can also be understood in this light. As Philippe Descola argues, one could sharply contrast the modern and primitive outlooks of the mind/body relation as opposite ways of accounting for that primal question of myth, the nature/culture division, two opposite ways of "worlding," as he puts it.[89]

If the modern assumption is that what we share with other natural beings is our bodies, and what distinguishes us from other natural beings is our minds or our souls, the "animistic" outlook considers what is common to us and other natural beings to be spirit or a spiritual substance, and what distinguish us are our bodies. In light of Benjamin's distinction between ensouled body (*Leib*) and corporeal substance (*Körper*), we could say that the modern outlook is one in which *Leib* is predominant, whereas in animistic "worlding" it is the other way around: we share a spiritual body, or a substance, we are of one flesh, and the more defined in our bodies, the more definition the substance as a whole attains (world soul). The spirit world is threatening precisely because it is bodiless—amorphous. Let us note as an aside that for Arendt, therein lies Plato's consequential "revaluation of values." In his myth of the cave, Plato reverses this relation: the shadowy realm of the underworld comes to stand for the realm of appearances, life in the cave, beyond which lies the supreme reality of light, the ideas. Arendt, therefore, locates in Plato's myth the precise moment in which philosophy overtook myth, so to speak.[90]

For Viveiros de Castro, in an animistic mindset what matters is the distinction between prey and hunter. As I may be prey to the tiger, I can also be the hunter. This is the basis for his case for a strong, ontological perspectivism, in which we can very well adopt other perspectives, or view them from "within." For all viewpoints are thus polarized, all beings divide the world between their prey and their hunters. In this way, a world can be created with multiple perspectives, which we can take up and reconstruct.[91] It is, we might say, one possible guideline for imitation. What allows for communion with other minds here, with the minds of animals, is precisely the reduction of viewpoint to the gaze of the hunter, an eye, if you will, that is in service of the mouth, orally driven.

Freud's memorable critique of the oceanic feeling, the sense of being connected to everything else, is venerated: the phantasy of being engulfed by being is in truth the phantasy of "swallowing" it whole.[92] At the same time, we get a sense of the dense reality of such an organizing fantasy, no less real than our own.

Taking the notion of "naturalizing" or "worlding" technologies, technologies of tradition, seriously, in fact, raises the opposite conundrum: not how there could be symbolic techniques, responsible, perhaps, for the great advantage of the unwritten (prehistoric, mythical) over the written (in both historical and structural terms: the long period of human prehistory in comparison with history, and the unshakable presence, within history, of the prehistoric), but rather, what it is that could have loosened the grip of the primal. What allowed our technological civilization to arise? Neither simplistic materialist nor "culturalist" accounts are here easily available, for what is at stake is the emergence of a society that organizes its world according to this very distinction. In societies in which symbolic technologies are fully effective—if such a thing is possible—one cannot sharply differentiate between symbolic exchange, the domain of culture, and productive labor, the exchange or "metabolism" between culture and nature. Insofar as nature is "alive," the exchange with it is symbolic; the earth does not bear fruit because we make it, but because we appease it.[93] This is to say, in such a cosmology one cannot yet distinguish properly between "production," which we understand as the metabolism of humans and nature and social relation, the "control over the means of production."

In leaning heavily on activity as the substratum of ontology, the ontological turn in anthropology should perhaps prompt us to reconsider some of Thorstein Veblen's more penetrating, if obscure, speculations, a theory, perhaps, as to the ruse mentioned by Benjamin, which drove a wedge between first and second technology.

SPLITTING THE MASTER, SPLITTING THE DIFFERENCE

Veblen begins his seminal study of the function and decline of the leisure class by a subtle yet crucial distinction, which can be read as an indirect critique of Hegel's master/slave dialectic (or of a common understanding of it). Veblen's account is motivated by a distinction between two kinds of human activity, the first of which he calls "industry" and the second "exploit." The first, Veblen will aim to show, carries the sense of dishonorable servitude, whereas the latter is the distinguishing feature of what is venerable and praiseworthy. Veblen sets out to disentangle two distinctions that modernity has come to fuse together: the distinction between what is venerable and free and what is base and subservient, and the distinction between human subjects and the domain of natural objects.

> The tacit, common-sense distinction [in our industrial times] is . . . in effect, that any effort is to be counted industrial only so far as its ultimate purpose

is the utilization of non-human things. . . . Man's "power over nature" is currently postulated as the characteristic fact of industrial productivity. The industrial power over nature is taken to include man's power over the life of the beasts and over all the elemental forces. A line is in this way drawn between mankind and brute creation.

In other times and among men imbued with a different body of preconceptions this line is not drawn precisely as we draw it to-day. . . . In all communities under the barbarian culture there is an alert and pervading sense of antithesis between two comprehensive groups of phenomena, in one of which barbarian man includes himself, and in the other, his victual. There is a felt antithesis between economic and non-economic phenomena, but it is not conceived in the modern fashion; it lies not between man and brute creation, but between animate and inert things.[94]

While premodern "barbarians" do in fact have a sense of a profound distinction between the life-sustaining "drudgery" of the economy and more noble pursuits, this distinction does not parallel a distinction between humans and nonhuman things, but rather accords with the type of engagement they call for; phenomena that are "formidable or baffling" are to be met with "a different spirit and with proficiency of a different kind from what is required in dealing with inert things. To deal successfully with such phenomena is a work of exploit rather than industry. It is an assertion of prowess, not of diligence."[95]

Much of Veblen's story can be pinned to the divergent meaning of "exploit" and "prowess." The two terms are ordinarily used to describe what for Heidegger would be subsumed under a technological, and for the Frankfurt school a utilitarian, approach. Veblen is after the element of the activity that made it possible for "exploit" to mean a feat, and for prowess to mean "bravery." In dealing with something unpredictable, something with the power to surprise us, we come to suspect it is of a teleological nature, having a mind of its own. In this sense, the computer that refuses our commands has a mind of its own. Veblen's point is a subtle one, and it is easy to miss its full significance. The distinction between teleology and mechanism is in one sense a stable fixture of the historical process, but at the same time it is what underlies profound historical change. Simply put, it is not that at some point in time, humans did not distinguish in the phenomenal world between subject and object, only that the distinction applied to a different category of objects. Many things could be taken to display what we would call subjectivity, and it is in dealing with them that one displayed praiseworthy behavior, behavior worthy of imitation. There, one's activities had the full significance of being human. What ultimately matters in Veblen's account, what originally determines the value of the activity, is its intersubjective character, which is derived from the confrontation with something displaying a purposive nature. If the activity is intersubjective, that is, if it is taken to be a confrontation with something opaque, that seems to have its own purposes, then the object is imbued with what we might call subjectivity, or spirit.

The historical process described by Veblen has two fundamental stages. First, with the development of private property, there develops something akin to Hegel's master-slave distinction. Superiority came to be imbued in the distinction between rule over people and rule over material objects. Status came to be bestowed upon those who are removed from the process of production, from "drudgery" or "industry."[96] In Veblen's account, this is the emergence of class distinction, and the beginning of the rise of the leisure class—a class whose economic function is to be noneconomic, unproductive. Priests and warriors belong to this class, and in Veblen's time their last, fading image is kept by the aristocracy.

Veblen's own time witnesses the decline of the leisure class. In an industrial society of strangers, one's superior status is no longer efficiently displayed by the old markers of distinction: decorum, taste, and higher learning, all of which require some interpersonal intercourse. Progressively, what comes to displace the old markers of status is consumption—the most efficient way to display one's standing above "industry" or "drudgery" is to buy and display items of luxury, that is, items that are of no material use.

What matters for our purposes here is the way in which, in this process, the display of wealth retains, albeit in a concealed form, the primal distinctive mark; it functions, effectively, as a display of symbolic superfluity, of the excess that had once distinguished between the boring activities of the day-to-day, drudgery, and the violently risky activities which were once the site for the display of what matters beyond survival. Simply put, as the excessive, symbolic dimension of ritual has lost its function, it has not stopped functioning. It appears, for example, in the excessive "busy-bodyness" discussed by Eric Santner, the unproductive restlessness that hovers over office life.[97] Working in an office, we could offer as a condensation of Santner's argument, is what happens when office, in its liturgical sense, no longer works. In its very unproductive excess, such work is of the same flesh as its ritual relative, only now being unproductive can no longer be sacralized; it lingers as an embarrassing, dirty little secret to be hidden from one's (equally unproductive) "bosses."[98]

According to Moishe Postone, what justifies the otherwise extremely crude separation between all modes of social and political organization and the modern, i.e., capitalist one, is precisely the abstraction of rule, in its social and political sense.[99] It is not that in modernity we do not have bosses, but our bosses too have bosses, and so on. We all seem to be subordinated to abstract systems, such as the exigencies of the labor market. For Postone, this is one of the primary effects of the abstraction and commodification of labor as analyzed by Marx. This is why the only answer is a revolutionary one; revolts would just not do, they would be the replacement of one functionary with another. To quote Kafka, "The animal wrests the whip from its master and whips itself in order to become master, not knowing that this is only a fantasy produced by a new knot in the master's whiplash."[100]

We might say that the commodification of labor does not so much sever the tie between social relations and relations of production but reverses it. We do not produce in order to exchange, but exchange—our labor and its products—as part of the production process. What happens in such an inversion is both the loss of status as a legitimate, justifiable form of social subordination and the effective subordination of all to abstract, quasi-natural rules.

Crucially, such an (abstraction and) inversion does not "cleanse" social relations of ethical significance, subduing everything to the logic of the market in ruthless efficiency, but rather taints all social exchange as inappropriate, obscene, misplaced market relations. With such an inversion, social ties themselves become suspect, if not directly obscene. Just consider how, within the order of law, the very "stuff" of social relations, gift exchange, turns into bribery. In the capitalist mode of exchange, symbolic exchange is degraded, as it can only be thought of in terms of material exchange. What is done in gift exchange societies in order to produce a nonsettleable debt, which is the social bond, becomes hopelessly entangled with a quid pro quo logic.

Contrary to the perceived wisdom, according to which in capitalism everything is included in the market, Noam Yuran advances a much more nuanced and indeed dialectical thesis: in capitalism, the economy includes what is excluded from exchange. Specifically, according to Yuran, capitalism can be defined and understood in relation to what, precisely, cannot be legitimately exchanged in it, namely, women. The explicit ban on the exchange of women—the primordial gift of ancient systems of exchange—has a dual effect: it inscribes an informal, obscene economy in all nonmarket relations (which is a way of seeing how the "material base" of the economy can only be detected in areas outside the understanding of the economists, i.e., in culture), and it endows economic exchange proper (the market) with an indelible erotic dimension.

It is as if the very attempt to sharply delineate material exchange (the market proper) from sociosymbolic exchange, the domain of culture, results in their desperate entanglement: the market economy is libidinally charged, becoming much more than a medium for the allocation of social goods needed for the continuous existence of society, and the domain of culture becomes an ultimately desperate attempt to provide the economy with what it needs most—something money cannot buy. Yuran's account renders Lacan's strange assertion, according to which in capitalism enjoyment became countable, understandable in economic terms. For how can enjoyment, which defies utilitarian reasoning, come to be calculable? Yuran renders this clear with an example drawn from Adam Smith himself. According to Smith, we pay an opera singer extra, precisely because we should not be paying; we compensate her, monetarily, for being forced to sell what in principle is beyond count and priceless: her talent and her enjoyment. In capitalism, we pay for paying.

In a similar vein, the violent, mythical, life-and-death confrontation has not so much disappeared as a long-forgotten, heroic if cruel way of life; its underlying logic has become ever more present as it has disappeared from our form of life as a concrete, common experience. Abstracted, it has become a structural function, a feature of functionality, objectified and impersonal. As an experience, it has never been more spectral. This speaks to a much broader issue, a very concrete form the "dialectics of the primal" takes: the supposed absorption of subjective violence into objective, systematic violence, the order of the state law. We no longer torture in order to inscribe equality in the bodies of group members; indeed, the very insistence of the body as a vehicle of punishment is an embarrassment to the rationale of contemporary penal systems.[101]

CRITIQUE OF VIOLENCE: POWER IS THE MESSAGE

If the law is to be anything at all, it has to be something substantially different from arbitrary violence. It must put some distance between humans and the powers of fate. But as we have seen, the notion of the unwritten law casts a long shadow of doubt over the sharp separation between law and violence, between necessity and contingency. What are the limits and repercussions of such critique? And is there an alternative articulation of the relation between law and violence?

In order to address these questions, let us turn our attention to Walter Benjamin's famous "Critique of Violence," in which he sets out to release our understanding of violence from the instrumental scheme, just as his essay on language was an attempt to uncover a dimension of language that is noninstrumental.

Violence—the term in German is *Gewalt*, whose semantic scope spans from the illegitimate violence of a crime or an arbitrary act of nature to something closer to the act of sovereignty or authority, that is, between what we take to be two opposites, the legitimate or sanctioned use of violence and the illegitimate—is, so Benjamin argues, ordinarily understood as a means. Its relation with justice is therefore either seen as one in which just ends justify the means undertaken to realize them, which Benjamin identifies with the view of natural law theories, or, vice versa, in which just means serve to justify ends. This would be the position, according to Benjamin, of legal positivism. The very legality (Weber) of the law, that is, the exercise of a fair, rational process, retroactively justifies its end, the law. The law here is not a means to an external—ahistorical—end of justice; but, if it accords with its notion, so to speak, it justifies itself. This would be a watered-down version of Hobbes: the centralized violence of the sovereign must prove itself superior to that of a state of nature. Legal violence, as an instrumentally reasoned use of violence—a technology, if you will—ought to prove itself superior to a "natural" state of affairs.

We might say that for Benjamin, natural law is useless in assessing legal violence as means because the ends that are to justify the violence of the law are external to the order of law and therefore, at its logical limit, entirely indifferent to it. An Augustinian, ontological gap between the kingdom of men and the kingdom of God renders historically concrete forms of legal violence insignificant, and therefore the most sacralized and most profane views of political violence, those of an Augustine or Thomas Aquinas and those of a Machiavelli, coincide: the end justifies the means, and the difference between these positions consists wholly in the source of ends, divine for Augustine, human for Machiavelli. A notion of naturally just ends leaves us with no criterion by which to evaluate the means to attain those ends.

Legal positivism, preferred by Benjamin precisely because of its grounding relation to history, relies, in this reading, on the distinction between lawmaking and law-preserving violence, and more broadly, on the successful separation between the violence of a state of nature and legal violence. If natural law was deemed irrelevant by Benjamin because of the gap separating the just ends from the (legal) means to achieve them, legal positivism depends on its success in establishing a significant enough distinction between legal violence—violence as a legal means to establish a just order—and sheer violence. It is in its legality—in its coherence as a system of law, its fairness, equity, and predictability—that law as a means has to distinguish itself from something like the mythic "state of nature," the limitless, unpredictable, chaotic violence that legal violence is meant to tame and contain. Legal violence must then, minimally, distinguish itself from arbitrary violence, if it is to be a "means" (legality) that justifies the end (rule of law). Law-making violence is to be "redeemed," justified, by law-preserving violence.

Benjamin's essay proceeds by considering symptoms that seem to undermine the legal positivistic logic of justification for legal, state violence. Approached symptomatically, the law is revealed to be driven by something which "legality" cannot seem to explain. The first thing that seems to elude the theoretical perspective of legal positivists is what we might call "legal imperialism," the tendency of the law toward a—growing—monopoly of violence, what Benjamin describes as the tendency to deny any use of violence for natural ends, even when these are not in themselves illegal. Benjamin is here implicitly raising a crucial question: What is it that drives the process of rationalization? Why does the law need to grow and expand? Indeed, Hobbes, arguably the philosophical father of legal positivism, took it for granted that sovereign intervention is a limiting and limited affair.[102] What are we to do, then, with a sovereign, legal violence's tendency to grow and accumulate more power itself?

In his *Civilization and Its Discontents* Freud is troubled by a similar problem. One of the primordial aspects of civilization, as understood by Freud, is an act of violence against the individual, the violence of a rule of law as such, in its very "leveling" effect. This "taming" of individuals by society seems necessary, as it were, in order to bring them together, and this empowers them in their otherwise hopeless struggle against nature. But why is it, Freud wonders in the essay, that civilization itself assumes an excessive, drivelike pressure? Why is it that the inhibition of drives, the curbing, by society, of unruly nature, seems destined to turn into a "drive for inhibition," infected, as it were, by the unruly nature it sought to reign in? The drive is uncannily manifest in the very attempts to overcome it, assuming its qualities. Drive is contagious, so contagious that even the prohibitions aimed at keeping it at arm's length can become infected by it.

To state the critical point as explicitly as possible: if the law is a means to bring order—equity, fairness, predictability—into the use of violence, why is it not satisfied with the ordering of state violence? Why does it tend to expand into domains not previously covered by law? What is it that drives the development of the law, the need to bring everything under its order? [103] Why does the law, so closely associated with the setting of boundaries, tend to transgress its own boundaries? Why is objectivity plagued by a stain of subjectivity, a hidden, underlying desire?

In the essay, Benjamin considers symptomatic perversions that undermine the logic of violence as a means, culminating in the decay of the famous distinction between law-preserving and law-making violence, a decay attested most clearly by, on the one hand, the "spectral" quality of the police, which, in its function as law-preserving is constantly, effectively, making new law, and, on the other hand, the inability of parliaments to make laws in a decisive manner. After considering these and other symptoms, Benjamin turns, in a way that seems rather abrupt, to the domain of myth.

> In its archetypical [urbildlichen] form, mythic violence is a mere
> manifestation of the gods. Not a means to their ends, scarcely even a
> manifestation of their will, but in the first instance a manifestation of their
> existence. But the legend of Niobe contains an outstanding example of this.
> To be sure, it could appear as though the action of Apollo and Artemis were
> only a punishment. But their violence establishes a law far more than it
> punishes the transgression of an existing one. Niobe's arrogance conjures
> up the disaster that befalls her not because it injures the law but because it
> challenges fate . . . violence thus closes in upon Niobe from the uncertain,
> ambiguous sphere of fate. [104]

This point in the essay cannot but strike the reader as a drastic shift in registers, as indeed it is. With the move into mythic and later divine violence, Benjamin has shifted the discussion away from a means-to-ends understanding of violence. The mythic dimension of violence is the dimension of manifestation. Violence here is not a means to an end, but a manifestation of the existence of power as such, that is, as a volatile potential, as the more everyday example provided by Benjamin clarifies.

> Everyday experience of life already shows a nonmediate [nicht mittelbare] function of violence like the one under investigation here. As regards a human being, rage [Zorn], for instance, leads to the most visible outbursts of violence that is not related as means to a predetermined end. This violence is not a means but a manifestation. And, in fact, this kind of violence admits of thoroughly objective manifestations on which it can be subjected to critique. It is of the highest significance that these can be found, above all, in myth.[105]

In its mythical mode of appearance, power is like a field of accumulated force, barely contained and ready to explode.[106] This is the inherently threatening nature of virtuality as power, of what we experience as unrealized. The unrealized is not only the amorphous pressure of the signification surplus but what is left deformed, so to speak, by our acts of conscious formations. It does not lie there in wait for us to symbolize, but in order to strike at the right moment. It has, we sense, a tendency to self-manifest in an imposing way. Hence its modality as a constant threat. Being in the presence of someone prone to rage is, for Benjamin, being confronted with mythic violence, a violence that is not simply arbitrary, outside any notion of guilt, but a violence that assigns guilt. Having triggered a violent response from a figure of authority, for example, a child inescapably asks herself where she erred, where was the line she should not have crossed.

Dramatic encounters with the mythical manifestation of power assign guilt. This is a primordial manifestation of the "lawfulness of the contingent," the way in which the most contingent is assigned the weightiest meaningfulness, as the individualization of fate. Relying on the story of Niobe, Benjamin argues that law emerges by an act of sacrifice that can only retroactively be constituted as punishment. The sacrifice marks a boundary that was previously invisible. The petrified Niobe is Benjamin's paradigm for this function of sacrifice. Niobe's petrified life marks the boundary between humans and the power of the gods. We might say that sacrifice, on this understanding, functions as a response to the desire expressed by the threatening, a way to appease and contain the eruptive powers of fate. A primordial answer to the question "What does the other want from me?" insofar as it—the other—is experienced, primarily, as mysteriously threatening. Sacrifice is a way to give a piece, a substitute, to that which threatens to annihilate, a bargaining compromise, a price to pay for "natural guilt," for the "surplus life" that drives us.[107]

Sacrifice is to be distinguished from gift exchange between peers: it is a gift we are returning to our superior, to whom we are indebted, and as such it may or may not be received. In its religious context, it is up to God to decide whether this gift is sufficient payment for the primordial debt of our lives and other gifts bestowed on us.[108] Interestingly, it is around the question of sacrifice that Benjamin offers the clearest of his juxtapositions between mythical and divine violence: "The former demands sacrifice, the latter assumes it [nimmt sie an]."[109] If the mythical is the ambivalence that demands sacrifice, and indeed may or may not accept it (it is forever ambivalent, opaque), the divine is that which assumes it, takes it on, accepts it as its duty. The divine, in this account, is the assurance that one's sacrifice was not in vain.

If myth is a mode of manifestation of violence, what are we to make of the entanglement of legal violence and mythical violence? A simple answer would be to say that the legal order merely veils what is much more readily manifest in mythical violence. Under the guise of instrumental reasoning, the mythical manifests itself, so to speak, as hidden in plain sight, in the symptomatic cracks of the legal system. These symptoms betray a dimension of legal violence that, by its own rationale, should have been superseded in the order of the law. Recall Benjamin's statement, quoted in chapter 2, according to which law was a triumph over the unwritten terrain of myth. And yet in the "Critique of Violence" essay the law turns out to be, to paraphrase von Ranke, a continuation of violence by (different) means; that is, the instrumental use of violence is revealed, by Benjamin's critique, as a medium for the (veiled) manifestation of mythic violence, rather than a way to conquer it. The mythical dimension of the law is made manifest only with the aid of Benjamin's probing, critical eye, uncovering a mythical dimension in the very cumulative nature of "technologies of power," the tendency of laws and rules to grow and expand beyond their own' "instrumental" reason,[110] in its propensity for punishment, etc.

Is the law ultimately merely the mask of primordial power? There are two problems with this suggestion. Firstly, as an interpretation of Benjamin, it fails to do justice to the sense in which, as Benjamin puts it in his essay on Kafka, the emergence of law has been, nonetheless, a victory over the forces of myth. If the law is merely—nothing but—a veiled extension of the mythic, unwritten dimension of the law, then it seems it deserves no credit for advancement. To the contrary, it only veils what was once much more directly manifest. Second, and more pressingly, it is precisely on the premise of such critical logic that the new right seeks today to assert its superiority: legality is merely a mask of power, and we will give you power unmasked.

On this point, it is worth comparing Benjamin's account with another, no less famous account of the connection between violence and the sacred. In his famous study of violence and the sacred, René Girard postulates a "pharmacological" theory of law and violence. Violence, for Girard, is a kind of primal substance, and the only way to contain it is by means of itself in diluted portions, a form of vaccination of which sacrifice is, for Girard, the paradigm. Sacrifice is the first form of violence that has the function of stopping the circle of violence, a violence that does not lead to further retribution.

For Girard, our modern "rule of law" is a much more efficient method of containment.

> Vengeance is a vicious circle whose effect on primitive societies can only
> be surmised. For us the circle has been broken, we owe our good fortune to
> one of our social institutions above all: our juridical system which serves to
> deflect the menace of vengeance. The system does not suppress vengeance;
> rather, it effectively limits it to a single act of reprisal, enacted by a sovereign
> authority specializing in this particular function. [111]

In this regard, Girard is an avid Hobbesian. Sovereign, legal violence is the most efficient machinery for the containment of violence. However, Girard notices a subtle dialectics at play in the process of "rationalization." The "desacralization" of the law is, for Girard, a forgetting of its own theological origin, but it also carries real effects. In shifting the burden of containing violence from the realm of unwritten customs to the legal machinery, modern societies indeed break free from their "ethical substance," but this is not without risks. Our societies have "automatized" the mechanisms of containing violence, a process that allows us some distance from the powers of myth:

> When the least false step can have dire consequences, human relationships
> may well be marked by a prudence that seems to us excessive and
> accompanied by precautions that appear incomprehensible. . . . Primitive
> societies do not have built into their structure an automatic brake against
> violence; but we do, in the form of powerful institutions whose grip
> grows progressively tighter as their role grows progressively less apparent.
> The constant presence of a restraining force allows modern man safely
> to transgress the limits imposed on primitive peoples without even
> being aware of the fact. In "policed" societies the relationship between
> individuals, including total strangers, is characterized by an extraordinary
> air of informality, flexibility, and even audacity. [112]

However, the very same procedure that allows for the loosening or desacralization of social relations has a rather massive side effect: it threatens to undermine the very frame in which it operates. The very spirit of "audacity" in the face of irrational customs can turn against itself, like an autoimmune disease.

> Our juridical system rationalizes revenge and succeeds in limiting and
> isolating its effects in accordance with social demands. The system treats the
> diseases without fear of contagion and provides a highly effective technique
> for the cure and, as a secondary effect, the prevention of violence. In the final
> analysis, then, the judicial system and the institution of sacrifice share the
> same function, but the judicial system is infinitely more effective. However,
> it can only exist in conjunction with a firmly established political power. And

like all modern technological advances, it is a two-edged sword, which can be used to oppress as well as to liberate. Certainly, that is the way it is seen by primitive cultures, whose view of the matter is indubitably more objective than our own.

If the function of the system has now become apparent, that is because it no longer enjoys the obscurity it needs to operate effectively. A clear view of the inner workings indicates a crisis in the system; it is a sign of disintegration. No matter how sturdy it may seem, the apparatus that serves to hide the true nature of legal and illegal violence from view eventually wears thin. The underlying truth breaks through, and we find ourselves face to face with a specter of reciprocal reprisal. This is not a purely theoretical concept belonging to the intellectual and scholarly realm, but a sinister reality; a vicious circle we thought we had escaped, but one we find has tightened itself, all unsuspected, around us. [113]

Our legal rationalism, Girard argues, can function only insofar as it retains a sense of its own, sacred function.

All this explains why our penetration and demystification of the system necessarily coincides with the disintegration of that system. The act of demystification retains a sacrificial quality and remains essentially religious in character for at least as long as it fails to come to a conclusion—as long, that is, as the process purports to be nonviolent, or less violent than the system itself. In fact, demystification leads to a constantly increasing violence, a violence perhaps less "hypocritical" than the violence it seeks to expose, but more energetic, more virulent, and the harbinger of something far worse—a violence that knows no bounds. [114]

Demystification is not a critical stance from outside; it is internal to the development of the law. It is, if you will, a kind of final irony of the law that its arrogance leads it to collide with what it sought to conquer—mythical, unbounded violence. In shedding all its ties to unwritten customs and their irrationality, the legal system finds itself to be the highest manifestation of the violence those primitive means were to contain.

ON THE ROT IN THE LAW: COMPLICITY AND CONTAINMENT

In her recent, powerful study of *Antigone*—a source, we have already seen, for both ancient and modern reflections on the unwritten law—Alenka Zupančič offers some penetrating insights as to the unwritten law and violence, allowing us to gather and order several dimensions of the unwritten law laid out above, and also come back to assess our contemporary situation. Zupančič sets out to undermine an interpretation of *Antigone* that views the confrontation central to the play as one between visible, subjective violence, embodied by Antigone, and the "transparent" objective violence of state law embodied by

Creon, the largely invisible violence entailed in maintaining the smooth running of things.[115]

As is well known, Antigone rebels against Creon's decrees because she sees in Creon's action a violation of unwritten laws. In Zupančič's interpretation, this violation has to do with the way in which, in forbidding Polyneices' burial, Creon had in fact effaced the distinction between subjective and objective violence. It is in the name of (objective) law that he performed his "gesture of excessive, subjective violence."[116]

Zupančič offers an explanation that touches on the core of what occupies us here and brings out some crucial features of the strange "topography" of the unwritten law:

> What Creon violates is not some other law (unwritten, divine laws), but an unwritten dimension of his own law . . . it is a matter of the other side of public, written laws. . . . At the core of every written, symbolic law there is (always) something like an "impossible crime" . . . it is not a crime like other crimes; it is, strictly speaking, the impossible crime that takes place in a territory that has no territory, no ground on which to stand; it constitutes an excluded interior of the state of the law. The constitution of law (or of the symbolic order in general) involves a discontinuity, a gap, something that cannot be based on anything other than itself, or derived linearly from the previous, "natural state."[117]

We might say that this impossible crime belongs to the constitutive, law-making dimension discussed by Benjamin. Such a constitutive act of violence would redeem itself, find its justification, had it risen to its own notion, so to speak, had it, indeed, succeeded in constituting a realm of law meaningfully separated from sheer violence. To make the connection to Zupančič's discussion clear, this would amount to successfully establishing state violence as objective, washing it clean of any residues of subjective violence. The residual "subjective" violence of law-making is to be redeemed by the very "objectivity" of the established order, by the manner in which the order of law manages to become objective in the full sense of the term, assuming an "objective," independent, reliable existence by being "objective" in the sense of fair, impartial, orderly.

However, such a clear demarking of the boundary between objective, "legitimized" violence and subjective, "criminal" violence cannot be established. It is here that Zupančič suggests we should introduce the unwritten laws under the name in which psychoanalysis knows them, taboos. Taboos are society's way to circumspect, with reverence, the very gap in the symbolic law, the sites in which it leaks. "The protecting at issue here is not simply about keeping it hidden, keeping it a dirty secret; rather, it is about keeping this criminal core from being drawn into the everyday workings of the rule of law, and thus from turning into the dirty but powerful secret weapon—supposedly 'neces-sary'—of this or that empirical rule."[118]

According to Zupančič, taboos and inhibitions, the "naturalized" aspect of the unwritten law, are in place in order to keep the unwritten in its mythical guise from overtaking the order of manmade, positive public law. The unwrit-ten laws so crucial for ethical substance are in this view what maintains the unstable boundary between the public order of law and its own mythical shadow. We can view this as an important, complementary view of the "com-plicity" of the unwritten law in establishing the order of law, noted already, if cynically, by Plato.[119] We can think of it as a technique that belongs to and responds to the mythical aspect of the law, not by erecting a boundary around it, as does the written, positive law, but by keeping a distance from the danger-ous, explosive "holes" where the written law and its mythical underside inter-penetrate. Finally, this account helps Zupančič explain the obscenity of Creon's actions, as an act of pushing the limit of the symbolic law: "it is pushing it at the precise point where it is porous; it is playing with fire."[120]

The obscenity of a Creon is here given some important precision: it is this meddling with the impossible-to-define but clearly felt line separating the positive order from its mythological shadow, and thereby blurring it, allowing the mythological dimension to bleed into that which is supposed to keep it at bay, that makes an action monstrously obscene. Zupančič is explicit as to the ramifications of her account for the new figures of authority which concerns us here.[121] Such obscene figures of authority need the public manifestation of the "primordial crime."

What is crucial to note is how this contemporary modality of power is, in this sense, not only immune to a critical perspective as to the relation between law and violence—it utilizes it directly. To the extent that Benjamin's point is a critical achievement, and it is one, the new right responds by affirming the mythical. If we cannot help but suspect that, underneath the neutral, objective violence of the state and more generally the maintenance of the status quo, there is an indelible stain of the subjective, mythical face of violence, what are we to do with a power that garners its appeal by promising to bring to the surface what polite society, or the order of law, seeks to safely ignore, kept at a distance?

If indeed taboo amounts to a kind of ethical tact (the unformalizable way in which we learn to circumspect certain areas of discourse), then violations of it are palpable, felt by a "gut reaction." A central question that concerns us here is indeed how the very primal reaction we seem to have to violations of unwritten laws has become a mode of legitimation of a new style of authori-tarianism. What allows the violation of taboo to claim authority over us? How does exposure come to function as obfuscation?

5

CAUGHT IN THE WEB: AUTHORITY AND POWER, MEDIA AND TECHNOLOGY

We cannot draw closed the net in which we are caught.
Walter Benjamin, "Capitalism as Religion"[1]

We have begun this exploration with a very concrete and troubling phenomenon: the proliferation, in recent years, of a new style of political legitimation, placing transgressive, obscene behavior front and center. We took our departure from theoretical accounts that wish to subsume the phenomenon under the concept of "populism," for their failure to account, precisely, for what it is that makes such behavior popular. The notion of "populism" tends to take for granted, rather than explain, the "popular" resentment of elites. Another difficulty such accounts face is the very global nature of the phenomenon. We would expect populism to be a relatively local affair in politics, having to do, precisely, with the particular grievances against elites.

One hypothesis as to the global nature of new-authoritarian legitimation patterns would be to link it to the development of new media. In order to establish the relation between a new politics and new media condition, it is necessary to address fundamental questions regarding new media. The fundamental question in this regard is what can be labeled the web's democratic paradox. In its first stages, the internet seemed to promise to advance democracy, enabling unprecedented freedom of speech and pluralism. This faith was founded on a firm base: the web's decentralized framework, the possibilities it opens for individual self-expression, and individually tailored use—all of these were perceived as the direct opposite of centralized, unidirectional, homogeneous broadcast media. While in some areas the web might have fulfilled its democratic promise, in other terrains it delivered the opposite outcome. Phenomena such as online shaming, conspiracy theories, and hate groups have found the internet to be fertile ground to their toxic social effects, displaying social behaviors that were associated in the nineteenth century with the "crowd": lack of judgment, loosening of the inhibitive effect of social norms, and diffusion of the limits of the self. John Suler coined the term "the disinhibition effect"[2] to describe how, paradoxically, online media enforce a new mode of disinhibition which is not experienced as a release of the self, but as an injury to its integrity.

The internet, which began as a promise to radically democratize human communications, a promise to deliver us from the remainders of authority inscribed in the very centralized nature of broadcast—which allows, as it were, for authority figures to speak at us, putting us in the position of passive spectators—has somehow come to host a culture ridden by conspiracy theories, shaming, and cyberbullying and a corresponding politics of obscenity, in which disinhibition endows certain politicians with a unique type of aura and authority, quite similar to that which, according to Freud's famed analysis, attaches to the leader of the crowd.[3] Only our crowd behavior, so to speak, is no longer eruptive but somehow integrated into our daily lives.

This raises a strange, temporal parallax: even the most historicist of analysts tend to find the obscene master to be an archaic, primal, even transhistorical figure. This holds even for Foucault, for whom the general trajectory of power seems to be from symbolic authority to technologies of power.[4] There is an insistence here on the master as an exceptional individual, echoing Freud's primal father, the leader of the horde or the crowd, a mythical deformation of the natural. And yet technology, inclusive of technologies of power, seem to be a matter of instrumentality gone wild, in which the tools developed by humans to master (nature or each other) are turned against them, deindividuating, posthuman in their very trajectory of development.[5] This, we argued, is not merely a problem of the scholarly division of labor, a matter of perspective. What is at stake is a profound puzzle regarding the very nature of power, its conceptual and historical bifurcation between authority and technologies of power.

Let us begin by developing conceptually the tension between authority and technology. Then we shall turn to Lacan in order to pose this (non-)relation more precisely, and in direct correspondence with the technological event of our time, namely, the emergence of a computer-networked world. With this, we shall come full circle in order to ask some fundamental questions about the relation between the medium of the web and the cultural contents that plague it, that is, between the structural features of the medium and the new crowds and new authoritarianism that inhabit it.

AUTHORITY AND TRADITION: A HERMENEUTIC CIRCLE

In her well-known essay "What Is Authority?," Arendt approaches the object of her essay obliquely, making clear right from the beginning that authority is no longer known to us; it is a thing of the past, felt by us only through the symptoms of its—probably fatal—crisis.

In order to avoid misunderstanding, it might have been wiser to ask in the title: What was—and not what is—authority? For it is my contention that we are tempted and entitled to raise this question because authority has vanished from the modern world. Since we can no longer fall back upon authentic and undisputable experience common to all, the very term has become clouded by controversy and confusion. Little about its nature appears self-evident or even comprehensible to everybody, except that the political scientist may still remember that this concept was once fundamental to political theory, or that most will agree that a constant, ever-widening and deepening crisis of authority has accompanied the development of the modern world in our century.[6]

So, authority is a thing of the past.[7] This brief formula captures both what is perhaps the most essential feature of authority and the reason for its epistemological unavailability. As we shall see, this unavailability or opacity of authority is a constant, and yet also what underwrites its profound transformation in modernity. Authority and tradition, I argue, form a hermeneutic circle, which, in one way, is precisely what had made authority such an elusive concept, and, in another way, tell all there is to know about both terms.

Let us begin with the modern, epistemological barrier: definitions of authority rely on a concept of tradition, whereas definitions of tradition rely on a concept of authority. We understand tradition to be that form of life in which authority is, or was, in full sway, and authority as a mode of power that relies on tradition for its legitimacy. This is why "traditional" societies are the original object of anthropology, what fascinated moderns about them— authority at its purest is the authority of a form of life, of the unwritten rules of society, without recourse to grand mechanisms of control and enforcement such as the law and state bureaucracy. What, in the absence of modern mechanisms of power, holds such societies in order? In the sociology of law, Maine's famous narrative of the development of law, "from status to contract," is a telling case in point. We move from an unwritten law that primarily seeks to order familial relations and secure inheritance, to the modern, contractual law seeking to explicitly order relations between and amongst individuals. As the law foregrounds individuals and individuation, inheritance and familial ties seem increasingly like murky, irrational phenomena, inherently "backgrounded"—part of our mythical background, ever present as archaic remainders we cannot quite grasp nor put to rest.[8]

Take Max Weber's classical discussion of the three sources of legitimacy: charisma, legality, and tradition.[9] Weber quickly puts to the side tradition as a source of legitimacy and focuses instead on legality and charisma, presumably as the latter two remain relevant to modern society. What is striking about the two is their polar opposition. The connection to the charismatic leader is personal, whereas legality is appealing in its impersonal impartiality. Whereas the charismatic leader is defined by his mandate, that is, in Weber's terms, he is judged on the basis of his ability to attain goals and purposes, the legitimacy of legality lies in its instrumental and formal rationality, standing above or underneath the political debate over values and goals. Legality is technical, instrumental. It is the mechanism required for the accomplishment of any policy and the appraisal of its reasonability, the very medium in which the political debate can take place.

Today the two sources of modern legitimacy mentioned by Weber seem to be locked in a direct confrontation. Legality has come under attack mostly from the political right as politically biased ("the deep state"), undermining its claim for neutrality. This politicization of the neutral medium is a main feature of the new right, arguably the core message of a new type of postideological charismatic authoritarianism. On the opposite side of the political fence, legality has become a strange political battle cry, which unwittingly participates in the politicization of something that draws its legitimacy from being a neutral medium.

Is there something outside the forced choice between charisma and legality? Perhaps there is something to be gained from what Max Weber has put to the side, namely, tradition. Unlike both charisma and legality, whose appealing rationale he thoroughly discusses, tradition's appeal is defined by Weber tautologically—it is the legitimacy afforded to "the eternal yesterday," to that which always already precedes us.[10] Tradition draws its authority from being tradition. Implicitly, we inherit from Weber a notion of traditional legitimation as uncritical, the unthinking acceptance of what comes down to us. As such, it is lost to modernity. We can no longer naively rely on what has come before.

And so it is certainly to Arendt's credit that she approaches authority as primordially lost to modernity. But she does not simply identify authority with the most primitive, with origin or beginning. Arendt famously argues that authority as a concrete cultural experience was absent from Greek culture, and thus comes to us from the Romans, who then, retroactively, constitute the Greeks as their—and therefore our—intellectual authorities or forefathers. In Arendt's account, Western political philosophy in its entirety emerges against this blank, this absence, which therefore could be said to occupy a position somewhat analogous to Heidegger's being, the forgetting of which constitutes in his account Western metaphysics.

For Arendt, our entire political tradition beginning with Plato and Aristotle is a massive forgetting of authority. The notion of authority, which implies an obedience in which freedom is retained, is inaccessible as long as we rely on the Greek view of despotic, coercive rule, natural in the household and illegitimate in the city, which is founded on freedom.[11] And yet the "origin" of authority is not sought by Arendt in the Greeks' own forerunners—she doesn't turn, as Heidegger did, to the pre-Socratics, or as an anthropologist might, to an even more traditional society—but rather to the Greek's successors, the Romans. Authority, as it emerges from Arendt's account, is at once primordially lost and somehow secondary, restorative, reactive. It is, as Arendt picks up from the etymology of the word, an act of augmentation, specifically of the foundations, thereby retroactively constituting them as such, as foundational. Authority is nothing but this circularity between establishment and reinforcement: a foundation operates as such—as truly foundational—only insofar as it has to be repeatedly augmented, only as long as we cannot tear it down and erect a new edifice in its stead. It is hallowed ground.

Implicit in Arendt's account of the secondary, retroactive place of authority in Western history is indeed a theory of its very historicality. It is because the West originally lacks an authoritative foundation that philosophy—not only political philosophy—is born, and the placing of that very philosophy as an authoritative foundation cannot but have a dialectical result, pushing us to search for firmer ground, and to undermine it, again and again. [12]

Compare, if you will, Lovejoy's famous thesis to Arendt's. For Lovejoy, "the great chain of being," which came to form the underlying ontological presupposition of the greater part of Western history, was a compromise formation, an attempt to account for conflicting demands, at once philosophical and religious, that the ground of reality would be both transcendent (otherworldly) and effective (in the realm of the senses). [13] Plato's ideas were the first philosophical articulation of such a double, contradictory demand.

For Arendt, Plato's theory of ideas as a transcendent standard emerges directly out of the absence, for the Greeks, of an experience of authority. In the absence of authority, standards lack, she suggests, an efficiency of their own, and can only become instrumental tools in the hands of philosopher kings. [14] Can we conceive of an efficacy that is different in kind from the compulsory action of one body on another? Echoing a line of thought central to Walter Benjamin, Arendt suggests that Plato comes close to conceiving such a power in those parts of his doctrine where he associates the idea with the beautiful, effective in its very unapproachability, but soon betrays this insight by availing himself of the ideas as tools to be handled by the philosopher king.

This, as we shall see, is indeed the problem raised by Arendt. Authority is eclipsed, for us, because we find it next to impossible to think of such a modality of power, a power which is not measured by its actualization. Its effectiveness is increased in direct proportion to its remaining virtuality. What makes authority difficult to grasp is precisely its strange, indirect presence. Its radiant beauty, if you will, or its glory, [15] the splendor, the effect of its semblance.

Since authority is unapproachable, inaccessible, we might get a better understanding of Arendt's interpretation of it if we follow her strategy and approach it through its very disappearance, by means of that which eclipses it. Significantly, Arendt views the rise of the functional view of society as the other side of the decline of authority.

> There exists a silent agreement in most discussions among political and social scientists that we can ignore distinctions and proceed on the assumption that everything can eventually be called anything else, and that distinctions are meaningful only to the extent that each of us has the right "to define his terms." Yet does not this curious right, which we have come to grant as soon as we deal with matters of importance—as though it were actually the same as the right to one's own opinion—already indicate that such terms as "tyranny," "authority," "totalitarianism," have simply lost their common meaning, or that we have ceased to live in a common world where the words we have in common possess an unquestionable meaningfulness. . . . [The] theory implicitly challenging the importance of making distinctions is, especially in the social sciences, the almost universal functionalization of all concepts and ideas. A convenient instance may be provided by the widespread conviction in the free world that communism is a new "religion," notwithstanding its avowed atheism, because it fulfills socially, psychologically, and "emotionally" the same function traditional religion fulfilled. [16]

For Arendt, the fact that we can speak of a function of authority already means that it is utterly lost to us. Although she doesn't quite spell it out, we may offer several different ways in which authority as it emerges from her essay is the obverse of the functional:

1. If authority is lost once we can speak of it as a function, this is because authority "functions" to the extent that it is taken for granted, presupposed, operative insofar as it forms the very background of our reality. "The ground-work" of the world, as Arendt puts it. [17] It is to be taken on trust, implicitly. To view it as a function is the first sign of its malfunctioning, so to speak, its loss of immediacy and transparency. If authority cannot be taken for granted, it cannot be taken at all, would be the idea. In this sense, authority is necessarily veiled, we are not to see behind its curtain. Recall the famous quote attributed to Bismarck, according to which laws and sausages are two things of which the public should not be made aware of the process of production. The function of authority is mysterious; indeed, the mystery as to its functioning is the essential ingredient of its unique functionality. This is one way of understanding the importance of ceremony, or what Walter Benjamin called "cult value" for traditional authority. [18] And hence the appearance of authority via the medium of crisis—it only comes to view when things are not quite right, when there is a significant enough disturbance to the smooth running of things. As Agamben notes, the authority of the senate was invoked, in Roman law, in the

"interregnum," in the time between one established or posited order, and the next, in the vacuum of power.[19]

2. Authority does not perform a function. It is profoundly anti-instrumental and cannot be viewed as a means to an end. We know this, although we hardly understand it—authority is not something to be executed, realized, but a virtual presence that accompanies power, giving it symbolic support, or withholding it. It ceremoniously augments acts and institutions by sanctioning them, permitting them a symbolic entrance into the space of possibility. This is perhaps the key to its fraught distinction and relation to power, as we commonly understand that term, a relation "at once antagonistic and supplementary."[20] Authority is not something to be enforced, it does not hinge on its realized effects, it is—"more than an advice, less than a command" as the famous quote from Mommsen describes it. Authority is superfluous, signatorial, and yet, as such, essential.

3. Authority is substantial, it attaches itself to concrete individuals—a person, a tradition. It is never, as Arendt emphasizes, "authority in general." It is rooted or seeks to be so, by no means something transferrable and translatable the way a function is. Put in problematic functional terms, it is precisely what endows a person, an institution, or an activity with substance, a dimension of depth, gravity, the density of a substance.

4. Authority belongs to a substantial *We*, a preindividual sense of community, of commitment to our way of life. To view it as a function is to view things from outside, as it were, from a sociological, scientific point of view, which can only conceive of society as a functional construct. Authority, we have already hinted, is directly linked to the mysterious way in which I am inscribed into a given community. It is a view from within a medium of tradition. Hence Arendt's turn to the particular history she sees herself as an heir to, the history of Western political thought. This is also why, in her account, when authority is intact, it brings together freedom and hierarchy. Properly authorized, things are in their right place, so to speak. There is an accepted hierarchy, a sacred order. Hierarchy and freedom coincide, insofar as I can see my concrete freedom as inseparable from the totality to which I belong. It is, say, as a father that I realize myself, as a son and a citizen of my country, as opposed to a liberal, formal-legal abstraction. It is an order in which differences—between the young and the old, between men and women, between nobles and serfs—have to be accepted and reinforced.

5. Authority is paradigmatic. It belongs to an order in which the singular is not poised as the opposite of the general rule, but as its expression or manifestation. The link between authority and charisma[21] has to do with this feature. Authority is not an office, a role—a function—that can be fulfilled. Terms like a position of authority, or "the authorities," betray the extent to which we can only understand authority in functional terms. The mystery raised by

Lorraine Daston as to the now lost meaning of paradigm as rule, and not as its opposition,[22] is not merely analogous to the eclipse of authority, but belongs to one and the same constellation. As emerges from Daston's study of rules, the capacities associated with learning from example (discretion) are inseparable from structures of authority, such as monasteries.[23] To learn the lessons of the paradigmatic exemplar is the other side of the coin, which could also be described as learning to respect authorities. Both aspects belong to, depend on, and reinforce a medium of tradition.

6. Finally, authority is grounded in the law insofar as it is both given and transcendent, a medium in which society is constituted rather than a constituted, man-made order. This is what distinguishes it from tyranny, according to Arendt:

> Even the most draconic authoritarian government is bound by laws. Its acts are tested by a code which was made either not by man at all, as in the case of the law of nature or God's commandments or the platonic ideas, or at least not by those actually in power. The source of authority in authoritarian government is always a force external and superior to its own power; it is always this source, this external force which transcends the political realm, from which authorities derive their "authority," that is, their legitimacy, and against which their power can be checked.[24]

The law is operative in an authoritarian structure insofar as it is precisely not a function anyone can master, that is, precisely insofar as the law has no human author, and no human can place himself in the position of its author.

AUTHORITY, OLD AND NEW

Although Arendt never quite fully spells it out, there is an intimate link between the topic of her most famous book, totalitarianism, and the topic of one of her most famous stand-alone essays, authority. While these two political concepts are in many ways diametrically opposed, both occupy a space that the major opposition in Western political thought, between legitimate rule and rule by force, seems to deny.

Totalitarianism is neither tyranny, the rule of one against all, based on violence and fear, nor democratically legitimate, the rule of the many against one, and the very same can be said of authority as explored by Arendt, which is undoubtedly legitimate, although its source of legitimacy is certainly one that transcends the polity and its freedom. There is an implicit thesis that emerges when we bring together Arendt's reflections on totalitarianism and her reflections on authority: totalitarianism lays claim to a direct contact with the transcendent, mysterious source of authority. We might say that in its modern blend of legitimate and illegitimate rule, of lawlessness and law, totalitarianism comes to occupy the logical space left open by the absence of authority.

In a way, much of the horror of totalitarianism is attributed by Arendt to its coming to assume the *function* of authority. In totalitarianism, it is precisely what cannot be thought of in functional terms, the very ground of the positive order, that is directly functionalized. The totalitarian ideologies of the last century avail themselves of the ideas grounding political reality, as if they were instrumentally available. In twentieth-century totalitarianism, this meant, in Arendt's analysis, the direct appeal to an impossible knowledge (gnosis) of nature (Nazism) or history (communism), as supplying the ideological meta-rule, in view of which all other laws can be suspended. Totalitarian terror, in direct opposition to the fear utilized by the tyrant, is not an instrument of rule, a means to an end, but an essential mode of expression of this new form of rule.[25]

What about contemporary, new authoritarianism? Arendt's account so far helps us appreciate the extent to which our new authoritarianism is structured as an antiauthoritarianism. If the unwritten law, for Arendt, is—we could say, as such, as unwritten—what serves as the ultimate standard of any authority figure; what are we to make of a Trump or Netanyahu, who are precisely capable of attaining authority and garnering legitimacy by means of transgressing these very unwritten laws? New authoritarianism, it would seem, lays no claim to a "higher law," say, the laws of nature, as in pseudo-biological racism, or history, as in communist interpretations of the laws of materialist dialectics governing the historical process. Instead, it makes direct contact with the unwritten law underlying authority, by calling attention to its elusive, implicit presence and defying it. The new, global right may not—at least so far—exercise terror to the extent we are familiar with from the previous century, but there is something horrifying in it, horrifying indeed, in the way it makes the horrifying mundane, everyday. What shocking new thing did he do today, we find ourselves asking, what new norms have they violated?

Authority as described by Arendt is one, historically significant way to make the mystery of language, the fact that it always already precedes us, a medium in which we are individuated, legitimate. The new modality of authority, on the contrary, is premised on the illegitimacy of anything we are called on to take on trust. "Do your own research!" is the injunction of the internet conspiracy theorists, their version of Kant's "dare to know!" The new authoritarian leader appears as the one who exposes the false pretense of established institutions and norms on which we rely. Rather than participating in the ceremonial mystery of authority, new authority figures appear to be radically anti-ceremonial, tearing down all the symbolic facades of power.

THE CENSOR, THE KING, AND THE PEN

In the classical modality of authority, the figure of authority, say the king, gives body (figure) to the unwritten law that authorizes him; he is not its source.

In his Seminar II, to which we shall return, Lacan gives this dimension of the "the law in so far as it is not understood" (in his words) a psychoanalytic name: censorship.

> By definition, no one is taken to be ignorant of the law, but it is never understood, for no one can grasp it in its entirety. The primitive who is caught up in the laws of kinship, of alliance, of the exchange of women, never has, even if he is very learned, a complete vision of what it is in this totality of the law that has a hold over him. . . . That is censorship. It is the law in so far it is not understood. [26]

Lacan's point about censorship is subtle and can be easily missed. Censorship turns an impossibility into a prohibition. The law has an unknowable, unwritten dimension. In order to become full subjects of the law, censorship forbids us from admitting something everybody knows all too well. In this way, censorship "symbolizes," by means of prohibition, what is structurally impossible in the law. What is untotalizable about the law, its unsayable, unknowable dimension—our very immersion in it, the way we are inscribed in it—is totalized by isolating special well-known things and making them forbidden to discourse. This is one way in which to understand the strange feature of "taboo," noted by Freud, its reference to both the prohibited, terrifying thing and the prohibition itself. [27] By making something "taboo," we isolate areas of discourse which we are to circumvent, so as not to encounter head on what, in discourse is for us thinglike, nondiscursive in its effect— sheer opacity.

Lacan makes his point by means of a rather humoristic—and strangely current—example, in which the law forbids us from saying that the king of England is an idiot under penalty of death by beheading.

> If it is forbidden to say that the king of England is an idiot, under pain of having one's head cut off, one will not say it, and in consequence of this sole fact, one will be led into not saying a great many other things—that is to say, everything which reveals the glaring reality that the king of England is an idiot. . . . The subject of the king of England has many reasons for wanting to express things which have a most direct relation with the fact that the king of England is an idiot. Let us say it passes into his dreams . . . the subject dreams that he has his head cut off. [28]

Censorship forbids us, that is, from making explicit what everybody knows, what can only be alluded to, hinted at, expressed indirectly, a driver of subtle subversion—that, underneath the crown, there is a human being just like us, more or less an idiot. He is merely fulfilling a function. To make the mechanics of authority explicit is tantamount to sacrilege—it points out the constructed, arbitrary structure of rule. To admit this is taboo. Making public what everybody knows involves a strange "reflective" twist. It transforms what "everybody knows" into something which "everybody knows that everybody knows." It discloses an open secret. From this point on, you may go on ignoring it, but you are, as it were, explicitly implicated in the act of censorship. The subject of such open secrets is a figure of the "big other" dubbed by Slavoj Žižek the other supposed to believe, the subject whose innocence must be protected. To bypass censorship is to make the "innocent" other aware of what everybody else already knows.

There is a crucial lesson here as to the nature and history of the unwritten law. As Žižek notes, in twentieth-century totalitarianism we witness an extra twist in this scheme: more than any forbidden content, what must never be avowed is the prohibition itself.[29] In this sense, censorship is always "self-censorship," it must always conceal its own act. However, if this is indeed a structural feature of the unwritten law—ingrained in its very unwrittenness—can we speak of significant historical changes? Paradoxical as this must sound, we might detect a general trajectory, in which the unwritten law becomes increasingly more unwritten, becoming, as it were, more and more itself, more and more fully transparent, and more and more present in its very transparency, the more everything is made explicit and comes into the open.

Consider Edith Wharton's *Age of Innocence* (1920). As is well known, the entire drama of the novel circles around the tension between the old world and its aristocratic code and the new world, already fully integrated into the capitalist system and its ethos of the bourgeoisie. But what, precisely, do we witness in this tension between the old and the new? The countess Olenska arrives from a world in which, to put things very simply, the open, public law is full of prohibition, enshrined in religion and tradition, whereas the unwritten law is a delicate dance of decadent transgression, a space of transgressive freedom. Call this the aristocratic code. It is truly old, and can be traced all the way back to Plato's "second-rank" law, according to which the fundamental unwritten law is the very splitting between a public realm of decency and a private realm of transgression. In the new world, on the contrary, culture leans toward explicit liberalism, the formal code being one of progressive individuals, much less formally bound to tradition and religion, and so it is up to the unwritten, informal law, to be a space of prohibition. In this modern, inverted constellation, prohibition is truly a private affair, no longer supported by a public moral code. As the unwritten law can no longer be identified with tradition and its private, aristocratic transgression, it becomes more properly unwritten, so to speak. It is now, itself, taboo, a set of prohibitions that are themselves a subject of censorship.[30] Foucault describes in similar terms the distinction between law and discipline: "In the system of the law, what is undetermined is what is permitted; in the system of disciplinary regulation, what is determined is what one must do, and consequently, everything else, being undetermined, is prohibited."[31]

So where are we now? Everyone is allowed, indeed incited, to say that the king of England is an idiot. It even seems to be inscribed into the ceremony of coronation—in a video that went viral, we all had to watch Charles III, during a signing ceremony, get annoyed at a pen, like him failing to fulfill its one and only function—to produce a signature![32] We are ceremoniously anticeremonial. Furthermore, we now have kings, authority figures, that ceaselessly display their idiocy, making themselves utterly immune from such ridicule. Not only immune—the more they are mocked, the stronger they seem to get. Has censorship been lifted? Are we no longer under the influence of the unwritten law, the law insofar as it is not understood? Does it no longer have a hold on us?

What interests Lacan in censorship is its productive function. The forbidden statement incites much psychic activity in the subjects of this king of England, and censorship appears by means of their dreams: being unable to say that the king is an idiot, the subject dreams that he has his head cut off. Censorship is productive of fantasies in which we may not directly fulfill the wish of lifting the censorship, say by dreaming that we are dancing and cursing on the king's grave, but rather in which we are punished for having thus transgressed. The transgression itself, mind you, appears only indirectly, implicit in our punishment. Today we can mock the king, the king makes a mockery of himself, but we still dream—now more than ever—that our heads have been cut off. Our fantasy of being seized by blind mechanisms of power, being headless subjects, is the clearest sign that censorship is more powerful than ever at the very moment it seems to have disappeared. It is within this dream that we need to search for what could be called the censorship of censorship.

FROM SUBSTANCE TO NETWORK

We have seen, on Arendt's part, that authority is occluded by functionality. Now let us turn to look at how things appear from the other side, as it were, from the side of the domain of intelligibility of functionality, namely, technology. Philosopher of technology Gilbert Simondon defines the technical mentality (and technical being) as juxtaposed to the rationale of religion, like figure to ground. "Technicity appears as a structure that resolves an incompatibility: it specializes the figural functions, while religions on their side specialize the functions of ground; the original magical universe, which is rich in potentials, structures itself by splitting in two."[33]

Simondon's juxtaposition, or bifurcation to use his terms, of technology and religion, it might be noted, is taken by him to be more primitive than the bifurcation between theory and practice. What he terms "magic" is his attempt to capture the primordial ground of intelligibility, "before" the seemingly primordial distinction between figure and ground, without automatically falling into the trap of "the night in which, as the saying goes, all cows are black,"[34] that is, a situation in which no significant difference can emerge. According to Simondon's account, in the magical phase of being, technology and religion are conjoined. Magic, for Simondon, is what can only be understood by us as religious technology, and technological religion. It is a "technique" serving religious purposes, and a "religion" organized around a unique, practical mastery of superhuman powers. This primal unity of technology and religion in magic is brought out by Simondon in his account of the centrality of singular points in space, such as mountaintops, in which there is a meeting between human and cosmic powers, affording equal standing, so to speak, to human and superhuman agency.[35] And so Simondon's magical phase is emphatically prehistorical. It is a present that can have no before and no after, a technology that is auratic through and through.[36] In it, space and time form privileged sites of conversion, where human, finite agency and the cosmic absolute come together. While concentrated in such privileged sites, it is unclear how such an ultimately flat ontology can allow for transformative events, for moments that introduce a gap between "before" and "after," that introduce a significant tear in the fabric of space and time thus woven together.

Nonetheless, rather inexplicably, this "magical" phase bifurcates, it cannot sustain the polarity it holds together, and the primal bifurcation is that between religion, which seeks to grasp things in their superphenomenal totality (that is, it inquires after the ground of being), and technology, which seeks to grasp things in their phenomenal partiality, what can be isolated, analyzed, torn apart and recombined. Technology thus arises as functional to its core, and in bifurcation with religion: "A mode of knowledge sui generis, that essentially uses the analogical transfer and the paradigm, and founds itself on the discovery of common modes of functioning—or of regimes of operation—in otherwise different orders of reality that are chosen just as well from the living or the inert as from the human or the non-human."[37]

If authority is effaced by the functional view, then it is precisely technology, or the technical mentality, that does the effacing. Consider the two postulates Simondon offers for the technical mentality:

1. The subjects are relatively detachable from the whole of which they are a part
2. If one wants to understand a being completely, one must study it by considering it in its entelechy, and not in its inactivity or its static state.[38]

If authority belongs to a substantial whole, technology is what tears it apart. If authority is to be grasped as pure virtuality, technology is all about actualization—specifically, however paradoxical—of the virtual as such. If authority preserves and sacralizes the past, technology finds its end in the open-ended future; it has to materialize itself in ever more concrete form. It is, so to speak, that which understands its own being as developmental, as that which, beginning abstractly, must find in development its concrete existence.[39] Simondon develops a full-blown philosophical account of technical objects, which hinges on the realization of the fundamentally deessentializing nature of the technical, its pure functionality. To paraphrase Heidegger, Simondon's point can be summed up by the slogan: The essence of technology is (that) nothing (is) essential. If authority belongs to a sacralizing intelligibility, technology is its direct opposite, desacralizing everything, stripping it down to its function. In terms of the distinction made famous by Kant, technology is the mother of understanding, and authority the mother of reason. Understanding analyzes and tears apart, whereas reason demands that things would be brought together into a comprehensible—if uncomprehended—totality.

This is why Simondon conceives of the network—what he has in mind is the power grid, but also communication networks—as the highest realization of the inessential nature of the technical. Indeed, without explicitly avowing it, it seems evident that in the technical network Simondon detects a new, perhaps higher phase of the primordially lost magic.

> It is the standardization of the subsets, the industrial possibility of the production of separate pieces that are all alike, that allows for the creation of networks. . . . It is not a question here of the rape of nature or of the victory of the human being over the elements, because in fact it is the natural structures themselves that serve as the attachment point for the network that is being developed; the relay points of the Hertzian "cables," for example, rejoin with the high sites of ancient sacredness above the valleys and the seas. Here, the technical mentality successfully completes itself and rejoins nature by turning itself into a thought-network, into the material and conceptual synthesis of particularity and concentration, individuality and collectivity—because the entire force of the network is available in each one of its points, and its mazes are woven together with those of the world, in the concrete and the particular.[40]

Note how the power grid is layered over the very same privileged points of conversion between human and superhuman agency, turning each of them into a node in the network. And so we arrive at our first possible definition of the network, from the standpoint of the philosophy of technology: The network is precisely a way to realize (in the dual sense of the term) the part-whole relation in a nonorganic, insubstantial way. Neither the part nor the whole is a substance, only their reticular relation, whose primary aim is to prevent them from stabilizing into anything resembling the philosophical notion of substance. From substance to network, if you will. Ultimately, for Simondon, the network is the way in which virtuality is actualized as such, paradoxical as this must be. To make this more readily graspable, let us take another look at how he describes the ideal (i.e., fully realized, concrete) technical object:

> The essential lies in this: in order for an object to allow for the development of the technical mentality and to be chosen by it, the object itself needs to be of a reticular structure. . . . If one imagines an object that, instead of being closed, offers parts that are conceived as being as close to indestructible as possible, and others by contrast . . . [with] a very high capacity to adjust each usage, one obtains an open object that can be completed, improved, maintained in the state of perpetual actuality. . . . The postindustrial technical object is the unity of two layers of reality—a layer that is as stable and permanent as possible, which adheres to the user and is made to last, and a layer that can be perpetually replaced, changed, renewed, because it is made up of elements that are all similar, impersonal, mass produced by industry and distributed by all the networks of exchange.[41]

This is quite a striking description of the smartphone, especially considering its author passed away in 1989. The point is that it is through participation in this network that the technical object always remains contemporary to its use, always new. A perfected technical object is a concrete manifestation of the network, and the network is actualized virtuality, a system for perpetual entelechy.

Let us address the major theoretical challenge we have stumbled upon here. In speaking about authority, we found ourselves talking about a certain relation to our linguistic being, our being in language, the way it always precedes us and is unknown by us. And while speaking about technology, we were made aware of its radically deessentializing, disruptive effect, perhaps culminating in the medium in which we find ourselves today. When it comes to inquiries about language and media, there seems to be something akin to the famous uncertainty principle in physics: the more one focuses on the effects of historically particular technical media, the less one is capable of grasping mediation as such, language, and vice versa.

We might get a little aid here from Marshall McLuhan, best known for his oft-quoted and mostly misunderstood slogan "The medium is the message."

> In a culture like ours, long accustomed to splitting and dividing all things as a means of control, it is sometimes a bit of a shock to be reminded that, in operational and practical fact, the medium is the message. . . . The instance of the electric light may prove illuminating in this connection. The electric light is pure information. It is a medium without a message,

as it were, unless it is used to spell out some verbal ad or name. This fact, characteristic of all media, means that the "content" of any medium is always another medium. The content of writing is speech, just as the written word is the content of print, and print is the content of the telegraph. . . . When the light is used for brain surgery or night baseball [it] is a matter of indifference. It could be argued that these activities are in some way the "content" of the electric light, since they could not exist without the electric light. This fact merely underlines the point that "the medium is the message" because it is the medium that shapes and controls the scale and form of human association and action. The content or uses of such media are as diverse as they are ineffectual in shaping the form of human association. Indeed, it is only too typical that the "content" of any new medium blinds us to the character of the medium. . . . The electric light escapes attention as a communication medium just because it has no "content." And this makes it an invaluable instance of how people fail to study media at all.[42]

McLuhan is not known for the clarity of his argumentation, and so it is easy to miss the full significance of what is here postulated. What is at stake is nothing short of the very distinction between a medium and a mean. We may therefore reconstruct his argument and pick up a few crucial points: A medium is not to be understood as a specific use of technology, a specialized function, say, a "means of communication." The medium is what emerges in the gap between the use of a technology, its function, what he calls content, and the message, we might say its significance—the way it reshapes our very "groundwork," the way we associate and act. The difficulty in studying media, the reason why McLuhan quite rightly argues that we mostly fail to study them, is precisely that the medium is an entity of the gap between our intentional use of things, as a means to ends, which is the viewpoint of technology—but also, mind you, of power—and what happens to us, the way we are, in our very activity, inscribed in a medium we cannot quite be cognizant of.

Does the foregrounding of functionality not equally describe the reversal in the relation between power and authority? More explicitly than anyone else, Foucault had advanced the notion of "technologies of power," often pitted against older, symbolic models of authorization. According to this understanding, the modern modality of power is technological. Power in modern societies has no center, and is very much understood as a sort of headless "instrumentality," a machine producing effects. While the process described by Foucault is real and of the highest significance, the problem is that this theoretical framework fails to account for the manner in which authority insists, precisely as that which is veiled by the very open, decentralized mechanisms of power. The message ingrained in the very manifestation of power. Authority, we have said following Arendt, is a thing of the past. But precisely as such, under modern conditions its mode of appearance is that of the return of the repressed: forgotten, but not gone. Foregrounding technology should not lead us to think of authority as historically outdated, but rather to consider its modes of insistence.

For our purposes here, what matters is the striking resemblance between McLuhan's account of media and Arendt's analysis of authority, as the ground-work and flipside of functionality. But it also adds a significant twist to it. In itself, the medium is totally transparent, indeed a matter of indifference, and it can only come to view when covered over by content, in its very eclipse, as it were. In this way, the content of technology comes to function as the veil of beauty, through which truth—the elusive totality of the medium—can shine forth. We need only add, as Lacan does, that this pertains also to our natural language.

As Lacan puts its apropos of the terms we used above of figure and ground, both are, as it were, manifestations of the gap: "Where is the background? Is it absent? No. Rupture, split, the stroke of the opening makes absence emerge— just as the cry does not stand against a background of silence, but on the con-trary, makes the silence emerge as silence."[43]

The background is not anterior to the discontinuity of the gap, but a prod-uct of it. It is only with the cry—something that breaks the silence, and stands out as the primordial signifier without a signified—that silence is made pres-ent precisely as a dense medium, the palpable presence of the unspoken, the unspeakable. Here Lacan takes us one important step beyond McLuhan: if indeed the content of a medium is always another medium, then the con-tent of speech, our natural medium, is silence as a medium, the presence of absence—or the unconscious. The medium as such, in its purity, is the gap between the lines, so to speak, the erotization of signification, the sense that something lurks in the background behind what is presented to us. This would be the zero point of intuition, the sense for sense.

What is important to note at this point, however, is the reversal that took place between the functional, or technical, and authority, reminiscent of Ben-jamin's famed opening thesis on history with its parable of the puppet and the dwarf. There Benjamin suggests that the seemingly automated puppet "his-torical materialism" would win consistently, as long as the ugly dwarf secretly operating it, "theology," was kept out of sight.[44] The power of the parable has much to do with the way in which it reverses the standard relations between technology and religion, where industrial technology replaces and renders superfluous religion by reinserting religion as the very invisible "driver" of the machine's automatism.

In Arendt's account, authority had to veil functionality, above all, its own. Had we known how it works, so to speak, the magic would be gone. And maybe it is. McLuhan offers his intervention at a point in which, on the contrary, functionality is foregrounded, and it is the media effect, the background structuring of our life, that is veiled by it.

In traditional authority, the eternal past of time immemorial is sacralized, and change is either absorbed by it or denied. In a technologically mediated environment, change is foregrounded, preservation of the past loses its internal rationale, and so the repetition that precedes us, so to speak, acquires instead the form of haunting insistence. As Joan Copjec put it:

> Modernity was founded on a definitive break with the authority of our ancestors, who were no longer conceived as the ground for our actions or beliefs. And yet this effective undermining of their authority confronted us with another difficulty; it is as if in rendering our ancestors fallible we had transformed the past from the repository of their already accomplished deeds and discovered truths into a kind of holding cell of all that was unactualized and unthought. The desire of our ancestors and thus the virtual past, the past that had never come to pass, or was not yet finished, weighed disturbingly on us, pressing itself on our attention.[45]

One primary function of tradition is the social organization of involuntary memory: festive days are collective occasions for the evocation of the mythical past—the form of signification that the past takes precisely insofar as it eludes articulation. As tradition loosens its hold, we are faced, individually, with the burden of the mythological, virtual past, which is why modernity is so often theorized in the context of the affect of anxiety.

> The break instituted by modernity did not cause the past to become effectively dead to us, its retreat turned out to be modal (that is, it became a matter of the virtual, not actual past) rather than total. We were thus not left simply alone in a cloistral present cut off from our ancestors, but found ourselves alone with something that did not clearly manifest itself. Anxiety is this feeling of being anchored to an alien self from which we are unable to separate ourselves nor to assume as our own, of being connected to a past that, insofar as it had not happened, was impossible to shed. Our implication in the past was thus deepened. For, while formerly a subject's ties to her past were strictly binding, they were experienced as external, as of the order of simple constraint. One had to submit to a destiny one did not elect and often experienced as unjust. But one could rail against one's destiny, curse one's fate. With modernity this is no longer possible. The "god of destiny" is now dead and we no longer inherit the debts of our ancestors, but become that debt. We cannot distance ourselves efficiently from the past to be able to curse the fate it hands us, but must, as Lacan put it, bear as jouissance the injustice that horrifies us.[46]

In modernity we are progressively faced with the unwritten law—a term, you will recall, which historically has been translated as both custom, tradition, and natural law—as such, that is, as unwritten, hauntingly present in its virtual, unrealized modality. It becomes, as it was for Benjamin, the form of appearance of the mythical as such. Differently put, traditional authority is a way to give a legitimate, indeed central, cultural place to (primary) repression. Primary repression is the emergence of the very space of repression, structurally preceding any repressed content.[47] It is, in this context, the very marking of an alien territory, extimate to the self. There is a knowledge the subject does not possess that is vital, crucial, to her very being. Indeed, it is the piece of her being which was, so to speak, sacrificed in "symbolic castration": the knowledge of what she desires, the missing piece that forms her unconscious. One way of describing a traditional way of life would be to say that in it, one attributes to tradition and its authority figures that very absent knowledge. It is, say, what the gods know, what we might get echoes of via their messengers, and through the mediation of those trained in reading their signs.

Or, somewhat more trivially, it is the automatic answer supplied by tradition as to how and who I am to be—what does it mean for me, say, to become a man? It is to become like my father. An impossibility, to be sure. Following the logic of this much simplified example we could say that in modernity, in part because of the increasing pace of technological transformation of our very surroundings, we find ourselves turning to a reversed, negative answer: what does it mean for me to be a man in the twenty-first century? Well, I don't know, but it certainly means being different from my father.[48]

As Freud taught us long ago, negation is a sure sign of repression.[49] But note that in this simplified narrative of ours, it is repression itself that is repressed. We know that we need not, cannot, and should not resemble what came before us. But do we thereby relieve ourselves of the weight of the past? To the contrary. With modernity, repression is repressed—it is precisely by knowing full well how things function that we are effectively mystified as to their effect on us. And so one dramatic consequence of this redoubled repression, or redoubled censorship, is a transformation of our relation to anxiety. It is as if the idea of censorship has become more terrifying for us than any terrifying content deserving of censorship. We can accept, maybe even welcome, the most terrifying reality, so long as we can consider it known by us, uncensored. As long as we witness limits transgressed, we can simultaneously admit and deny the limits we are approaching.

Hence the strange appeal of transgressive authority figures—in their transgression, they seem to be exposing the myriad unwritten rules governing the public space of political appearances. There is a strange enjoyment that accompanies our witnessing of such behavior, as if it comforts us by confirming our worst expectations and bringing them into the open.

ON THE "MAGIC" OF THE OBSCENE

Obscenity is linked to the mythical, daemonic underside of the law. In his work on obscene words, Sándor Ferenczi notes that, in his clinical practice, patients avoid certain words having to do with sexual or excremental objects and processes, preferring to use other, cleaner terms instead. "How is it," Ferenczi wonders, "that it is so much harder to designate the same thing with one term than with another?"[50] The reason, as he goes on to speculate, has to do with the special status of the obscene words, which he also calls word-images. Drawing on a line of argument from Freud's work on obscene jokes,[51] Ferenczi comes to the following, generalized conclusion: "An obscene word has a peculiar power of compelling the hearer to imagine the object it denotes, the sexual organ or function, in *substantial actuality*."[52]

The obscene word does not *represent* the object; rather, it functions as if it were, directly, the object, in all its carnality. In a twist on Swift's philosophers of Lagado,[53] the utterance of an obscene word functions much like "pulling the cat out of the bag," and displaying the object directly, with the emphasis put on "pulling it out," that is to say on the act of exhibition. Words that behave like things are far from being convenient modes of communication, as they are imagined to be by Swift's philosophers. They belong to a precommunicative dimension of language. Ferenczi's obscene words are what contemporary philosophers would call "performatives." Ferenczi points to oaths[54] as refined sublimations of obscene words, and notes that they "do not at all belong . . . to conceptual speech; they do not serve the needs of conscious communication but represent reactions to a stimulus which are nearly related to gestures."[55] These are words that function like acts or objects, fully materialized.

For Ferenczi, obscene words carry the traces of "attributes that have belonged to all words in some early stage of psychical development."[56] At this stage, before the interference of, and gradual compromise with, the reality principle, which, in imposing limitations on the child's will, teaches him to distinguish the wish-idea from real gratification, "the idea is . . . treated as equivalent to reality."[57] The capacity for abstract thought and representation is coeval with the separation of wish and reality, word and image, but this separation is not absolute, and the potential of regression remains, as is evidenced by the "magical power" retained in obscene words.

So much, then, for direct representation: obscene words do not represent but rather exhibit, in an immediate fashion, the pre-Oedipal, primordial thing which words (that is to say, our normal, discursive use of language, and the assumption of linguistic "aboutness") put at a distance. Obscene words operate, on a miniature scale, a regression to infantile sexuality. It is not only the specific object that comes to view with the utterance of the obscene word but the very murky background, the preontological void to which it belongs, in which reality itself, as an objective limit and a world, has not yet been established. The pleasure—and horror—of the obscene has to do with the collapse of the gap that separates a wish from its fulfillment, or, for that matter, a command from its execution. In this sense, it might be better to distinguish between the objective violence of the state and the violence of the object disclosed by the obscene, that is, the way in which, in the obscene, we encounter an objectivity that is presubjective. The "truth effect" of the obscene has much to do with the way in which it seems to manifest something more primitive than our subjectivity, a real which our objective reality primordially represses. It seems compelling because primordial, belonging to a more archaic dimension of our being.

What are we to make of the relation between the obscene and the magical, or sacred? As a linguistic phenomenon, we know from our everyday experience that obscene words are interchangeable with evocations of the holy, in their grammatical function as expletives, words that add emphasis but do not add meaning. In his famed introduction to Marcel Mauss, Lévi-Strauss leaned on precisely this "grammatical" insight, to critique the various "emic" words anthropologists relied on as conveying a sense of magic, words like hau, or mana. What anthropologists failed to take note of, so ran Lévi-Strauss's critique, was that such words served their function precisely by having no signified. They were floating signifiers, stabilizing the primordial surplus of sense, the overwhelming excess of being over language, that is, what we cannot make sense of.[58]

It is possible to condense an entire history of "disenchantment" into the observation that what anthropologists discovered as oh so many "proper names" for a grammatical function amongst "primitive people" we moderns have, quite properly, named, well, "it." We speak of someone "having it," and account for what exceeds our causal-mechanistic explanations by "(sh)it happens." We might think that we have thereby overcome "magical thinking," replacing fate with contingency, and properly naming that which we cannot name, je ne sais quoi. But of course, naming "it" does not rob it of its powers, which is why there is a need for psychoanalysis. Psychoanalysis is quite famously the science of "it," the German Es, translated as "id," which is the clear, grammatical expression of the unconscious, that something within us that is totally alien to us, the very stuff of analysands' complaints: all of those things that just keep happening to us.

God is unconscious. Now we know. But what happens when we come to realize that? Now that, with the advent of psychoanalysis, the phallic function has stopped being unwritten, does God, or the divine, cease to be unconscious, or, having been able to name it, have we altered our relation to our very unconscious? The phallic function is the castrating effect of the symbolic, the way in which entrance to the symbolic universe is tantamount to a (primordial) loss of nonlinguistic being, a loss "symbolized" in the symbol as such, in the promise of an enigmatic, floating signifier, to hold within its fold all that was (primordially) lost for the speaking subject. To say that it became writable is to say that we can now speak of this as a function.[59] We can describe this objectively, as it were, not as enthralled believers but as cool researchers, thereby imagining ourselves to be outside its grip. Symbols are for them, for those who believe in them, not for us, who understand their function. Seeing how things function has become our way to deny their effect on us. It is as if we cannot stop drawing phallic symbols as a way to prove that the phallic function is no more.

But does the fact that obscene words and evocations of the sacred share a grammatical function erase the distinction between the obscene and the sacred? That would be the ultimate, cynical conclusion, but it would also be too hasty.

Lévi-Strauss's floating signifier is certainly a close cousin of Lacan's master signifier, which is also defined, in part, as having no signified. And indeed Lacan, at the very end of Seminar XVII, draws a direct connection between his master signifier and the obscene.

> It does have to be said that it is unusual to die of shame. Yet it is the one sign—I have been talking about this for a while now, how a signifier becomes a sign—the one sign whose genealogy one can be certain of, namely, that it is descended from a signifier. After all, any sign can fall under the suspicion of being a pure sign, that is to say, obscene.[60]

In evoking the relation between the signifier and the sign, Lacan is suggesting a strong theory of expression. For him, a signifier represents a subject to another signifier; that is the way in which subjectivity is inscribed in language as merely alluded to, present in its absence, so to speak. A sign is what signifies a subject to another subject. Lacan's favored example is smoke, signaling the faraway presence of another human subject. In calling shame the one sign whose genealogy one can be sure of, Lacan is suggesting that the affect of shame bears a direct testimony of the unconscious. Shame indicates, immediately, to another subject, the presence of another subject's unconscious. Feeling ashamed, even in private, signals to us the presence of another subject. At this most intimate juncture between the private and the public, between the unconscious and the conscious, where the public gaze is most interiorized, and the most private is radically exposed to the gaze of others, we experience a certain intimacy with our extimacy, so to speak, we are close to what is irreducibly foreign to us.

Shame seems to be the objective reality of the subject. Blushing exteriorizes on the body what we feel inside; it is an affect that is directly legible for others, like the mark of Cain. We might say that in blushing, as blood, the inner fluid of life, rushes to our face, our body becomes flesh. Our flesh shines through our body's "natural" mask, the face, and we have a strong sense of our bodies as what exposes us to, rather than hides us from, the gaze of others, the window to our flesh.[61] They can see right through me, we think to ourselves.

Indeed, we may put this reflexively—shame is the feeling that our feelings are out there for all to see, that our interiority is exposed. We are shamed by the way shame discloses our shame. By the same token, someone else's shame is never something we witness disinterestedly, as if taking note of a state of affairs. While ever so private, shame is directly a social event, in which we are involved.[62] Ordinarily, we feel a share of the shame of others, we feel implicated by someone else being shamed.

What then is the substance of Lacan condemnations? At first blush, it seems that he is merely producing a reactionary, conservative position, scolding his audience for having lost a sense of shame. Lacan seems to speak to his audience like a preacher to his parish which had been led astray: "The more unworthy, obscene, the better off you are."[63] But Lacan's point is more complex. This scolding comes at the last session of a seminar held against the background of the great unrest of '68, a seminar dedicated to both the permutations and the persistence of what Lacan calls the "master's discourse." In the seminar he develops an account of a new social link he believes has become dominant with capitalism, which he calls university discourse, a social link that does not so much replace the old master's discourse but rather obfuscates and represses it.

In this final session of his seminar, Lacan is indeed suggesting that there is a weakening of the efficacy of the master signifier, indicated by it becoming more and more a rarity for people to die of shame, to die, as it were, directly because of the presence of a master's discourse. In this Lacan is echoing a narrative of modernity as the decline of "status." In a more traditional setting, let us say, where social mores are directly obligatory, what Lacan refers to here by alluding to "honor culture," where, to employ Girard's terminology, mores are directly responsible for the containment of violence, one is much more likely to be willing to risk death rather than shame than in a hedonistic, capitalist, postideological society.

It is because the master's discourse has receded to the background that we find it more difficult to subjectify shame, which is a mode of appearance of what is overwhelming in being, but that does not mean that shame is simply out of the picture. On the contrary, it is because we are less capable of feeling ashamed that we produce a wide range of symptoms. It is the business of psychoanalysis to discover, behind those varied symptoms, what Lacan calls the "shame of living": "Shame of living is what psychoanalysis discovers. It's justified by the fact that you do not die of shame, that is, by maintaining with all your force a discourse of the perverted master—which is the university discourse. Rhegel yourself!"[64]

What Lacan expects his audience to be ashamed of is their complicity with a "perverse master," a master that does not put them to shame but rather commands for them to "enjoy!"[65]

Shamelessness is not simply the evidence of a receding master. Rather, the decrease in subjective shame indicates for Lacan the rise in what might be called objective, systemic shame. This is even more apparent in our contemporary culture of online shaming. In shaming strangers online, we encounter what could be labeled as "shameless shame."[66] Outrage is being scandalized by other people's shamelessness: they should be ashamed of themselves! We shame people whom we take to have no shame, and we do so self-righteously, the very opposite sentiment of shame: pride in being without blame. It is our righteous function to shame those who have sinned, to expose to social violence that dimension of transgression that legal punishment doesn't quite reach, its libidinal charge, the flesh of the sin. Shaming is a supplement of legal violence, directed to the same, elusive ground of the transgressive act which has introduced the expert on the soul into modern mechanisms of punishment. Moral indignation becomes an extension of the law, serving punishment where no punishment would do.

Ours is an unapologetic shame. Which is to say that apology today is effective only when withheld. Those shamed fall into two groups: those who apologize, and those who refuse to. The former take upon themselves a ritual distinguished by its constitutive lack of effect: they have to follow the script, talk about how this—the exposure of their shameful behavior—has been an education for them, etc., knowing full well no apology will do. They are to disappear, that is what is expected from them, nothing else. Wanting to disappear is a marker of shame, and now it is "they" who want it from you, it arrives as an explicit demand from the outside. And so their apologies are merely buying time, staying in the public eye for a minute longer than they should, proving they are not sufficiently shamed. These are shameful apologies, only adding to the shame. The other group, on the contrary, would rather go to jail than apologize. They know, on some primal level, that apologizing is the one thing that would instantaneously rob them of their charisma: it would imply that they too are, after all, subjects to shame.

But the juxtaposition between shaming as a quasi-objectified instrument of social punishment and openly transgressive behavior, "subjectively shameless," is misleading. Subjectified shamelessness, the open transgressive behavior of new figures of authority, declaring itself to be without shame, is effective precisely because of its "objective" dimension. Openly transgressive behavior has an effect of truth precisely by addressing our sense of shame; the more shameful their behavior, the more they seem to be revealing our own, shameful transgressivity. This is what makes their behavior "transgressive," and our reaction complicit: being shamed, however much we may want to distance ourselves in our "outrage," we confirm their act as an act of exposure, exposing things we would have preferred to remain hidden. Their lack of shame is direct evidence of objective shame, shame as a duty we cannot escape, though one we are no longer capable of assuming.

Undermining traditional master figures, exposing and shaming them, is an act of desacralization, uncovering the obscene enjoyment behind official, sacred, substantial values. But the predicament of our contemporary society is such that what is truly dominant is not old masters, speaking in the name of sacred, timeless values, but rather the obscene enticement to enjoy, which is much harder to subvert. It is harder to subvert in no small part because of the "truth effect" of obscenity, the way it presents itself as the dirty secret coming to light. To combat the inevitability of cynical wisdom, it is therefore crucial to scrutinize this much more elusive mode of concealment by means of exposure. What is veiled in exposure?

THE TRUTH EFFECT OF ENJOYMENT

What is it that makes obscene power compelling? How does it draw us into its net, presenting itself as utterly inescapable? Once power moves into the terrain of unwritten laws, winking at us, as it were, it becomes so much harder to imagine a way out. To a large extent, obscene power is compelling because it makes us complicit.[67] Simply put, we cannot break out because we enjoy—which is to say not only because there is a certain pleasure or seduction in the ways in which we are under the hold of power, but also, more significantly, that we feel guilty, responsible, because we were forced to want it, so to speak. That, at least, is the illusion at stake here. And it is a powerful one.

As Zupančič makes clear, enjoyment presents itself as an answer to the unanswerable question of desire.[68] What do I want? What am I to want? Such is the question that instigates discourse, that coconstitutes our barred subjectivity, missing the crucial piece of its being that would make it whole, and the big other, who holds that piece of the puzzle. The effectiveness of enjoyment lies precisely in that it presents itself as the answer to that constitutive question. You want to enjoy! We may not like this as an answer to what we desire most, but we also find it uncannily hard to shake off. As much as we dislike it, and as much as we might know better, there is something of a compulsion to that obscene answer.

If desire is anything, it is insatiable. Desire is discontent. For the object cause of its desire is constitutively lacking; it only exists in absentia. Desire has an object *cause* of desire, structurally missing, which is to say there is no object that can fill its place. Why and how, then, are we tempted to cede our desire to enjoyment? What is it about our contemporary modes of enjoyment that impresses such a sense of objectivity on us? That is capable of eliciting not only compliance but indeed a deep sense of complicity, a sense that it is our guilty secret that has been exposed?

Perhaps the key lies in this: enjoyment presents itself as evidence of our true desire, precisely because we do not want it. Isn't it precisely in its forced aspect, the way it feels imposed on us, overwhelming, that we feel most intimately implicated by it? We don't want it, we feel ashamed, exposed by it, which is why we suspect it must be what we truly want. Its "object" nature, so to speak, what is objectionable about it, is directly what impresses us as its objectivity, its status as the ultimate secret we would have liked to keep secret from ourselves. It is precisely because the object cause of desire is in a strict sense supraphenomenal that enjoyment is such an effective semblance of it.

We have a constitutively missing object, Lacan's objet a—what better way to "feel in touch" with it can we have than to have something presented to us as the secret wish we would not want to admit to? The transgressive aspect of enjoyment is—as such—an immensely effective semblance of the impossibility of the objet a, "translating" the impossible to the censored. Censorship, you will recall, is such a translation of the impossible to the forbidden. And it is this function of censorship that we have now effectively censored. The censorship of censorship we are discussing here is by no means the abolishment of censorship in the name of truth and liberty; to the contrary, it is the blind reliance on the truth of the censored coming to light, the ultimate fetishization of the impossible. We have finally found a way to directly experience the impossible, we delude ourselves, by bathing in what is shameful. Our shame is direct evidence that we are touching on the impossible "real." We can thus use even traumatic encounters with the real as covers for the traumatic negativity of the real; we satiate ourselves with the "surplus reality" of obscenity so as not to encounter the radical void of the real.

What we are encountering here is the erosion between perversion and hysteria (neurosis). We are made to believe that objectified enjoyment reveals the true, perverse core of our desire, our unconscious desire to be instruments of the other's desire. Precisely this perversion functions as a unique lie, lying by telling the truth about something of which no truth can be asserted (the truth can only be half-said.[69] The terrifying, ontological negativity of desire, the structural absence of an answer to the question "what do I want?" (what does the other want from me?), is given an answer—the other wants to enjoy me, and so I want to be the instrument of its enjoyment. In this way the other and I complete each other, form a whole. What "I" is all about is the saturation of the other, and the other is nothing but the desire to see us fulfill our duty, serve our purpose, that is, serving it (for our benefit). This is the radical evil of perversion: by "satiating" the big other, we effectively treat the ground as existing.[70] That which can only ex-sist, so to speak, conditioning and uncondi-tioned, the symbolic order in which we are inscribed, is animated for us (has a hold on us) by appearing to hold the object cause of our desire, the answer to the question "what do I want?" Perversion is not the ultimate truth of our being (our relation to Being, the big other), but a kind of defense against the horror of the unanswerable question "what do you want?," our complex, cut-ting entanglement with it—the abyss of freedom.[71] Perversion sees the lack in the big other, but interprets it directly as its own proper place. In face of the horrifying abyss of primary repression, the opacity of the big other, present-ing us with the question "what do you want?" (what are we to want, what the other wants us to want), the pervert inverts the unanswerable question into an answer—what the other wants is for me to plug its hole, to make it whole. I have a task, to be the instrument of the other's desire. I have to make the other whole, which is to say, paradoxically, to make it real, realize it, by taking it to be real, that is, not the virtual ground of my freedom, but a strange substance, unlike any other. It is not the other who holds the secret of my desire, but I, the little pervert, who is the answer to her desire.

Everything boils down to this dual interpretation of the negativity of desire (subjectivity): desire wants to want, its eternal motto being "this is not it." It is because of this that enjoyment is such an effective semblance of the *objet a*—it must be what we truly want, because we clearly don't want it—but also, for the very same reason, why we must insist on the ontological (as opposed to moral) innocence of desire. Perverse enjoyment tells us that this is it, but the truth of desire is that we are structurally ignorant about what "it" is like.[72]

And so we can come back to our comparison between the master signifier and the obscene word: yes, there is an obvious similarity—both are nonrepre-sentational. The difference, however, though subtle, is all-important. A master signifier both "solidifies" and undermines the representational order, func-tioning as its constitutive or sovereign exception. The obscene word seems to belong to a completely different order of language. Put differently, the master signifier "pretends" to belong to the order of reason and representation, but "secretly" transgresses it. The obscene word, on the contrary, "pretends" to be nonlinguistic violence, self-identical like a slap in the face. What it thereby masks is precisely its mediated character, the way its violence is only operative against the background of a representational order which it disturbs.

Enjoyment does effectively present itself, paradoxically, as what we truly want precisely when it shames us, precisely when we do not, cannot, want to want it. And so the more shameful, the more degrading, the more it strikes us as the real thing. We couldn't possibly want this, so no doubt this is the real we have been hiding from ourselves. Here we can see how the notion of objective enjoyment helps articulate what remains unthought in objective knowledge

(Marx), namely, the way in which confronting our enjoyment without us, so to speak, in its objectivity, reducing ourselves to its instruments, affects us as uncovering the secret of what we truly are, a kind of emptied-out essence.

This point is crucial for spelling out the link between the two aspects of the phenomenon that have occupied us throughout, namely, the drive to objectify, to give an objectlike nature to enjoyment, which we saw as central to technology, and the "truth effect" of obscenity, the way in which, in making things explicit, it endows an empirical petty little pleasure with the aura of the impossible real, a kind of sublimation in reverse.

KNOWLEDGE WITHOUT KNOWERS: LACAN, BETWEEN SCIENCE AND AUTHORITY

What are we to make, then, of the "coincidence" of obscene master figures and network technology? From the very beginning and until the end of his teaching, Lacan was constantly and explicitly struggling to position himself precisely in light of the tension we have discussed above, under the terms of authority and technology. Psychoanalysis, as he understood it, is a technique, with serious, deep commitments to science,[73] one indeed that Lacan does much to formalize, and yet it has an author, and one Lacan sees himself committed to augment, to borrow Arendt's language.

This is not to say that Lacan follows the ideal of science, the wish that psychoanalysis would become scientific; in fact, this would be a concise way to distinguish Lacan's approach to science from that of the author of psychoanalysis, Freud. If anything, Lacan's commitment to science has to do with its forceful, anti-idealizing effect.[74] It is in this that Lacan identifies the direct connection between Freud and modern science: in separating the ego from the subject of the unconscious, Freud has been part of the movement of science which dislodges thinking from subjective self-consciousness.[75] Modern science discovers and brings about a world of objective knowledge, knowledge that exists independently of its knowers, indifferent to them, exceedingly formal. It dislodges the subject from the center of the universe. Psychoanalysis is the science of this decentered subject.

Famously, Seminar II, dedicated to the "technique of psychoanalysis," includes a stand-alone lecture given by Lacan on psychoanalysis and cybernetics. Lacan was well aware of the tremendous stakes raised by what was then known as cybernetics.[76] In the seminar, Lacan articulates what he takes to be the common ground of cybernetics and psychoanalysis, why, that is, cybernetics should be of interest to those, like him, committed to a psychoanalytic framework. "Why are we so astonished by these machines? It may have something to do with the difficulties Freud encountered. Because cybernetics also stems from a reaction of astonishment at rediscovering that this human language works almost by itself, seemingly to outwit us."[77]

Both cybernetics and psychoanalysis stem from the astonishment that human language presents itself as working by itself—almost. What will advance Lacan's thinking here is what looks like a rhetorical flourish—the "almost," which allows one to pay attention rather to its malfunctions, and the way such an encounter with language seems designed to outwit us, that is, the game of temptation and deception integral to our being in language, its erotic dimension.

One way to condense the lesson emerging from Lacan in this and subsequent seminars is to say that science and authority are divided by a common object, for which we might propose the catchy name of a knowledge without knowers, the mode of knowledge that has the unwritten law as its object. Notions like structure, system, network are ways to describe a phenomenon that behaves as if it was purposively organized, as if it knew what it was doing. Its lawfulness is not exterior to it.[78] This would be language in itself, so to speak, language as distinct from a means of communication, used by human speakers like an instrument. Lacan's term for this is "knowledge in the real."[79] Even if we suspend or even preclude the possibility of their intelligent design by an external subject, that is, the notion of an author, the word "self" seems to impose itself in their description: they are self-organizing, self-regulating, etc. Only they do not have a self. Or do they? No doubt it is the fascination with this question that is in no small part responsible for our current forays into artificial intelligence. Can something lifeless, of our own creation, become like us? And if so, will it prove to have gained the mysterious spark of life, or will it prove that we never had it?

As a first—very problematic, as we shall soon see—approximation, we could say that authority, for which psychoanalysis proposes the name "transference," as understood by Lacan, is a way to view this knowledge without knowers—it would be better to say "with without," to mark the positive aspect of what is missing—from within, as something we are primordially entangled in, caught in the web of as it were, whereas technoscience is a way to view it from without. As to the first, consider the following definition of the unconscious, proposed by Lacan in Seminar II:

> The unconscious is the discourse of the other . . . not the discourse of the abstract other, the other in the dyad, of my correspondent, nor even my slave, it is the discourse of the circuit in which I am integrated. I am one of its links. It is the discourse of my father for instance, in so far as my father made mistakes which I am absolutely condemned to reproduce.[80]

We are inscribed in the circuit as a domain of fate, encountering a certain insistence from the past, which we are bound to repeat. Note that the discourse of the father, the inscription in a chain of tradition, is already presented by Lacan as one way in which one may be inscribed within the network of signifiers, one way in which we might inscribe ourselves in language, one way to subjectify the fact that "everything is always there."

It is precisely Lacan's "functionalization" of language, his viewing it as a network, that allows him later to condense the primary inscription within a network of signifiers—or primary repression—with the formula "a signifier represents the subject to another signifier," which he will never tire of repeating.[81] He was justifiably proud of it—it captures the coemergence of a split subject or a subject of the unconscious and a quasi-totalized network, a language that "almost" functions by itself, and also captures the erotic nature of our inscription within a network, the troubled relation we have with what supports us in the symbolic, the master as a signifier, that incites us into language by its very mysterious nature, suggesting to us that somewhere, behind our backs as it were, lies the knowledge we are missing, the knowledge that would make us whole. This is not just any piece of knowledge; what the big other holds is the very missing part of our being, what we lost by becoming speaking beings.

Lacan pushes a "functional" view all the way back, to describe the emergence of a speaking subject. At the same time, he is acutely aware of the ways in which electronic, indeed digital media, which he sees as a realization or materialization of the symbolic, alter in a fundamental way our "native" inscription within language: "the entire movement of the theory converges on a binary symbol, on the fact that anything can be written in terms of o and 1. What else is needed before what we call cybernetics can appear in the world?"[82]

Here Lacan emerges as an indispensable resource for thinking about the technologically realized network, the internet. In his lecture on cybernetics and psychoanalysis, he presents the function of the symbolic, as he will again and again, with reference to the door. As he puts it in the lecture, what makes the door symbolic is that "there is an asymmetry between the opening and the closing . . . the door is a real symbol, the symbol par excellence, that symbol in which man is passing."[83]

We can read this as a condensed version of themes that he will later elaborate: our entrance to the symbolic has to do with it being more closed than open, so to speak, the way in which its closing is what makes the idea of an opening alluring. This would be the general function of the veil, so to speak, the sense that there is something beyond appearances.

And yet something in the emerging technology, which makes the game of presence and absence into its prime operator, seems to transfer the symbolic from the terrain of the human sciences, which Lacan calls the science of conjecture, into the realm of technoscience, thereby altering it radically: "Once it has become possible . . . to construct an enclosure, that is to say a circuit, so that something passes when it is closed, and doesn't when it is open, that is when the science of the conjuncture passes into the realm of realization of cybernetics."[84]

There is much to be said about this dense paragraph, and the lecture to which it belongs, but for now let us only take from it another possible definition of the network: a network is that which opens by closing, and closes by opening. In that respect, the web is structured like the unconscious.[85] We may not yet have cracked the "hard problem" of consciousness[86] with our artificial creations, but we may already have been constructing, for a while now, an artificial unconscious. This materialized unconscious, in its strange structure, also crosses paths with the fraught subject known to social studies as the "masses" or "crowds."

IS TABOO TABOO?

But how can this be so? Isn't our reaction to the violation of taboo absolutely primal? This is indeed a central insight of Freud's work on the notion of "taboo": "the oldest human unwritten code of laws. It is generally supposed that taboo is older than gods and dates back to a period before any kind of religion existed."[87] Although we should take care, as Freud sometimes neglects to, to avoid identifying the primal with "the oldest" or first, it should be noted that there is an important point to be rescued from this account. Freud insists on a certain logical primacy of taboos to any ideological system that would make sense of them.

> Taboo restrictions are distinct from religious or moral prohibitions. They are not based upon divine ordinance but may be said to impose themselves on their own account. They differ from moral prohibitions in that they fall into no system that declares quite generally that certain abstinence must be observed and gives reasons for that necessity. Taboo prohibitions have no grounds and are of unknown origin. Though they are unintelligible to us, to those who are dominated by them they are taken as a matter of course.[88]

The primal, we might say, can be manifest, equally, as "a matter of course" and as "unintelligible." What we are pursuing here is the way in which the unintelligibility, for us, of the unwritten is the very mode in which we are under its spell, or rather, the way in which we register it as a matter of course. What draws Freud to the term "taboo" is its uncanny ambiguity, the way it seems to signify both a thing to be avoided and the techniques taken to circumspect it:

> The meaning of "taboo," as we see it, diverges in two contrary directions. To us it means, on the one hand, "sacred," "consecrated," and on the other "uncanny," "dangerous" "forbidden," "unclean." The converse of "taboo"

in Polynesian is "noa," which means "common" or "generally accessible." Thus "taboo" has about it a sense of something unapproachable, and it is principally expressed in prohibitions and restrictions. Our collocation "holy dread" would often coincide in meaning with "taboo."[89]

Taboo is the forbidden, dangerous thing, and the prohibition itself. It is common, everyday, and sacred. Somehow, in the obscene, both dimensions come together.

CROWDS AND POWER: THE TWO FACES OF THE MASSES

The discourse around the term "crowd," which garnered considerable theoretical attention at the turn of the twentieth century, directed the focus of sociological thought toward the ostensibly threatening and disorganized facets of "the people," the amorphous, mythical apparition of the political subject.

As we have learned from Reinhart Koselleck, in many European languages, the word for "people" has a double and often contradictory meaning:[90] it references the polity from which the political system draws its meaning, the subject in whose name political leaders are able to govern, as in "we the people"; and the popular masses, devoid of political or social order, that constitute a main threat to the moral order—the segment of the population that has abandoned the official values of the polity and endangers its stability. It is worth noting that, at the same time that anthropology began to move away from the image of the "savage" as underdeveloped and wild and began to study, precisely, the unwritten laws of "primitive people," something like a collective "savagery," a new barbarism, had made its impression at the very heart and center of modern, urban life, in the figure of the "crowd." The notion of the "crowd" was rejected, yet subtly integrated by mainstream sociological theory in notions such as Durkheim's effervescences, the "magical" bond of the social.[91] It is as if the "primal" which disappeared from the "undeveloped" cultures, now no longer treated as lawless "savages," has returned at the very heart of modern, urban life. As Fredric Jameson noted long ago, it took the "real abstraction" of custom as an effective medium for organizing the lives of Europeans for the abstract notion of the social to appear as an object to be studied scientifically.[92]

Gustave Le Bon became a pioneer in the field when he pointed to what seemed to be unique psychological traits proper to the crowd: not a mere collection of individuals, the crowd fused into a very strange, indeed paradoxical unity with its own, unique psychology.[93] When we study the crowd as a subject with its own personality and psychology, we see that there is a unique element of freedom in it, despite, or perhaps because of, its threatening nature—the freedom from individuality.[94] It is perhaps no accident that the very same Le Bon saw himself as the true originator of the mass-energy equivalence, made so consequential by Einstein's equations.[95] In the psychology of the crowd, what Le Bon detects is profoundly analogous to nuclear fission—the explosive surplus energy[96] derived from the release of the energy invested in holding the unit together. Elias Canetti captured this transformation best in his book *Crowds and Power*:[97]

> There is nothing that man fears more than the touch of the unknown. . . . All the distances which men create around themselves are dictated by this fear. They shut themselves in houses which no-one may enter, and only there feel some measure of security. . . . It is only in a crowd that man can become free of this fear of being touched. That is the only situation in which the fear changes into its opposite. . . . As soon as a man has surrendered himself to the crowd, he ceases to fear its touch. Ideally, all are equal there; no distinctions count, not even that of sex. The man pressed against him is the same as himself. He feels him as he feels himself. Suddenly it is as though everything were happening in one and the same body.[98]

The crowd frees the person from their individuality, from the partitions erected between their private space and whatever is external and foreign to it. That is the source of both its charm and its horror. But the same goes for the collective. The crowd is distinguished from all other modes of collectivity. It is the potential energy released when the energy invested in containing the social unit erupts. Canetti begins his analysis by distinguishing between the "open crowd" and the "closed crowd," even though it might be more accurate to term them the "opening crowd" and the "closing crowd." The former's intention is set on removing boundaries, while the latter aims to erect and preserve them:

> The natural crowd is the open crowd; there are no limits whatever to its growth; it does not recognize houses, doors or locks and those who shut themselves in are suspect. . . . In its spontaneous form it is a sensitive thing. The openness which enables it to grow is, at the same time, its danger. . . . The closed crowd renounces growth and puts the stress on permanence. . . . It establishes itself by accepting its limitation. It creates a space for itself which it will fill. This space can be compared to a vessel into which liquid is being poured and whose capacity is known. The entrances to this space are limited in number, and only these entrances can be used; the boundary is respected whether it consists of stone, of solid wall, or of some special act of acceptance, or entrance fee.[99]

Canetti here distinguishes between two orders of social organization. The natural order is that of the open crowd, and therefore its domestication, in the form of the closed crowd, can only be partial. Of course, the appeal of the open crowd, which according to Canetti manifests itself in the desire to overcome the barriers at the foundation of social life, raises questions about the precedence of this kind of organization: without boundaries and barriers, what is there for it to open or remove? Since the open crowd is described as a kind of anticultural drive, an impulse to remove the partitions put up by culture, it presupposes the existence of these partitions. What Canetti puts forth here is a notion of preindividual social substance, what predates any individuated subject by definition, the primordial, mythological "soup" from which individuation arises and to which it returns (even if such a primordial ground is retroactively projected by the individual).

Unsurprisingly, for Freud the distinction between the crowd and the organized group, a distinction analogous to Canetti's open and closed crowds, is smaller than we would like to imagine. In his essay on group psychology, Freud disputes the sharpness of the distinction between the wild, or open, and the civilized crowds: "Groups of the first kind stand in the same sort of relation to those of the second as a high but choppy sea to a ground swell."[100]

What Canetti likens to a dynamic, formless liquid and the receptacle that wishes to contain it, Freud compares to another vast liquid mass—the ocean. The formations of crowds are like waves breaking on the beach; although it is their visible power that makes an impression on the onlookers, this power is only a pale expression of their underlying power, the power of the deep currents—the permanent if elusive "substance" of the social order.[101] As if he had intuited the mass-energy equivalence implied in mass psychology, where other observers see disorder, Freud sees an expression of the most primordial elements of order. What explodes in the crowd is the same power that, under normal conditions, holds the social unit together.

Freud makes an illuminating remark in this context: not only are the members of the group themselves not released from inhibitions, their inhibitions are in fact what make them a group.[102] The crowd, despite its common reputation, is not deprived of restraint; on the contrary, it becomes a crowd because of its collective inhibitions. Only the leader is (relatively) free of restraint; the crowd is only following his commands.

Freud describes identification with the transgressive leader as a process by which "the individual gives up his ego ideal and substitutes for it the group ideal as embodied in the leader."[103] In other words, the leader directly embodies the "commonness" of the masses, their (at least potential) lack of boundaries through his uninhibited behavior. This behavior, in turn, leads the crowd to live up to the transgressiveness attributed to it through the power of "suggestion," the Freudian equivalent of Tarde's "imitation."[104] What Canetti, and others like him, see as spontaneous and leaderless manifestations, Freud perceives in terms of a complex mechanism of identification, driven by the transgressive elements of the masses. Where others see a leaderless mass, Freud sees an expression of a deep yearning for the worst kind of leader, a leader in the image of the primal father Freud outlined in *Totem and Taboo*. The unique identification mechanism Freud describes in his essay explains the complex relationship between the masses and the liberated leader—a leader unfettered by inhibition. He sees evidence of this in the contrary phenomenon— the panic that seizes a truly leaderless crowd, which ultimately leads to its dispersion.[105] A rallying crowd, even one that is wild and riled up, according to Freud, is always under some form of leadership, even if it is but an idea of leadership (the way that Jesus is the leader of the Church). The transgressive leader of the crowd is the functional equivalent of any other, insofar as he sustains the transference of the group. What is unique to his brand of "leadership" is the way in which he binds, directly, the unbinding power (so to speak: what erupts in nuclear fission). The "substance" of his power is directly the force, the intensity that holds the unit together in its explosive modality. In his display of disinhibition, the crowd leader imitates the crowd, so to speak, giving body to the essence-defying substance by translating the intensive and limitless to the transgressive and explosive; this, in turn, gives shape and cohesion to the crowd as they rally.

Freud does not pass up the opportunity to remind his readers of the fragility of their independence, and of the arrogance of their self-image as individuals who are distinct from the crowd, protected behind ironclad doors and steeped in self-consciousness. Nevertheless, he also admits that the same primeval human characteristic which serves as the focal point of his essay—the elimination of the self in favor of an uninhibited leader—is equally characteristic of the transient crowd. The crowd that Canetti terms "open" is for Freud only a surface manifestation of primordial structures of control. However, it is a temporary, fleeting manifestation. It would appear, in light of this fundamental contradiction, that a profound transformation must take place in the transition from the transient to the permanent crowd, a transition that allows for the emergence of an open-closed crowd, a stable or semistable transgressive group. This transformation, the emergence of stable masses bearing the characteristics of the transient, as well as the global nature of the phenomenon, calls for an examination of the changes that have taken place in the public arena, and in particular the changes in the media landscape.

OPENING MEDIUM, CLOSING MEDIUM: THE CROWD BETWEEN TELEVISION AND THE INTERNET

While Canetti's distinction between two kinds of crowds may not be entirely convincing with respect to its original object, it might be useful in describing the difference between types of media. Indeed, in the spirit of Canetti's distinction between open and closed crowds, Noam Yuran offers a distinction between television and the internet in terms of their social significance.

Television, argues Yuran, drawing on Durkheim, is a sacred space because it splits humanity into two: those who are on television and those who can only watch it from the outside. Crossing this boundary constitutes a dramatic transformation, akin to crossing the line between the sacred and the profane. One may say that being on television is a way to differentiate and extricate oneself from the anonymous crowd of television viewers. The internet, on the other hand, does not offer this same kind of polarized division of reality. In Yuran's words, "The spatial structure of the Internet does not allow for holiness, because the Web does not divide reality into two. Unlike television, the Internet does not provide the possibility of distinguishing the inside from the outside." [106]

Yuran proposes a media-oriented analysis of a difference expressed in everyday speech, the fact that, unlike television, you can never be "on the Internet." Unlike a broadcast, a term containing the idea that "everyone" is watching the same thing at the same time, a kind of tribal gathering at the bonfire, one might say, the internet does not have a center from which content is broadcast and to which our collective gaze is turned; in the same way, it does not guarantee a space of shared meaning. On the other hand, it is also impossible to be completely off the internet.

This lack of interiority explains why the internet is the medium of rumors. The rumor is an archaic model of viral propagation, which on the internet replaces the centralized model of the broadcast. As Mladen Dolar explains, rumors are able to spread widely due to the fact that there is no need to internalize them: we do not have to believe the rumor in order to pass it on. We can even explicitly disbelieve it and still spread it ("I don't believe it of course, but I heard that . . ."). [107]

There is another sense in which gossip serves as a "primal" social substance: sharing a piece of gossip is an old modality of forging intimate bonds, enacting the minimal structure of society as a bond between two to the exclusion of a third party. This excluded third is a prototypical figure of the big other as the sustainer of the public sphere, an innocent agent supposed to believe, the agent for the sake of which we "keep up appearances" in public. The internet emerges as a public forum for intimate transgression. And so the internal logic of the rumor also defines our relationship with the medium: we hear about what happens on the internet, whether we want to or not. Even if we are not active online ourselves, our friends' friends' friends are; even if not, we will still hear about it on television.

At this point, it is useful to go back to Canetti's definition, not as a distinction between two kinds of crowds, but as a second-order distinction between two ways of mediating the crowd. Television is a closed medium, or rather a closing medium, one that frames and differentiates between outside and inside. The internet, on the other hand, is an open medium, or rather an opening medium; that is to say, it erodes the distinction between the open crowd and the closed crowd.

Canetti's original terminology was intended to define the erosion of the distance between the private and the public in an open crowd, Freud's unstable crowd, on the point of discovering the wondrous phenomenon of the loss of the ego. Translating Canetti's thought process to means of communication allows us to add a crucial nuance to his thesis regarding the degradation of the border between the private and the public: what is eroded is not the border between the private and the public, but the border between a complete elimination of the border, the terrifying liberated mass, and a hunkering down within the border. This erosion may offer a preliminary explanation for the emergence of the semipermanent "open" crowd, a phenomenon that various thinkers thought necessarily transient, while at the same time suggesting why such a crowd fails to provide the satisfaction of the transient open crowd.[108]

MEDIA REFLECTIVITY AND THE PLURALITY OF SOCIAL MEDIA

It is a commonplace observation that a medium becomes what it is, so to speak, reaching its self-reflectivity, with the emergence of a new medium. The camera, precisely by being a superior technology, better equipped to capture reality, made painting aware of itself as a medium, propelling painting into what we today call modernism, the exploration of its means of expression: color, shape, etc. Along similar lines, we have seen how the internet reveals to us what broadcast was—it was essentially a medium drawing a sharp, ontological line between being in it and watching it from outside. This is why its self-reflective moment is to be found in reality TV shows, exploring what it is to be on TV, exploring the unique media effect of television.

The network, by contrast, has no proper inside or outside. Its lack of interiority is made clear when we consider, for instance, that the mark of a true internet celebrity, or event, is precisely its spilling over into old media, being reported about in television and newspapers, what many today call "legacy media," and which we predominantly consume—if at all—via the internet. With Lacan we might say that to be in the circuit is to be outside of it, and vice versa. .

The internet as a medium is organized around this very problem. We might say that both platforms and algorithms, the "machinery" of the internet, and its users are inescapably asking themselves what it is to be in a network—they are asking this in their practice, of course, not explicitly. The reason why there must be social networks in the plural is that each platform proposes a specific answer to this paradoxical being. Certainly, social networks are business ventures, aiming to make a profit. But in order to do so, they need to offer a new way of being in the network. And while what distinguishes one social network from the other is precisely their unique answer to that question, they all share this one feature of oscillation: we oscillate between being outside of them, incapable of getting in, and inside, incapable of getting out. The infamous addictive character of social networks has everything to do with this erotic dimension. Anyone who has ever dipped his toes, so to speak, into a new social network can attest to this experience: at first, one is seduced, and repelled, precisely by the experience of being an outsider. There are unwritten rules—some social, some technical—that make it hard to become an insider. Other people will tell you: you only get it once you have so many followers (Twitter), or once you have given this much opportunity for the algorithm to study your embarrassing, unconscious preferences (TikTok). After a certain imperceptible threshold is crossed, you haven't arrived, but you are caught. All of a sudden, it is hard to get out. You become not an insider but an addict, having acquired a "bad habit" you cannot quite break.

One simple way in which TV reveals itself as a medium is when we turn it on in the background—the content is clearly irrelevant, it is the background presence that is enjoyed. Can one turn on the internet in the background? Clearly not, which goes to show that we can never turn it off. This feature of the web, always lurking in the background, never quite there, is incarnated by the new social type produced by the internet—the creep.

If, as Foucault teaches us, the figure of the sinner mutated, in disciplinary societies, into the figure of the pervert, then certainly in our age the pervert has mutated into the creep, lurking in the background. Lurking is the way passive spectators on social networks—such as myself—are described, their suspected presence creeping everybody out. Those who cannot seem to manage to make an entrance, no doubt out of fear of creeping everybody out, serve the function of making the strange absent presence of the network appear. For Foucault, the dangerous individual, with his "lesser body," oscillating between the written law and the unwritten norm, was the polar corollary to the sovereign's second body.[109] If the creep is a form of "sublation" of perversion, a way to make everyone potentially a "mild" pervert, a "perve," sitting behind the screen naked, then new authoritarian figures tailor out of the very same nudity their new emperor's clothing; their attire and insignia, the ritual objects which endow them with authority, are their "open" transgression, their nudity seemingly breaking through all screens.[110]

The political polarization of internet culture, between right-wing trolls who get a kick out of offending the sensibilities of progressives who in their turn get a kick out of being outraged by the trolls' transgressiveness, expresses,[111] on the level of content, the formal truth of the medium. It is precisely because of the felt absence of a solid symbolic space in the sense developed by Arendt that social boundaries need to be constantly transgressed, and regimented. Paradoxically, we feel the pressure of the unwritten law ever more acutely, ever more confusingly, the more we try to exorcize it and render it explicit.

Can these features of the network illuminate the new type of authoritarianism everywhere on the rise? As an empirical statement of fact, new authoritarian leaders seem to be, very often, masters of new media. Trump was the Twitter president, and anyone who follows Israeli politics cannot fail to note that Netanyahu has become, in the process of rising again to power, the TikTok candidate. Should this be written off as effective propaganda, a more efficient manipulation of the medium?

The hypothesis we have been advancing suggests a more substantive relation here. What is unique about the charisma of such figures of power is the way they lie by means of an act of exposure. We are fascinated by their very capacity to transgress the unwritten law, increasingly felt as a transparent web spun around us. In this sense, the conspiracy theorists who support them are closer to the truth than outside observers: their dear leaders do indeed uncover a secret power that lurks in the background, out of sight, only that power has no center, no author, and no substance until it is transgressed.

FROM SPIRIT TO SEX . . . AND BACK?
THE OBSCENE AND ITS SHADOW

So far, the bad news. Is there any good news? We have seen how, as the "primal technologies" of tradition and authority recede into the background, what we get is a depressing mixture of new media and archaic, obscene authority. Is there any emancipatory potential in this development, or are we just left exposed to the now desacralized powers of myth, left to revel, as it were, in the "objectivity of the obscene," the "taboo" substance, with no recourse to the technologies of "taboo" to keep it at bay?

Rather than look for good news to compensate us for what is lost, we might do better to look at the productivity of the wounding loss itself. What, we might ask, comes to light as primal, ritual technology recedes into the background? Interestingly, for Benjamin, what is to be resurrected from the ruins of first technology are questions of life and death:

> For the more the collective makes the second technology its own, the more keenly individuals belonging to the collective feel how little they have received of what was due them under the dominion of the first technology. In other words, it is the individual liberated by the liquidation of the first technology who stakes his claim. No sooner has the second technology secured its initial revolutionary gains than vital questions affecting the individual—questions of love and death which had been buried by the first technology—once again press for solutions.[1]

How are we to understand the notion that "first technology" "buries" this aspect of primal nature? And in what way can its "liquidation" be emancipating? Primal nature—love and death—seem precisely to be those aspects of natural life that cannot be mastered, that can only be experienced as dramatic encounters with fate, the "stuff" around which our life narratives turn. These are conditions or limits of our experience, not directly experiences. As Girard put it, "Sexuality is one of those primary forces whose sovereignty over man is assured by man's firm belief in his sovereignty over it."[2]

However, Girard makes this remark in the context of his attempt to downplay the significance of sexuality as an object of social ordering and subordinate it to the problems of violence. This is one of his major points of contention with Freud, whose theory of the origins of law in an act of sacrificial violence Girard sets out to defend, insisting as Freud does on the empirical reality of such a primal, constitutive crime. From a psychoanalytic perspective, however, not only is the idea of an original crime highly dubitable, the very idea of ordering the relation between violence and sexuality is to be rejected. From a psychoanalytic perspective, namely, one that takes up the question regarding sex as a profound ontological challenge, indeed a stumbling block for ontology, both terms are—problematically—conjoined in the notion of jouissance. Why is it that violence has to take on a dramatic, symbolic appearance in ritual acts? Why, in other words, must it be redoubled, repeated, thereby displaying a libidinal, erotic charge? It is not enough to argue, as Girard does, that sexuality is a major cause of social unrest, leading to violence. Violence itself, as portrayed by Girard, is itself "sexualized."

But perhaps it is this, precisely, that enables us to see what the objects of first technology are, what it aims to do—it aims to separate, and thus order, the relations between sexuality and violence, or the lethal. It is precisely since they cannot be neatly theoretically separated, once and for all, that their severance has to be enacted, and performed, again and again.

First technology, in dealing with primal phenomena that defy mastery, responds in kind. Love and death are the prime objects of "ritual technology": they are the objects of taboos, and they are "handled with" by means of ceremonies—funerals and weddings, rituals that order the synchronic and diachronic differentiation of a given group, its kinship: its relation to ancestors, the relation between generations, and its relation to "foreigners," with whom one might go to war and/or enter into a sexual exchange. From a psychoanalytic perspective, the ceremonial "ordering" of love and death has much to do with their separation into two distinct "elements."

Let us begin with death: funeral rites are a symbolic technique to sever the uncanny connection between death and sexuality. Death is not just something human societies have tended to symbolize. In his famous analysis of *Antigone*, Hegel writes about the primordial duty inscribed in death, the duty of mourning:

> The duty of the member of a family is on that account to add this aspect,
> in order that the individual's ultimate being, too, shall not belong solely to
> Nature and remain something irrational, but shall be something done, and
> the right of consciousness be asserted in it. Or rather, the meaning of the

action is that because in truth the calm and universality of a self-conscious being do not belong to nature, the illusory appearance that the death of the individual results from a conscious action on the part of nature may be dispelled, and the truth established.[3]

Death as a natural fact brings nothing to rest. To the contrary, it bestows a unique, primordial duty on us to bring the departed to rest, and thereby transform the flawed natural end, an unnerving process of decay, to something accomplished by human activity. Death cannot settle for being a fact and must be put to rest in the ethical realm of deeds. Death calls for symbolization, and an element of death sticks to the act of symbolizing—the activity of symbolizing is a matter of putting things to rest, changing the very essence of a thing by assigning it a social-linguistic place.

But what is it that makes death into such an unrestful affair? As Alenka Zupančič explains, it is the entanglement of sexuality and death that charges death with an excess, undead quality.[4] As for marriage, the ordering of sexual relations in complex rules of exogamy and endogamy distinguishes, as it were, between two kinds of relatives while distinguishing between two kinds of "foreigners"—those we can sleep with and those we cannot. We could say that, in imposing the regulations of "incest," human societies attempt to contain the very surplus of sexuality, what in sexuality cannot be reduced to sexual reproduction, and in fact can act as a stumbling block for it, which in psychoanalysis is precisely the drive dimension, beyond the pleasure principle. Simply put, human sexuality is "strange" because its nonreproductive element is both a necessary support to "normal" sexual relations and cannot be entirely harmonized with it. Rules of marriage are an attempt to introduce a distinction between sex proper and nonsexual relations, by means of a distinction between proper sexual relations and improper ones. If technology consists of exteriorization, then this is a prime example—it is by dividing the domain of objects in regard to their sexual permissibility that such an impossible line is demarcated.

Sexuality does not have a proper limit. This is what accounts for its conceptual oddity, which drew the attention of Freud.[5] Drawing clear lines between those with whom we can have sexual intercourse and those with whom we cannot is a primal social technique invested in drawing limits between sexuality "proper" and its excessive drive dimension. Seeing that there is no way to separate sexuality itself from its excesses, distinctions are instead drawn between objects classified as appropriate and inappropriate for sexual exchange. And so "perverse" sexual relations are defined by object choices. To take an age-old and seemingly undying, example, homosexuality[6] would be a way to isolate artificially the "perverse," i.e., nonreproductive sexual component which is always present in sexuality in the preferred object choice. The way to introduce "right and wrong," proper and improper to sexuality, is to codify particular objects of desire as perverse, incestuous, "against nature," threatening the reproductive function itself.

ORIGIN IS THE GOAL: FROM THE TRANSFERENCE OF THE NEW TO NEW TRANSFERENCE

Lacan links Koyré's grand thesis as to the transition in modern science, *From the Closed World to the Infinite Universe* (1957), with a longer process of desexualizing the cosmos, beginning with the Hebrew God's "ferocious ignorance" regarding enjoyment.[7] Perhaps the emancipatory potential that lies in the liquidation of primal technology has to do with the very coming to light of the nonrelation, what Benjamin calls "the interplay" with nature.

With the demise of tradition, love and death, indeed their very relation, are once again pressing questions, no longer given any satisfactory answers by society and its traditions. Why do we still have families, we might ask, either finding a new rationale or abolishing the institution? What is there to transmit from one generation to the other? Which is to say, what new technology does, or should do, is to open up the question of communism.

This is one way to understand the famous polarization Benjamin offers between the fascist aestheticization of politics and the communist politicization of aesthetics.[8] As the patriarchal model of society declines—which is not to say that it is gone but that it appears either obsolete, dysfunctional, an archaic leftover of a bygone world, or as an incessant insistence of the obscene, primal father—we are confronted with two versions of the "aestheticization of politics," two versions, that is, of creating a link between nature and freedom.

The modern paradox of freedom can be articulated in terms of the nonrelation between nature and freedom: is freedom a matter of liberation from (mythical) nature, the establishment of clear boundaries between human society and nature and its perils? Or is it a matter of liberating nature, so to speak, from the constraints of society? The first is the trajectory of modern political philosophy in the wake of Hobbes, and its most monstrous manifestation, so far, has been the totalitarian attempt to create a new, artificial man, a society liberated from its natural, suprahistorical limitations. The alternative, the liberation of nature from the constraints of society, might have been romantic resonances, but its actual political manifestation has been the free market ideology, seeking to unleash desire and allow the "spontaneous order" of the economy its natural freedom.

To these intimately linked variations of the aestheticization of politics, we must juxtapose the politicization of the aesthetic, the taking up of the complex of the "aesthetic body." Only now, released from the traditional technologies in which it was buried, can it emerge, complete, as an object of resurrection, a project of political experimentation, asserting the nonrelation between nature and freedom as a site of "interplay."

What could it possibly mean to "master" an interplay, to master a nonrelation, an entanglement between two quasi entities that can be neither separated nor harmonized? In an earlier essay, Benjamin makes an interesting analogy, and perhaps more than just that, between the mastery of nature and the mastery involved in education, one of the three impossible professions.[9]

> The mastery of nature (so the imperialists teach) is the purpose of all technology. But who would trust a cane wielder who proclaimed the mastery of children by adults to be the purpose of education? Is not education, above all, the indispensable ordering of the relationship between generations and therefore mastery (if we are to use this term) of that relationship, and not of children? And likewise, technology is the mastery not of nature but of the relation between nature and man. Men as a species completed their development thousands of years ago; but mankind as a species is just beginning. In technology, a *physis* is being organized through which mankind's contact with the cosmos takes a new and different form from that which it had in nations and families. . . . In the nights of annihilation of the last war, the frame of mankind was shaken by a feeling that resembled the bliss of the epileptic. And the revolts that followed it were the first attempt of mankind to bring the new body under its control. The power of the proletariat is the measure of its convalescence. If it is not gripped to the very marrow by the discipline of this power, no pacifist polemics will save it. Living substance conquers the frenzy of destruction only in the ecstasy of procreation.[10]

The violence employed on nature by technology should be likened to the violence involved in education. Its purpose is surely not the mastery of children, but an ordering of the very relations of transmission. Consider, by way of further elucidation, Arendt's insistence on the indispensability of authority in education. In her account, authority is needed if any relation between the old and the new is to be established, a mediation that prevents them from canceling each other. Authority is the disposition necessary in order to welcome the newcomers, children, into the old, the world as what is always already there, rather than allowing the old to crush the new or the new to annihilate the old.[11] Any type of "worlding," in this account, would have to order the relation between adults and children.[12]

Perhaps, then, we can take our clue for the potential released in "annihilation," in the liquidation of the old technologies, from the field of education. This would allow us to recast the question of "bad" news versus "good" news in a new light. Why, we should ask, when it comes to our contemporary relation to technology, does even the good news appear, immediately, as bad news?[13] Can the wounds of the spirit no longer heal?[14]

Consider the prospect of AI shattering the system of education. The worry, for anyone involved in higher learning, is whether humans will still bother to learn challenging texts, such as Benjamin's or Lacan's, now that AI can manufacture college essays for them.

Why can we not say instead that, now that AI can finally write papers and the pointlessness of the university system has been revealed, we are finally free to learn?[15] Now, finally, machines can relieve us of the burden of, well, proving that we too are machines. Under the university discourse, we are constantly engaged in reverse Turing tests, in which humans have to prove to machines (bureaucracies and their representatives) that they too are machines. Why do we have such difficulty envisioning the reduction of human use to a minimum, which Benjamin identified as key to second technology as an emancipatory prospect? What is it that chains us to hard labor, regardless of any real productivity?

What would it take for us to see the closure of the era of reverse Turing tests as a possibility for a new social relationship? If learning is to be established as freedom, it would also have to be reestablished as a passionate engagement, which is inseparable from transference. As old relations of transference are entering total crisis—not only interpersonal but now also institutional transference, what Eric Santner calls the "crisis of investiture"[16]—freedom is not achieved. Freedom is not freedom from transference, but freedom to form new bonds of transference. As transference seems destined to utter decay, there emerges the chance, for the first time, to reveal its true nature, to release it, as it were, as a good in itself.

The university has been, until recently, an institution that, in its very conservative tendencies, allowed a modicum of true, erotic engagement with study. It had allowed, here and there, for a dialectics of novelty, so to speak, in which the engagement with old texts could produce new insights, avoiding the opposition between traditional conservatism and the pseudo-novelty of fashion, the form of appearance, in modernity, of the "eternal return of the same." That was the redeeming grace of the humanities, for as long as it was able to survive in the university. In recent years, it seems, passionate engagement with subject matter had appeared, within the university walls, as itself antiquarian, a remnant of a bygone world, if not outright obscene. As this space closes with the increasing absorption of the economic discourse of productivity and efficiency in academia, we may perhaps be in a position to achieve a dialectical reversal.

In a fine example of contemporary ideology, a few years ago the Harvard Business School offered a class titled How to Talk Gooder in Business and Life. Researchers have "discovered" that machines are much better than humans at "reading" the nonverbal signs that disclose what their interlocutors want to hear, and, based on this machine-produced knowledge, they are now teaching students to converse better. The machine will teach them how to signal to the other exactly what she wants to hear. In this, the art of seduction goes mainstream: we would be able to push all the right buttons and get what we want from the other (as long as we have the proper business education, or online training in the art of seduction, that is).[17]

The idea is clear—machines are far better equipped for reading all the tacit, implicit cues that disclose a person's inner mental state, and so humans have to learn from machines how to interact more efficiently and transparently. While this seems extreme, the cutting edge of the direction in which we are going, one can find in campuses around the world special classes and seminars designed to teach the unwritten rules of the profession, to help students understand the job market, the politics of publishing, and so on. What was once learned by example, in initiation, in relations of transference is now brought into the open and discussed explicitly. What was once delivered as a mystery of the form of life of academics is finally broken down to practical advice, open to everyone equally, as to how to navigate an increasingly difficult career. By the very nature of the beast, such instructions do not achieve their goal of rendering the "business" of academia more transparent, far from it, but they do assign an added sense of guilt to those who, inevitably, fail to navigate these murky waters: "Why didn't you just do as you were told? What's stopping you from performing the explicitly encouraged display of self-promotion? What's with the outdated insistence on the value of ideas?"

Still, this utter and complete demystification is by no means to be lamented. If transference is now viewed as nothing but an outmoded remnant, an antiquated instrument to get people involved in learning, which should be eliminated, the space is finally opened to see the truth: learning is a way, perhaps the purest, to establish transference. Now that transference, the establishment of relations of authoritative transmission, can no longer be taken for granted, indeed now that it no longer serves its purpose, it may finally appear as something to be realized, an object of desire, a good in itself. May this be our lesson—lessons are still to be had, more than ever, now that they serve no institutional purpose.

There is, in teaching, direct evidence of the "spontaneous" communism of ideas. Anyone who has ever struggled to communicate a difficult idea knows this at some level: an idea is only had, owned, and possessed once successfully passed along, communicated in a way that makes it accessible to others. Ideas are only privatized, individualized, and internalized as they are made common, something others can partake in. Only as my student makes an idea she learned from me her own can I be said to have ever "possessed" it. Mastery in the realm of ideas is a matter of transference, in that it is only attained when transferred.[18]

NOTES

PREFACE

1. Slavoj Žižek, "The Big Other Doesn't Exist," *Journal of European Psychoanalysis: Humanities, Philosophy, Psychotherapies*, no. 5 (Spring-Fall 1997).

2. Walter Benjamin, "On the Concept of History," in Benjamin, *Selected Writings*, 4 vols., ed. Michael W. Jennings et al. (Cambridge, MA: Harvard University Press, 1996–2003), 4:392.

1 FATHER KNOWS WORST

1. Immanuel Kant, "An Answer to the Question What Is Enlightenment," in *Kant's Political Writings*, ed. Hans Reiss, trans. H. B. Nisbet (Cambridge: Cambridge University Press, 1991), 54–60.

2. Jacques Lacan, *Television*, trans. Denis Hollier, Rosalind Kraus, and Annette Michelson, ed. Joan Copjec (New York: W. W. Norton, 1990), 54.

3. A sentiment shared by the otherwise very different approaches of Maurice Blanchot and Mark Fisher. Fisher gave the name *Boring Dystopia* to his anti-Facebook Facebook page. Blanchot analyzed the "disappointing" aspect of the manner in which we seem to be sleepwalking into catastrophe: see "The Apocalypse Is Disappointing" in *Friendship*, trans. Elizabeth Rottenberg (Stanford: Stanford University Press, 1997).

4. Michel Foucault, "Truth and Power: An Interview with Michel Foucault," in *Critique of Anthropology* 4, no. 13–14 (1979): 131–137.

5. Lacan's seminar titled . . . or *Worse* puts his notion of the absence of sexual relations, his more elaborate theory of symbolic castration, on the other side of the worse, instead of the father. We might say that the infamous "name of father" is thereby revealed to be only one agent, however historically influential, of something more fundamental. See Jacques Lacan, *Seminar XIX: . . . or Worse*, ed. Jacques-Alain Miller, trans. A. R. Price (Cambridge, UK: Polity Press, 2018).

6. See Alain Badiou, *The Century* (Cambridge, UK: Polity Press, 2007).

7. Mark Fisher, *Capitalist Realism: Is There No Alternative?* (Ropley, UK: O Books, 2009), 60. See also Jürgen Link, "From the 'Power of the Norm' to 'Flexible Normalism': Considerations after Foucault," trans. Mirko M. Hall, *Cultural Critique*, no. 57 (Spring 2004): 14–32.

8. *HyperNormalisation*, dir. Adam Curtis (United Kingdom, 2016).

9. Alenka Zupančič, "Perverse Disavowal and the Rhetoric of the End," *Filozofski vestnik* 43, no. 2 (2022): 94.

10. Max Horkheimer, "The Jews and Europe," in *The Frankfurt School on Religion: Key Writings by the Major Thinkers*, ed. Eduardo Mendieta (New York: Routledge, 2005), 226.

11. Yanis Varoufakis, *Technofeudalism: What Killed Capitalism* (Brooklyn, NY: Melville House, 2024).

12. Max Weber, *On Charisma and Institution Building: Selected Papers by Max Weber*, ed. S. N. Eisenstadt (Chicago: University of Chicago Press, 1968), 248.

13. A comparison with left-wing populism makes this point even more conspicuous. Bernie Sanders, the left-wing populist candidate in the United States, has been employing rhetoric and suggesting policies that connote radical change to the existing political order: ridding the political system of dependence on large donors, nationalized healthcare, the "Green New Deal," and so on. For better or for worse, he was giving his voters clear and specific criteria by which to measure his success, if he should be elected to the White House.

14. Peter Sloterdijk, *Critique of Cynical Reason*, trans. Michael Eldred (Minneapolis: University of Minnesota Press, 1987), 5.

15. Robert Pfaller, *On the Pleasure Principle in Culture: Illusions without Owners*, trans. Lisa Rosenblatt (London: Verso, 2014).

16. Weber, *On Charisma and Institution Building*, 25.

17. Claude Lefort, *The Political Forms of Modern Society: Bureaucracy, Democracy, Totalitarianism*, ed. David Thompson (Cambridge, MA: MIT Press, 1986), 181–272.

18. Slavoj Žižek, *Like a Thief in Broad Daylight: Power in the Era of Post-humanity* (London: Penguin, 2019), 90.

19. Octave Mannoni, "I Know Well, but All the Same," in *Perversion and the Social Relation*, ed. Molly Anne Rothenberg, Dennis A. Foster, and Slavoj Žižek (Durham: Duke University Press, 2003), 68–92.

20. John W. Martens, *One God, One Law: Philo of Alexandria on the Mosaic and Greco-Roman Law* (Boston: Brill, 2003).

21. Walter Benjamin, *Selected Writings*, 4 vols., ed. Michael W. Jennings et al. (Cambridge, MA: Harvard University Press, 1996–2003), 1:236–252.

22. Henri Bergson, *Laughter: An Essay on the Meaning of the Comic*, trans. Cloudesley Brereton and Fred Rothwell (New York: Macmillan, 1913), 18–21.

23. Richard Tuck, *The Rights of War and Peace: Political Thought and the International Order from Grotius to Kant* (Oxford: University Press, 2001). As Tuck shows, the unwritten laws of war and peace (i..e., exchange and commerce) that govern relations between strangers (i.e., between groups in the absence of a shared body of law) form the background of conceptions developed in modern political theory regarding the state of nature. The influence of this murky background can be traced in much of modern political thought, from the war of all against all theorized by Hobbes to the "civil society" that would become the center of liberal thought.

24. Michael Polanyi and Amartya Sen, *The Tacit Dimension* (Chicago: University of Chicago Press, 2009).

25. Hans Kelsen, *Pure Theory of Law* (Berkeley: University of California Press, 1967); Weber, *On Charisma and Institution Building*, 16–17.

26. Maurice Bloch, "What Goes Without Saying: The Conceptualization of Zafimaniry Society," in *Conceptualizing Society*, ed. Adam Kuper (London: Routledge, 1992), 127–146.

27. Adam Kotsko, *Awkwardness* (Winchester: John Hunt Publishing, 2010).

28. Benjamin, *Selected Writings*, 1:249.

29. Weber, *On Charisma and Institution Building*, 23–24.

30. "It is also written in your law, that the testimony of two men is true. I am one that bears witness of myself, and the Father that sent me beareth witness of me" (John 8:17–18). See also Matthew 5:17–44.

31. See Rudolf Sohm, *Kirchenrecht: Die geschichtlichen Grundlagen* (Munich: Duncker & Humblot, 1923). Another genealogical branch, linking Weber's "charisma" with "magical" terms such as "mana," was hotly debated by religious scholars and anthropologists in Weber's time. See, for example Martin Riesebrodt, "Charisma in Max Weber's Sociology of Religion," *Religion* 29, no. 1 (1999): 1–14.

32. Salena Zito, "Taking Trump Seriously, Not Literally," *Atlantic*, September 23, 2016, https://www.theatlantic.com/politics/archive/2016/09/trump-makes-his-case-in-pittsburgh/501335/

33. Immanuel Kant, *Religion within the Boundaries of Mere Reason: And Other Writings*, ed. Allen W. Wood and George Di Giovanni (Cambridge: Cambridge University Press, 2016), 59–60.

34. Gilles Deleuze, *Difference and Repetition*, trans. Paul Patton (New York: Columbia University Press, 1994), 150–153.

35. Eli Friedlander, "Metaphysics and Magic: Echoes of the *Tractatus* in Wittgenstein's Remarks on Frazer," in *Wittgenstein's Tractatus at 100*, ed. Martin Stokhof and Hao Tang (Cham, Switzerland: Palgrave Macmillan, 2023), 104.

36. Theodor W. Adorno, "Freudian Theory and the Pattern of Fascist Propaganda," in *Psychoanalysis and the Social Sciences*, vol. 3, ed. Géza Róheim (New York: International Universities Press, 1951), 279–300.

37. Hannah Arendt, *The Origins of Totalitarianism* (London: Penguin Classics, 2017), 333, 348–350, 353, 382.

38. See Sigmund Freud, *Civilization and Its Discontents*, trans. James Strachey (New York: W. W. Norton, 1989); Friedrich Nietzsche, *On the Genealogy of Morality*, ed. Keith Ansell-Pearson, trans. Carol Diethe (London: Cambridge University Press, 2006; Norbert Elias, *The Civilizing Process: Sociogenetic and Psychogenetic Investigations* (Oxford: Blackwell, 2000).

39. For example, in Hobbes's influential writings, the need for sovereign power emerges from the potentially destructive perversion of human desire. Contrary to common notion, Hobbes does not assume the natural state as a starting point, but infers it from his observations of human nature, that is to say, the particularity of man in relation to nature. Humans crave power—a means to achieve goals, rather than a specific goal. This dimension makes human desire infinite and, therefore, unlimitedly competitive, antisocial, and dangerous to others. This is why the social fabric is a potential "war of all against all" that must be restrained by appealing to a power that is external and above all competition: the sovereign. See Thomas Hobbes, *Leviathan*, ed. J. C. A. Gaskin (Oxford: Oxford University Press, 1998), 82–106.

40. Michel Foucault, *The History of Sexuality*, vol. 1, trans. Robert Hurley (New York: Pantheon Books, 1978), 47.

41. In her book *What IS Sex?* Alenka Zupančič undertakes a close examination of the strange ontological status of sexuality in psychoanalysis. See Alenka Zupančič, *What IS Sex?* (Cambridge, MA: MIT Press, 2017).

42. The term "populism" is of course notoriously ambiguous. See Margaret Canovan, *Populism* (New York: Harcourt Brace Jovanovich, 1981). For a thorough overview of the different approaches and definitions of the term, see Danny Filc, פופוליזם והגמוניה בישראל [Populism and hegemony in Israel] (Tel Aviv: Resling, 2006).

43. Chantal Mouffe, *The Democratic Paradox* (London: Verso, 2009), 2–3.

44. See Yascha Mounk, *The People vs. Democracy: Why Our Freedom Is in Danger and How to Save It* (Cambridge, MA: Harvard University Press, 2018), 44–147. Lately, Orbán has also started employing the term "Christian democracy." One cannot help but note the dubious honor that Israel can claim in being the first to adopt a regime in which democracy is bundled together with a religious-ethnic identity, the main purpose of which is the disenfranchisement of large segments of the country's population.

45. See Slavoj Žižek, *Did Somebody Say Totalitarianism? Five Interventions in the (Mis)use of a Notion* (London: Verso, 2001).

46. Samuel Moyn, *Liberalism against Itself: Cold War Intellectuals and the Making of Our Times* (New Haven: Yale University Press, 2023).

47. See Noam Chomsky and Edward S. Herman, *Manufacturing Consent* (New York: Pantheon Books, 1988).

48. See Jacob Leib Talmon, *The Origins of Totalitarian Democracy* (London: Mercury Books, 1956).

49. See David Runciman, *How Democracy Ends* (London: Profile Books, 2018), 16–24, 53.

50. Arendt, *The Origins of Totalitarianism*, 328.

51. Theodor W. Adorno, *Introduction to Sociology*, trans. Edmund Jephcott, ed. Christoph Göde (Stanford: Stanford University Press, 2000).

52. Arendt, *The Origins of Totalitarianism*, 461.

53. Ibid., 328.

54. Ibid., 336

55. Hannah Arendt, *The Human Condition*, 2nd ed. (Chicago: University of Chicago Press, 1998), 22–28, 68–73.

56. Arendt, *The Origins of Totalitarianism*, 331

57. Ibid., 332.

58. This should be enough to undermine the philosophical and political fascination with anarchy. Being exposed to that which is without principle and origin is not freedom from rule. It is to be given over to a kind of lawfulness without law, dictated by the very absent origin.

59. See Rémi Brague, *The Law of God: The Philosophical History of an Idea* (Chicago: University of Chicago Press, 2020).

60. Like rumor, the unwritten law's position is not only lower than knowledge (episteme) but even lower than opinion (doxa), which were indistinguishable in early philosophy, and like rumor, its source is absent. The disturbing power of the rumor lies in the fact that there is no need to believe it in order to take part in its dissemination. "I do not know, but I've heard" is the phrasing that usually accompanies the transmission of a rumor. Even agnosticism is not a requirement: outright rejection of the content doesn't hurt its status as a rumor either ("I'm sure it's not true, but they say . . ."). The epistemic weakness of the rumor is the secret of its power. Just as the effectiveness of the rumor does not depend on the ability to verify or refute it, so the unwritten law does not depend

on enforcement. See ibid and Mladen Dolar, "On Rumors, Gossip and Related Matter," in *Objective Fictions: Philosophy, Psychoanalysis, Marxism*, ed. Adrian Johnston, Boštjan Nedoh, and Alenka Zupančič (Edinburgh: Edinburgh University Press, 2022), 144–164.

61. Plato, *Laws*, ed. T. L. Pentangle (Chicago: University of Chicago Press, 1988), 181.

62. Ibid., 229.

63. Ibid., 232–233.

64. At this point in the dialogue we come to understand the rationale behind the strange turn, in book I of the *Laws*, from a discussion of virtues, courage, etc., to the Athenian's strange obsession with drinking parties, and his philosophical defense of the Athenian custom of getting drunk in public, old and young together: being this publicly and collectively shamed creates a powerful bond, so powerful it even allows the Athenians to display the unique public courage of criticizing their own. See ibid., 19–31.

65. See Slavoj Žižek, *For They Know Not What They Do: Enjoyment as a Political Factor* (London: Verso, 2008), lxi.

66. For more on political hypocrisy see Judith Shklar, *Ordinary Vices* (Cambridge, MA: Belknap Press, 1985); David Runciman, *Political Hypocrisy: The Mask of Power from Hobbes to Orwell and Beyond* (Princeton: Princeton University Press, 2008). On the "noble lie" see Leo Strauss, *The City and Man* (Chicago: University of Chicago Press, 1978).

67. Slavoj Žižek, *The Plague of Fantasies* (London: Verso, 1997), 37–38.

68. Henry Sumner Maine, *Ancient Law: Its Connection to the History of Early Society* (London: J. M. Dent & Sons, 1912).

69. See Giorgio Agamben, "What Is a People?," in *Means without End: Notes on Politics*, trans. Vincenzo Binetti and Cesare Casarino (Minneapolis: University of Minnesota Press, 2000), 29–35; and Reinhart Koselleck, *Critique and Crisis: Enlightenment and Pathogenesis of Modern Society* (Oxford: Berg, 1988).

70. Various political thinkers have spoken to the two-faced nature of the *demos*, the people, as the subject of democracy. To use Agamben's terms, this is the difference between *bios*, organized political life, and *zoe*, "bare" life outside of the social order. See Giorgio Agamben, *Homo Sacer: Sovereign Power and Bare Life* (Stanford: Stanford University Press, 1998); Giorgio Agamben, *Stasis: Civil War as a Political Paradigm* (Stanford: Stanford University Press, 2015). Jacques Rancière views the Greek *demos* as the prototype of the concept of the proletariat in Marxist philosophy, the group whose exclusion from the centers of power is what makes it the champion of revolutionary universalism. Rancière examines how the *demos*, a category that applied first and foremost to the common people, those deprived of all privilege who, as Aristotle puts it, "had no part in anything," gave its name to the universal principle of democracy. As those who had nothing but their freedom, the *demos* provided the foundational principle of a system in which they found no representation. See Jacques Rancière, *Disagreement: Politics and Philosophy*, trans. Julie Rose (Minneapolis: University of Minnesota Press, 1999), 8–9. Étienne Balibar argues the central importance of the ambivalent attitude toward the "masses" in modern democracy as a fundamental problem of political philosophy from Spinoza onward. Modern democracy relies, both symbolically and practically, on the power of the people, the power of the masses, and yet it is this power that threatens the very logic that drives it. Étienne Balibar, *Masses, Classes, Ideas: Studies on Politics and Philosophy before and after Marx* (London: Routledge, 2013). Awareness of the threat posed by the "mob" to the representational logic of liberalism can be found in writings as early as Hegel's. Georg Wilhelm Friedrich Hegel, *Elements of the Philosophy of Right*, trans. H. B. Nisbet (Cambridge: Cambridge University Press, 1991), 266–267. The rabble,

Hegel admits, are justified to feel despair regarding the political order wherein they find themselves at the bottom. See Frank Ruda, *Hegel's Rabble: An Investigation into Hegel's Philosophy of Right* (London: Bloomsbury Academic, 2011). For Arendt it is quite essential that the subject of totalitarianism is the "masses," a modern variation of "the mob." In her account, the masses are, in some ways, the quality of quantity, that is, the quality of that which has been stripped of any and all of its individuating qualities. These are people stripped of any meaningful identification with both class and nation, and it is their political mobilization that is one of the first signs of the pretotalitarian condition. Why, from the perspective of liberal democracy, does the political "awakening" of those utterly disinvested in public, political life present itself as a threat, like the awakening of slumbering titans, supposedly put to rest with the emergence of civilization?

71. Agamben, "What Is a People?"

72. The distinction central to Agamben's philosophy, the formative distinction law forces upon nature, is formulated for the Greeks in terms of the distinction between the written and the unwritten law. Thus, for Aristotle, nature is the space of unwritten law, while society is the space where the law splits into written and unwritten law. Unwritten law is the way by which that which is outside the law is preserved at the heart of the social order. See Aristotle, *Rhetoric*, trans. Edward Meredith Cope and John Edwin Sandys (Cambridge: Cambridge University Press, 2010), 189, 245, 254–255, 269, 271.

73. See Žižek, *For They Know Not What They Do*.

74. Maine, *Ancient Law*.

75. Michel Foucault, *Security, Territory, Population: Lectures at the Collège de France, 1977–78*, ed. Arnold I. Davidson, trans. Graham Burchell (Basingstoke, UK: Palgrave Macmillan, 2007), 43–44.

76. Raymond Williams, *The Country and the City* (New York: Oxford University Press, 1973), 3, 304.

77. See Adorno, *Introduction to Sociology*, 10–19.

78. See Raymond Williams, *Culture and Society 1780–1950* (New York: Doubleday, 1960); Elias, *The Civilizing Process*, 5–44.

79. Michel Foucault, *Abnormal: Lectures at the Collège de France 1974–1975*, trans. Graham Burchell (London: Verso, 2003).

80. See Kojin Karatani, *The Structure of World History: From Modes of Production to Modes of Exchange*, trans. Michael K. Bourdaghs (Durham: Duke University Press, 2014).

81. Slavoj Žižek, *Living in the End Times* (London: Verso, 2010), 139; Adam Komisaruk, "Žižek's Jews," *Comparatist* 46, no. 1 (2022): 156–175.

82. Immanuel Kant, *Critique of Judgment*, trans. Werner S. Pluhar (Indianapolis: Hackett, 1987), 351–355.

83. Isaiah Berlin, *The Roots of Romanticism* (Princeton: Princeton University Press, 2013).

84. Angela Nagle, *Kill All Normies: Online Culture Wars from 4chan and Tumblr to Trump and the Alt-Right* (Winchester: John Hunt Publishing, 2017).

85. Agamben, *Stasis*, 22.

86. Ibid., 53.

87. We address the topic of myth extensively in chapters 2 and 4. For now let us only note in passing that in Aeschylus's *Eumenides*, what allows for the transformation of ire and vengeance into a blessing is the split between inner unity, now understood as an extended

kinship, and what lies outside the political community, the space of war. See Maine, *Ancient Law*, 24–25. Athena manages to harness the power of vengeance for the service of justice inside Athens and to unleash their full rage outside, relying on the following (implicit) thesis: for citizenship to function as kinship, to attain the tight bond of a family, of blood relations, blood must be spilled outside the community. Contemporary authoritarianism seems to be invested, instead, in pushing the bond of citizenship to its breaking point, that is, threatening to divide the populace to such an extent that it might not stand as one against a common enemy. In this, they make the existence of common enemies the most important, and forever present feature of the civil union, the only thing tentatively holding the "family" together. Agamben bases his analysis of stasis on Nicole Loraux, who in turn bases much of her study of stasis on this element of the *Eumenides*. See Nicole Loraux, *The Divided City: On Memory and Forgetting in Ancient Athens*, trans. Corrine Pache and Jeff Fort (New York: Zone Books, 2006), 15–44; Nicole Loraux, "War in the Family," trans. Adam Kotsko, *Parrhesia* 27 (2017): 13–47.

88. Žižek, *Like a Thief in Broad Daylight*, 90.

89. See Jan-Werner Müller, *What Is Populism?* (Philadelphia: University of Pennsylvania Press, 2016), 76–79, 85–93; Jan-Werner Müller, *Democracy Rules* (London: Penguin, 2021), 43–50.

90. Lefort, *The Political Forms of Modern Society*.

91. Žižek, *For They Know Not What They Do*.

92. Lefort, *The Political Forms of Modern Society*.

93. Ibid., 258.

94. https://winstonchurchill.org/resources/quotes/the-worst-form-of-government/.

95. See Sandor Ferenczi, *First Contributions to Psycho-analysis* (London: Routledge, 2018).

96. See Anatole France, *Le Lys rouge* (1894), ch. 7.

97. Foucault, *Abnormal*, 11–12.

98. Claude Lefort, *Democracy and Political Theory* (Minneapolis: University of Minnesota Press, 1988), 244.

99. Žižek, *For They Know Not What They Do*, 254–255.

100. Foucault, *Abnormal*, 14.

101. See Jacques Lacan, *Seminar XI: The Four Fundamental Concepts of Psychoanalysis*, trans. Alan Sheridan (New York: W. W. Norton, 1988), 123–203.

102. Foucault, *Abnormal*, 13.

103. Ibid., 15.

104. Balibar discusses the medical-legal doublet as an aporia of the public and the private, constitutive of the modern, bourgeois, citizen-subject. See Étienne Balibar, *Citizen-Subject: Foundations for Philosophical Anthropology* (New York: Fordham University Press, 2016), 213–226.

105. Foucault, *Abnormal*, 16.

106. See Michel Foucault, *The Order of Things: An Archaeology of the Human Sciences* (London: Routledge, 2005).

107. Mark Andrejevic, *Automated Media* (London: Routledge, 2019), 123.

108. Ibid., 120.

109. Ibid., 2.

110. Antoinette Rouvroy and Thomas Berns, "Algorithmic Governmentality and Prospects of Emancipation: Disparateness as a Precondition for Individuation through Relationships?," *Réseaux* 177, no. 1 (2013): 163–196.

111. Ed Finn, *What Algorithms Want: Imagination in the Age of Computing* (Cambridge, MA: MIT Press, 2017), 25–26.

112. Jean-Pierre Dupuy, *On the Origins of Cognitive Science: The Mechanization of the Mind*, trans. M. B. DeBevoise (Cambridge, MA: MIT Press, 2009), 27–42.

113. See Giorgio Agamben, *What Is an Apparatus? and Other Essays*, trans. David Kishik and Stefan Pedatella (Stanford: Stanford University Press, 2009), 14; Gilles Deleuze, "Postscript on the Societies of Control," *October* 59 (Winter 1992): 3–7.

114. Andrejevic. *Automated Media*, 3–4.

115. Boris Groys, *Under Suspicion: Phenomenology of the Media* (New York: Columbia University Press, 2000), 12.

116. Ibid., 55.

117. See Noam Yuran, *What Money Wants: An Economy of Desire* (Stanford: Stanford University Press, 2014).

118. Carl Schmitt, *The Nomos of the Earth* (New York: Telos Press, 2003); Carl Schmitt, *Theory of the Partisan*, trans. G. L. Ulmen (New York: Telos Press, 2007); Carl Schmitt, *The Concept of the Political*, expanded ed. (Chicago: University of Chicago Press, 2008).

2   GROUND AND SHADOW

1. Hermann Cohen, *Religion of Reason out of the Sources of Judaism*, trans. Simon Kaplan (Atlanta: Scholars Press, 1995), 83.

2. Leo Strauss, *Philosophy and Law: Contributions to the Understanding of Maimonides and His Predecessors* (Albany: SUNY Press, 1995); Peter Fitzpatrick, *Modernism and the Grounds of Law* (Cambridge: Cambridge University Press, 2001).

3. We could think of this as the historical-political manifestation of Schelling's philosophical account of the primordial entanglement between evil and freedom, arising from the very gap between ground and existence. See Friedrich Wilhelm Joseph Schelling, *Philosophical Investigations into the Essence of Human Freedom*, trans. Jeff Love and Johannes Schmidt (Albany: SUNY Press, 2006).

4. Immanuel Kant, *Critique of Judgment*, trans. Werner S. Pluhar (Indianapolis: Hackett, 1987), 351–355.

5. Leo Strauss, *Natural Right and History* (Chicago: University of Chicago Press, 1953), 82–83, 90.

6. Ibid., 91.

7. See ibid., 81–119. Also Giorgio Agamben, *Creation and Anarchy: The Work of Art and the Religion of Capitalism*, trans. Adam Kotsko (Stanford: Stanford University Press, 2019); Reiner Schürmann, *Heidegger on Being and Acting: From Principles to Anarchy*, trans. Christine-Marie Gros (Bloomington: Indiana University Press, 1987).

8. See Friedrich Hayek, "The Use of Knowledge in Society," *American Economic Review* 35, no. 4 (1945): 519–530; Friedrich Hayek, *The Constitution of Liberty* (Chicago: University of Chicago Press, 1960); Friedrich Hayek, *Law, Legislation and Liberty* (London: Routledge, 1982). Hayek seems to have coined the term in *The Constitution of Liberty* but had already made use of the idea in the essay "The Use of Knowledge in Society."

9. See Michael Stolleis, "The Legitimation of Law through God, Tradition, Will, Nature and Constitution," in *Natural Law and the Laws of Nature in Early Modern Europe: Jurisprudence, Theology, Moral and Natural Philosophy*, ed. Lorraine Daston and Michael Stolleis (London: Routledge, 2008).

10. Hobbes's status as a founding father for modern political philosophy is not without notoriety. *Leviathan* has been taken to be a scandalous book by authors from Hegel to Schmitt and onward. See Georg Wilhelm Friedrich Hegel, *Lectures on the History of Philosophy: The Lectures of 1825–1826*, ed. Robert F. Brown (Berkeley: University of California Press, 1990), 181; and Carl Schmitt, *The Leviathan in the State Theory of Thomas Hobbes*, trans. George Schwab (Westport, CT: Greenwood Press, 1996), 5.

11. David Runciman and Mónica Brito Vieira, *Representation* (Cambridge, UK: Polity Press, 2008); Hanna F. Pitkin, *The Concept of Representation* (Berkeley: University of California Press, 2023).

12. Ori Belkind, "Unnatural Acts: The Transition from Natural Principles to Laws of Nature in Early Modern Science," *Studies in History and Philosophy of Science Part A* 81 (2020): 62–73.

13. See Joseph Vogl, *The Specter of Capital*, trans. Joachim Redner and Robert Savage (Stanford: Stanford University Press, 2015).

14. See Albert O. Hirschman, *The Passions and the Interests: Political Arguments for Capitalism before Its Triumph* (Princeton: Princeton University Press, 1977).

15. See Vogl, *The Specter of Capital*.

16. See Hayek *The Constitution of Liberty*; Hayek, *Law, Legislation and Liberty*.

17. Michel Foucault, *Security, Territory, Population: Lectures at the Collège de France, 1977–78*, ed. Arnold I. Davidson, trans. Graham Burchell (Basingstoke, UK: Palgrave Macmillan, 2007), 102.

18. These questions are further explicated and discussed in chapter 4.

19. Alenka Zupančič, *What IS Sex?* (Cambridge, MA: MIT Press, 2017).

20. See Robert Pippin, *Modernism as a Philosophical Problem: On the Dissatisfactions of European High Culture* (Malden, MA: Blackwell, 1999), 120; Fitzpatrick, *Modernism and the Grounds of Law*; Strauss, *Natural Right and History*.

21. Robert Pippin, *The Persistence of Subjectivity* (Cambridge: Cambridge University Press, 2005); Slavoj Žižek and Markus Gabriel, *Mythology, Madness, and Laughter: Subjectivity in German Idealism* (London: Bloomsbury Publishing, 2009), 95–121.

22. Giorgio Agamben, *Homo Sacer: Sovereign Power and Bare Life* (Stanford: Stanford University Press, 1998), 35.

23. Elizabeth Anscombe, "Modern Moral Philosophy," *Philosophy* 33, no. 124 (1958): 1–19.

24. Robert Brandom, *A Spirit of Trust: A Reading of Hegel's Phenomenology* (Cambridge, MA: Harvard University Press, 2019), 469–758.

25. Robert Pippin, "Heidegger on Nietzsche on Nihilism," in *Political Philosophy Cross-Examined: Recovering Political Philosophy*, ed. T. L. Pangle and J. H. Lomax (New York: Palgrave Macmillan, 2013).

26. See Rahel Jaeggi, *Alienation* (New York: Columbia University Press, 2014).

27. They therefore share what Peter Sloterdijk deemed to be the repressed anxiety of cynical wisdom: "Psychologically, present-day cynics can be understood as borderline melancholics, who can keep their symptoms of depression under control and can remain more or less able to work. Indeed, this is the essential point in modern cynicism: the ability

of its bearers to work—in spite of anything that might happen, and especially, after anything that might happen. . . . For cynics are not dumb, and every now and then they certainly see the nothingness to which everything leads. Their psychic (*seelisch*) apparatus has become elastic enough to incorporate as a survival factor a permanent doubt about their own activities. . . . Behind the capable, collaborative, hard facade, it covers up a mass of offensive unhappiness and the need to cry. In this, there is something of the mourning for a 'lost innocence,' of the mourning for better knowledge, against which all action and labor are directed." Peter Sloterdijk, *Critique of Cynical Reason*, trans. Michael Eldred (Minneapolis: University of Minnesota Press, 1987), 5.

28. More on the normative force of tradition and the problematic of technology in chapter 5.

29. Pierre Clastre, *Society against the State: Essays in Political Anthropology*, trans. Robert Hurley (New York: Zone Books, 1989).

30. Friedrich Nietzsche, *On the Genealogy of Morality*, ed. Keith Ansell-Pearson, trans. Carol Diethe (London: Cambridge University Press, 2006), 35–40, 142.

31. Walter Benjamin, *Selected Writings*, 4 vols., ed. Michael W. Jennings et al. (Cambridge, MA: Harvard University Press, 1996–2003), 4:403.

32. Nietzsche, *On the Genealogy of Morality*, 53.

33. Karl Marx, *Grundrisse: Foundations of the Critique of Political Economy*, trans. Martin Nicolaus (London: Penguin, 1973), 104–105.

34. Kant, *Critique of Judgment*, 217, 404.

35. Johann Wolfgang von Goethe, *Naturwissenschaftliche Schriften* (Munich: C. H. Beck, 1998), 24–25.

36. Eli Friedlander, "Wittgenstein, Benjamin, and Pure Realism," in *Wittgenstein and Modernism*, ed. Michael LeMahieu and Karen Zumhagen-Yekplé (Chicago: University of Chicago Press, 2016).

37. Georg Wilhelm Friedrich Hegel, *Phenomenology of Spirit*, trans. A. V. Miller (Oxford: Oxford University Press, 1977), 261–262.

38. Ibid.

39. Eli Friedlander, "The Measure of the Contingent: Walter Benjamin's Dialectical Image," *boundary 2* 35, no. 3 (August 2008): 1–26.

40. Friedrich Wilhelm Joseph Schelling, *Philosophy of Art*, trans. Douglas W. Stott (Minneapolis: University of Minnesota Press, 1989), 34–35.

41. Friedrich Wilhelm Joseph Schelling, *Historical-Critical Introduction to the Philosophy of Mythology*, trans. Mason Richey (Albany: SUNY Press, 2012).

42. Claude Lévi-Strauss, *Structural Anthropology*, trans. Claire Jacobson and Brooke Grundfest Schoepf (New York: Basic Books, 1973), 210–211, 229; Claude Lévi-Strauss, *Myth and Meaning* (New York: Schocken Books, 1978).

43. I owe this point to Attay Kremer. See Hegel, *Phenomenology of Spirit*, 91.

44. The Greek myths themselves reveal this tension, the dual face of the mythical, in the guise of the overthrow of the titanic, chthonic order, by the Olympians. The Olympian gods are already a mythical victory over the titanic order of the eternal return of the same, preventing things from emerging out of chaos once and for all. Out of the endless cycle of incest and cannibalism, in which it is first Gaia, the primordial, maternal ground locked in copulation with the sky (Uranus) that allows nothing to spring forth decisively, and then Chronos, time, who swallows his offspring, it takes Zeus to violently open up

verticality and place the gods on Mount Olympus. Myth is the drama of individuation—the precarious emergence of individuated being out of the preontological chaos of indifference, and the eternal return of indifference. In myth, we marvel at the emergence of a world in which everything is young and full of potential and witness how everything returns to indifference. See David Graeber and David Wengrow, *The Dawn of Everything: A New History of Humanity* (London: Penguin, 2021), 202. In this schema, the Olympian gods arise as introducing the difference that finally makes a difference, the difference between high and low, the space inhabited by humans. The difference, to be more precise, between a symbolic order of differences that swallows back everything that emerges out of it as distinctive, and the notion of a space in which virtuality must, out of inner necessity, express itself. With Antigone, Hegel is presenting us not with the inner logic of myth, but with the clash with myth internal to history, the way in which myth appears in history. Here, in tragedy, we get a certain confrontation with the mythical as such.

45. Benjamin, *Selected Writings*, 2:797.

46. Henry Sumner Maine, *Ancient Law: Its Connection to the History of Early Society* (London: J. M. Dent & Sons, 1912).

47. Foucault's analysis as to the return, with a vengeance, of the murky realm of the unwritten, at the very moment when a clear boundary between the realms was to be erected, is well aligned with the Kafkaesque, and in the pages that follow we shall attempt to gain a firmer grasp of the strange logic that seems to govern this paradoxical outcome, which is precisely at the center of Benjamin's interrogations of the entanglement of law, fate, and myth.

48. Eli Friedlander, "Goethe et Benjamin: De la nature à l'histoire," in *Goethe, le second auteur: Actualité d'un inactuel*, ed. Christoph König and Denis Thouard (Paris: Hermann Éditeurs, 2022).

49. Walter Benjamin, *The Arcades Project* (Cambridge, MA: Harvard University Press, 1999), 462.

50. Benjamin, *Selected Writings*, 1:103.

51. Robert Pfaller, *On the Pleasure Principle in Culture: Illusions without Owners*, trans. Lisa Rosenblatt (London: Verso, 2014), 12–16, 66–67; Paul Veyne. *Did the Greeks Believe in Their Myths? An Essay on the Constitutive Imagination*, trans. Paula Wissing (Chicago: University of Chicago Press, 1988).

52. The line comes from Hugo von Hofmannsthal's *Death and the Fool* (1894), and recurs several times in Benjamin's oeuvre.

53. We could consider Benjamin's engagement with Kant as an afterlife of the Schelling-Hegel feud. Like Schelling, Benjamin is pursuing a kind of metaphysical empiricism, but one whose experiential basis, so to speak, is the Hegelian "substance is subject," the way in which subject names the split as ontological. See Friedrich Wilhelm Joseph Schelling, *Grounding of Positive Philosophy: The Berlin Lectures*, trans. Bruce Matthews (Albany: SUNY Press, 2007), 171–192.

54. Jean-Claude Milner, *A Search for Clarity: Science and Philosophy in Lacan's Oeuvre* (Evanston: Northwestern University Press, 2020).

55. See Immanuel Kant, *Critique of Pure Reason*, trans. Werner S. Pluhar (Indianapolis: Hackett, 1996), A297–298/B353–355.

56. The issue didn't entirely elude Kant. In the *Opus Postumum*, he reopens the central questions of the critical project in an unfinished attempt to bridge the gap between metaphysics and physics. He does so by way of a doctrine of self-affection, wherein he

conceptualizes the sense in which physics takes phenomena to be things in themselves. To do so, he differentiates between appearances and the appearances of appearances—a kind of second-order phenomena, which capture what the phenomena produce in an affected subject perceiving them. This opens the way to a new kind of amphibole, this time belonging to the power of judgment, that confuses the appearance of appearance with the appearance itself. Together with the amphiboles of the first *Critique*, this shows that the confusion between ground and figure is not something that one can be rid of, but rather a haunting presence that exists at all levels of the analysis of experience and its conditions. See Immanuel Kant, *Opus Postumum*, trans. Eckhart Förster and Michael Rosen (Cambridge: Cambridge University Press, 1993). For commentary on this, see Frederick Beiser, *German Idealism: The Struggle against Subjectivism, 1781–1801* (Cambridge, MA: Harvard University Press, 2008), 180–214. I owe this reference to Attay Kremer.

57. Wilfrid Sellars, *Empiricism and the Philosophy of Mind* (Cambridge, MA: Harvard University Press, 1997), 253–329.

58. Call it "conceptual supremacy," the unspoken rule according to which all is to be understood conceptually.

59. For Cassirer, it seems, it is the artificial, manufactured function of modern myths that distinguishes them from the old. Myth, Cassirer well understands, is mostly an unconscious phenomenon; with modernity, it comes to be utilized intentionally. Ernst Cassirer, *Language and Myth* (New York: Dover, 1953), 282.

60. See Alexandre Koyré, "The Political Function of the Modern Lie," *October* 160 (2017): 143–151; Frank Ruda, "(From the Lie in the Closed World to) Lying in an Infinite Universe," in *Objective Fictions: Philosophy, Psychoanalysis, Marxism*, ed. Adrian Johnston, Boštjan Nedoh, and Alenka Zupančič (Edinburgh: Edinburgh University Press, 2022), 144–164.

61. Eric L. Santner, "Psychoanalysis and the Enigmas of Sovereignty," *Qui Parle* 11, no. 2 (1999): 1–19.

62. Schelling, *Philosophical Investigations into the Essence of Human Freedom*, 19–21.

63. Alenka Zupančič, *Why Psychoanalysis? Three Interventions* (Uppsala: NSU Press, 2008), 6–19.

64. Zupančič, *What IS Sex?*, 11.

65. Jean Laplanche and Jean Bertrand Pontalis, "Fantasy and the Origins of Sexuality," in *Unconscious Phantasy*, ed. Riccardo Steiner (London: Karnac Books, 2003), 130.

66. Sigmund Freud, "Formulations on the Two Principles of Mental Functioning," in Steiner, *Unconscious Phantasy*, 70.

67. Laplanche and Pontalis, "Fantasy and the Origins of Sexuality," 132–133.

68. In the famous correspondence with Einstein, Freud speaks to the presence of myth in scientific theory: "All this may give you the impression that our theories amount to species of mythology and a gloomy one at that! But does not every natural science lead ultimately to this—a sort of mythology? Is it otherwise today with your physical sciences?" See Sigmund Freud, *New Introductory Lectures on Psycho-Analysis and Other Works*, trans. James Strachey (London: Hogarth Press, 1964), 211. This is not so strange sounding if we consider Benjamin's point: any theoretical account seeks to fix the subjective and objective. It is precisely in this that it is a mythology: it is an attempt to capture the ground, the unity of apperception if you will, which precedes the conscious subject.

69. Freud, *New Introductory Lectures on Psycho-Analysis and Other Works*, 95.

70. In this respect, Lévi-Strauss might have had it right when he spoke of psychoanalysis as modern shamanism. See Lévi-Strauss, *Structural Anthropology*, 186–206.

71. Laplanche and Pontalis, "Fantasy and the Origins of Sexuality," 133.

72. It is significant that Freud's own, concentrated treatment of the ubiquity of the subject in phantasy is developed in the context of the complex role of perversion in neurotic phantasy. "A child is being Beaten" is a fundamental way in which perversion enters a neurotic's phantasy. See Sigmund Freud, *An Infantile Neurosis and Other Works* (London: Hogarth Press, 1955), 175–204. The ever-elusive distinction between "normal" perversion, which is the kernel of neurosis, and perversion "proper," the notion according to which perversion is the negative or the inverse of neurosis is, at first approximation, "settled" by the idea that the perverts do what neurotics dream of. See Sigmund Freud, *A Case of Hysteria, Three Essays on Sexuality and Other Works* (London: Hogarth Press, 1953), 165. The pervert will reenact, again and again, the sadomasochistic phantasy repressed by the neurotic, giving support to his libidinal economy. The problem, of course, is that this situates the pervert as the (perverse) realization of a neurotic's phantasy, signaling the very phantasmatic function of the pervert in neurotic phantasy, as the one who really enjoys, the one who goes through with it.

73. Sigmund Freud, *The Interpretation of Dreams*, trans. James Strachey (New York: Basic Books, 1955), 528.

74. Benjamin, *Selected Writings*, 1:72.

75. Eli Friedlander, *Walter Benjamin: A Philosophical Portrait* (Cambridge, MA: Harvard University Press, 2012), 117.

76. Eli Friedlander, "Wittgenstein and Goethe: The Life of Colors," *L'art du comprendre*, no. 20 (July 2011), ed. Christiane Chauviré.

77. See Jacques Lacan, *Seminar XI: The Four Fundamental Concepts of Psychoanalysis*, trans. Alan Sheridan (New York: W. W. Norton, 1988), 35–36; Jacques Lacan, *Écrits*, trans. Bruce Fink (New York: W. W. Norton, 2006), 429–430; Jacques Lacan, *Seminar XVII: The Other Side of Psychoanalysis*, trans. Russell Grigg (New York: W. W. Norton, 2007), 103.

78. Alenka Zupančič, "The Second Death," *Angelaki* 27, no. 1 (2022): 26–34.

79. Jacques Lacan, *Seminar XX: The Limits of Love and Knowledge, 1972–1973*, ed. Jacques-Alain Miller, trans. Bruce Fink (New York: W. W. Norton, 1999), 93.

80. Ibid., 34–35.

81. Ibid., 31.

82. Ibid.

83. Barbara Cassin, *Dictionary of Untranslatables: A Philosophical Lexicon*, trans. Steven Rendall, Christian Hubert, Jeffrey Mehlman, Nathanael Stein, and Michael Syrotinski (Princeton: Princeton University Press, 2014), 1133–1137.

84. Aristotle, *Metaphysics: Books Z and H*, trans. David Bostock (Oxford: Clarendon Press, 1994), xi.

85. Erwin Sonderegger, "Zur Bildung des Ausdrucks τὸ τί ἦν εἶναι durch Aristoteles," *Archiv für Geschichte der Philosophie* 65, no. 1 (1983): 18–39 (available at https://www.researchgate.net/publication/344339607_Die_Bildung_des_Ausdrucks_to_ti_en_einai_durch_Aristoteles_-_Dieser_Artikel_erschien_erstmals_im_Archiv_fur_Geschichte_der_Philosophie_65_1983_18-39).

86. Aristophanes, *Acharnians*, trans. Alan H. Sommerstein (Warminster, UK: Aris & Philips, 1980).

87. Sonderegger, "Zur Bildung des Ausdrucks τὸ τί ἦν εἶναι durch Aristoteles," quotation near the end of section 3; my translation.

88. Ibid.

89. Aristotle, *Metaphysics*, trans. Hugh Lawson-Tencred (London: Penguin Classics, 1998), 148.

90. Hannah Arendt, *The Human Condition*, 2nd ed. (Chicago: University of Chicago Press, 1998), 22–27.

91. Lacan, *Seminar XVII: The Other Side of Psychoanalysis*, 62.

92. Lacan, *Seminar XX: The Limits of Love and Knowledge*, 44.

93. Ibid., 34.

94. Ibid., 119.

95. The explication of Lacan's reference to Gödel was to a large extent wrought out in discussion with Attay Kremer, on whose mathematical expertise I rely here. For Gödel's treatment, see Kurt Gödel, *On Formally Undecidable Propositions of Principia Mathematica and Related Systems* (Chelmsford, MA: Courier Corporation, 1992).

96. See Friedrich Wilhelm Joseph Schelling, *First Outline of a Philosophy of Nature*, trans. Keith R. Peterson (Albany: SUNY Press, 2004), 202–203; Schelling, *Philosophical Investigations into the Essence of Human Freedom*, trans. Jeff Love and Johannes Schmidt (Albany: SUNY Press, 2006), 4, 21–23, 27–29, 31–32.

97. See Walter Benjamin, *Origin of the German Trauerspiel*, trans. Howard Eiland (Cambridge, MA: Harvard University Press, 2019), 45, 55.

98. Ibid., 43.

99. Eli Friedlander, *Walter Benjamin and the Idea of Natural History* (Stanford: Stanford University Press, 2024), 80.

100. Ibid., 82.

101. Joan Riviere, "Womanliness as a Masquerade," *International Journal of Psychoanalysis* 10 (1929): 303–313.

102. Karen Horney, *Neurotic Personality of Our Time*, vol. 10 (New York: W. W. Norton, 1937), 107–121.

103. This would be a way to speak of the direct, immediate link between being "me" and being at all, in the anxiety of femininity. See Zupančič, *What IS Sex?*, 56.

104. Alenka Zupančič, *Ethics of the Real: Kant and Lacan* (London: Verso, 2012), 132.

105. Lacan, *Seminar XX: The Limits of Love and Knowledge*.

106. Ibid., 61.

3   THE MACHINE'S NEW BODY

1. Bernard Stiegler, *Technics and Time 1: The Fault of Epimetheus*, trans. Richard Beardsworth and George Collins (Stanford: Stanford University Press, 1998), 21.

2. Sigmund Freud, *Totem and Taboo: Some Points of Agreement between the Mental Lives of Savages and Neurotics*, trans. James Strachey (London: Routledge, 1950), 91–92.

3. Gilles Deleuze, "Postscript on the Societies of Control," *October* 59 (Winter 1992): 3–7.

4. Bernard Stiegler, *The Age of Disruption: Technology of Madness in Computational Capitalism*, trans. Daniel Ross (Cambridge, UK: Polity Press, 2019), 52.

5. Ibid., 232–233.

6. Timothy Snyder, "Ukraine Holds the Future: The War between Democracy and Nihilism," *Foreign Affairs*, September/October 2022.

7. Jean-Pierre Dupuy, *On the Origins of Cognitive Science: The Mechanization of the Mind*, trans. M. B. DeBevoise (Cambridge, MA: MIT Press, 2009), 28–41; Jean-Pierre Dupuy, *The Mark of the Sacred*, trans. M. B. DeBevoise (Stanford: Stanford University Press, 2013), 67–81.

8. There is a definition of complexity here that merits a bit of unpacking. A complex system is one in which fabrication does not equate to understanding. The relation between structure and behavior is inverted. It is much easier to explain the behavior of a clock—the way it shows time—than its structure, its inner mechanism. Complexity is the moment in which the relation is reversed: it is much easier to explain the basic structure of a given society (patriarchal, industrial, etc.) than to describe its behavior. See Dupuy, *On the Origins of Cognitive Science*, 141.

9. Hannah Arendt, *The Human Condition*, 2nd ed. (Chicago: University of Chicago Press, 1998), 231.

10. Aristotle, *Physics: Books I and II*, trans. William Charlton (Oxford: Clarendon Press, 1983), 40.

11. Immanuel Kant, *Critique of Judgment*, trans. Werner S. Pluhar (Indianapolis: Hackett, 1987), 170–178, 181–188.

12. Ibid., 174.

13. The distinction between doing and making is made explicit, famously, by Aristotle. *Techne* is an action that has an end separate from the action, i.e., the product. See Aristotle, *Nicomachean Ethics*, ed. Roger Crisp (Cambridge: Cambridge University Press, 2014), 105. For Aristotle, the debate revolves around intellectual virtues and the faculties of the soul. But in Plato, the discussion is much more directly ontological, which is perhaps why it mostly goes overlooked. Plato's hierarchy of activities, corresponding to degrees of reality, is famous for the lowly status it preserves for art, understood as imitation. So lowly in fact, it should be exiled from the city. "For each thing there are these three crafts, one that uses it, one that makes it, and one that imitates it." See Plato, *Complete Works*, ed. John M. Cooper and Douglas S. Hutchinson (Indianapolis: Hackett, 1997), 1205. Implicit in Plato's reasoning here is a hierarchy of knowledge and being, in which, we might say, the more closely intertwined knowledge and being are, the more reality and value is bestowed upon the object and the subject of the activity alike. Indeed, the more ideal the object—higher in goodness and being, closer to the unity of being and goodness which is the Idea. Plato's initial premise is a simple one: The expert on the quality of a thing is the one who knows how to put it to use. Implicit in this, however, is a hierarchy of arts. In the higher arts, such as government, the knowledge involved in using and making is one and the same, for knowing how to put a city to use, knowing, that is, how to govern well, simply is what produces a well governed state. Using and making are the same activity, rooted in one and the same knowledge. This is even more strongly the case when it comes to thought: Knowing how to "apply" thought, to put it to use, knowing how to evaluate its quality, is thinking well. And all the way up to the top: To know the good is to be good. In the lower arts, corresponding to lesser objects, using and making come apart, and with them we witness a decrease in the reality and value of the object, indeed, the very opening of a gap between reality and value. "A flute player, for example, tells a flute maker about the flutes that respond well in actual playing and prescribes what kind of flutes he is to make" (1206). And so making is distinguished from higher arts, for in it we produce something of which we lack the knowledge to evaluate. We can bring it into being, without knowing its value, whether it is good or bad. The division of labor between knowers here speaks to the growing distance between the brute existence of a thing, and its goodness or value. This gap in itself is where, for Plato, evil sneaks in (this is why we can speak of an evil

demiurge, but not an evil creator: a craftsman can bring an evil world into existence, not a creator, for whom goodness and existence are one and the same). Art, as the imitation of a thing, is therefore twice removed from the unity of being, knowledge and value, or virtue. The imitator knows nothing of value, and his knowledge is not serious, it has no being of its own, no sturdiness to it. As a copy of a copy, art is no feeble thing, an echo of an echo, etc. Art realizes the gap: it bestows value on things that do not exist, and brings into existence things that have no intrinsic value. The disaster entailed in art has to do with its transformative power—it destroys the world of ideas, making its world out of the gap between value and existence. In a sense, in imitating a thing art renders that initial gap opened up in craft invisible: all we see now are things and copies, the "world-picture" has taken over our thought and action. We cannot fathom a unity of being and value, a good that exists and a being whose existence is a good in itself, for we are forced to picture them—existence and value—as distinct, apart. Only the "copy of the copy" sediments the status of craft as already nothing but a copy, and now it copies all the way down (and up).

14. Eric Schatzberg, *Technology: Critical History of a Concept* (Chicago: University of Chicago Press, 2018); Sacha Loeve, Xavier Guchet, and Bernadette Bensaude-Vincent, eds., *French Philosophy of Technology: Classical Readings and Contemporary Approaches* (Cham: Springer, 2018), 5–8.

15. Gilbert Simondon, *Individuation in Light of Notions of Form and Information*, trans. Taylor Adkins (Minneapolis: University of Minnesota Press, 2020), 42.

16. Jürgen Renn, *The Evolution of Knowledge: Rethinking Science for the Anthropocene* (Princeton: Princeton University Press, 2020), 32.

17. Ludwig Wittgenstein, *The Mythology in Our Language: Remarks on Frazer's Golden Bough*, trans. Stephanie Palmie (Chicago: Hau Books, 2020), 54; Robert Pfaller, *On the Pleasure Principle in Culture: Illusions without Owners*, trans. Lisa Rosenblatt (London: Verso, 2014).

18. Jürgen Renn speaks of a "generative ambiguity" intrinsic to "external representations": while their function is to stabilize meaning for transmission, their very "tool character" opens them up for innovation. In this, Renn aims to inherit Hegel's "cunning of reason." It is the gap between material encodings of knowledge and their "internal" meaning that opens up the "horizon of possibility" for exploration and development. See Renn, *The Evolution of Knowledge*, 56–57. We might here speak of a further reflective twist of this notion: there is a "generative ambiguity" as to what constitutes the very externality of a representation, the limit between language and matter.

19. Ibid., 49–50.

20. For a discussion of different historical renegotiations of the boundary between art and nature, see Bernadette Bensaude-Vincent and William R. Newman, eds., *The Artificial and the Natural: An Evolving Polarity* (Cambridge, MA: MIT Press, 2007). Our discussion here offers a perspective from which we might understand both the persistence of the "polarity" and its tendency toward historical reappearance as problematic and even as involving fundamental changes (dialectical twists and reversals).

21. Nature as process is something we seem to be unable to think of without some reference to teleology, especially what Kant called inner-purposiveness, an inherent part-whole logic that makes it at the very least analogous to what is "alive."

22. Friedrich Wilhelm Joseph Schelling, *First Outline of a Philosophy of Nature*, trans. Keith R. Peterson (Albany: SUNY Press, 2004), 202–203.

23. And indeed we would have to turn to theories of art to tease out the hostility that such an imitation entails. Consider Alois Riegl's notion of art's competition with nature. See

Alois Riegl, *Historical Grammar of the Visual Arts*, trans. Jacqueline E. Jung (New York: Zone Books, 2004). With this Riegl inherits Aristotle's analysis of human skill and adds, in a Schopenhauerian vein, an implicit theory as to its unity, what holds together imitation and completion. Competition with nature is the attempt to be more nature than nature itself, a mimetic mirror which is a very ambivalent relation, as we know from psychoanalytic theory. In speaking of a will to art, Riegl should not be taken to be describing a human endeavor that confronts nature from the outside; to the contrary, the will to art should be understood in the spirit of Schopenhauer, as a dimension in which human strivings are an expression of the noumenal dimension of nature, supraphenomenal. Nature, we could say, realizes itself beyond itself through human art. As humans go about trying to compete with nature, producing art, the will to art is working through them. Their artistic achievements, their victory over nature, is "second nature," nature's self-realization. In this way, competitive imitation is an agent of nature's completion.

24. See Marcel Mauss, *Techniques, Technology and Civilization*, ed. Nathan Schlanger (New York: Berghahn Books, 2006), 35–40. The distinction is fundamental for the study of "prehistory," which is to a large extent the study of material objects, for it effectively marks the boundary between societies and their broader civilizational area, which is why it had recently drawn the attention of Graeber and Wengrow, in their attempt to open up the "cold case" of civilizational development (2022, 288–292). See David Graeber and David Wengrow, *The Dawn of Everything: A New History of Humanity* (London: Penguin, 2021), 288–292.

25. Simondon, *Individuation in Light of Notions of Form and Information*, 171–172, 177–178.

26. Stiegler, *Technics and Time* 1, 136–141.

27. Gilbert Simondon, *On the Mode of Existence of Technical Objects*, trans. Cecile Malaspina and John Rogove (Minneapolis: Univocal Publishing, 2017).

28. Walter Benjamin, *Selected Writings*, 4 vols., ed. Michael W. Jennings et al. (Cambridge, MA: Harvard University Press, 1996–2003), 2:735.

29. Sigmund Freud, *Beyond the Pleasure Principle, Group Psychology and Other Works*, trans. James Strachey (New York: W. W. Norton, 1955).

30. Sigmund Freud, *The Future of an Illusion*, trans. James Strachey (London: Penguin Classics, 2008), 10.

31. On the temporalities implied in the names of the two titan brothers see Jean-Pierre Vernant and Marcel Detienne, *The Cuisine of Sacrifice among the Greeks* (Chicago: University of Chicago Press, 1989), 125–126.

32. Plato, *Complete Works*, 1765–1768.

33. Johann Gottfried Herder, *Philosophical Writings*, trans. Michael N. Forster (Cambridge: Cambridge University Press, 2002), 65–166; Roberto Esposito, *Bios: Biopolitics and Philosophy*, trans. Timothy Campbell (Minneapolis: University of Minnesota Press, 2008), 48; and Yuval Noah Harari, *Sapiens: A Brief History of Humankind* (New York: Random House, 2014), 11.

34. See Gaston Bachelard, *The Psychoanalysis of Fire*, trans. Alan C. M. Ross (Boston: Beacon Press, 1987).

35. Sigmund Freud, *Civilization and Its Discontents*, trans. James Strachey (New York: W. W. Norton, 1989), 90.

36. Hesiod, *Theogony. Works and Days. Testimonia*, trans. Glenn W. Most (Cambridge, MA: Harvard University Press, 2006), 47–49.

37. Jacques Lacan, *Seminar XI: The Four Fundamental Concepts of Psychoanalysis*, trans. Alan Sheridan (New York: W. W. Norton, 1988), 196–198.

38. Ibid.

39. Ibid.

40. Freud, *Beyond the Pleasure Principle, Group Psychology and Other Works*, 45–46.

41. Lacan, *Seminar XI: The Four Fundamental Concepts of Psychoanalysis*, 198.

42. Alenka Zupančič, "The Second Death," *Angelaki* 27, no. 1 (2022): 26–34.

43. Interestingly, for Simondon, this causes a serious problem to the amoeba's individuation: "Amoeba . . . are not strictly speaking veritable individuals; these beings are capable of regeneration by exchanging one nucleus with another being, and after a period of time they can reproduce by dividing into two parts. . . . In this case and properly speaking, there is no distinction between the individual and the species; individuals do not die but divide. Individuality can only appear with the death beings; death is the correlate of individuality." See Simondon, *Individuation in Light of Notions of Form and Information*, 181.

44. See Freud, *Beyond the Pleasure Principle, Group Psychology and Other Works*, 58. Riffing on Aristophanes' myth of the origin of sexual difference, Freud dares speculate that "living substance, at the time of its coming to life was torn apart into small particles, which have ever since endeavored to reunite through the sexual instincts." Sexed life is driven by the splintering of "living substance." If there is something that pushes the drives toward unification, it is the very splintering of "living substance." One can hardly avoid thinking about Schelling here.

45. This is the core of Benjamin's justifiably famous reading of the story of the fall: it is the fall into an instrumental view of language as a means of communication, identified with judgment, or the perspective of human understanding. See "On Language as Such and the Language of Man," in Benjamin, *Selected Writings*, 1:62–74.

46. Hesiod, *Theogony. Works and Days*.

47. See Francis Bacon, *The New Organon*, ed. Lisa Jardine and Michael Silverthorne (Cambridge: Cambridge University Press, 2000), 98. Hadot sees this as part of a long judicial metaphoric, dating back to the Hippocratic text and to be found again in Kant. See Pierre Hadot, *The Veil of Isis: An Essay on the History of the Idea of Nature*, trans. Michael Chase (Cambridge, MA: Harvard University Press, 2006).

48. Hadot, *The Veil of Isis*, 10.

49. With Plato, nature becomes a divine art. Aristotle introduces a crucial distinction between the external finality of human art and the internal finality of nature (ibid., 18–21).

50. Nature is personified as a goddess in the stoics. The great secret is nature herself, that is, the invisible reason or force of which the visible world is only a manifestation (ibid., 34).

51. Bacon, *The New Organon*, 100.

52. Lacan, *Seminar XI: The Four Fundamental Concepts of Psychoanalysis*, 185.

53. Octave Mannoni, "I Know Well, but All the Same," in *Perversion and the Social Relation*, ed. Molly Anne Rothenberg, Dennis A. Foster, and Slavoj Žižek (Durham: Duke University Press, 2003), 68–92.

54. Francis Bacon, *New Atlantis and The Great Instauration*, ed. Jerry Weinberger (Chichester, UK: Wiley-Blackwell, 1989), 71.

55. See Mladen Dolar, "'I Shall Be with You on Your Wedding Night': Lacan and the Uncanny," *October* 58 (Fall 1991): 5–24.

56. See Chris Baldick, In *Frankenstein's Shadow: Myth, Monstrosity, and Nineteenth-Century Writing* (Oxford: Clarendon Press, 1990).

57. See Dolar, "'I Shall Be with You on Your Wedding Night.'"

58. As Joan Copjec notes, there is reason to believe that Frankenstein's invention fails, and that the monster arises from his scientific failure. See Joan Copjec, "Vampires, Breast-Feeding, and Anxiety," *October* 58 (1991): 25–43.

59. Mary Shelley, "Frankenstein," in *Three Gothic Novels*, ed. Peter Fairclough (London: Penguin, 1968), 318.

60. See Jean-Jacques Rousseau, *Essay on the Origin of Languages and Writings Related to Music*, trans. and ed. John T. Scott (Hanover, NH: University Press of New England, 1998).

61. Dolar, "'I Shall Be with You on Your Wedding Night.'"

62. Ibid.

63. Simondon, *Individuation in Light of Notions of Form and Information*, 343.

64. Jean Baudrillard, *The System of Objects*, trans. James Benedict (London: Verso, 1996), 113.

65. Ibid., 117.

66. Ibid., 120–121.

67. Alan Turing, "Computing Machinery and Intelligence," *Mind* 59, no. 236 (1950): 433.

68. Joan Riviere, "Womanliness as a Masquerade," *International Journal of Psychoanalysis* 10 (1929): 303–313.

69. One is tempted to venture that the centrality of the figure of the transgender in our times is not unrelated to this undermining of human essentiality. We are all taught that nothing is essential, but it is only in sexuality that this is given a concrete form. The reason transgender women, in particular, have come to occupy such a major place in contemporary cultural politics is the way they exhibit, more than any "biological" woman, the elusive "essence" of femininity. Only a transsexual identity, a woman "trapped in a man's body," can give body to the X that makes a woman.

70. Catherine Malabou, *The Future of Hegel: Plasticity, Temporality, and Dialectic* (London: Routledge, 2004).

71. Or to sell us as products, which, in the internet "big data" economy, tends to amount to the same thing. See Shoshana Zuboff, *The Age of Surveillance Capitalism: The Fight for a Human Future at the New Frontier of Power* (New York: Hachette, 2019); and Antoinette Rouvroy and Thomas Berns, "Algorithmic Governmentality and Prospects of Emancipation: Disparateness as a Precondition for Individuation through Relationships?," *Réseaux* 177, no. 1 (2013): 163–196.

72. Significantly, she does so by translating human thought into desire, and that desire into stimulation, into functional interest—a mechanism thoroughly deciphered and one that reaches its full potential of use. Enjoyment can be used to create Ava because it has first been reduced to a predictable, behaviorist mechanism. This is the ambiguity ingrained in the project of "mechanization of the mind." See Dupuy, *On the Origins of Cognitive Science*.

73. Simondon, *Individuation in Light of Notions of Form and Information*.

74. Simondon, *On the Mode of Existence of Technical Objects*, 25–29.

75. Gilbert Simondon, "Technical Mentality," in *Being and Technology*, ed. Arne De Boever, Alex Murray, Jon Roffe, and Ashley Woodward (Edinburgh: Edinburgh University Press, 2012), 3.

76. This is, of course, a broader symptom pertaining to the technical. Stiegler detects comparable difficulties in Bertrand Gilles and Leroi-Gourhan. See Stiegler, *Technics and Time*, 43–49, 116, 135–138, 141–142.

77. Simondon, *Individuation in Light of Notions of Form and Information*.

78. Marshall McLuhan, *Understanding Media: The Extensions of Man* (Cambridge, MA: MIT Press, 1994), 46.

79. Jacques Lacan, *Seminar II: The Ego in Freud's Theory and in the Technique of Psycho-analysis, 1954–1955*, trans. Sylvana Tomaselli, ed. Jacques-Alain Miller (New York: W. W. Norton, 1991), 297–298.

80. Deleuze, "Postscript on the Societies of Control," 5.

81. Ibid.

82. Ibid, 5–6. Compare Benjamin, *Selected Writings*, 1:288.

83. Michel Feher, "Self-Appreciation; or, The Aspirations of Human Capital," *Public Culture* 21, no. 1 (January 2009): 21–41.

84. William S. Burroughs, *Naked Lunch* (New York: Grove Press, 1992), 81.

85. See Wendy Hui Kyong Chun, *Control and Freedom: Power and Paranoia in the Age of Fiber Optics* (Cambridge, MA: MIT Press, 2006).

86. Norbert Wiener, *The Human Use of Human Beings: Cybernetics and Society* (1950; London: Free Association Books, 1989).

87. Karl Marx, *Grundrisse: Foundations of the Critique of Political Economy*, trans. Martin Nicolaus (London: Penguin, 1973), 692–694.

88. Ibid.

89. This is Zupančič's "technical" definition of incest: "Perhaps we can even say that incest is precisely that which is more than its technical definition." See Alenka Zupančič, *Let Them Rot: Antigone's Parallax* (New York: Fordham University Press, 2023), 69

90. Marx, *Grundrisse*, 695; my emphasis.

91. Agamben's notion of the "Act of Impotentiality" seems to aim at a similar effect; the presence, in the actuality of the act, of its possibility not to be actualized would be its dimension of freedom, the appearance of a gift (grace, talent). Giorgio Agamben, *Potentialities: Collected Essays in Philosophy*, trans. Daniel Heller-Roazen (Stanford: Stanford University Press, 1999), 177–185. On the manner in which habit can come to manifest freedom see Félix Ravaisson, *Of Habit*, trans. Claire Carlisle and Mark Sinclair (London: Bloomsbury Publishing, 2008). My emphasis, however, is on the way in which such grace is an appearance of disappearance, so to speak, the way in which in such graceful performance what we enjoy is the very negative presence of laboriousness.

92. Lacan, *Seminar XI: The Four Fundamental Concepts of Psychoanalysis*, 47.

93. Even horrifying knowledge, say, the cold, calculated assessment of the existential risks humanity is facing, can be used as a way to defend from acknowledging that very same knowledge. Acknowledging would be to step outside the false security of cognition and recognize the way in which our very being is gripped by the threat. It would mean shifting from passive understanding to anxious, engaged activity. See Jacques Lacan, *Seminar III: The Psychoses, 1955–1956*, trans. Russell Grigg (New York: W. W. Norton, 1993), 265–267.

94. Jacques Lacan, *Seminar XVII: The Other Side of Psychoanalysis*, trans. Russell Grigg (New York: W. W. Norton, 2007), 22–23.

95. See Karl Marx, *Capital: A Critique of Political Economy*, trans. Ben Fowkes, 3 vols. (New York: Vintage, 1977), 1:163–164; Slavoj Žižek, *The Sublime Object of Ideology* (London: Verso, 2008), 28.

96. Kant, *Critique of Judgment*, 367–370.

97. Giorgio Agamben, *What Is an Apparatus? and Other Essays*, trans. David Kishik and Stefan Pedatella (Stanford: Stanford University Press, 2009), 1–24.

98. Vilém Flusser, *Towards a Philosophy of Photography*, trans. Anthony Mathews (London: Reaktion Press, 1983), 21–32.

99. Ibid., 26–28.

100. See Fredric Jameson, *The Prison-House of Language: A Critical Account of Structuralism and Russian Formalism* (Princeton: Princeton University Press, 1974).

101. Pfaller, *On the Pleasure Principle in Culture*.

102. Jean-Luc Nancy, *The Sense of the World*, trans. Jeffrey S. Librett (Minneapolis: University of Minnesota Press, 2008), 8.

103. Ibid., 50.

104. See Isabel Millar, *The Psychoanalysis of Artificial Intelligence* (Cham: Palgrave Macmillan, 2022), vii–viii.

105. Perhaps, then, it is no accident that the most philosophically potent voice of the speculative turn in philosophy, Quentin Meillassoux, is also the prophet of a "possible" Jesus.

106. Slavoj Žižek, *Pandemic! COVID-19 Shakes the World* (New York: OR Books, 2020), 63–64.

107. Yuval Kremnitzer, "The Frameless Life," *Angelaki* 27, no. 1 (2022): 140–151.

4   HUMAN, NATURE

1. See Michel Foucault, *The Order of Things: An Archaeology of the Human Sciences* (London: Routledge, 2005); Ihab Hassan, "Prometheus as Performer: Towards a Posthumanist Culture?," in *Performance in Postmodern Culture*, ed. Michael Benamou and Charles Caramella (Madison, WI: Coda Press, 1977); N. Katherine Hayles, *How We Became Posthuman: Virtual Bodies in Cybernetics, Literature, and Informatics* (Chicago: University of Chicago Press, 2000).

2. Immanuel Kant, *Anthropology from a Pragmatic Point of View*, trans. Mary J. Gregor (The Hague: Nijhoff, 1974), 151–160; Immanuel Kant, *Critique of Judgment*, trans. Werner S. Pluhar (Indianapolis: Hackett, 1987), 171–172.

3. Martin Heidegger, *The Question Concerning Technology and Other Essays*, trans. William Lovitt (New York: Harper, 1977).

4. Walter Benjamin, *Selected Writings*, 4 vols., ed. Michael W. Jennings et al. (Cambridge, MA: Harvard University Press, 1996–2003), 4:101–133; 3:251–283.

5. Friedlander speaks here of a balance between the two poles essential to the power of art, expressing the "veiled character of the shining forth of beauty." Eli Friedlander, *Walter Benjamin and the Idea of Natural History* (Stanford: Stanford University Press, 2024), 229.

6. Ibid., 1:393.

7. Ibid., 1:394. Also see Eric L. Santner, *The Royal Remains: The People's Two Bodies and the Endgames of Sovereignty* (Chicago: University of Chicago Press, 2011); Eric L. Santner, *The Weight*

of All Flesh: On the Subject-Matter of Political Economy, ed. Kevis Goodman (Oxford: Oxford University Press, 2016).

8. Benjamin, Selected Writings, 1:393–401.

9. See Immanuel Kant, Critique of Pure Reason, trans. Werner S. Pluhar (Indianapolis: Hackett, 1996), B414–426.

10. See Friedrich Wilhelm Joseph Schelling, The Unconditioned in Human Knowledge: Four Early Essays 1794–1796, trans. F. Marti (Lewisburg, PA: Bucknell University Press, 1980); Paul Franks, All or Nothing: Systematicity, Transcendental Arguments, and Skepticism in German Idealism (Cambridge, MA: Harvard University Press, 2005), 260–336.

11. Friedlander, Walter Benjamin and the Idea of Natural History, 147.

12. Benjamin, Selected Writings, 1:396.

13. See Santner, The Weight of All Flesh, 84.

14. Benjamin, Selected Writings, 1:394.

15. Ibid., 1:95–96, 103.

16. Ibid., 1:105.

17. Intoxication is, according to Benjamin, the most intense modality of pleasure and pain. See ibid., 1:394. We might say that in intoxication, or ecstasy [Rausch], both are equally present: there is pleasure in pain and pain in pleasure. But precisely in focusing on such a limit experience, we fail to see the way pleasure and pain (together, flesh) are present in ordinary perception.

18. See ibid., 1:101.

19. Benjamin, Selected Writings, 4:313–355.

20. Benjamin is relying here on Freud's Beyond the Pleasure Principle. It would have been interesting to compare Benjamin's notion of "shock experience" with Freud's account of fetishistic disavowal. The gap between the state of affairs recorded and its (practical) significance is most extreme in fetishistic disavowal, where it merits, in Freud's view, speaking of in terms of the splitting of the ego. See Sigmund Freud, New Introductory Lectures on Psycho-Analysis and Other Works, trans. James Strachey (London: Hogarth Press, 1964), 271–278.

21. See Benjamin, Selected Writings, 4:313–355.

22. Theodor W. Adorno and Walter Benjamin, The Complete Correspondence, 1928–1940 (Cambridge, MA: Harvard University Press, 1999), 326.

23. See Benjamin, Selected Writings, 4:318; 1:3–5.

24. Ibid., 1:288–291.

25. Santner, The Royal Remains, xxi, 21–32.

26. Benjamin, Selected Writings, 1:391.

27. See Arthur Schopenhauer, The World as Will and Representation, vol. 1, trans. and ed. Judith Norman, Alistair Welchman, and Christopher Janaway (Cambridge: Cambridge University Press, 2010), 14, 41, 125–126, 217.

28. Ludwig Wittgenstein, Philosophical Investigations, trans. G. E. M. Anscombe (Oxford: Basil Blackwell, 1958), 89–106.

29. Benjamin, Selected Writings, 1:396–397.

30. In the "Orientation" essay, orientation without concept, advancing, as it were, from the "blindness" of intuition toward concepts, is likened by Kant to the utilization of the

sense of "right and left" in a dark room. In the third critique, he develops the notion of aesthetic judgment (one arm of reflective judgment) as serving the same function of ascending to concepts, rather than subsuming particulars under concepts (determining judgment). Reflection is a pleasure in judging, which supplies judgment with orientation in the absence of concepts. In this sense, pleasure (and pain, here as what to avoid, then in the sublime as the very measure of transcendence) is the "inner differentiation" of right and left, which situates judgment in horizontal as well as lateral directionality, speaking to the presence of the idea in the very possibility of a path, or accord, between concepts and intuitions. See *Kant's Political Writings*, ed. Hans Reiss, trans. H. B. Nisbet (Cambridge: Cambridge University Press, 1991), 667–681; Jean-François Lyotard, *Lessons on the Analytic of the Sublime*, trans. Elizabeth Rottenberg (Stanford: Stanford University Press, 1994), 31–35; Eli Friedlander, *Expressions of Judgment: An Essay on Kant's Aesthetics* (Cambridge, MA: Harvard University Press, 2015), 17–20, 44–45.

31. In an early fragment, titled "Perception Is Reading" Benjamin writes: "In perception, the useful (the good) is true. Pragmatism. Madness is a form of perception alien to the community." See Benjamin, *Selected Writings*, 1:92. The attunement of perception to an order in which the good is identified with the true evokes the identity, in the idea, of the good, the beautiful, and the true. Such an apparently idealistic picture is evidenced, for Benjamin, in perception: perception is not indifferent toward its objects; it is oriented by "enjoyment," by the pleasure and pain that underlie it. Which is not to say that perception is pleasure-seeking. On the contrary, perception is often drawn to the painful, to what exerts a demand on it.

32. For both Kant and Schelling, the problem of radical evil concerns the way in which we must perceive our very dispositions, what seems (pre)determined in us, as the product of our own choice, even if that choice is atemporal. See Friedrich Wilhelm Joseph Schelling, *Philosophical Investigations into the Essence of Human Freedom*, trans. Jeff Love and Johannes Schmidt (Albany: SUNY Press, 2006), 51–52; Immanuel Kant, *Religion within the Boundaries of Mere Reason: And Other Writings*, ed. Allen W. Wood and George Di Giovanni (Cambridge: Cambridge University Press, 2016), 41–62, 72–105.

33. Indeed, one of the earliest articulations of Benjamin's notion of the aura appears in the context of his critical analysis of Socrates. Benjamin scolds Socrates for his indiscrete relation to the truth; his probing which makes truth accessible is also what discounts its essential distance, its auratic dimension. The short essay is an early attempt to think the relation between spirit and sexuality. See Benjamin, *Selected Writings*, 1:52–54.

34. Ibid.

35. See Walter Benjamin, *Origin of the German Trauerspiel*, trans. Howard Eiland (Cambridge, MA: Harvard University Press, 2019), 55.

36. Benjamin, *Selected Writings*, 1:201–206, 398.

37. The psychoanalytic notion of sublimation as a destiny of the drive, distinct from repression, could be productively linked with this notion. See Sigmund Freud, *On the History of the Psycho-Analytic Movement, Papers on Metapsychology and Other Works* (London: Hogarth Press, 1957), 126.

38. See Benjamin, *Selected Writings*, 4:251–283.

39. Ibid., 1:397.

40. Ibid., 4:389.

41. Ibid., 4:390.

42. Ibid., 3:305–306.

43. Ibid., 1:395.

44. Ibid., 2:474.

45. Georg Wilhelm Friedrich Hegel, *Phenomenology of Spirit*, trans. A. V. Miller (Oxford: Oxford University Press, 1977), 10.

46. Benjamin, *Selected Writings*, 3:107.

47. Ibid., 3:253.

48. Ibid., 3:108.

49. Analyzing the desire underlying Spinoza's vision of a deterministic universe, which reduces us to the role of spectators, Schelling notes: "The necessity to save one's ego from all objective determination and, accordingly, to still think of oneself in every instance, is illustrated by two contradictory yet very common experiences. Now and again, our thought of death and not-being is connected with aggregable feelings, and for no other reason than this, that we presuppose a pleasure in not-being, that is, we presume a continuation of ourselves even during not being." See Schelling, *The Unconditioned in Human Knowledge*, 182.

50. Giorgio Agamben, "Archaeology of the Work of Art," in Agamben, *Creation and Anarchy: The Work of Art and the Religion of Capitalism*, trans. Adam Kotsko (Stanford: Stanford University Press, 2019), 1–13.

51. Benjamin, *Selected Writings*, 3:107.

52. See Theodor W. Adorno and Max Horkheimer, *Dialectic of Enlightenment*, trans. Edmund Jephcott (Stanford: Stanford University Press, 2002); Max Horkheimer, *Critique of Instrumental Reason* (London: Verso, 2013); Heidegger, *The Question Concerning Technology and Other Essays*.

53. See Ernst Cassirer, *Language and Myth* (New York: Dover, 1953), 186. Compare with Durkheim's conceptualization of the sacred as founded on separation: Emile Durkheim, *The Elementary Forms of the Religious Life*, trans. Joseph Ward Swain (Chelmsford, MA: Courier Corporation, 2008).

54. Cassirer, *Language and Myth*, 133.

55. Jacques Lacan, *Seminar XI: The Four Fundamental Concepts of Psychoanalysis*, trans. Alan Sheridan (New York: W. W. Norton, 1988), 44, 84, 101, 106, 132, 138–143.

56. Ludwig Wittgenstein, *The Mythology in Our Language: Remarks on Frazer's Golden Bough*, trans. Stephanie Palmie (Chicago: Hau Books, 2020), 68.

57. This is the "magic" that ties beautiful semblance to life. See Benjamin, *Selected Writings*, 1:224.

58. Wittgenstein, *The Mythology in Our Language*, 34.

59. Ibid., 43.

60. Ibid., 145.

61. Ibid., 40.

62. See E. E. Evans-Pritchard, *Witchcraft, Oracles and Magic among the Azande* (Oxford: Clarendon Press, 1963); James T. Siegel, *Naming the Witch* (Stanford: Stanford University Press, 2006).

63. Wittgenstein, *The Mythology in Our Language*, 42.

64. Ibid., 54.

65. See Sigmund Freud, *Beyond the Pleasure Principle, Group Psychology and Other Works*, trans. James Strachey (New York: W. W. Norton, 1955), 175–204.

66. See Schelling, *Philosophical Investigations into the Essence of Human Freedom*, 34.

67. Wittgenstein, *The Mythology in Our Language*, 58.

68. Gilbert Simondon, *On the Mode of Existence of Technical Objects*, trans. Cecile Malaspina and John Rogove (Minneapolis: Univocal Publishing, 2017), 174.

69. Ibid.

70. Wittgenstein, *The Mythology in Our Language*, 46.

71. Ibid., 54.

72. See Benjamin, *Selected Writings*, 2:684–685, 694–698, 720–722.

73. Eli Friedlander, "Wittgenstein, Benjamin, and Pure Realism," in *Wittgenstein and Modernism*, ed. Michael LeMahieu and Karen Zumhagen-Yekplé (Chicago: University of Chicago Press, 2016).

74. Benjamin, *Selected Writings*, 2:239.

75. Ibid., 2:721.

76. See Friedlander, *Walter Benjamin and the Idea of Natural History*.

77. "The body," writes Benjamin, "is a moral instrument. It was created to fulfill the commandments. It was fashioned at the creation according to this purpose. Even its perceptions indicate how far they draw the body away from its duty or bind it close." Benjamin, *Selected Writings*, 1:396. There is a direct link between the normative and perception in Benjamin's metaphysical empiricism: there is a primordial (sense of) purpose given in the most nuanced and developed expression precisely of what strikes us as opaque.

78. Slavoj Žižek, "Ideology II: Competition Is a Sin," *Lacan.com* 4 (2008).

79. See Henry Sumner Maine, *Ancient Law: Its Connection to the History of Early Society* (London: J. M. Dent & Sons, 1912), 111; Thorstein Veblen, *The Theory of the Leisure Class* (Oxford: Oxford University Press, 2007), 34–37.

80. Benjamin, *Selected Writings*, 2:722.

81. Sigmund Freud, "Obsessive Acts and Religious Practices," trans. James Strachey, in *Jensen's "Gradiva" and Other Works* (London: Hogarth Press, 1959), 115–128.

82. David Graeber and David Wengrow, *The Dawn of Everything: A New History of Humanity* (London: Penguin, 2021), 190–192.

83. Ibid., 191–196.

84. Pierre Clastre, *Society against the State: Essays in Political Anthropology*, trans. Robert Hurley (New York: Zone Books, 1989), 183–186.

85. See Moshe Halbertal, *On Sacrifice* (Princeton: Princeton University Press, 2012).

86. See A. M. Hocart, *Kingship* (London: Oxford University Press, 1969); Marshall Sahlins and David Graeber, *On Kings* (Chicago: Hau Books, 2017), 1–22, 23–64, 72, 377–464.

87. This is perhaps why "traditional" society produces unique, singularly skilled members and fosters long experience. Singular life experience goes hand in hand with traditional, hierarchical mimetic relations, in which we seek to learn, by apprenticeship, from the eldest.

88. Graeber and Wengrow, *The Dawn of Everything*, 61–68.

89. See Philippe Descola, *In the Society of Nature: A Native Ecology in Amazonia* (Cambridge: Cambridge University Press, 1994).

90. Hannah Arendt, *Between Past and Future: Eight Exercises in Political Thought* (New York: Viking, 1961), 36–37.

91. Eduardo Viveiros de Castro, "Cosmological Deixis and Amerindian Perspectivism," *Journal of the Royal Anthropological Institute* (1998): 469–488.

92. Sigmund Freud, *Civilization and Its Discontents*, trans. James Strachey (New York: W. W. Norton, 1989), 11–13.

93. See Descola, *In the Society of Nature*.

94. Veblen, *The Theory of the Leisure Class*, 12–13.

95. Ibid., 14.

96. Interestingly, Simondon advances a similar theory as to the defects of Aristotelian hylomorphism. The notion of form as the active ingredient imposing itself on passive matter is the outlook of a master issuing commands, not that of a worker familiar with the process of production. See Gilbert Simondon, *Individuation in Light of Notions of Form and Information*, trans. Taylor Adkins (Minneapolis: University of Minnesota Press, 2020), 36, 45.

97. Santner, *The Weight of All Flesh*.

98. David Graeber, *Bullshit Jobs: A Theory* (New York: Simon and Schuster, 2018).

99. Moishe Postone, *Time, Labor, and Social Domination: A Reinterpretation of Marx's Critical Theory* (Cambridge: Cambridge University Press, 1995).

100. Franz Kafka, *The Blue Octavo Notebooks*, ed. Max Brod (Cambridge, MA: Exact Change, 2004).

101. See Michel Foucault, *The History of Sexuality*, vol. 1, trans. Robert Hurley (New York: Pantheon Books, 1978), 11.

102. This point is quite crucial for the distinction between legal violence and the ever-threatening violence of the (mythical) state of nature. Contrary to the textbook version of Hobbes's philosophy, the state of nature is not the beginning point, a state which Hobbes simply presupposes. What drives the hostility which makes the war of all against all at least a potential reality? The reason underlying the potential violence of human society has to do precisely with the perverse relation toward power as a means. It is because power is viewed as a means to attain ends that the desire for it is perversely unlimited, and inherently competitive, making the prospect of an equal share in power inherently problematic, and making the postulate of power above and beyond competition—sovereign power—necessary. Only a power above all others, above competition, can limit, equally, the power of all members of society, and thus secure peace. See Thomas Hobbes, *Leviathan*, ed. J. C. A. Gaskin (Oxford: Oxford University Press, 1998), 62–70.

103. As an aside, we might add that this tendency of the law is by no means a universal feature, but rather is inseparable from its modernity. For Henry Maine, this was indeed the distinguishing feature of Western law. In juxtaposition to what he labeled customary law, ossified by its ceremonial character, the Western legal tradition has its own developmental key, indeed, a quasi-Hegelian tendency toward its own notion, forever progressing toward equity. Leaving aside the laudatory aspect of this analysis, to the extent that the Western legal tradition has in fact managed to offer itself as the universal standard and model of the law, it has done so, perhaps, thanks to its capacity for radical transmutation, the capacity to remain—or become—itself, through *revolutionary* change. See Harold J. Berman, *Law and Revolution: The Impact of the Protestant Reformations on the Western Legal Tradition* (Cambridge, MA: Harvard University Press, 1983).

104. In the following discussion we do not cite the usual *Selected Writings* edition of the text, but rather the new translation: Walter Benjamin, *Towards the Critique of Violence: A Critical Edition*, trans. and ed. Peter Fenves and Julia Ng (Stanford: Stanford University Press, 2021), 55.

105. Ibid., 54.

106. Power held in abeyance, in reserve, can also be understood as a specific experience with the modality of the possible, a certain sense of its actuality as unrealized. This sense of the potential as there, standing in reserve, underlies hubris, or arrogance (Friedlander), the original sin of myth—to hold on to power as if it was a possession is to play with fire. This is the "sin" of power understood as means, the self-delusional logic underlying its "accumulation." See Eli Friedlander, "Assuming Violence: A Commentary on Walter Benjamin's 'Critique of Violence,'" *boundary 2* 42, no. 4 (November 2015): 159–185.

107. From a psychoanalytic perspective, it is impossible to ignore the very specific context in which mythic violence intervenes in Niobe's myth, which marks her particular arrogance and the bitter irony inscribed in her "punishment." The irony of mythic violence is "the answer from the real," the way in which what is rejected from symbolization returns with a vengeance. In bragging about the superiority of her reproductive achievements—Niobe has 14 offspring, whereas Latona, mother of Apollo and Artemis, only has two—in having produced more offspring than the gods, Niobe's vulgarity of counting her offspring is not a mere sin against individuality, the uniqueness of individuated being; it "forgets" the real line separating the mortals from the immortals, namely, the primal connection between sexual reproduction and death, which is part and parcel of human individuation. And so the gods strike some but not all of her children, and they leave her as an eternal witness, neither alive nor dead: petrified, turned into a stone, Niobe is caught between the "two deaths" forever, a forerunner of Antigone.

108. See Halbertal, *On Sacrifice*.

109. Benjamin, *Towards the Critique of Violence*, 58.

110. The mythical is manifest in the sacrifice demanded by legal punishment which is disclosed in the threatening dimension of the law, which Benjamin, *pace* utilitarian interpretations of threat and deterrence, understands through the chance, however remote, of escaping punishment and the disproportionality of punishment

111. René Girard, *Violence and the Sacred*, trans. Patrick Gregory (Baltimore: Johns Hopkins University Press, 1977), 15.

112. Ibid., 20.

113. Ibid., 23.

114. Ibid., 24–25.

115. See Slavoj Žižek, *Violence: Six Sideways Reflections* (New York: Picador, 2008).

116. Alenka Zupančič, *Let Them Rot: Antigone's Parallax* (New York: Fordham University Press, 2023), 10.

117. Ibid., 11.

118. Ibid., 12.

119. See the discussion of Plato in the first chapter.

120. Ibid., 13.

121. See ibid., 18.

5 CAUGHT IN THE WEB

1. Walter Benjamin, *Selected Writings*, 4 vols., ed. Michael W. Jennings et al. (Cambridge, MA: Harvard University Press, 1996–2003), 1:288.

2. John Suler, "The Online Disinhibition Effect," *Cyberpsychology and Behavior* 7, no. 3 (2004): 321–326.

3. Sigmund Freud, *Totem and Taboo: Some Points of Agreement between the Mental Lives of Savages and Neurotics*, trans. James Strachey (London: Routledge, 1950), 102.

4. Michel Foucault, *Abnormal: Lectures at the Collège de France 1974–1975*, trans. Graham Burchell (London: Verso, 2003), 12–16.

5. See Gilles Deleuze, "Postscript on the Societies of Control," *October* 59 (Winter 1992): 3–7; and Mark Andrejevic, *Automated Media* (London: Routledge, 2019).

6. Hannah Arendt, *Between Past and Future: Eight Exercises in Political Thought* (New York: Viking, 1961), 91.

7. See Mladen Dolar, "The Future of Authority?," *Philosopher* 109, no. 2 (2022).

8. See Henry Sumner Maine, *Ancient Law: Its Connection to the History of Early Society* (London: J. M. Dent & Sons, 1912), 359–383; Mahmood Mamdani, *Define and Rule* (Cambridge, MA: Harvard University Press, 2012), 21–23.

9. Max Weber, *From Max Weber: Essays in Sociology*, trans. and ed. H. H. Gerth and C. Wright Mills (New York: Oxford University Press, 1946), 77–128.

10. Ibid., 78–79.

11. See Arendt, *Between Past and Future*, 105–106. Nicole Loraux's impressive study of the structural, mythical presence of stasis—civil war—in Greek culture and thought can be interpreted as lending credence to Arendt's claim. The Greeks developed against an experience of a centuries-long civil struggle, organized to a large extent around the tension between a form of rule derived from the oikos, the family household bound to the necessities of nature, and the polis, the city. See Nicole Loraux, *The Divided City: On Memory and Forgetting in Ancient Athens*, trans. Corrine Pache and Jeff Fort (New York: Zone Books, 2006), 15–44. Authority, it is implied in Arendt's account, is neither familial nor political, but rather resides in their point of extimacy, precisely the place Agamben reserves for stasis. See Giorgio Agamben, *Stasis: Civil War as a Political Paradigm* (Stanford: Stanford University Press, 2015), 16. Elsewhere, Agamben explicitly links the question of authority to civil war. There, he seems to imply, the struggle is to a large extent around the very possibility of authority's existence alongside power. See Giorgio Agamben, *State of Exception*, trans. Kevin Attell (Chicago: University of Chicago Press, 2005), 86–87.

12. See Leo Strauss, *Philosophy and Law: Contributions to the Understanding of Maimonides and His Predecessors* (Albany: SUNY Press, 1995); Peter Fitzpatrick, *Modernism and the Grounds of Law* (Cambridge: Cambridge University Press, 2001); Hermann Cohen, *Religion of Reason out of the Sources of Judaism*, trans. Simon Kaplan (Atlanta: Scholars Press, 1995).

13. Arthur O. Lovejoy, *The Great Chain of Being: A Study of the History of an Idea* (Cambridge, MA: Harvard University Press, 1964), 45–46.

14. Arendt, *Between Past and Future*, 110.

15. See Giorgio Agamben, *The Kingdom and the Glory: For a Theological Genealogy of Economy and Government*, trans. Lorenzo Chiesa (Stanford: Stanford University Press, 2011).

16. Arendt, *Between Past and Future*, 102

17. Ibid., 95.

18. Benjamin, *Selected Writings*, 1:7.

19. Agamben, *State of Exception*, 79.

20. Ibid., 80.

21. Ibid., 83–84.

22. See Lorraine Daston, *Rules: A Short History of What We Live By* (Princeton: Princeton University Press, 2022), 8.

23. Ibid., 41–44.

24. Arendt, *Between Past and Future*, 97.

25. Hannah Arendt, *The Origins of Totalitarianism* (London: Penguin Classics, 2017), 344.

26. Jacques Lacan, *Seminar II: The Ego in Freud's Theory and in the Technique of Psycho-analysis, 1954–1955*, trans. Sylvana Tomaselli, ed. Jacques-Alain Miller (New York: W. W. Norton, 1991), 127.

27. Freud, *Totem and Taboo*, 21.

28. Lacan, *Seminar II: The Ego in Freud's Theory and in the Technique of Psycho-analysis*, 128.

29. Slavoj Žižek, *The Plague of Fantasies* (London: Verso, 1997), 37–38.

30. Yuval Kremnitzer, "The Princess Learns to Wink: Lubitsch and the Politics of the Obscene," in *The Ethics of Ernst Lubitsch: Comedy without Relief*, ed. Ivana Novak and Gregor Moder (Lanham, MD: Rowman & Littlefield, 2024), 115–135.

31. Michel Foucault, *Security, Territory, Population: Lectures at the Collège de France, 1977–78*, ed. Arnold I. Davidson, trans. Graham Burchell (New York: Palgrave Macmillan, 2007), 69.

32. https://www.youtube.com/watch?v=bJYOKWL8kMQ

33. Gilbert Simondon, *On the Mode of Existence of Technical Objects*, trans. Cecile Malaspina and John Rogove (Minneapolis: Univocal Publishing, 2017), 169.

34. Georg Wilhelm Friedrich Hegel, *Phenomenology of Spirit*, trans. A. V. Miller (Oxford: Oxford University Press, 1977), 9.

35. Simondon, *On the Mode of Existence of Technical Objects*, 180–181.

36. Benjamin, *Selected Writings*, 3: 103–104.

37. Gilbert Simondon, "Technical Mentality," in *Being and Technology*, ed. Arne De Boever, Alex Murray, Jon Roffe, and Ashley Woodward (Edinburgh: Edinburgh University Press, 2012), 1.

38. Ibid., 3–4.

39. Simondon, *On the Mode of Existence of Technical Objects*, 25–29.

40. Simondon, "Technical Mentality," 9.

41. Ibid., 12.

42. Marshall McLuhan, *Understanding Media: The Extensions of Man* (Cambridge, MA: MIT Press, 1994), 7–9.

43. Jacques Lacan, *Seminar XI: The Four Fundamental Concepts of Psychoanalysis*, trans. Alan Sheridan (New York: W. W. Norton, 1988), 26.

44. Benjamin, *Selected Writings*, 3: 389.

45. Joan Copjec, "The Descent into Shame," *Studio: Israeli Art Magazine* (Tel Aviv), no. 168 (March 2007).

46. Ibid.

47. See Sigmund Freud, *Beyond the Pleasure Principle, Group Psychology and Other Works*, trans. James Strachey (New York: W. W. Norton, 1955).

48. Modernity is not the loss of innocence but the loss of the technique of losing one's innocence, a technique that transmutes disillusionment to an investment in the

continuation of the form of life. With Casanova, we have the horror of finding ourselves in the position of the duped. See Yuval Kremnitzer, "The Frameless Life," *Angelaki* 27, no. 1 (2022): 140–151.

49. See Sigmund Freud, *On the History of the Psycho-Analytic Movement, Papers on Metapsychology and Other Works* (London: Hogarth Press, 1957), 435–442; and Alenka Zupančič, "Not-Mother: On Freud's Verneinung," *E-flux online*, 2012.

50. Sandor Ferenczi, *First Contributions to Psycho-analysis* (London: Routledge, 2018), 135.

51. Sigmund Freud, *Group Psychology and the Analysis of the Ego*, trans. James Strachey (London: Hogarth Press, 1949), 97–98.

52. Ferenczi, *First Contributions to Psycho-analysis*, 137.

53. Jonathan Swift, *Gulliver's Travels* (New York: Signet Classics, 2008), 173.

54. On the oath as paradigmatic of the symbolic efficacy, or "magic," of language, see Giorgio Agamben, *The Sacrament of Language: An Archaeology of the Oath*, trans. Adam Kotsko (Stanford: Stanford University Press, 2010). For a very different take on the magic of symbolic efficacy in connection with the perverse mode, see Robert Pfaller, *On the Pleasure Principle in Culture: Illusions without Owners*, trans. Lisa Rosenblatt (London: Verso, 2014).

55. Swift, *Gulliver's Travels*, 151.

56. Ferenczi, *First Contributions to Psycho-analysis*, 138.

57. Ibid.

58. Claude Lévi-Strauss, *Introduction to the Work of Marcel Mauss* (London: Routledge, 1987).

59. Lacan, *Seminar XI: The Four Fundamental Concepts of Psychoanalysis*, 29.

60. Jacques Lacan, *Seminar XVII: The Other Side of Psychoanalysis*, trans. Russell Grigg (New York: W. W. Norton, 2007), 180.

61. Insofar as it is an expression of the flesh, or corporeal substance, there is no wonder that Benjamin rejected the notion of blushing as exteriorization: you will recall that the flesh has no inside nor outside to speak of—it is not a unity of form.

62. Mladen Dolar, *Hontology* (Durham: Duke University Press, 2023).

63. Lacan, *Seminar XVII: The Other Side of Psychoanalysis*, 183.

64. Ibid., 182.

65. Jacques Lacan, *Seminar X: Anxiety*, trans. Adrian R. Price (Cambridge, UK: Polity Press, 2014), 80.

66. I owe this formulation to Simon Hajdini.

67. See Kremnitzer, "The Princess Learns to Wink."

68. Alenka Zupančič, "Perversion vs. Desire," conference presentation at "Perversion and Its Discontents," Ljubljana, Slovenia, 2023, https://www.youtube.com/watch?v=_2TZVFGfQpM.

69. Jacques Lacan, *Seminar XX: The Limits of Love and Knowledge, 1972–1973*, ed. Jacques-Alain Miller, trans. Bruce Fink (New York: W. W. Norton, 1999), 92.

70. Friedrich Wilhelm Joseph Schelling, *Philosophical Investigations into the Essence of Human Freedom*, trans. Jeff Love and Johannes Schmidt (Albany: SUNY Press, 2006), 34.

71. Slavoj Žižek, *The Sublime Object of Ideology* (London: Verso, 2008), 124–125; Žižek, *The Plague of Fantasies*, 3–18.

72. Kremnitzer, "The Princess Learns to Wink."

73. See Jason Glynos and Yannis Stavrakakis, eds., *Lacan and Science* (London: Routledge, 2018); Jean-Claude Milner, *A Search for Clarity: Science and Philosophy in Lacan's Oeuvre* (Evanston: Northwestern University Press, 2020).

74. Milner, *A Search for Clarity*, 18–19.

75. Ibid., 24.

76. See Lydia H. Liu, *The Freudian Robot: Digital Media and the Future of the Unconscious* (Chicago: University of Chicago Press, 2010).

77. Jacques Lacan, *Seminar II: The Ego in Freud's Theory and in the Technique of Psycho-analysis*, 119.

78. See Niklas Luhmann, *Introduction to Systems Theory*, trans. Dirk Baecker and Peter Gilgen (Cambridge, UK: Polity Press, 2013); Ludwig von Bertalanffy, "An Outline of General System Theory," *British Journal for the Philosophy of Science* 1, no. 2 (1950): 134–165.

79. See Samo Tomšič, "From the Orderly World to the Polluted Unworld," in *Objective Fictions: Philosophy, Psychoanalysis, Marxism*, ed. Adrian Johnston, Boštjan Nedoh, and Alenka Zupančič (Edinburgh: Edinburgh University Press, 2022), 64–84.

80. Lacan, *Seminar II: The Ego in Freud's Theory and in the Technique of Psycho-analysis*, 89–90.

81. Jacques Lacan, *Écrits*, trans. Bruce Fink (New York: W. W. Norton, 2006), 694.

82. Lacan, *Seminar XI: The Four Fundamental Concepts of Psychoanalysis*, 302.

83. Ibid.

84. Ibid.

85. Ibid., 143.

86. David Chalmers, "Facing Up to the Problem of Consciousness," *Journal of Consciousness Studies* 2, no. 3 (1995): 200–219.

87. Freud, *Totem and Taboo*, 22.

88. Ibid.

89. Ibid., 21.

90. Reinhart Koselleck, *Critique and Crisis: Enlightenment and Pathogenesis of Modern Society* (Oxford: Berg, 1988), 176.

91. Christian Borch, *The Politics of Crowds: An Alternative History of Sociology* (Cambridge: Cambridge University Press, 2012), 70–78.

92. Fredric Jameson, "On Goffman's Frame Analysis," *Theory and Society* 3 (1976): 119–133.

93. Gustave Le Bon, *The Crowd: A Study of the Popular Mind* (Chelmsford, MA: Courier Corporation, 2002), 2.

94. Ibid., 4.

95. Gustave Le Bon, *The Evolution of Matter*, trans. F. Legge (London: Walter Scott, 1909); Max Jammer, *Concepts of Mass in Contemporary Physics and Philosophy* (Princeton: Princeton University Press, 2009), 72.

96. In this "vindicating" Hermann Cohen's idealistic history of the natural sciences' path from substance to energy. See Hermann Cohen, "The Relationship of Logic to Physics," in *The Neo-Kantian Reader*, ed. Sebastian Luft (London: Routledge, 2015).

97. Metamorphosis and power are the two grand themes of Canetti's project in the book. He defines power, in contradistinction to force, as what opens up the space where force can be applied. Elias Canetti, "The Torch in My Ear," in *The Memoirs of Elias Canetti*, trans. Joachim Neugroschel (New York: Farrar, Straus and Giroux, 1990), 281, 353. As Malabou

suggests, power and crowds are identical for Canetti: Catherine Malabou, *Plasticity: The Promise of Explosion* (Edinburgh: Edinburgh University Press, 2022), 119. Power and mass are without essence, they are the state of existence of potential for transformation, like a cat waiting in silence for its prey. For Canetti, it would seem, ultimately it is in the explosive release of energy—the very power that holds the space of action open—that we find its truth kernel. It is when power itself is released, made manifest, that we glimpse the fluid, plastic substance of the social.

98. Elias Canetti, *Crowds and Power*, trans. Carol Stewart (New York: Farrar, Straus and Giroux, 1984), 15–16.

99. Ibid., 16–17.

100. Freud, *Group Psychology and the Analysis of the Ego*, 26.

101. Benjamin speaks of flesh, corporeal substance, as that in which currents flow (*Selected Writings*, 1:395).

102. Freud, *Group Psychology and the Analysis of the Ego*, 91–92.

103. Ibid., 102.

104. ibid., 99–100.

105. Ibid., 45–46.

106. Noam Yuran, "Being and Television: Producing the Demand to Individualize," tripleC: Communication, Capitalism and Critique 17, no. 1 (2019): 56–71.

107. Mladen Dolar, "On Rumors, Gossip and Related Matter," in Johnston, Nedoh, and Zupančič, *Objective Fictions*, 144–164.

108. Suler, "The Online Disinhibition Effect."

109. Foucault, *Security, Territory, Population*, 28–29.

110. Jean Baudrillard, "The Ecstasy of Communication," trans. John Johnston, in *The Anti-Aesthetic: Essays on Post-Modern Culture*, ed. Hal Foster (New York: New Press, 2002), 130.

111. See Angela Nagle, *Kill All Normies: Online Culture Wars from 4chan and Tumblr to Trump and the Alt-Right* (Winchester: John Hunt Publishing, 2017).

1. Benjamin, *Selected Writings*, 3:124.

2. René Girard, *Violence and the Sacred*, trans. Patrick Gregory (Baltimore: Johns Hopkins University Press, 1977), 34.

3. Hegel, *Phenomenology of Spirit*, 270.

4. Alenka Zupančič, *Let Them Rot: Antigone's Parallax* (New York: Fordham University Press, 2023), 25, 30–39.

5. Alenka Zupančič, *What IS Sex?* (Cambridge, MA: MIT Press, 2017), 6–7.

6. Leo Bersani, *Homos* (Cambridge, MA: Harvard University Press, 1996); Leo Bersani, *Is the Rectum a Grave? And Other Essays* (Chicago: University of Chicago Press, 2019).

7. Lacan, *Seminar XVII: The Other Side of Psychoanalysis*.

8. Benjamin, *Selected Writings*, 3:122.

9. See Sigmund Freud, *Moses and Monotheism, An Outline of Psycho-Analysis and Other Works* (London: Hogarth Press, 1964), 271–278.

10. Benjamin, *Selected Writings*, 1:487.

11. Arendt, *Between Past and Future*, 173–196.

12. This highlights what is so deeply troubling about contemporary culture's tendency to treat adults as children, to effectively erase the distinction. See Robert Pfaller, *Erwachsenensprache: über ihr Verschwinden aus Politik und Kultur* (Frankfurt: S. Fischer Verlag, 2017).

13. Slavoj Žižek, *Like a Thief in Broad Daylight: Power in the Era of Post-humanity* (London: Penguin, 2019), 22.

14. See Hegel, *Phenomenology of Spirit*, 407; Slavoj Žižek, *Absolute Recoil: Towards a New Foundation of Dialectical Materialism* (London: Verso, 2015), 140–141.

15. Zack Brown, "ZIZEK: that AI will be the death of learning & so on; to this, I say NO! My student brings me their essay, which has been written by AI, & I plug it into my grading AI, & we are free! While the 'learning' happens, our superego satisfied, we are free now to learn whatever we want," December 7, 2022, 10:07 PM, https://twitter.com/Luminance Bloom/status/1600598003391266816?lang=en.

16. Eric L. Santner, *My Own Private Germany: Daniel Paul Schreber's Secret History of Modernity* (Princeton: Princeton University Press, 1997).

17. See Noam Yuran, "The Eroticism of Technology and Finance," in A. Samman and E. Gammon, *Clickbait Capitalism: Economies of Desire in the Twenty-First Century* (Manchester: Manchester University Press, 2023), 61–80.

18. This is one way to interpret Benjamin's demand that the coming philosophy become doctrine (*Lehre*), teachings. Teachings, those things to be handed down and commented upon, are to be resurrected; no longer the given, but what is to be given. See Benjamin, *Selected Writings*, 1:109–110.

BIBLIOGRAPHY

Adorno, Theodor W. *Aspects of the New Right-Wing Extremism*. Trans. Wieland Hoban. Cambridge, UK: Polity Press, 2020.

Adorno, Theodor W. "Freudian Theory and the Pattern of Fascist Propaganda." In *Psychoanalysis and the Social Sciences*, vol. 3, ed. Géza Róheim, 279–300. New York: International Universities Press, 1951.

Adorno, Theodor W. *Introduction to Sociology*. Trans. Edmund Jephcott, ed. Christoph Göde. Stanford: Stanford University Press, 2000.

Adorno, Theodor W., and Walter Benjamin. *The Complete Correspondence, 1928–1940*. Cambridge, MA: Harvard University Press, 1999.

Adorno, Theodor W., and Max Horkheimer. *Dialectic of Enlightenment*. Trans. Edmund Jephcott. Stanford: Stanford University Press, 2002.

Agamben, Giorgio. *Creation and Anarchy: The Work of Art and the Religion of Capitalism*. Trans. Adam Kotsko. Stanford: Stanford University Press, 2019.

Agamben, Giorgio. *Homo Sacer: Sovereign Power and Bare Life*. Stanford: Stanford University Press, 1998.

Agamben, Giorgio. *The Kingdom and the Glory: For a Theological Genealogy of Economy and Government*. Trans. Lorenzo Chiesa. Stanford: Stanford University Press, 2011.

Agamben, Giorgio. *Pilate and Jesus*. Stanford: Stanford University Press, 2015.

Agamben, Giorgio. *Potentialities: Collected Essays in Philosophy*. Trans. Daniel Heller-Roazen. Stanford: Stanford University Press, 1999.

Agamben, Giorgio. *The Sacrament of Language: An Archaeology of the Oath*. Trans. Adam Kotsko. Stanford: Stanford University Press, 2010.

Agamben, Giorgio. *Stasis: Civil War as a Political Paradigm*. Stanford: Stanford University Press, 2015.

Agamben, Giorgio. *State of Exception*. Trans. Kevin Attell. Chicago: University of Chicago Press, 2005.

Agamben, Giorgio. *What Is an Apparatus? and Other Essays*. Trans. David Kishik and Stefan Pedatella. Stanford: Stanford University Press, 2009.

Agamben, Giorgio. "What Is a People?" In *Means without End: Notes on Politics*, trans, Vincenzo Binetti and Cesare Casarino, 29–35. Minneapolis: University of Minnesota Press, 2000.

Andrejevic, Mark. *Automated Media*. London: Routledge, 2019.

Anscombe, Elizabeth. "Modern Moral Philosophy." *Philosophy* 33, no. 124 (1958): 1–19.

Arendt, Hannah. *Between Past and Future: Eight Exercises in Political Thought*. New York: Viking, 1961.

Arendt, Hannah. *The Origins of Totalitarianism*. London: Penguin Classics, 2017.

Arendt, Hannah. *The Human Condition*. 2nd ed. Chicago: University of Chicago Press, 1998.

Aristophanes. *Acharnians*. Trans. Alan H. Sommerstein. Warminster, UK: Aris & Phillips, 1980.

Aristotle. *Metaphysics*. trans. Hugh Lawson-Tencred. London: Penguin Classics, 1998.

Aristotle. *Metaphysics: Books Z and H*. Trans. David Bostock. Oxford: Clarendon Press, 1994.

Aristotle. *Nicomachean Ethics*. Ed. Roger Crisp. Cambridge: Cambridge University Press, 2014.

Aristotle. *Physics: Books I and II*. Trans. William Charlton. Oxford: Clarendon Press, 1983.

Aristotle. *Rhetoric*. Trans. Edward Meredith Cope and John Edwin Sandys. Cambridge: Cambridge University Press, 2010.

Bachelard, Gaston. *The Psychoanalysis of Fire*. Trans. Alan C. M. Ross. Boston: Beacon Press, 1987.

Bacon, Francis. *New Atlantis and The Great Instauration*. Ed. Jerry Weinberger. Chichester, UK: Wiley-Blackwell, 1989.

Bacon, Francis. *The New Organon*. Ed. Lisa Jardine and Michael Silverthorne. Cambridge: Cambridge University Press, 2000.

Badiou, Alain. *The Century*. Cambridge, UK: Polity Press, 2007.

Baldick, Chris. *In Frankenstein's Shadow: Myth, Monstrosity, and Nineteenth-Century Writing*. Oxford: Clarendon Press, 1990.

Balibar, Étienne. *Citizen Subject: Foundations for Philosophical Anthropology*. New York: Fordham University Press, 2016.

Balibar, Étienne. *Masses, Classes, Ideas: Studies on Politics and Philosophy before and after Marx*. London: Routledge, 2013.

Baudrillard, Jean. "The Ecstasy of Communication." Trans. John Johnston. In *The Anti-Aesthetic: Essays on Post-Modern Culture*, ed. Hal Foster. New York: New Press, 2002.

Baudrillard, Jean. *The System of Objects*. Trans. James Benedict. London: Verso, 1996.

Beiser, Frederick. *German Idealism: The Struggle against Subjectivism, 1781–1801*. Cambridge, MA: Harvard University Press, 2008.

Belkind, Ori. "Unnatural Acts: The Transition from Natural Principles to Laws of Nature in Early Modern Science." *Studies in History and Philosophy of Science Part A* 81 (2020): 62–73.

Benjamin, Walter. *The Arcades Project*. Cambridge, MA: Harvard University Press, 1999.

Benjamin, Walter. *Origin of the German Trauerspiel*. Trans. Howard Eiland. Cambridge, MA: Harvard University Press, 2019.

Benjamin, Walter. *Selected Writings*. 4 vols. Ed. Michael W. Jennings et al. Cambridge, MA: Harvard University Press, 1996–2003.

Benjamin, Walter. *Towards the Critique of Violence: A Critical Edition*. Trans. and ed. Peter Fenves and Julia Ng. Stanford: Stanford University Press, 2021.

Bensaude-Vincent, Bernadette, and William R. Newman, eds. *The Artificial and the Natural: An Evolving Polarity*. Cambridge, MA: MIT Press, 2007.

Bergson, Henri. *Laughter: An Essay on the Meaning of the Comic.* Trans. Cloudesley Brereton and Fred Rothwell. New York: Macmillan, 1913.

Berlin, Isaiah. *The Roots of Romanticism.* Princeton: Princeton University Press, 2013.

Berman, Harold J. *Law and Revolution: The Impact of the Protestant Reformations on the Western Legal Tradition.* Cambridge, MA: Harvard University Press, 1983.

Bersani, Leo. *Homos.* Cambridge, MA: Harvard University Press, 1996.

Bersani, Leo. *Is the Rectum a Grave? And Other Essays.* Chicago: University of Chicago Press, 2019.

Bertalanffy, Ludwig von. "An Outline of General System Theory." *British Journal for the Philosophy of Science* 1, no. 2 (1950): 134–165.

Blanchot, Maurice. "The Apocalypse Is Disappointing." In *Friendship,* trans. Elizabeth Rottenberg. Stanford: Stanford University Press, 1997.

Bloch, Maurice. "What Goes Without Saying: The Conceptualization of Zafimaniry Society." In *Conceptualizing Society,* ed. Adam Kuper, 127–146. London: Routledge, 1992.

Borch, Christian. *The Politics of Crowds: An Alternative History of Sociology.* Cambridge: Cambridge University Press, 2012.

Brague, Rémi. *The Law of God: The Philosophical History of an Idea.* Chicago: University of Chicago Press, 2020.

Brandom, Robert. *A Spirit of Trust: A Reading of Hegel's Phenomenology.* Cambridge, MA: Harvard University Press, 2019.

Brown, Zack. "ZIZEK: that AI will be the death of learning & so on; to this, I say NO! My student brings me their essay, which has been written by AI, & I plug it into my grading AI, & we are free! While the 'learning' happens, our superego satisfied, we are free now to learn whatever we want." December 7, 2022, 10:07 PM. https://twitter.com/Luminance Bloom/status/1600598003391266816?lang=en.

Burroughs, William S. *Naked Lunch.* New York: Grove Press, 1992.

Canetti, Elias. *Crowds and Power.* Trans. Carol Stewart. New York: Farrar, Straus and Giroux, 1984.

Canetti, Elias. "The Torch in My Ear." In *The Memoirs of Elias Canetti,* trans. Joachim Neugroschel. New York: Farrar, Straus and Giroux, 1990.

Canovan, Margaret. *Populism.* New York: Harcourt Brace Jovanovich, 1981.

Cassin, Barbara. *Dictionary of Untranslatables: A Philosophical Lexicon.* Trans. Steven Rendall, Christian Hubert, Jeffrey Mehlman, Nathanael Stein, and Michael Syrotinski. Princeton: Princeton University Press, 2014.

Cassirer, Ernst. *Language and Myth.* New York: Dover, 1953.

Chalmers, David. "Facing Up to the Problem of Consciousness." *Journal of Consciousness Studies* 2, no. 3 (1995): 200–219.

Chomsky, Noam, and Edward S. Herman. *Manufacturing Consent.* New York: Pantheon Books, 1988.

Chun, Wendy Hui Kyong. *Control and Freedom: Power and Paranoia in the Age of Fiber Optics.* Cambridge, MA: MIT Press, 2006.

Clastre, Pierre. *Society against the State: Essays in Political Anthropology.* Trans. Robert Hurley. New York: Zone Books, 1989.

Cohen, Hermann. "The Relationship of Logic to Physics." In *The Neo-Kantian Reader*, ed. Sebastian Luft. London: Routledge, 2015.

Cohen, Hermann. *Religion of Reason out of the Sources of Judaism*. Trans. Simon Kaplan. Atlanta: Scholars Press, 1995. 117–136.

Conant, James. "The Search for Logically Alien Thought." *Philosophical Topics* 20, no. 1 (1992): 115–180.

Copjec, Joan. "The Descent into Shame." *Studio: Israeli Art Magazine* (Tel Aviv), no. 168 (March 2007).

Copjec, Joan. "Vampires, Breast-Feeding, and Anxiety." *October* 58 (1991): 25–43.

Daston, Lorraine. *Rules: A Short History of What We Live By*. Princeton: Princeton University Press, 2022.

Deleuze, Gilles. *Difference and Repetition*. Trans. Paul Patton. New York: Columbia University Press, 1994.

Deleuze, Gilles. "Postscript on the Societies of Control." *October* 59 (Winter 1992): 3–7.

De Man, Paul. "Theory of Metaphor in Rousseau's 'Second Discourse.'" *Studies in Romanticism* 12, no. 2 (1973): 475–498.

Derrida, Jacques. *Of Grammatology*. Trans. Gayatri Chakravorty Spivak. Baltimore: Johns Hopkins University Press, 1976.

Descola, Philippe. *In the Society of Nature: A Native Ecology in Amazonia*. Cambridge: Cambridge University Press, 1994.

Descola, Philippe. "Modes of Being and Forms of Predication." *Journal of Ethnographic Theory* 4 (2014): 271–280.

Dolar, Mladen. "The Comic Mimesis." *Critical Inquiry* 43, no. 2 (2017): 570–589.

Dolar, Mladen. "The Future of Authority?" *Philosopher* 109, no. 2 (2022).

Dolar, Mladen. *Hontology*. Durham: Duke University Press, 2023.

Dolar, Mladen. "'I Shall Be with You on Your Wedding Night': Lacan and the Uncanny." *October* 58 (Fall 1991): 5–24.

Dolar, Mladen. "Lifting the Veil." *South Atlantic Quarterly* 119, no. 4 (2020): 671–680.

Dolar, Mladen. "On Rumors, Gossip and Related Matter." In *Objective Fictions: Philosophy, Psychoanalysis, Marxism*, ed. Adrian Johnston, Boštjan Nedoh, and Alenka Zupančič, 144–164. Edinburgh: Edinburgh University Press, 2022.

Dupuy, Jean-Pierre. *The Mark of the Sacred*. Trans. M. B. DeBevoise. Stanford: Stanford University Press, 2013.

Dupuy, Jean-Pierre. *On the Origins of Cognitive Science: The Mechanization of the Mind*. Trans. M. B. DeBevoise. Cambridge, MA: MIT Press, 2009.

Durkheim, Emile. *The Elementary Forms of the Religious Life*. Trans. Joseph Ward Swain. Chelmsford, MA: Courier Corporation, 2008.

Elias, Norbert. *The Civilizing Process: Sociogenetic and Psychogenetic Investigations*. Oxford: Blackwell, 2000.

Esposito, Roberto. *Bios: Biopolitics and Philosophy*. Trans. Timothy Campbell. Minneapolis: University of Minnesota Press, 2008.

Evans-Pritchard, E. E. *Witchcraft, Oracles and Magic among the Azande*. Oxford: Clarendon Press, 1963.

Feher, Michel. "Self-Appreciation; or, The Aspirations of Human Capital." *Public Culture* 21, no. 1 (January 2009): 21–41.

Ferenczi, Sándor. *First Contributions to Psycho-analysis.* London: Routledge, 2018.

Filc, Danny. פופוליזם והגמוניה בישראל [Populism and hegemony in Israel]. Tel Aviv: Resling, 2006.

Finn, Ed. *What Algorithms Want: Imagination in the Age of Computing.* Cambridge, MA: MIT Press, 2017.

Fisher, Mark. *Capitalist Realism: Is There No Alternative?* Ropley, UK: O Books, 2009.

Fitzpatrick, Peter. *Modernism and the Grounds of Law.* Cambridge: Cambridge University Press, 2001.

Flusser, Vilém. *Towards a Philosophy of Photography.* Trans. Anthony Mathews. London: Reaktion Press, 1983.

Foucault, Michel. *Abnormal: Lectures at the Collège de France 1974–1975.* Trans. Graham Burchell. London: Verso, 2003.

Foucault, Michel. *Discipline and Punish.* Trans. Alan Sheridan. London: Vintage, 1995.

Foucault, Michel. *The History of Sexuality,* vol. 1. Trans. Robert Hurley. New York: Pantheon Books, 1978.

Foucault, Michel. *The Order of Things: An Archaeology of the Human Sciences.* London: Routledge, 2005.

Foucault, Michel. *Security, Territory, Population: Lectures at the Collège de France, 1977–78.* Ed. Arnold I. Davidson, trans. Graham Burchell. Basingstoke, UK: Palgrave Macmillan, 2007.

Foucault, Michel. "Truth and Power: An Interview with Michel Foucault." In *Critique of Anthropology* 4, no. 13–14 (1979): 131–137.

Franklin, Seb. *Control: Digitality as Cultural Logic.* Cambridge, MA: MIT Press, 2015.

Franks, Paul. *All or Nothing: Systematicity, Transcendental Arguments, and Skepticism in German Idealism.* Cambridge, MA: Harvard University Press, 2005.

Freud, Sigmund. *Beyond the Pleasure Principle, Group Psychology and Other Works.* Trans. James Strachey. The Standard Edition, vol. 18. New York: W. W. Norton, 1955.

Freud, Sigmund. *A Case of Hysteria, Three Essays on Sexuality and Other Works.* The Standard Edition, vol. 7. London: Hogarth Press, 1953.

Freud, Sigmund. *Civilization and Its Discontents.* Trans. James Strachey. New York: W. W. Norton, 1989.

Freud, Sigmund. "Formulations on the Two Principles of Mental Functioning." In *Unconscious Phantasy,* ed. Riccardo Steiner. London: Karnac Books, 2003.

Freud, Sigmund. *The Future of an Illusion.* Trans. James Strachey. London: Penguin Classics, 2008.

Freud, Sigmund. *Group Psychology and the Analysis of the Ego.* Trans. James Strachey. London: Hogarth Press, 1949.

Freud, Sigmund. *An Infantile Neurosis and Other Works.* The Standard Edition, vol. 17. London: Hogarth Press, 1955.

Freud, Sigmund. *The Interpretation of Dreams.* Trans. James Strachey. New York: Basic Books, 1955. (Reprinted from the Standard Edition, vols. 4–5.)

Freud, Sigmund. *Moses and Monotheism, An Outline of Psycho-Analysis and Other Works.* The Standard Edition, vol. 23. London: Hogarth Press, 1964.

Freud, Sigmund. *New Introductory Lectures on Psycho-Analysis and Other Works*. Trans. James Strachey. The Standard Edition, vol. 22. London: Hogarth Press, 1964.

Freud, Sigmund. "Obsessive Acts and Religious Practices." Trans. James Strachey. In *Jensen's "Gradiva" and Other Works*, 115–128. The Standard Edition, vol. 9. London: Hogarth Press, 1959.

Freud, Sigmund. *On the History of the Psycho-Analytic Movement, Papers on Metapsychology and Other Works*. The Standard Edition, vol. 14. London: Hogarth Press, 1957.

Freud, Sigmund. *Totem and Taboo: Some Points of Agreement between the Mental Lives of Savages and Neurotics*. Trans. James Strachey. London: Routledge, 1950.

Friedlander, Eli. "Assuming Violence: A Commentary on Walter Benjamin's 'Critique of Violence.'" *boundary 2* 42, no. 4 (November 2015): 159–185.

Friedlander, Eli. *Expressions of Judgment: An Essay on Kant's Aesthetics*. Cambridge, MA: Harvard University Press, 2015.

Friedlander, Eli. "Goethe et Benjamin: De la nature à l'histoire." In *Goethe, le second auteur: Actualité d'un inactuel*, ed. Christoph König and Denis Thouard. Paris: Hermann Éditeurs, 2022.

Friedlander, Eli. "The Measure of the Contingent: Walter Benjamin's Dialectical Image." *boundary 2* 35, no. 3 (August 2008): 1–26.

Friedlander, Eli. "Metaphysics and Magic: Echoes of the *Tractatus* in Wittgenstein's Remarks on Frazer." In *Wittgenstein's Tractatus at 100*, ed. Martin Stokhof and Hao Tang. Cham, Switzerland: Palgrave Macmillan, 2023.

Friedlander, Eli. *Walter Benjamin and the Idea of Natural History*. Stanford: Stanford University Press, 2024.

Friedlander, Eli. *Walter Benjamin: A Philosophical Portrait*. Cambridge, MA: Harvard University Press, 2012.

Friedlander, Eli. "Wittgenstein and Goethe: The Life of Colors." *L'art du comprendre*, no. 20 (July 2011), ed. Christiane Chauviré.

Friedlander, Eli. "Wittgenstein, Benjamin, and Pure Realism." In *Wittgenstein and Modernism*, ed. Michael LeMahieu and Karen Zumhagen-Yekplé. Chicago: University of Chicago Press, 2016.

Girard, René. *Violence and the Sacred*. Trans. Patrick Gregory. Baltimore: Johns Hopkins University Press, 1977.

Glynos, Jason, and Yannis Stavrakakis, eds. *Lacan and Science*. London: Routledge, 2018.

Gödel, Kurt. *On Formally Undecidable Propositions of Principia Mathematica and Related Systems*. Chelmsford, MA: Courier Corporation, 1992.

Goethe, Johann Wolfgang von. *Naturwissenschaftliche Schriften*. Munich: C. H. Beck, 1998.

Graeber, David. *Bullshit Jobs: A Theory*. New York: Simon and Schuster, 2018.

Graeber, David, and David Wengrow. *The Dawn of Everything: A New History of Humanity*. London: Penguin, 2021.

Grigg, Russell, Dominique Hecq, and Craig Smith, eds. *Female Sexuality: The Early Psychoanalytic Controversies*. London: Karnac Books, 2015.

Groys, Boris. *Under Suspicion: Phenomenology of the Media*. New York: Columbia University Press, 2000.

Hadot, Pierre. *The Veil of Isis: An Essay on the History of the Idea of Nature*. Trans. Michael Chase. Cambridge, MA: Harvard University Press, 2006.

Halbertal, Moshe. *On Sacrifice*. Princeton: Princeton University Press, 2012.

Harari, Yuval Noah. *Sapiens: A Brief History of Humankind*. New York: Random House, 2014.

Hassan, Ihab. "Prometheus as Performer: Towards a Posthumanist Culture?" In *Performance in Postmodern Culture*, ed. Michael Benamou and Charles Caramella. Madison, WI: Coda Press, 1977.

Hayek, Friedrich. *The Constitution of Liberty*. Chicago: University of Chicago Press, 1960.

Hayek, Friedrich. *Law, Legislation and Liberty*. London: Routledge, 1982.

Hayek, Friedrich. "The Use of Knowledge in Society." *American Economic Review* 35, no. 4 (1945): 519–530.

Hayles, N. Katherine. *How We Became Posthuman: Virtual Bodies in Cybernetics, Literature, and Informatics*. Chicago: University of Chicago Press, 2000.

Hegel, Georg Wilhelm Friedrich. *Elements of the Philosophy of Right*. Trans. H. B. Nisbet. Cambridge: Cambridge University Press, 1991.

Hegel, Georg Wilhelm Friedrich. *Lectures on the History of Philosophy: The Lectures of 1825–1826*. Ed. Robert F. Brown. Berkeley: University of California Press, 1990.

Hegel, Georg Wilhelm Friedrich. *Phenomenology of Spirit*. Trans. A. V. Miller. Oxford: Oxford University Press, 1977.

Heidegger, Martin. *Nietzsche*. Vol. 1. Trans. David Farrell Krell. New York: Harper Collins, 1991.

Heidegger, Martin. *The Question Concerning Technology and Other Essays*. Trans. William Lovitt. New York: Harper, 1977.

Herder, Johann Gottfried. *Philosophical Writings*. Trans. Michael N. Forster. Cambridge: Cambridge University Press, 2002.

Hesiod. *Theogony. Works and Days. Testimonia*. Trans. Glenn W. Most. Cambridge, MA: Harvard University Press, 2006.

Hirschman, Albert O. *The Passions and the Interests: Political Arguments for Capitalism before Its Triumph*. Princeton: Princeton University Press, 1977.

Hobbes, Thomas. *Leviathan*. Ed. J. C. A. Gaskin. Oxford: Oxford University Press, 1998.

Hocart, A. M. *Kings and Councillors: An Essay in the Comparative Anatomy of Human Society*. Chicago: University of Chicago Press, 1970.

Hocart, A. M. *Kingship*. London: Oxford University Press, 1969.

Horkheimer, Max. *Critique of Instrumental Reason*. London: Verso, 2013.

Horkheimer, Max. "The Jews and Europe." In *The Frankfurt School on Religion: Key Writings by the Major Thinkers*, ed. Eduardo Mendieta. New York: Routledge, 2005.

Horney, Karen. *Neurotic Personality of Our Time*. Vol. 10. New York: W. W. Norton, 1937.

Jaeggi, Rahel. *Alienation*. New York: Columbia University Press, 2014.

Jameson, Fredric. "On Goffman's Frame Analysis." *Theory and Society* 3 (1976): 119–133.

Jameson, Fredric. *The Prison-House of Language: A Critical Account of Structuralism and Russian Formalism*. Princeton: Princeton University Press, 1974.

Jammer, Max. *Concepts of Mass in Contemporary Physics and Philosophy*. Princeton: Princeton University Press, 2009.

Kafka, Franz. *The Blue Octavo Notebooks*. Ed. Max Brod. Cambridge, MA: Exact Change, 2004.

Kant, Immanuel. *Anthropology from a Pragmatic Point of View*. Trans. Mary J. Gregor. The Hague: Nijhoff, 1974.

Kant, Immanuel. *Critique of Judgment*. Trans. Werner S. Pluhar. Indianapolis: Hackett, 1987.

Kant, Immanuel. *Critique of Pure Reason*. Trans. Werner S. Pluhar. Indianapolis: Hackett, 1996.

Kant, Immanuel. *Kant's Political Writings*. Ed. Hans Reiss, trans. H. B. Nisbet. Cambridge: Cambridge University Press, 1991.

Kant, Immanuel. *Opus Postumum*. Trans. Eckhart Förster and Michael Rosen. Cambridge: Cambridge University Press, 1993.

Kant, Immanuel. *Religion within the Boundaries of Mere Reason: And Other Writings*. Trans. and ed. Allen W. Wood and George Di Giovanni. Cambridge: Cambridge University Press, 2016.

Karatani, Kojin. *The Structure of World History: From Modes of Production to Modes of Exchange*. Trans. Michael K. Bourdaghs. Durham: Duke University Press, 2014.

Kelsen, Hans. *Pure Theory of Law*. Berkeley: University of California Press, 1967.

Komisaruk, Adam. "Žižek's Jews." *Comparatist* 46, no. 1 (2022): 156–175.

Koselleck, Reinhart. *Critique and Crisis: Enlightenment and Pathogenesis of Modern Society*. Oxford: Berg, 1988.

Kotsko, Adam. *Awkwardness*. Winchester: John Hunt Publishing, 2010.

Koyré, Alexandre. *From the Closed World to the Infinite Universe*. Baltimore: Johns Hopkins Press, 1957.

Koyré, Alexandre. "The Political Function of the Modern Lie." *October* 160 (2017): 143–151.

Kremnitzer, Yuval. "The Frameless Life." *Angelaki* 27, no. 1 (2022): 140–151.

Kremnitzer, Yuval. "The Princess Learns to Wink: Lubitsch and the Politics of the Obscene." In *The Ethics of Ernst Lubitsch: Comedy without Relief*, ed. Ivana Novak and Gregor Moder, 115–135. Lanham, MD: Rowman & Littlefield, 2024.

Lacan, Jacques. *Écrits*. Trans. Bruce Fink. New York: W. W. Norton, 2006.

Lacan, Jacques. *Seminar II: The Ego in Freud's Theory and in the Technique of Psycho-analysis, 1954–1955*. Trans. Sylvana Tomaselli, ed. Jacques-Alain Miller. New York: W. W. Norton, 1991.

Lacan, Jacques. *Seminar III: The Psychoses, 1955–1956*. Trans. Russell Grigg. New York: W. W. Norton, 1993.

Lacan, Jacques. *Seminar X: Anxiety*. Trans. Adrian R. Price. Cambridge, UK: Polity Press, 2014.

Lacan, Jacques. *Seminar XI: The Four Fundamental Concepts of Psychoanalysis*. Trans. Alan Sheridan. New York: W. W. Norton, 1988.

Lacan, Jacques. *Seminar XVII: The Other Side of Psychoanalysis*. Trans. Russell Grigg. New York: W. W. Norton, 2007.

Lacan, Jacques. *Seminar XIX: . . . or Worse*. Ed. Jacques-Alain Miller, trans. A. R. Price. Cambridge, UK: Polity Press, 2018.

Lacan, Jacques. *Seminar XX: The Limits of Love and Knowledge, 1972–1973*. Ed. Jacques-Alain Miller, trans. Bruce Fink. New York: W. W. Norton, 1999.

Lacan, Jacques. *Television*. Trans. Denis Hollier, Rosalind Kraus, and Annette Michelson, ed. Joan Copjec. New York: W. W. Norton, 1990.

Laplanche, Jean, and Jean Bertrand Pontalis. "Fantasy and the Origins of Sexuality." In *Unconscious Phantasy*, ed. Riccardo Steiner. London: Karnac Books, 2003.

Le Bon, Gustave. *The Crowd: A Study of the Popular Mind*. Chelmsford, MA: Courier Corporation, 2002.

Le Bon, Gustave. *The Evolution of Matter*. Trans. F. Legge. London: Walter Scott, 1909.

Lefort, Claude. *Democracy and Political Theory*. Minneapolis: University of Minnesota Press, 1988.

Lefort, Claude. *The Political Forms of Modern Society: Bureaucracy, Democracy, Totalitarianism*. Ed. David Thompson. Cambridge, MA: MIT Press, 1986.

Leroi-Gourhan, André. *Gesture and Speech*. Trans. Anna Bostock Berger. Cambridge, MA: MIT Press, 1993.

Lévi-Strauss, Claude. *Introduction to the Work of Marcel Mauss*. London: Routledge, 1987.

Lévi-Strauss, Claude. *Myth and Meaning*. New York: Schocken Books, 1978.

Lévi-Strauss, Claude. *Structural Anthropology*. Trans. Claire Jacobson and Brooke Grundfest Schoepf. New York: Basic Books, 1973.

Link, Jürgen. "From the 'Power of the Norm' to 'Flexible Normalism': Considerations after Foucault." Trans. Mirko M. Hall. *Cultural Critique*, no. 57 (Spring 2004): 14–32.

Liu, Lydia H. *The Freudian Robot: Digital Media and the Future of the Unconscious*. Chicago: University of Chicago Press, 2010.

Loeve, Sacha, Xavier Guchet, and Bernadette Bensaude-Vincent, eds. *French Philosophy of Technology: Classical Readings and Contemporary Approaches*. Cham: Springer, 2018.

Loraux, Nicole. *The Divided City: On Memory and Forgetting in Ancient Athens*. Trans. Corrine Pache and Jeff Fort. New York: Zone Books, 2006.

Loraux, Nicole. "War in the Family." Trans. Adam Kotsko. *Parrhesia* 27 (2017): 13–47.

Lovejoy, Arthur O. *The Great Chain of Being: A Study of the History of an Idea*. Cambridge, MA: Harvard University Press, 1964.

Luhmann, Niklas. *Introduction to Systems Theory*. Trans. Dirk Baecker and Peter Gilgen. Cambridge, UK: Polity Press, 2013.

Lyotard, Jean-François. *Lessons on the Analytic of the Sublime*. Trans. Elizabeth Rottenberg. Stanford: Stanford University Press, 1994.

Maine, Henry Sumner. *Ancient Law: Its Connection to the History of Early Society*. London: J. M. Dent & Sons, 1912.

Maine, Henry Sumner. *Lectures on the Early History of Institutions*. Cambridge, MA: Harvard University Press, 1914.

Malabou, Catherine. *The Future of Hegel: Plasticity, Temporality, and Dialectic*. London: Routledge, 2004.

Malabou, Catherine. *Plasticity: The Promise of Explosion*. Edinburgh: Edinburgh University Press, 2022.

Mamdani, Mahmood. *Define and Rule*. Cambridge, MA: Harvard University Press, 2012.

Mannoni, Octave. "I Know Well, but All the Same." In *Perversion and the Social Relation*, ed. Molly Anne Rothenberg, Dennis A. Foster, and Slavoj Žižek, 68–92. Durham: Duke University Press, 2003.

Martens, John W. *One God, One Law: Philo of Alexandria on the Mosaic and Greco-Roman Law*. Boston: Brill, 2003.

Marx, Karl. *Capital: A Critique of Political Economy*. 3 vols. Trans. Ben Fowkes. New York: Vintage, 1977.

Marx, Karl. *Grundrisse: Foundations of the Critique of Political Economy*. Trans. Martin Nicolaus. London: Penguin, 1973.

Mauss, Marcel. *Techniques, Technology and Civilization*. Ed. Nathan Schlanger. New York: Berghahn Books, 2006.

McLuhan, Marshall. *Understanding Media: The Extensions of Man*. Cambridge, MA: MIT Press, 1994.

Millar, Isabel. *The Psychoanalysis of Artificial Intelligence*. Cham: Palgrave Macmillan, 2022.

Milner, Jean-Claude. *A Search for Clarity: Science and Philosophy in Lacan's Oeuvre*. Evanston: Northwestern University Press, 2020.

Mouffe, Chantal. *The Democratic Paradox*. London: Verso, 2009.

Mounk, Yascha. *The People vs. Democracy: Why Our Freedom Is in Danger and How to Save It*. Cambridge, MA: Harvard University Press, 2018.

Müller, Jan-Werner. *Democracy Rules*. London: Penguin, 2021.

Müller, Jan-Werner. *What Is Populism?* Philadelphia: University of Pennsylvania Press, 2016.

Nagle, Angela. *Kill All Normies: Online Culture Wars from 4chan and Tumblr to Trump and the Alt-Right*. Winchester: John Hunt Publishing, 2017.

Nancy, Jean-Luc. *The Sense of the World*. Trans. Jeffrey S. Librett. Minneapolis: University of Minnesota Press, 2008.

Nietzsche, Friedrich. *On the Genealogy of Morality*. Ed. Keith Ansell-Pearson, trans. Carol Diethe. London: Cambridge University Press, 2006.

Paul, Ian Alan. "Are Prisons Computers?" https://www.ianalanpaul.com/are-prisons-computers/. 2022.

Pfaller, Robert. *Erwachsenensprache: über ihr Verschwinden aus Politik und Kultur*. Frankfurt: S. Fischer Verlag, 2017.

Pfaller, Robert. *On the Pleasure Principle in Culture: Illusions without Owners*. Trans. Lisa Rosenblatt. London: Verso, 2014.

Pippin, Robert. "Heidegger on Nietzsche on Nihilism." In *Political Philosophy Cross-Examined: Recovering Political Philosophy*, ed. T. L. Pangle and J. H. Lomax. New York: Palgrave Macmillan, 2013.

Pippin, Robert. *Modernism as a Philosophical Problem: On the Dissatisfactions of European High Culture*. Malden, MA: Blackwell, 1999.

Pippin, Robert. *The Persistence of Subjectivity*. Cambridge: Cambridge University Press, 2005.

Pitkin, Hanna F. *The Concept of Representation*. Berkeley: University of California Press, 2023.

Plato. *Complete Works*. Ed. John M. Cooper and Douglas S. Hutchinson. Indianapolis: Hackett, 1997.

Plato. *Laws*. Ed. T. L. Pentangle. Chicago: University of Chicago Press, 1988.

Polanyi, Michael, and Amartya Sen. *The Tacit Dimension*. Chicago: University of Chicago Press, 2009.

Postone, Moishe. *Time, Labor, and Social Domination: A Reinterpretation of Marx's Critical Theory*. Cambridge: Cambridge University Press, 1995.

Rancière, Jacques. *Disagreement: Politics and Philosophy*. Trans. Julie Rose. Minneapolis: University of Minnesota Press, 1999.

Ravaisson, Félix. *Of Habit*. Trans. Claire Carlisle and Mark Sinclair. London: Bloomsbury Publishing, 2008.

Renn, Jürgen. *The Evolution of Knowledge: Rethinking Science for the Anthropocene*. Princeton: Princeton University Press, 2020.

Riegl, Alois. *Historical Grammar of the Visual Arts*. Trans. Jacqueline E. Jung. New York: Zone Books, 2004.

Riesebrodt, Martin. "Charisma in Max Weber's Sociology of Religion." *Religion* 29, no. 1 (1999): 1–14.

Riviere, Joan. "Womanliness as a Masquerade." *International Journal of Psychoanalysis* 10 (1929): 303–313.

Rousseau, Jean-Jacques. *Essay on the Origin of Languages and Writings Related to Music*. Trans. and ed. John T. Scott. Hanover, NH: University Press of New England, 1998.

Rouvroy, Antoinette, and Thomas Berns. "Algorithmic Governmentality and Prospects of Emancipation: Disparateness as a Precondition for Individuation through Relationships?" *Réseaux* 177, no. 1 (2013): 163–196.

Ruda, Frank. "(From the Lie in the Closed World to) Lying in an Infinite Universe." In *Objective Fictions: Philosophy, Psychoanalysis, Marxism*, ed. Adrian Johnston, Boštjan Nedoh, and Alenka Zupančič, 144–164. Edinburgh: Edinburgh University Press, 2022.

Ruda, Frank. *Hegel's Rabble: An Investigation into Hegel's Philosophy of Right*. London: Bloomsbury Academic, 2011.

Runciman, David. *How Democracy Ends*. London: Profile Books, 2018.

Runciman, David. *Political Hypocrisy: The Mask of Power from Hobbes to Orwell and Beyond*. Princeton: Princeton University Press, 2008.

Runciman, David, and Mónica Brito Vieira. *Representation*. Cambridge, UK: Polity Press, 2008.

Sahlins, Marshall, and David Graeber. *On Kings*. Chicago: Hau Books, 2017.

Santner, Eric L. *My Own Private Germany: Daniel Paul Schreber's Secret History of Modernity*. Princeton: Princeton University Press, 1997.

Santner, Eric L. "Psychoanalysis and the Enigmas of Sovereignty." *Qui Parle* 11, no. 2 (1999): 1–19.

Santner, Eric L. *The Royal Remains: The People's Two Bodies and the Endgames of Sovereignty*. Chicago: University of Chicago Press, 2011.

Santner, Eric L. *The Weight of All Flesh: On the Subject-Matter of Political Economy*. Ed. Kevis Goodman. Oxford: Oxford University Press, 2016.

Schatzberg, Eric. *Technology: Critical History of a Concept*. Chicago: University of Chicago Press, 2018.

Schelling, Friedrich Wilhelm Joseph. *First Outline of a Philosophy of Nature*. Trans. Keith R. Peterson. Albany: SUNY Press, 2004.

Schelling, Friedrich Wilhelm Joseph. *Grounding of Positive Philosophy: The Berlin Lectures*. Trans. Bruce Matthews. Albany: SUNY Press, 2007.

Schelling, Friedrich Wilhelm Joseph. *Historical-Critical Introduction to the Philosophy of Mythology*. Trans. Mason Richey. Albany: SUNY Press, 2012.

Schelling, Friedrich Wilhelm Joseph. *Philosophical Investigations into the Essence of Human Freedom*. Trans. Jeff Love and Johannes Schmidt. Albany: SUNY Press, 2006.

Schelling, Friedrich Wilhelm Joseph. *Philosophy of Art*. Trans. Douglas W. Stott. Minneapolis: University of Minnesota Press, 1989.

Schelling, Friedrich Wilhelm Joseph. *The Unconditioned in Human Knowledge: Four Early Essays 1794–1796*. Trans. F. Marti. Lewisburg, PA: Bucknell University Press, 1980.

Schmitt, Carl. *The Concept of the Political.* Expanded ed. Chicago: University of Chicago Press, 2008.

Schmitt, Carl. *The Leviathan in the State Theory of Thomas Hobbes.* Trans. George Schwab. Westport, CT: Greenwood Press, 1996.

Schmitt, Carl. *The Nomos of the Earth.* New York: Telos Press, 2003.

Schmitt, Carl. *Theory of the Partisan.* Trans. G. L. Ulmen. New York: Telos Press, 2007.

Schopenhauer, Arthur. *The World as Will and Representation.* Vol. 1. Trans. and ed. Judith Norman, Alistair Welchman, and Christopher Janaway. Cambridge: Cambridge University Press, 2010.

Schürmann, Reiner. *Heidegger on Being and Acting: From Principles to Anarchy.* Trans. Christine-Marie Gros. Bloomington: Indiana University Press, 1987.

Sellars, Wilfrid. *Empiricism and the Philosophy of Mind.* Cambridge, MA: Harvard University Press, 1997.

Shelley, Mary. "Frankenstein." In *Three Gothic Novels,* ed. Peter Fairclough. London: Penguin, 1968.

Shklar, Judith. *Ordinary Vices.* Cambridge, MA: Belknap Press, 1985.

Siegel, James T. *Naming the Witch.* Stanford: Stanford University Press, 2006.

Simondon, Gilbert. *Individuation in Light of Notions of Form and Information.* Trans. Taylor Adkins. Minneapolis: University of Minnesota Press, 2020.

Simondon, Gilbert. *On the Mode of Existence of Technical Objects.* Trans. Cecile Malaspina and John Rogove. Minneapolis: Univocal Publishing, 2017.

Simondon, Gilbert. "Technical Mentality." In *Being and Technology,* ed. Arne De Boever, Alex Murray, Jon Roffe, and Ashley Woodward. Edinburgh: Edinburgh University Press, 2012.

Sloterdijk, Peter. *Critique of Cynical Reason.* Trans. Michael Eldred. Minneapolis: University of Minnesota Press, 1987.

Snyder, Timothy. "Ukraine Holds the Future: The War Between Democracy and Nihilism." *Foreign Affairs,* September/October 2022.

Sohm, Rudolf. *Kirchenrecht: Die geschichtlichen Grundlagen.* Munich: Duncker & Humblot, 1923.

Sonderegger, Erwin. "Zur Bildung des Ausdrucks τὸ τί ἦν εἶναι durch Aristoteles." *Archiv für Geschichte der Philosophie* 65, no. 1 (1983): 18–39.

Stiegler, Bernard. *The Age of Disruption: Technology of Madness in Computational Capitalism.* Trans. Daniel Ross. Cambridge, UK: Polity Press, 2019.

Stiegler, Bernard. *Technics and Time 1: The Fault of Epimetheus.* Trans. Richard Beardsworth and George Collins. Stanford: Stanford University Press, 1998.

Stolleis, Michael. "The Legitimation of Law through God, Tradition, Will, Nature and Con-stitution." In *Natural Law and the Laws of Nature in Early Modern Europe: Jurisprudence, Theology, Moral and Natural Philosophy,* ed. Lorraine Daston and Michael Stolleis. London: Routledge, 2008.

Strauss, Leo. *The City and Man.* Chicago: University of Chicago Press, 1978.

Strauss, Leo. *Natural Right and History.* Chicago: University of Chicago Press, 1953.

Strauss, Leo. *Philosophy and Law: Contributions to the Understanding of Maimonides and His Predecessors.* Albany: SUNY Press, 1995.

Suler, John. "The Online Disinhibition Effect." *Cyberpsychology and Behavior* 7, no. 3 (2004): 321–326.

Swift, Jonathan. *Gulliver's Travels.* New York: Signet Classics, 2008.

Talmon, Jacob Leib. *The Origins of Totalitarian Democracy*. London: Mercury Books, 1956.

Tomšič, Samo. "From the Orderly World to the Polluted Unworld." In *Objective Fictions: Philosophy, Psychoanalysis, Marxism*, ed. Adrian Johnston, Boštjan Nedoh, and Alenka Zupančič, 64–84. Edinburgh: Edinburgh University Press, 2022.

Turing, Alan. "Computing Machinery and Intelligence." *Mind* 59, no. 236 (1950): 433.

Varoufakis, Yanis. *Technofeudalism: What Killed Capitalism*. Brooklyn, NY: Melville House, 2024.

Veblen, Thorstein. *The Theory of the Leisure Class*. Oxford: Oxford University Press, 2007.

Vernant, Jean-Pierre, and Marcel Detienne. *The Cuisine of Sacrifice among the Greeks*. Chicago: University of Chicago Press, 1989.

Veyne, Paul. *Did the Greeks Believe in Their Myths? An Essay on the Constitutive Imagination*. Trans. Paula Wissing. Chicago: University of Chicago Press, 1988.

Viveiros de Castro, Eduardo. "Cosmological Deixis and Amerindian Perspectivism." *Journal of the Royal Anthropological Institute* (1998): 469–488.

Vogl, Joseph. *The Specter of Capital*. Trans. Joachim Redner and Robert Savage. Stanford: Stanford University Press, 2015.

Weber, Max. *From Max Weber: Essays in Sociology*. Trans. and ed. H. H. Gerth and C. Wright Mills. New York: Oxford University Press, 1946.

Weber, Max. *On Charisma and Institution Building: Selected Papers by Max Weber*. Ed. S. N. Eisenstadt. Chicago: University of Chicago Press, 1968.

Weller, Shane. *Literature, Philosophy, Nihilism: The Uncanniest of Guests*. London: Palgrave Macmillan, 2008.

Wiener, Norbert. *The Human Use of Human Beings: Cybernetics and Society*. 1950; London: Free Association Books, 1989.

Williams, Raymond. *The Country and the City*. New York: Oxford University Press, 1973.

Williams, Raymond. *Culture and Society 1780–1950*. New York: Doubleday, 1960.

Wittgenstein, Ludwig. *The Mythology in Our Language: Remarks on Frazer's Golden Bough*. Trans. Stephanie Palmie. Chicago: Hau Books, 2020.

Wittgenstein, Ludwig. *Philosophical Investigations*. Trans. G. E. M. Anscombe. Oxford: Basil Blackwell, 1958.

Yuran, Noam. "Being and Television: Producing the Demand to Individualize." *tripleC: Communication, Capitalism and Critique* 17, no. 1 (2019): 56–71.

Yuran, Noam. "The Eroticism of Technology and Finance." In A. Samman and E. Gammon, *Clickbait Capitalism: Economies of Desire in the Twenty-First Century*, 61–80. Manchester: Manchester University Press, 2023.

Yuran, Noam. "Home Economics: Why We Treat Objects Like Women." *Problemi International* 3, no. 3 (2019): 29–64.

Yuran, Noam. *What Money Wants: An Economy of Desire*. Stanford: Stanford University Press, 2014.

Zito, Salena. "Taking Trump Seriously, not Literally." *Atlantic*, September 23, 2016. https://www.theatlantic.com/politics/archive/2016/09/trump-makes-his-case-in-pittsburgh/501335/

Žižek, Slavoj. *Absolute Recoil: Towards a New Foundation of Dialectical Materialism*. London: Verso, 2015.

Žižek, Slavoj. *The Abyss of Freedom*. Ann Arbor: University of Michigan Press, 1997.

Žižek, Slavoj. "The Big Other Doesn't Exist." *Journal of European Psychoanalysis: Humanities, Philosophy, Psychotherapies*, no. 5 (Spring-Fall 1997).

Žižek, Slavoj. *Did Somebody Say Totalitarianism? Five Interventions in the (Mis)use of a Notion.* London: Verso, 2001.

Žižek, Slavoj. *For They Know Not What They Do: Enjoyment as a Political Factor.* London: Verso, 2008.

Žižek, Slavoj. "Ideology II: Competition Is a Sin." *Lacan.com* 4 (2008).

Žižek, Slavoj. *Like a Thief in Broad Daylight: Power in the Era of Post-humanity.* London: Penguin, 2019.

Žižek, Slavoj. *Living in the End Times.* London: Verso, 2010.

Žižek, Slavoj. *Pandemic! COVID-19 Shakes the World.* New York: OR Books, 2020.

Žižek, Slavoj. *The Plague of Fantasies.* London: Verso, 1997.

Žižek, Slavoj. *The Sublime Object of Ideology.* London: Verso, 2008.

Žižek, Slavoj. "Tolerance as an Ideological Category." *Critical Inquiry* 34, no. 4 (2008): 660–682.

Žižek, Slavoj. *Violence: Six Sideways Reflections.* New York: Picador, 2008.

Žižek, Slavoj, and Markus Gabriel. *Mythology, Madness, and Laughter: Subjectivity in German Idealism.* London: Bloomsbury Publishing, 2009.

Zuboff, Shoshana. *The Age of Surveillance Capitalism: The Fight for a Human Future at the New Frontier of Power.* New York: Hachette, 2019.

Zupančič, Alenka. *Ethics of the Real: Kant and Lacan.* London: Verso, 2012.

Zupančič, Alenka. *Let Them Rot: Antigone's Parallax.* New York: Fordham University Press, 2023.

Zupančič, Alenka. "Not-Mother: On Freud's Verneinung." *E-flux online*, 2012.

Zupančič, Alenka. "Perverse Disavowal and the Rhetoric of the End." *Filozofski vestnik* 43, no. 2 (2022): 89–103.

Zupančič, Alenka. "Perversion vs. Desire." Conference presentation at "Perversion and Its Discontents," Ljubljana, Slovenia, 2023.

Zupančič, Alenka. "The Second Death." *Angelaki* 27, no. 1 (2022): 26–34.

Zupančič, Alenka. *What IS Sex?* Cambridge, MA: MIT Press, 2017.

Zupančič, Alenka. *Why Psychoanalysis? Three Interventions.* Uppsala: NSU Press, 2008.